P9-CDT-069

An Inconve

Also by the Author:

The Real America

nient Book

Real Solutions to the World's Biggest Problems

WRITTEN AND EDITED BY:

Glenn Beck

Kevin Balfe

WRITERS

Steve "Stu" Burguiere, John Bobey, Dan Andros, Paul Starke

CONTRIBUTORS

Carol Lynne, Virginia Leahy, Evan Cutler, Patricia Balfe

ILLUSTRATIONS

Paul Nunn

THRESHOLD EDITIONS

NEW YORK LONDON TORONTO SYDNEY

To my wife, Tania—my guide, my strength,
my inspiration, my eternal partner

Threshold Editions
A Division of Simon & Schuster, Inc.
1230 Avenue of the Americas
New York, NY 10020

First Threshold Editions trade paperback edition May 2009

THRESHOLD EDITIONS and colophon are trademarks of Simon & Schuster, Inc.

For information about special discounts for bulk purchases, please contact Simon & Schuster Special Sales at 1-800-456-6798 or business@simonandschuster.com.

The Simon & Schuster Speakers Bureau can bring authors to your live event. For more information or to book an event contact the Simon & Schuster Speakers Bureau at 1-866-248-3049 or visit our website at www.simonspeakers.com.

Designed by Timothy Shaner, nightanddaydesign.biz

Manufactured in the United States of America

3 5 7 9 10 8 6 4

Library of Congress Cataloging-in-Publication Data

An inconvenient book : real solutions to the world's biggest problems / written and edited by Glenn Beck, Kevin Balfe ; writers Steve "Stu" Burguiere . . . [et al.] ; contributors Carol Lynne ; illustrations Paul Nunn. — 1st Threshold Editions hardcover ed.
p. cm.

1. United States—Civilization—1970– 2. United States—Social conditions—1980– 3. Social problems—United States. 4. United States—Politics and government—1989– 5. Civilization, Modern—1950– 6. Social history—1970– 7. Social problems. 8. World politics—1989–
I. Beck, Glenn. II. Balfe, Kevin. III. Burguiere, Steve.
E169.12.B335 2007
973.92—dc22
2007026246

ISBN-13: 978-1-4165-5219-2 (hc)
ISBN-10: 1-4165-5219-7 (hc)

ISBN-13: 978-1-4165-6044-9 (pb)
ISBN-10: 1-4165-6044-0 (pb)

CONTENTS:

An Inconvenient Update: The More Things Change. vi

1 Global Warming, Storming, and Conforming 1

2 Marriage, Porn, Adultery, and Divorce: The Circle of Life . . 24

3 Radical Islam: Politically Incorrect 36

4 Body Image: The New Hotness 58

5 Blind-Dating: Playing the Powerball of Love 70

6 The Income Gap: The Rich Get Richer, Good for Them 80

7 America's Oil Dependence: The Peak of Stupidity 90

8 Education through Indoctrination 108

9 Political Games: America's on a Losing Streak 118

10 Sleepytime! The Weekend Movie Rental 130

11 Media Bias: An All-New Fairness Doctrine 138

12 You Can't Say That! The Politics of Correctness 150

13 Gratuities: I've Reached My Tipping Point 164

14 Child Molesters: A Fiery Solution 172

15 The UN: Truth, Justice, and the Anti-American Way 188

16 How to Remember Names, by Glenn—something or other . . 202

17 Minimum Wage, Maximum Politics 210

18 Aging: God's System of Depreciation 224

19 Opinion Polls: Our Country's Real Leader 234

20 Poverty Prozac 252

21 Parenting: The Case for Abstinence 266

22 Illegal Immigration: Behind the Lies 276

Acknowledgments 296

An Inconvenient Update: The More Things Change . . .

WHEN I ORIGINALLY WROTE THIS BOOK I realized that it probably wouldn't solve *all* of America's problems overnight. After all, issues like illegal immigration and dependence on foreign oil have been building for decades—one little book can't solve them.

But now that America has a new president, I have a whole new perspective on how to solve the 22 issues covered in this book: Hope for change.

That's it.

We don't need fancy new laws to fight child molesters, or cutting-edge technologies to battle global warning. We just need hope. And change.

But mostly hope.

Of course, what I didn't know when I originally wrote this book—what I *couldn't have known* when I wrote this book—was that the person who would make me see the light was a junior senator whose experience included eight years as a state legislator and a lost election to the U.S. House of Representatives. Silly me!

Anyway, I now realize that I wasted a lot of pages (and needlessly killed a lot of trees—my bad) talking about "solutions." Solving problems is so 1983 . . . these days, politicians earn power and respect by *talking* about solving problems, but then making them a thousand times worse.

Let's see . . . the energy crisis? Thanks to decades of broken promises by politicians, things were already pretty bad. But then the government got fully involved, determined that corn ethanol would be our savior, developed mandatory mileage standards for cars, and—poof!—we had four-dollar gas and a nearly bankrupt auto industry. Thanks, Washington!

Then there's illegal immigration. Politicians have talked the issue to death, but losing money to special interest groups (not to mention votes from huge swaths of voters) was just too much to take—they had to get involved. Ironically, it was the politicians' disastrous economic policies that slowed illegal immigration far more than their committee hearings and lobbyist luncheons.

A.D.D. MOMENT Isn't it kind of sad that we had to actually lower the standard of living for all Americans in order to stop people from trying to sneak in here? You'd think there'd be a more convenient way . . . like, I don't know, building a couple of fences.

I guess what confuses me the most is how Americans' frustration with our politicians is obvious, yet we continually vote to give them more and more power. It's like being the CEO of a corporation who keeps calling the worst-performing employees into his office to promote them. "Listen, Bob, I know you've sexually harassed half of the sales staff and have cheated us out of thousands on your expense reports and . . . I love it! Pack your things, you're moving into the corner office!"

Honestly, how poorly do our leaders need to perform before people start to realize that it's not about the parties, it's about power? Most politicians may think they stand for something, but once elected their entire focus shifts to one major policy: how to get reelected.

The more responsibility and power we give the government (especially in exchange for personal liberties), the more they use it to figure out new ways to rape and pillage the villagers. Pretty soon, those villagers will get fed up and will either leave . . . or—well, let's just say the alternative is worse (think torches and pitchforks). Remember, while "We hold these truths to be self-evident . . . " is the most famous part of the Declaration of Independence, the most meaningful lines appear much later in the document:

Since we're on the subject of political parties and our founding fathers, how about this little ditty from George Washington's 1796 farewell speech?

The alternate domination of one faction over another, sharpened by the spirit of revenge, natural to party dissension, which in different ages and countries has perpetrated the most horrid enormities, is itself a frightful despotism. But this leads at length to a more formal and permanent despotism. The disorders and miseries which result gradually incline the minds of men to seek security and repose in the absolute power of an individual; and sooner or later the chief of some prevailing faction, more able or more fortunate than his competitors, turns this disposition to the purposes of his own elevation, on the ruins of public liberty.

Loose translation: Parties breed partisanship; partisanship breeds disenfranchisement; disenfranchisement breeds rebellion; and rebellion results in tyranny. Hmm, now where do you think we are on that little road map conveniently laid out for us over 210 years ago?

A.D.D. MOMENT

In every stage of these oppressions we have petitioned for redress in the most humble terms: our repeated petitions have been answered only by repeated injury. A prince, whose character is thus marked by every act which may define a tyrant, is unfit to be the ruler of a free people.

Sound familiar? Here we are, centuries later, feeling exactly the same way. Why won't they listen to us? Why are our seemingly humble requests ignored or, worse, met with arrogance, as if there's no way we "average Americans" could ever understand the complexities of what the really smart people in New York and Washington are dealing with?

If the *people* really ran America, do you think that Fannie Mae and Freddie Mac would've been given our "implicit backing"? Do you think we would've caved to the pressure of special interest groups and passed ridiculous laws mandating mortgages for everyone? Do you think we would've promised trillions in benefits to future generations without making sure we actually had a way to pay for them? And, most of all, if "We the People" were really in charge, do you think we would've allowed our leaders to treat our Constitution as if it's merely a list of *suggestions*?

Follow the Leaders!

"The problems in the subprime market seems likely to be contained."

—Ben Bernanke, Federal Reserve chairman, March 28, 2007

The Dow lost over 28 percent from the day Bernanke gave that speech to the end of 2008, clearly signaling that our problems were anything but "contained."

Yet, those things have all happened, and the truth is that we have only ourselves to blame. We're the ones who keep lending the same people our power year after year (after year, after year) because they have a last name we recognize or because we've been brainwashed into believing that experience is more important than competence (it's funny how rarely they go hand in hand). The reality is that experience breeds complacency, and complacency is what stops people from asking the simple questions that could keep us out of trouble.

A.D.D. MOMENT A great question circa 2004 might have been something like: "So what happens if housing prices ever start to decline?"

Have Robert Byrd (first elected to Congress in 1952), Joe Biden (1972), John Dingell (1955), or Daniel Inouye (1962) really done such a great job in office that they essentially deserve to be politicians for life? I bet if we listed their policies and accomplishments on the ballot instead of their names, they'd lose every election.

When we find out that the people we've allowed to lead us for decades are crooks (i.e., Ted Stevens, elected in 1968) we act shocked, as if people being corrupted by having too much power for too long is something new.

The whole thing is really laughable, especially when you consider that the politicians who are now responsible for "saving" us are some of the same people who brought us to this point. How is everyone up in arms over CEO salaries or expensive corporate retreats, yet hardly anyone is calling for the firing of people like Barney Frank and Chris Dodd, two politicians who were at the very center of the housing and credit bubbles and who have taken barely an ounce of personal responsibility for what they've done to us?

We seem to have lost perspective on what it means to be a leader. Good leaders don't measure their success by the number of elections won, the size of their donor war chests, or how high they rank in popularity polls. They measure success in thank-you letters, tearful phone calls, and hugs.

The one thing that's become apparent since I wrote the original version of this book is that America no longer looks at itself the way it once did. The financial crisis had a lot to do with speeding up the process, but the underlying tenets of this shift have been gathering steam for a while. "Big government" is no longer seen as an insult, it's a solution to our problems. Even "socialism" isn't the slur that it once was.

Follow the Leaders!

"I don't think the government ought to be involved in bailing out companies."

—President George W. Bush, July 15, 2008

Since that statement the government has bailed out Fannie Mae, Freddie Mac, AIG, GMAC, the Big Three automakers, and countless other financial companies by way of the $700 billion "TARP" bill.

I was recently in a taxi with a guy who had immigrated here decades ago from the former Soviet Union. He took it upon himself to talk nonstop about how New York City's government is corrupt, how they've squandered billions in taxpayer money without any results, and how his taxes and tolls go up each and every year without any increase in salary or improvement in service. It was a *very* long ride.

I asked him if he had any fear that the United States was at the early stages of looking like the country he had left so long ago. I expected him to say yes and then spend the rest of the ride telling me how America was losing what was once great about it. Instead he looked at me in the rearview mirror as if I were crazy. (It's a look I've gotten used to over the years.)"Actually," he said with a thick Russian accent, "I think that if they would just marry communism with capitalism we might finally have the perfect system."

I shouldn't have been shocked, but I was. Here was a guy who'd just spent an hour telling me how government screws everything up now advocating that the government have *more* power.

Before I could open the door and jump out, he continued, "That way, the rich people will stay rich and the poor people like me will just get money from the government and the rich. Everybody wins!"

If you're laughing, stop. This guy wasn't kidding, and, unfortunately, there are millions of others who think the same way. To them it's a simple matter of common sense: Those who are wealthy would still do fine, they'd just be a little *less* wealthy, but the poor would all be promoted to the middle class. Everybody wins!

Of course, what those people fail to acknowledge is that that their beloved system has never worked one time in the history of civilization. Believe me, if it had, every country on earth would be using it. Unfortunately, the people who value hope over facts (like my cabdriver) aren't exactly interested in historical case studies.

> **Follow the Leaders!**
>
> "We have more capital than we need, so we can say to the market that we don't need more injections. We can confirm that we have tackled the problem."
>
> —John Thain, former CEO, Merrill Lynch, March 16, 2008
>
> Less than six months later Merrill Lynch was bought by Bank of America in an emergency fire sale.

As you already know, it's impossible to set up a system of government whereby you reap huge rewards if you succeed, yet there are no penalties for failure. Absolutely impossible. The recent bailouts and nationalizations should serve as great examples of that, as should the case of alleged Ponzi-schemer Bernard Madoff.

Here was a guy who promised investors the same thing that so many Americans now seem to want: risk-free returns. No matter the market . . . no matter the economy . . . his funds were always up. But instead of questioning how he did it, investors simply took it at face value. They didn't care about the repercussions or consequences (remember that word . . . *consequences*?) so long as they saw their balances increasing every year. And then it all caved in and those investors quickly learned a lesson that will soon be taught to all of us if we continue down this path: You can't get something for nothing; there is no such thing as risk-free return.

But since a growing number of people seem to disagree, the chances that we'll see real socialism in America have grown exponentially. The *will*—at least among the vocal minority—is already there; now all it will take is the *way*.

That is generally the point at which you lose the people who laugh at the idea of a socialist America. *You'd never get those kinds of laws passed here,* they say. And they might be right. But what they're wrong about is that you don't need *laws* to shift us into a country where the government explicitly controls everything—there are far easier ways.

The EZ Socialist Policy Creator!

If you think that creating socialist policy is too difficult, stop worrying! We've constructed an easy-to-use chart that allows politicians to mix 'n' match fancy-sounding items to create great new laws.

If you think this fast-and-loose approach feels less like a "plan" rooted in sound logic and more like an idealized, nonsensical whim—well . . . you're right! But you better keep that under your hat, because "The State" hates that kind of talk. (And "reeducation" won't include recess.) Now let's have some fun!

Choose one item from each column, jam your law down the throats of unsuspecting Americans under the guise of an "emergency," then sit back and enjoy!

Who's It For?	What's the Rationale?	End It with a Bang!
The American	Recovery and Reinvestment	Initiative
The International	Infrastructure Improvement	Act
The Federal	Protection of Children	Strategy
The State	Safety and Sacrifice	Policy
The Multilateral	Health and Hope	Proposition
The Cross-Border	Security Preparedness	Effort
The Collective	Alternative Thinking	Proposal
The Joint	Social Responsibility	Program
The Universal	Tax and Fairness	Reform
The Continental	Defense of the Weakest	Plan
The Hemispheric	Peace and Prosperity	Platform

Laws require all sorts of pesky votes and signatures. But smart politicians know that they can accomplish just as much (if not more) by using carrots instead of sticks, and President Obama is nothing if not smart. One of his plans before taking office was to offer states $7 billion in incentives if they agreed to change key provisions of their unemployment laws. To cash-strapped states, that's a lot of money—probably too much to turn down—but to get it, they would have to make decisions that would result in major long-term changes to their social programs.

For example, Obama wanted states to allow more part-time workers to receive unemployment benefits. While that may sound okay to some people while the economy is down, what happens when things turn around? Should states really be responsible for permanently providing a social safety net to people who are actually working? And what about Medicaid? In exchange for a piece of that $7 billion, states would have to agree to allow laid-off workers to buy into their program. Who ends up eventually footing the bill? Employers do . . . which means that those costs would eventually be passed on to consumers in the form of higher prices.

By dangling a few billion out there, a savvy politician is able to expand government health care and achieve massively expanded insurance benefits without a vote ever being taken or a law ever being passed.

Another good example of how the government can slowly move us toward socialism is via financial control over the media. Some people consider the media to be our fourth branch of government—and they might be right. An independent, unbiased, well-financed media provides at least as many checks and balances as Congress. But what happens when the media isn't "independent, unbiased, or well financed"? What happens when circulation slips so low that newspapers begin to start folding?

Bailouts.

Momentum for "rescues" (that's the new PC term for "bailouts") of media companies is already building in places like central Connecticut, where several hometown papers are on the verge of bankruptcy. The rationale is that you can't let newspapers fail (especially local ones) because they serve the public good—but the result would be nothing short of catastrophic. What happens if a newspaper being funded by the government is critical of that government? Is their funding cut off? It's a giant leap toward state-controlled media—and it can happen without a law ever being passed.

That's just one small example of the "socialist creep"—but the truth is that a lot of the issues we face are ripe for exploitation by those who think Putin is onto something. Issues like . . .

GLOBAL WARMING, STORMING, AND CONFORMING

Believe what you want about man-made global warming, but it's hard to dispute that the main focus of those offering solutions is the redistribution of wealth. Redistribution from the rich to the poor, from the private sector to the public sector, and, ultimately, from the United States to the rest of the world.

If there is an upside to the economic crisis, it's that it has served as kryptonite to the Superman that is the "end global warming" movement. Even ardent supporters have realized that asking companies to pay millions of additional dollars because of an invisible gas is a recipe for both political and economic disaster. Fortunately (or unfortunately, depending on how you look at it) the economy will recover sooner or later, and when it does, the kryptonite will lose its power—right along with America.

For a sneak preview at how this will likely play out, just look at Europe. Unlike us nasty Americans, they actually care about the environment, so, in 2005, the European Union began issuing permits to companies for the right to emit carbon dioxide. The idea was that if you exceed your limit you have to go to the marketplace to buy excess capacity from those companies who did a better job conserving. Here in unsophisticated America we call that program "Cap & Trade," but, whatever you call it, there's one common characteristic: It doesn't work.

Here's what the *New York Times* recently said about the EU's program:

> *". . . [Their] plan unleashed a lobbying free-for-all that led politicians to dole out favors to various industries, undermining the environmental goals. Four years later, it is becoming clear that system has so far produced little noticeable benefit to the climate—but generated a multibillion-dollar windfall for some of the Continent's biggest polluters."*

I don't know about you, but I was just thinking the other day that the one thing we're missing in America is a way for politicians to get cozier with lobbyists. If only we could usher in a "lobbying free-for-all" like the Europeans, that would fix everything! A.D.D. MOMENT

Yes, that's actually from the *New York Times*. I'm serious. No, there's no catch, they really wrote that.

Of course, all of that lobbying is about one thing: money. To proponents of radical new programs and policies, cutting profits is more important than cutting carbon. If you're not convinced, then consider that $80 billion will be transferred around Europe in 2008 as a result of these permits. And that's just the beginning; once this program goes worldwide the market will be substantially larger.

So who "pays" for of all that money changing hands? (Unlike our politicians, most of us understand that you can't throw billions around without *someone* paying a price for it.) It's simple: We all do.

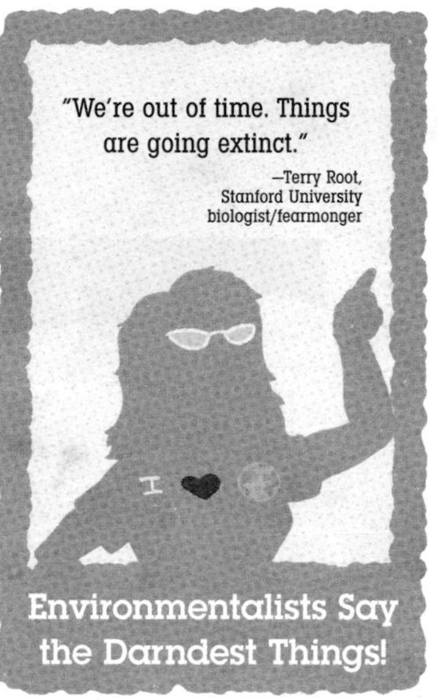

"We're out of time. Things are going extinct."
—Terry Root, Stanford University biologist/fearmonger
I
Environmentalists Say the Darndest Things!

A great illustration of how this works is the German power company RWE. As Europe's largest carbon emitter, RWE was exactly the kind of company that the EU's shiny new Cap & Trade program was meant to restrain. But unfortunately, Government-Run Markets + Billions of Dollars + Politicians and Lobbyists = Unmitigated Disaster.

Here's what happened. Instead of permitting RWE to emit 3 percent less carbon than they had the year before, the company got permits allowing them to emit 3 percent more. RWE then traded that excess capacity on the open market, earning themselves a tidy $6.4 billion over the first three years.

But it gets even better! RWE then claimed that the new permits were costing them money, so they raised their prices by about 5 percent a year—earning them millions more from their unsuspecting customers (i.e., German families).

But none of that qualifies as a true "disaster." For that, you have to look to RWE's actual carbon emissions. Remember, the whole point of this bureaucratic nightmare was to save the environment by slashing CO_2. So, did it work?

Not so much.

While making billions selling permits, RWE was also *emitting more carbon*. How much more? Thirty-eight million tons over the first two years of the program; an increase of 32 percent!

The really scary thing is that RWE wasn't exactly an anomaly. All across Europe consumer prices have increased right along with carbon dioxide output. Emissions by plants and factories that participated in the "experiment" were up 0.4 percent in 2006 and *another* 0.7 percent in 2007.

So where did all the money go? Good question . . . and the answer you'd get from supporters would likely sound very similar to the one given by President Obama when asked how we could've spent all of those billions on bailouts with seemingly very little progress: Imagine how bad off we'd be if we *didn't* spend all of that money!

What a great line! You never have to account for the money—you just have to scare people into believing that carbon or foreclosures or bankruptcies (or whatever you were trying to prevent) would be much worse if you *hadn't* acted.

Who Said It?

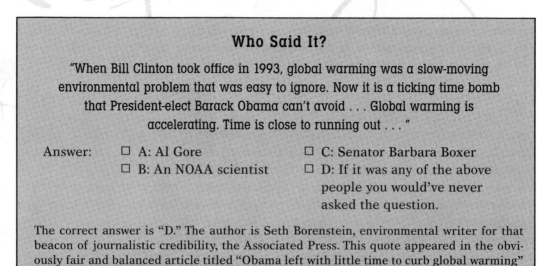

"When Bill Clinton took office in 1993, global warming was a slow-moving environmental problem that was easy to ignore. Now it is a ticking time bomb that President-elect Barack Obama can't avoid . . . Global warming is accelerating. Time is close to running out . . . "

Answer:
- ☐ A: Al Gore
- ☐ B: An NOAA scientist
- ☐ C: Senator Barbara Boxer
- ☐ D: If it was any of the above people you would've never asked the question.

The correct answer is "D." The author is Seth Borenstein, environmental writer for that beacon of journalistic credibility, the Associated Press. This quote appeared in the obviously fair and balanced article titled "Obama left with little time to curb global warming" in December 2008.

Unfortunately, Cap & Trade, in one form or another, is coming to America. Higher consumer prices, lobbyist free-for-alls, and even more CO_2 emissions are likely the short-term consequences, but for a preview of the endgame you have to once again look to Germany. Wolfgang Clement, the German economic minister during the time the EU Cap & Trade program was launched, paints a frightening scenario. "At the end of their policy," he recently told the *New York Times*, "is the deindustrialization of Germany."

There is no reason to think that those who are promoting radical shifts in policy and massive transfers of wealth here in America aren't aiming for exactly the same thing.

THE INCOME GAP: THE RICH GET RICHER, GOOD FOR THEM!

I added an exclamation mark to the heading above because I wanted to make sure that people are reading it the right way: *Good for them!!!!!!* Why have we lost that perspective in America?

The "rich" are so often made out to be evil corporate CEOs making $10–$20 million a year while their stock price collapses and their plants are closed, forcing poor Sally Muckenfutch and her four kids into foreclosure. But that's the cartoon version of rich. There is a real difference between being "wealthy" and being "greedy." The former is a goal; the latter is one of the seven deadly sins. Saying that all wealthy people are greedy is like saying that all poor people deal crack. It's simply not true.

The more realistic version of the rich in America is the family making $350,000 a year, putting a few kids through college, paying a big mortgage on a nice house, maybe employing some people in a business, and, oh yeah—paying the majority of this country's tax bill.

No one is saying that family deserves your sympathy, but they certainly don't deserve your scorn, either.

There are a lot of opinions on how best to help the poor rise out of poverty, but, as typically happens with issues that get politicized, the debate has turned into a manufactured battle between the classes. The lower class is angry that the upper class supposedly gets all the breaks, the middle class is angry that they're supposedly vanishing, and the upper class is angry that everyone apparently wants them to *actually* vanish.

The great myth is that one class can succeed only to the detriment of others—and that myth is now so commonly accepted that's it hardly ever challenged. For example, Michelle Obama recently said, "The truth is, in order to get things like universal health care and a revamped education system, then someone is going to have to give up a piece of their pie so that someone else can have more."

Sorry, Michelle, the truth is that that's absolutely *not* the truth. The only people who look at financial success as slices of pie are those who believe that you can't make it on your own; people who think that the only way you'll ever get more pie is if you take it away from others.

What a terrible way to look at things. A much better way (especially if you want to stick with the bakery examples . . . which I'm never opposed to) is that every single one of us is *making* our own pie using a virtually limitless supply of ingredients. Some people are really good at it and they make extra-large pies that they're able to share it with others. Other people make small but tasty pies that they're perfectly happy with. But, at no time during all of this baking, is anyone taking pie away from others who want to make it themselves. The only people restricting us from making more and more pie is the government, because they control most of the ingredients.

Best Pie of All Time:
Strawberry Rhubarb
A.D.D. MOMENT

Instead of being territorial about our own pies we should be far more motivated to help others get better at baking their own. After all, the more people with larger pies the better, because they're our nation's safety net; they have food when others are hungry.

Unfortunately, this vilification of the financially successful is one of the issues that I think has a real chance to spiral out of control over the next few years. Let's face it—the *real* economy is in tatters. America is technically bankrupt. We have trillions in unfunded promises and our creditors (like China) can stop financing us anytime they'd like. So guess where America's bailout money going to come from . . .

Yes, the wealthy.

They'll pay more in federal, state, and, in many cases, local taxes. Their deductions will be limited, the Alternative Minimum Tax will be increased, and payroll taxes will go up. And if you're sitting here reading all of that and thinking "cry me a river," then just consider the end result: an entire class of people who are unable to continue baking the pies that so many others have come to count on.

MEDIA BIAS: AN ALL-NEW FAIRNESS DOCTRINE

I saw an article in the paper recently about how MTV is introducing 16 new reality shows to their lineup. One of the executives said that the programs won't be the typical *Real World*–type shows we're used to. Instead, he explained, the shows will be about inspiration and doing good, because those are the values of the "Obama Generation."

Really? I find it hard to believe that a) Obama already has a "generation" named after him, and b) A first-term president with no meaningful accomplishments has magically altered the television viewing habits of millions of American youths.

What's much more likely is that MTV (along with all of the other media outlets that are suddenly faced with declining ratings and revenue) has finally figured out that American values, like hard work, honesty, charity, and personal responsibility, never went away—and, best of all, they still sell. Obama might be a convenient excuse to incorporate those values into their programming, but they've always been here.

That, I suppose, is one of the lessons I've learned in the time since this book was initially published. For all of the obvious media bias that we covered in that chapter (and for the nauseating bias that happened during the campaign) the truth is that the goal of most media companies is simple: to make a lot of money. If they can make money while also promoting their agendas, even better—but when that bias begins to cost them, things change fast.

For most of its existence, MSNBC had no real identity. Then Keith Olbermann came along with his in-your-face liberal activism ridiculously masquerading as Edward R. Murrow–like journalism. His anti-Bush "Special Comments" resonated with viewers, ratings swelled, and soon people like Chris Matthews ("I felt a thrill running up my leg" after an Obama speech), David Gregory, and Rachel Maddow filled the primetime lineup.

I can't blame MSNBC for that (although blending their news division with clearly biased commentators was a terrible idea—and the audience let them know it), just as I can't blame any other outlet for trying to attract other niche groups. Whether that means conservatives, blacks, or peg-legged Asian midgets—if that's where they think the money is, then that's the direction the programming will (and should) go.

In fact, it's when companies *stop* going after the markets they think will make them money and *start* running their businesses based on government regulations or a misplaced sense of elitism that they end up getting into trouble. The *New York Times* is a great example. Back when my fiction book *The Christmas Sweater* was number one on their bestseller list we wondered whether they would review it. (We didn't wonder, however, what that review would've said.) Not surprisingly, they didn't. In fact, best as I can tell, they reviewed only *one* of the books that made the top ten that week—you know, the books that hundreds of thousands of people were *actually buying.*

Instead, the *Times* chose to review books like *The World Is What It Is: The Authorized Biography of V. S. Naipaul* (review excerpt: "A monument truly worthy of its subject . . . " It's sold about 7,000 copies); *The Superorganism: The Beauty, Elegance, and Strangeness of Insect Societies* (". . . an astonishing account"; sold about 7,400 copies). I'm sure those are both tremendous books, but I'm also sure that most readers of the *Times* don't care.

The truth is that the *Times* thinks they are better than you and their "reporting" proves it. That's why they have the audacity to write scathing editorials about how the war in Iraq is completely lost (see July 8, 2007, "The Road Home") and then never bother to apologize/explain/recant once they've been proven dangerously wrong.

But when people or companies don't hold themselves accountable, others will. (I submit the *Times*' subscriber base as Exhibit A.) The only exception, of course, is when that accountability is trumped by politically expedient bailouts. The Big Three U.S. automakers, for instance, tried to take responsibility for their poor decisions far too late. The result *should've* been organized bankruptcies, but that was, at least temporarily, avoided by the government's insistence on giving them billions more of our tax dollars.

> **Here's** how that should-be-infamous-but-isn't *Times* editorial on Iraq started: "It is time for the United States to leave Iraq, without any more delay than the Pentagon needs to organize an orderly exit . . . Whatever [Mr. Bush's] cause was, it is lost." Wow, you guys really nailed that one!
>
> **A.D.D. MOMENT**

The point is that we're succeeding in turning a very simple capitalist concept (survival of the fittest) into a very complicated system where your survival depends on some black-box formula involving your revenue, union contracts, lobbyist payments, and the chance that your demise will trigger that always frightening "systemic collapse" of our entire economy.

Take talk radio, for instance. It's a business and, like any business, the goal is to make money. Democrats, many of whom don't like the fact that conservative talk is successful, want to change the rules of the game. Profits don't matter, they argue. What matters is serving the public good—and that means balancing out conservative viewpoints with opposing liberal ones.

A.D.D. MOMENT I wonder how the *New York Times* would've felt if the Bush administration decided that they'd had enough of their liberal editorials and mandated that each left-leaning opinion be balanced by one with an opposing view printed right next to it.

A.D.D. MOMENT Actually—maybe the better question is how the *New York Times* shareholders would've felt. After all, they're the ones down about 85 percent over the last five years.

I can't believe I have to ask this, but doesn't anyone still believe that the public good has something to do with what kind of programming the public decides *is* good?

The beauty of our system (that we're now ruining) is that the market gets to decide what they like and they vote with their wallets. While the failed liberal radio network Air America is usually cited as an example of how those votes have turned out, the truth is that liberal talk has been tried time and again (both locally and nationally) and the result is almost always the same.

Fort Lauderdale conservative talk station WFTL recently tried to experiment by giving a show to a liberal journalist. It didn't go well. "Our listeners did not like that," said Ken Pauli, director of news and operations. "That's no reflection on [his] talent. But when his show came on, conservatives turned us off and liberals didn't come looking for him."

Imagine if Senator Byrd were put in charge of programming America's radio stations? We'd all be forced to listen to groups of white guys playing big band. A.D.D. MOMENT

It's at this point when those who are in favor of ideas like the Fairness Doctrine step in and say, "Well, just because people aren't listening doesn't mean that his show should be off the air! Ratings are secondary to balance—and that's why airtime needs to be allocated through legislation." In other words, the American people are too stupid to know what they like or to realize that there are other points of view out there and other places to get them. Of course, what's unspoken is that we need the politicians to swoop in and save us because, as always, they know best.

Fortunately (at least if you're a believer in free markets), not everyone has fallen for the idea that we need a federal bailout of liberal talk. Randi Rhodes, who hosts a liberal show that would undoubtedly benefit from any kind of Fairness Doctrine revival, told the *Miami Herald* that she doesn't want to be successful because of a federal mandate. "I'm not into legislating my way onto the air," she said. "I would never do that, I would never want that, I would never want the negative press that would go with something like that—'She's just on the radio because of the FCC.' I'd rather go into a board meeting and make the case for great radio. Stations should pick up my show because it's great radio, not because of the Fairness Doctrine."

Holy cow, Randi Rhodes and I agree on something! But, more importantly, what does it say about how we value success in America when a statement like that is so rare that I'm actually citing it in a book?

AMERICA'S OIL DEPENDENCE: THE PEAK OF STUPIDITY

When I originally wrote the chapter on oil I had no idea just how quickly America would face $150/barrel oil head-on. Yet, despite all of the congressional hearings, press conferences, and political promises . . . what has really changed?

The cost of plane tickets went up and experts called for the end of air travel as we know it. Now the ticket costs are back down but we're still paying to check a bag or eat something other than peanuts.

The cost of gas went up, Detroit got hurt, and now here we are with billions in loans to the Big Three even as consumers again start to test-drive the "evil" SUVs that were supposedly to blame for everything.

ANWR is still closed, ethanol is still subsidized, and the Kennedys still don't have to worry about wind turbines impeding their beautiful Cape Cod oceanfront view anytime soon. In other words, America after the 2008 energy crisis looks remarkably like the America before it.

"It's a sad characteristic of our society," James Schlesinger, America's first energy secretary, recently told the *Wall Street Journal*, "that energy issues get no political attention until prices run up." Then, when those prices inevitably fall, the politicians move on to something else and everything "goes back to normal."

When you look back, that's exactly what's happened—and not just with the oil issue. After 9/11 we were told that the only issue worth talking about was Islamic extremism and homeland security. That morphed into the wars in Afghanistan and Iraq, and all of the hearings and debates that came along with them. Then, in 2007, Iraq shared the spotlight with illegal immigration. Cue more hearings and debates. That bill was shot down, the politicians gave up, and 2008 brought us the energy issue on a silver platter. More hearings, debates, and inaction followed—and here we are now with the economy as the issue du jour.

It's like the whole country has my level of ADD. We frantically go from issue to issue, immersing ourselves in each of them, and then we move on to the next thing without solving anything (or, in most cases, we leave things much worse).

How bad have we done with the energy issue over the decades? When Jimmy Carter left office in 1981, renewable energy was responsible for about 7 percent our country's energy use. In 2007, after years of stops and starts, taxes and tax credits, mandates and regulations—renewable energy was responsible for about 6.7 percent.

Impressive!

Even more impressive is the way the U.S. auto industry has responded to the challenges of our time. A recent article in the *Wall Street Journal* summed it up like this: "The combined car and light truck fleet in 1981 had a fuel-efficiency rate of around 20.5 miles per gallon . . . Today, it clocks in at 20.8 miles per gallon, an improvement of just 1.5% in 27 years."

Whew, am I glad we bailed those guys out! How would we ever live without that kind of progress?!

The truth is that we are no closer to getting ourselves on a path toward energy stability now than we were a year, two years, or 18 years ago. And the short-term solution I offered, which was to buy time while we encourage the innovators to innovate, has been ignored only slightly less than Michael Moore's health-care advice.

Which brings us to President Obama. While many people believe that we can end our addiction to oil and fight global warming simultaneously by doing time-tested, common-sense things (like building more nuclear power plants), progressives see an opportunity to go much farther. Using the recession as an excuse, they'll pass enormously expensive programs designed to fund "renewable energy" projects and "green jobs"—all under the guise of economic recovery. But a government-funded job is really just a government job, which means that we'll soon not only still be calling the Saudi king to beg for more oil, but we'll also be calling the Chinese paramount leader to beg for more cash.

WHAT I'VE LEARNED

In 1961 Yale University professor Stanley Milgram performed a now-famous experiment in which he asked people to press a button that administered increasingly painful electrical shocks to unseen participants.

In reality, the button did nothing, but Milgram's subjects didn't know that. The result was that 82.5 percent of them kept pressing the button even after hearing the actor on the receiving end cry out in pain. In fact, most of the subjects kept cranking the voltage all the way up to the maximum of 450 volts.

In 2008, that experiment was repeated with just a few small tweaks. The result? Seventy percent of participants continued to administer shocks even after hearing the actor complain about the pain. "What we found," said the new experiment's coordinator, Jerry Burger of Santa Clara University in California, "is validation of the same argument—if you put people into certain situations, they will act in surprising, and maybe often even disturbing, ways."

So what does all of this have to do with America? Well, between the election and the economy it's been a trying time. Watching all of the lying, the broken promises, and the bailouts has brought me to an important realization . . . a realization that was underscored by the results of that experiment: You have to know and understand exactly what you believe in, because the day will soon come when those beliefs will be put to the ultimate test.

No one went into the Milgram or Burger experiments thinking that they were the type of person who would readily agree to torture others. But most of them did it anyway. Why?

Because they were ordered to.

Likewise, the vast majority of us believe in little things like the individual right to bear arms, freedom of speech, or the right to privacy. But how many of us would be willing to compromise on those values if we were ordered to? How many of us when faced with someone at our door demanding to search our home for guns would open it? How many of us when faced with a government order to shut down our blog that was critical of that very government would do it?

Putting your trust in people to do the right thing, especially those people to whom we've lent our power, will almost always result in disappointment. That's why you have to put your trust in things that are everlasting; things that won't ebb and flow with the times or change their core values based on some poll.

Things like our Constitution and our Creator.

The words contained in our Constitution, while written by our founding fathers, come directly from God—as do the rights they grant us.

Read them. Know them. Believe in them.

When everything around us is crumbling, *they* will be our only true guide.

I guess that what I've learned over the last year is really something that I've known all along: The best way to solve whatever problems we face and keep America great is by putting our **trust** in God, our **faith** in the Constitution, and, most importantly, neither of those things into the people we elect.

Or . . . we could just sit back and hope for change. The choice is yours.

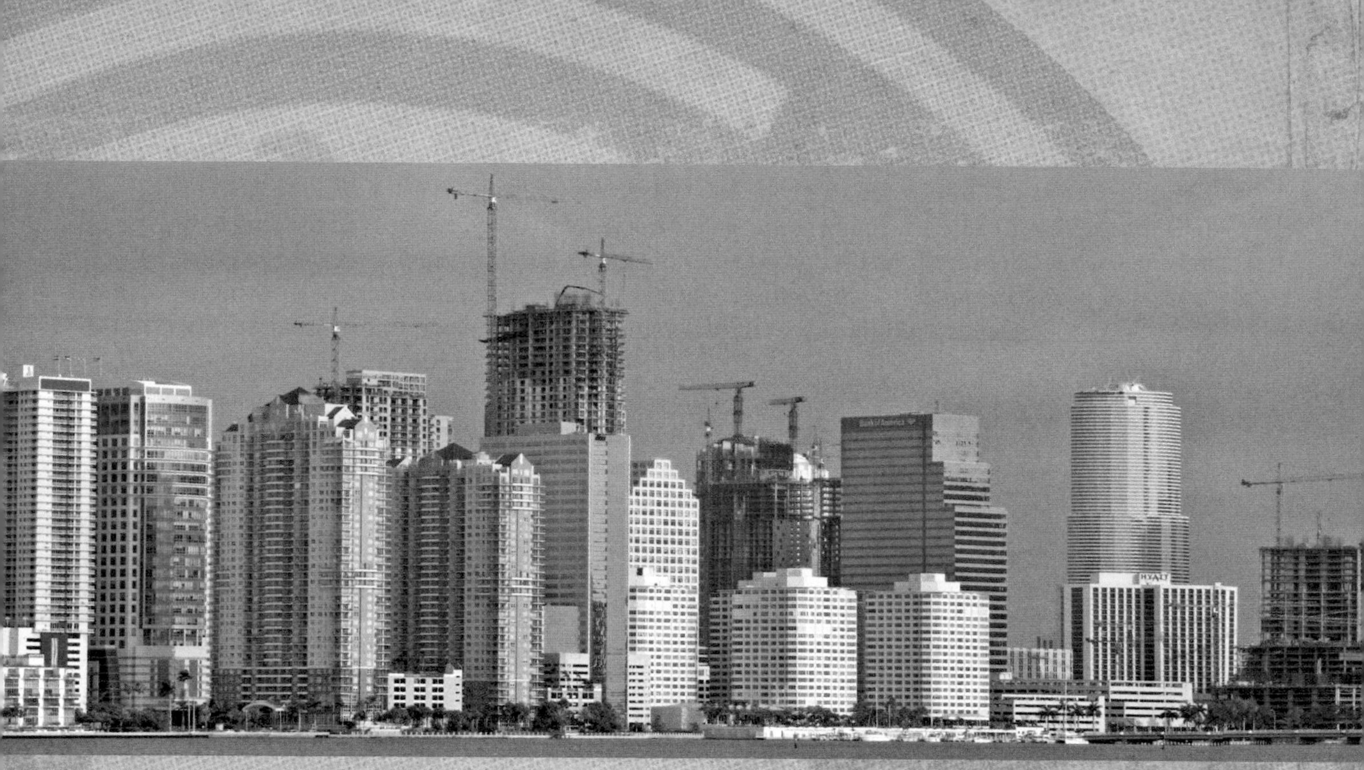

Chapter 1

Global Warming, Storming, and Conforming

THE SKYLINE OF MIAMI is a spectacular sight, but not because of the lights, the sunsets, or even the flesh-covered plastic that's wrapped in bikinis lying on the beaches in the distance. It's the cranes. There are dozens of them.

It looks as if every two buildings in the city are divided by one that's under construction, topped with a crane like the star on top of a Christmas tree. It truly is southern Florida's capitalist equivalent of the birth of Christ. In the next few years alone, approximately 100 skyscrapers will be somewhere between the stages of just finished or about to be started—and that's just in downtown Miami. Drive across to Miami Beach or down to Fort Lauderdale, and you'll see similar, if not quite as dramatic, development. Even 60 miles north of Miami, the far-from-fabulous, overly underwhelming oceanfront Briny Breezes trailer park has caught the eye of developers. They offered to buy the land from the 411 Briny Breeze residents for $510 million, a deal that would have made all of them instant millionaires.

Of course, South Florida is also a haven for the rich and famous. Lenny Kravitz, Ricky Martin, Enrique Iglesias, Anna Kournikova, Diddy (or "The Didster," as I call him), Gloria Estefan, Beyoncé, Matt Damon, Calvin Klein, Hulk Hogan, and Rosie O'Donnell are just a few who own houses there.

Yes, the overwhelming scientific consensus is that people want to live in Miami.

The question is . . . why? Have they not seen *An Inconvenient Truth?* Don't they know the risks of global warming? Why are people so passionate about living in a place that will soon be under water?

There seems to be an incredible disconnect between what Al Gore says and what people do. Why is that?

Some, of course, will blame a mass disinformation campaign (funded by Evil Big Oil) that can only be deciphered by the enlightened 21 percent of Americans who think that greenhouse gases are the most important factor causing global warming. But the truth is that most people never even hear honest questioning on this issue because, when it comes to global warming, dissent has its price.

Here are just a few quick highlights of what "the enlightened" say about those who dare to ask logical questions about global warming:

- Heidi Cullen, climatologist at The Weather Channel, suggested disagreement should mean a loss of meteorological certification: "If a meteorologist can't speak to the fundamental science of climate change, then maybe the AMS shouldn't give them a Seal of Approval."
- Ellen Goodman, from the *Boston Globe*, wrote: "Let's just say that global warming deniers are now on a par with Holocaust deniers, though one denies the past and the other denies the present and future."
- David Roberts, of climate website *Grist,* wrote: "When we've finally gotten serious about global warming, when the impacts are really hitting us and we're in a full worldwide scramble to minimize the damage, we should have war crimes trials for these bastards—some sort of climate Nuremberg."
- In fact, the Nazi references are quite popular with this crowd; I was even called "CNN's chief corporate fascism advocate" by Robert F. Kennedy Jr. When asked by the *Washington Post* why I was a fascist (or a fascism advocate), Kennedy said that he recalled that I was "voicing doubts about global warming a few weeks back." How dare I! But the fact is that

A.D.D. MOMENT

It may be time to review exactly what the word *fascist* means, since it's now being constantly thrown around. First of all, I have not killed anywhere near 7 million Jews. In fact, I can't personally remember even killing 1 million. I did drink quite a bit back in the day, but I think I'd remember something like that. Second, one of the key elements of fascism was controlling public thought by using fear to silence dissent. Hmm . . . which side of the argument is doing that? Those who are encouraging questions and debate or those who refer to the Holocaust when they run into disagreement? I'd say RFK Jr. is a fascist, but I doubt he's killed any Jews either. Let me know if I'm wrong on that one, Bob.

Ocala

Orlando

John Travolta

FLORIDA

Tampa

Stephen King

Celine Dion

Donald Trump

Jupiter Island

Lake Okeechobee

Casey Key

Drew Barrymore

Palm Beach

Andy Roddick

Fort Myers

Rosie O'Donnell

Boca Raton

P. Diddy

Current Coastline

Predicted Coastline

Gloria Estefan

Star Island

Anna Kournikova

Miami Beach

> RFK Jr. "recalled" (translation: some blog told him) incorrectly. I simply asked questions about whether or not man is primarily responsible, which, as you'll see, is an entirely reasonable question.

Since I know that I'll be taken out of context and made to say what I don't believe, let me try to make my position perfectly clear.

1. Yes, I think the globe has warmed a bit! Approximately 0.74 degree Celsius (+/– 0.18 degree) in the last 100 years. (0.74 +/– 0.18? Isn't that a 24 percent margin of error?)
2. Yes, I think that man might be responsible for some part of that warming, although I'm not 100 percent convinced of how much (126 percent margin of error).
3. I believe that natural changes are also playing a part in the warming and that the only thing constant about the climate *is* change.
4. I believe that we don't fully understand the climate yet, and we must be careful until we do.
5. I don't believe that so-called solutions, such as the Kyoto Protocol, are the answer for a myriad of reasons (see 4 above).
6. I believe that science, governments, and the media must stop shutting down dissenting views.
7. Because I live in the Northeast, I would like approximately 30 degrees of global warming in the winter, followed by a 10-degree global cooling in the summer. A gentle global breeze would be nice too.

"Climate change (provides) the greatest chance to bring about justice and equality in the world."
"No matter if the science is all phony, there are still collateral environmental benefits (to global warming policies)."
—Christine Stewart, Canada's former environment minister
I
Environmentalists Say the Darndest Things!

PLEASE BLIND THEM FROM THE SCIENCE

I am not a scientist. I have never sat in a lab with beakers and test tubes and poured bubbling liquids together to make smoky gases. But I am a thinker. I've tried to boil down a ridiculous amount of information into some of the more interesting arguments from actual scientists known as "skeptics." Warning: There's a reason scientists don't have girlfriends; this stuff can get a tad boring at times. I'll do my best to keep it short and as little like physical torture as possible.

In the Deep End

An Inconvenient Truth pumped more graphs, charts, and animations into the American airwaves in one movie than is normally allowed by the EPA in a century. But one of the more famous visuals was the previously mentioned drowning peninsula of Florida, where the ocean rises up to cover Florida as if it were a raft that a really fat person had just stepped on. The water engulfs everything from the southern tip of Florida to about 100 miles north and connects Lake Okeechobee to the Atlantic Ocean.

But Gore's apocalyptic yet tropical (apoca-tropical) vision of the future was based on a water level rise that is about 17 times higher than what the United Nations International Panel on Climate Control is expecting. In fact, it's even five times higher than the *high* end of the *worst-case scenario* painted by scientists who thought the UN report was too conservative.

A.D.D. MOMENT When I say that those who disagree with the "consensus" on global warming are routinely attacked, I should point out an important caveat. You seem to be criticized only if you say there will be *less* devastation. When Gore says there will be far more than the UN, he's not only embraced, he wins Oscars.

Lung Cancer Causes Smoking

Another one of the most powerful moments in *An Inconvenient Truth* is when Al Gore gets on his fancy hydraulic lift and stands in front of a gigantic screen featuring a graph that shows carbon dioxide (CO_2) and temperature moving in unison for hundreds of thousands of years. Since I'd gone to see the movie with an open mind, I initially thought to myself, "Wow, there might very well be something to this!" Sure, Al Gore is kind of creepy and robotic and without a doubt is giving a tabloid version of the facts, but there seems to be a pretty obvious correlation.

Not surprisingly, there is a reason the chart was zoomed out so far. It's because perspective is everything. If you zoom in, you'll start to see that in many cases, the temperature rises *before* the CO_2 rises; sometimes between 800 and 1,000 years earlier. As geologist and paleoclimate expert Dr. Bob Carter puts it, to say that CO_2 is the primary cause of temperature change is like saying that lung cancer causes smoking.

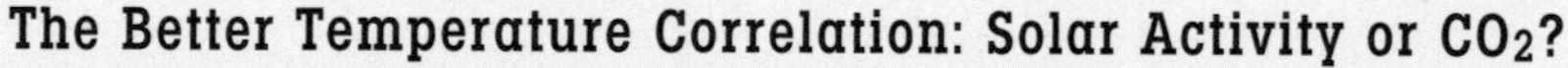

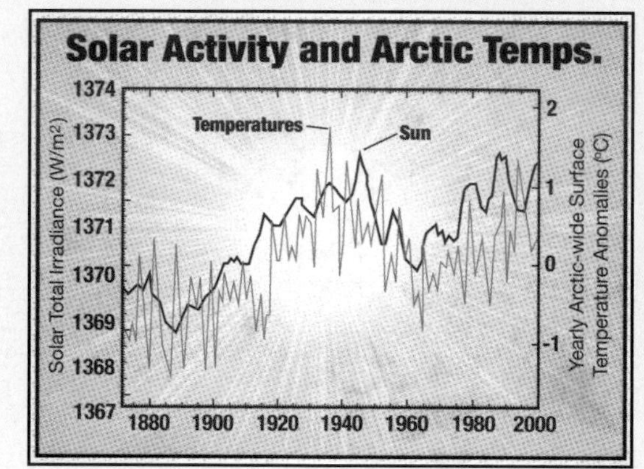

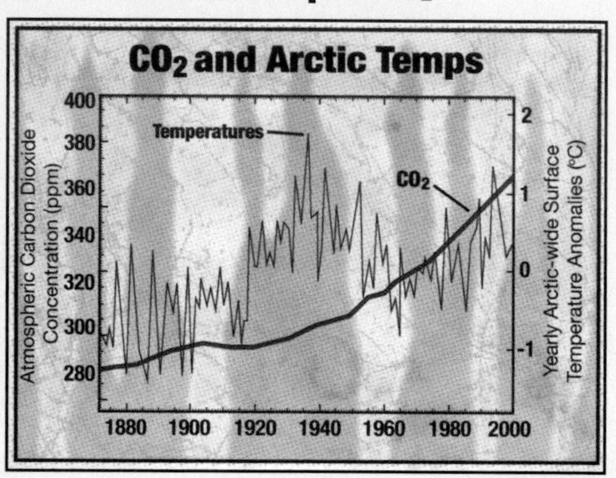

Great Ball of Fire

Have you noticed that from the time you wake up in the morning to the middle of the day, the globe seems to warm? Have you also noticed how that warming seems to correspond with that giant ball of light in the sky? It's so weird!

I strongly advocate the introduction of sunscreen on the atmosphere. No less than SPF 15.

A.D.D. MOMENT

Actually, many scientists do believe the activity of the sun is at an 8,000-year high over the past 60 years and may very well be at least partially responsible for the recent warming trend.

The correlation between solar activity and temperature is unmistakable, but scientists are still debating how much influence the sun really has. In 2004, Paula Reimer, a paleoclimate expert at Queens University in Belfast, said, "Whether solar activity is a dominant influence in these [climate] changes is a subject of intense debate." But just two years later, in September 2006, she updated her opinion: "A couple of years ago, I would not have said that there was any evidence for solar activity driving temperatures on Earth. . . . Now I think there is fairly convincing evidence."

3 Billion Ford Expeditions

Environmentalists like to say that the solution to global warming is for every person to do his or her part. The truth is that their ideas about how we should all do that are almost always symbolic gestures that do nothing to actually change CO_2 emissions.

Honestly, if buying a hybrid would really help, I would gladly do it. What black-hearted nightmare of a human being is going to put the fact that a Honda Insight looks like a retarded space ship ahead of the future of the entire globe?

But what these same environmentalists don't tell you is just how small a piece of the puzzle your choice of automobile really is. So let me try to put this into perspective for you. Just the *increase* in the amount of coal that China will burn by 2020 will send as much CO_2 into the atmosphere as 3 billion Ford Expeditions, each driven 15,000 miles a year. That's right. The increased burning of *one* source of energy by *one* country is equal to the CO_2 emissions from 3 billion giant Ford Expedition SUVs. At its current pace, it would take Ford 15,000 years even to sell that many.

What about another "personal solution" constantly presented to us: the compact fluorescent lightbulb. Australia has implemented one of the most aggressive campaigns in the world, and they expect old-style incandescent lightbulbs to be completely phased out by 2010. The Australian government bragged that the program will save an average of 800,000 metric tons of CO_2 per year for the next four years. Wow! That *must* make a huge difference, right?

> **Be particularly** and immediately suspicious of anyone expressing environmental benefits in the form of "number of cars taken off the road." The U.S. Energy Star program says that if every home in America replaced one normal lightbulb with a fluorescent (using that realistic standard of "full compliance"), it would be the equivalent of taking 800,000 cars off the road. Sure, that sounds like a lot, but it's less than 0.1 percent of registered vehicles worldwide. Plus, transportation accounts for only about one-fifth of global emissions anyway. The people making these claims are undoubtedly aware of these facts; they are just trying to influence your behavior by making their ideas seem far more significant than they actually are.
>
> A.D.D. MOMENT

Wrong. What they left out is that the savings equate to a paltry 0.21 percent of Australian emissions. To put it another way, an *entire continent* being forced to use fluorescent lightbulbs will reduce world emissions by 0.003 percent. Of course, increases in other sectors would nullify the entire cut in approximately five hours. (Full disclosure: It's possible the plan's savings could skyrocket to 0.011 percent of projected world emissions by 2015.)

If you want to buy a hybrid or use a fluorescent lightbulb, go ahead. Please don't take this dose of truth as my way of telling you not to do so. But, as with the *American*

Idol contestant with no talent, it's time someone breaks the news to you: These changes will make essentially no difference in the problem you're trying to solve. Now I feel like Simon Cowell (minus an English accent and tens of millions of dollars).

Supermodels in Heat

Call me old-fashioned, but I have a hard time basing my planning for the future of the globe on the same device that brings me to YouTube to watch videos like "Boy Falls off Roof, Lands on Cat."

Computer models have drastically improved our understanding of everything from the climate to how to be a proficient minesweeper, but they are far from infallible. In a 2007 report largely ignored by the media, David Bromwich, researcher with the Byrd Polar Research Center at Ohio State University, found that temperatures in Antarctica aren't matching up with what climate models have been predicting: "The best we can say right now is that the climate models are somewhat inconsistent with the evidence that we have for the last 50 years from continental Antarctica. . . . We're looking for a small signal that represents the impact of human activity and it is hard to find it at the moment."

Remember, computer models are dependent on the humans that design them—humans who often already have their minds made up. If these things are wrong, even by a few tenths of a degree per decade, we could easily be facing another global-cooling hysteria like in the 1970s.

> **A.D.D. MOMENT** To truly test computer models, I had my producer Stu run an in-depth experiment using quite possibly the most advanced simulation software of all time: a computer program with more than $2 trillion invested in it so far: Madden 2007, for PlayStation 3. He ran 20 simulations of the 2006–07 NFL season (which, in reality, ended with the Colts defeating the Bears 29–17 in the Super Bowl), but our Madden simulations predicted the Colts getting to the Super Bowl only three times and the Bears only twice. It correctly predicted both teams in the game just once—which was the same number of times it matched up the Oakland Raiders and the Detroit Lions, the two worst teams in the league. So much for simulations.

Global Warming: It's What's for Dinner

As soon as it's released, the main report from the UN IPCC is always immediately embraced by the mainstream media. But the UN released another report on climate change in November 2006 that barely received any coverage at all. It was the same organization talking about the same topic, but *this* report didn't fit neatly into the media's political agenda, so it was largely ignored.

The report stated that livestock and the industry revolving around it are responsible for 18 percent of all greenhouse gases when measured in CO_2 equivalent. That's more than the entire worldwide transportation sector.

My first reaction was to support the brutal murder of all cows. "Attention, Hollywood vegans: You're either with us or you're with the bovines." But I quickly reminded myself about the law of supply and demand: The more juicy porterhouse you eat, the more cows they'll bring into this world to kill our lovely planet.

Livestock is responsible for 65 percent of a less publicized greenhouse gas—nitrous oxide—that warms the planet 296 times more than CO_2. In addition, livestock's "natural emissions" produce methane, which warms the planet 23 times as much as CO_2 (and is infinitely more fragrant). Since meat consumption is due to double by 2050, it's only going to get worse.

In addition, because methane cycles out of the atmosphere in less than one-twelfth of the time that CO_2 does, avoiding meat is a far quicker and more effective way of cutting greenhouse gases. I know that Al Gore is forced to travel around the globe in private jets to give his fancy slide shows, but he doesn't *have* to eat meat. Neither do global warming campaigners Bill Clinton, Arnold Schwarzenegger, or John McCain; but they all do it anyway. At least we finally have one piece of science that *is* settled: Any global warming activist who isn't a vegan is a hypocrite.

Global Warming Car Shopping

If, as environmentalists claim, global warming will cause catastrophic flooding that can only be solved by world governments playing nicely and working together, we're totally screwed. So why not plan for the inevitable by buying smart for the coming floods?

Sure, the Toyota Prius *looks* really cool, but when the floods arrive, you'll only have a five-inch ground clearance. But if you pick up a Hummer H1 instead, you'll not only get 16 inches of ground clearance but also the ability to drive comfortably in up to 30 inches of water! Another bonus is that you get to maintain some level of manhood.

A.D.D. MOMENT If the coastline floods, will we finally make the lowered, pimped-out Honda Civics a thing of the past? If so, I'm going to Lowe's to buy the longest garden hose I can find, run it from my faucet to the ocean, and leave it on until I stop seeing 1985 Toyota Corollas with ground effects. Yes, we might lose another 14 *The Fast and the Furious* sequels, but that's a risk I'm willing to take.

an inconvenient toot
A GLOBAL BROILING

FUN WITH FUNDS

One of the more amusing attacks on those who dare to doubt any piece of the wide-ranging global-warming "consensus" is to accuse them of receiving funding from Big Oil or some evil equivalent. If they haven't been paid directly by ExxonMobil, they surely know someone who knows someone, whose great-aunt teaches at a school where one of her students' brother was given a green Hess truck for Christmas in 1987. (When one of those links isn't available, the scientist is simply a hack. But that's another story.)

Honestly, who is a big-oil company going to give its money to: the politician it believes is giving it a fair shot or the politician who is literally saying its product is killing the earth? In reality, people and companies give their money to politicians and groups who believe what they believe. It's normally not too sinister. But the obvious implication of these attacks is that a scientist or a politician who receives funding from an organization cannot be depended on to fairly analyze information about their cause.

With that in mind, here are the top 10 recipients of environmental special-interest cash from 2000 to 2004 (the campaign years). Do I even need to include their party affiliation?

1. John Kerry .... '04
2. Al Gore .... '00
3. Paul Wellstone .... '02
4. Barbara Boxer .... '04
5. Bill Bradley .... '00
6. Mark Udall .... '00
7. Jay Inslee .... '00
8. Jeanne Shaheen .... '02
9. Jean Carnahan .... '02
10. Barack Obama .... '04

(From the Center for Responsive Politics)

"To capture the public imagination, we have to offer up some scary scenarios, make simplified dramatic statements and little mention of any doubts one might have. Each of us has to decide the right balance between being effective, and being honest."

—Stephen Schneider, lead 2007 UN IPCC report author and climate alarmist, who made this statement back in 1989. He also wrote one of the reports that led to the global-cooling scare of the 1970s. How does this guy still have a job?

Environmentalists Say the Darndest Things!

SCARE TACTICS 101

When science, reason, and political attacks alone can't win a battle of ideas, it's time to start thinking like the director of a horror movie. How long until one of the sequels to *Saw* has some half-dressed 18-year-old girl being tortured by the evils of global warming? You know it's coming.

Here are some of my favorite scare tactics used in the media recently. Boo!

Polar Bear Cannibalism

"Polar Bears May Turn to Cannibalism," ABC News, June 13, 2006.

This one is a little confusing. I guess I don't want a bunch of cuddly white-furred Jeffrey Dahmers lounging around in the Arctic, but what kind of polar bears are we talking about? The cute animated ones from the Coke commercials or the *real* ones that could rip your chest open as if it's the plastic wrap on a package of ground beef? If it's *those* polar bears, then let 'em eat each other.

An Inconvenient Nuke!

Does Al Gore use scare tactics? Of course not! Look at these three sequential screen shots from the trailer for *An Inconvenient Truth*. There's a car that's underwater and what I would describe as a sad forest without leaves. But in between? A nuclear explosion? Is that an underreported effect of global warming?

Can the media scare little Billy?

Let's see how he reacts to each scare tactic.

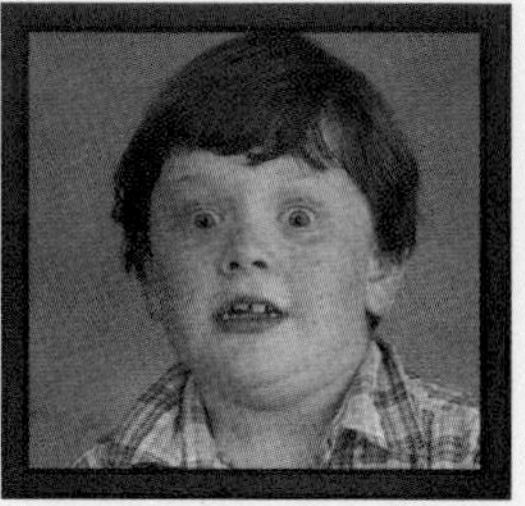

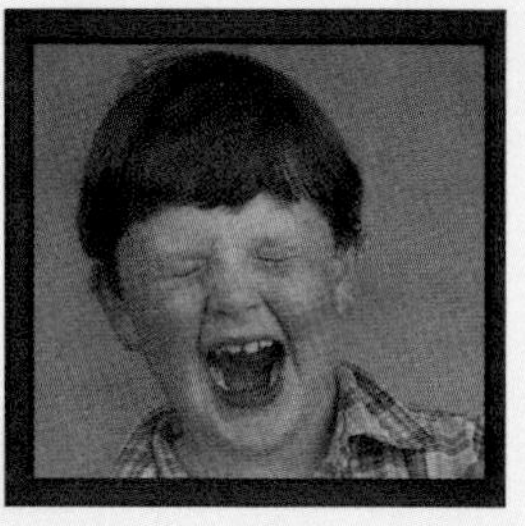

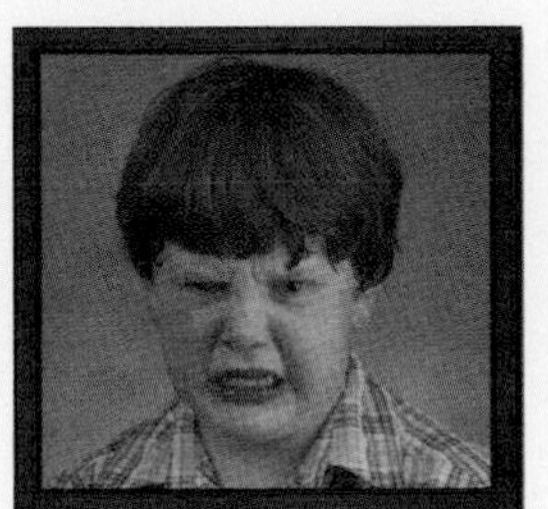

The Day After Tomorrow!

Obviously, the idea of Statue of Liberty–sized waves and oil tankers frozen in the streets of New York City is a tad ridiculous. But follow me on this one: *The Day After Tomorrow* made a bunch of money, leading to more acting jobs for Jake Gyllenhaal, which led to two dudes in a tent on *Brokeback Mountain*.

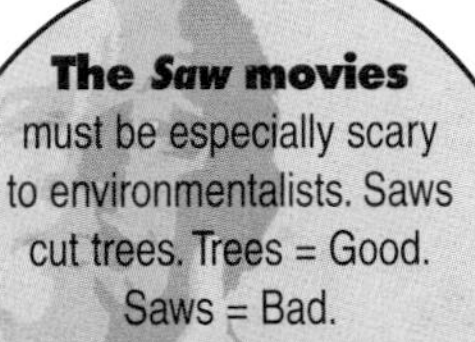

The *Saw* movies must be especially scary to environmentalists. Saws cut trees. Trees = Good. Saws = Bad.

Scientists Say It's Already Too Late!

"It's much too late to sweat global warming,"
San Francisco Chronicle, *February 13, 2005.*

Oookkaayyyy . . . so if there's nothing anyone can do about it, why am I going to do anything about it?

Science Fun For Kids!

Play at home with mom and dad!

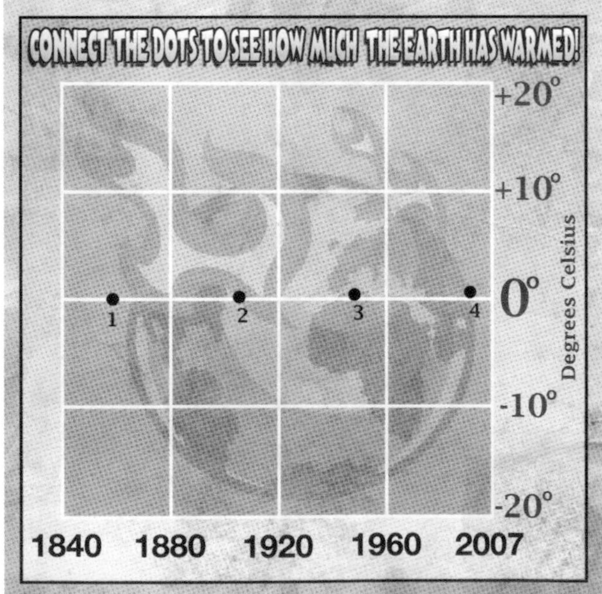

CONNECT THE DOTS TO SEE HOW MUCH THE EARTH HAS WARMED!

Hedgehogs Are Losing Their Prickles!

A hedgehog named Glen "is having to make do without any prickles—apparently thanks to global warming,"
Daily Mail, *U.K., January 31, 2007.*

This is a very ineffective scare tactic. People don't like prickles on animals. I'm sure, on the surface, hedgehogs aren't excited about their version of male pattern balding, but maybe if they didn't have skin covered in needles, they'd make more snuggly pets.

Hornets Are Living Longer!

"Swarms of giant hornets renowned for their vicious stings and skill at massacring honeybees have settled in France. . . . Global warming has largely been blamed,"
Telegraph, *U.K., February 22, 2007.*

Asian hornets are supposedly living longer because of global warming and are becoming a threat to European beehives. So hornets are endangering bees? That seems like the kind of sectarian violence I can get behind!

Horror Movies Spawn Lots of Sequels

Interestingly, scare tactics seem to lead to bizarre and extreme measures to solve problems. Look at how far we've come from the global-cooling scare of the 1970s.

THE "SOLUTION" THEN: "Climatologists are pessimistic that political leaders will take any positive action to compensate for the climatic change, or even to allay its effects. They concede that some of the more spectacular solutions proposed, such as melting the arctic ice cap by covering it with black soot or diverting arctic rivers, might create problems far greater than those they solve," *Newsweek,* April 28, 1975.

THE "SOLUTION" NOW: A "layer of pollution deliberately spewed into the atmosphere to help cool the planet. . . balloons bearing heavy guns be used to carry sulfates high aloft and fire them into the stratosphere," *Washington Post*, November 16, 2006, by Nobel Prize–winning climatologist Paul J. Crutzen ("The reception on the whole is more positive than I thought," he said.)*

***An Inconvenient Footnote:** This period of horrific swings and misses called "global cooling" is usually dismissed by saying that there wasn't as much certainty then as there is now. You'd be hard-pressed to find that sentiment in the *Newsweek* article itself. In fact, there are grandiose statements in the exact opposite direction: *"The evidence in support of these predictions has now begun to accumulate so massively that meteorologists are hard-pressed to keep up with it."*

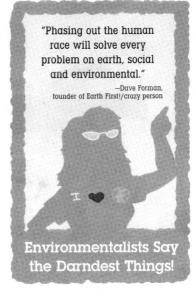

> "Phasing out the human race will solve every problem on earth, social and environmental."
>
> —Dave Forman, founder of Earth First!/crazy person
>
> **Environmentalists Say the Darndest Things!**

But the global-cooling age was far from the first climate scare. The *New York Times* wrote scary articles about cooling in 1924, warming in 1935, back to cooling in 1975, and, of course, warming again today. *Time* did essentially the same thing: cooling in 1924, warming in 1939, back to cooling in 1974, and then warming again today.

Some will say "1975 was a long time ago; science has improved so much since then!" Obviously, that's true. Scientists have done an immeasurable amount of good, usually as a result of allowing a full, honest, and open debate, the sort of debate not afforded to scientists from Switzerland in 1990.

While discussing the Montreal Treaty, which was designed to close the hole in the ozone layer, Swiss scientists said that changing to the chemicals being discussed could make another problem much worse: global warming. In fact, the new chemicals that scientists and environmentalists approved (without listening to Switzerland's objections) can harm the envi-

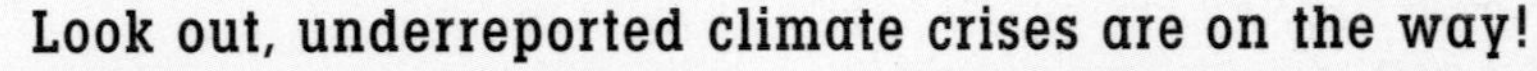

Look out, underreported climate crises are on the way!

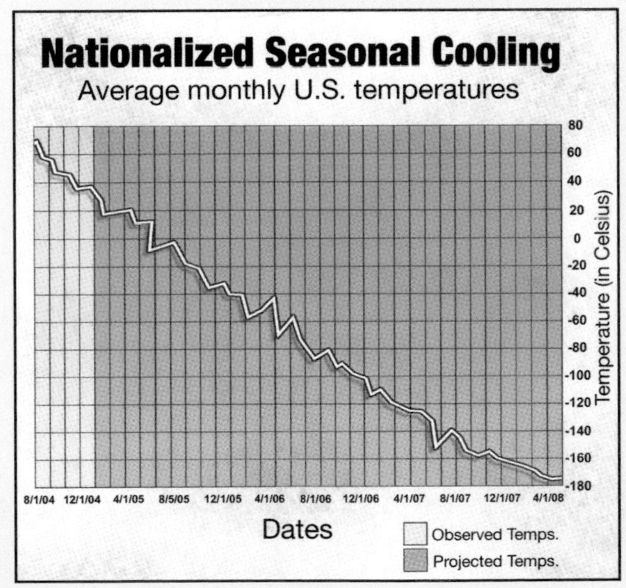

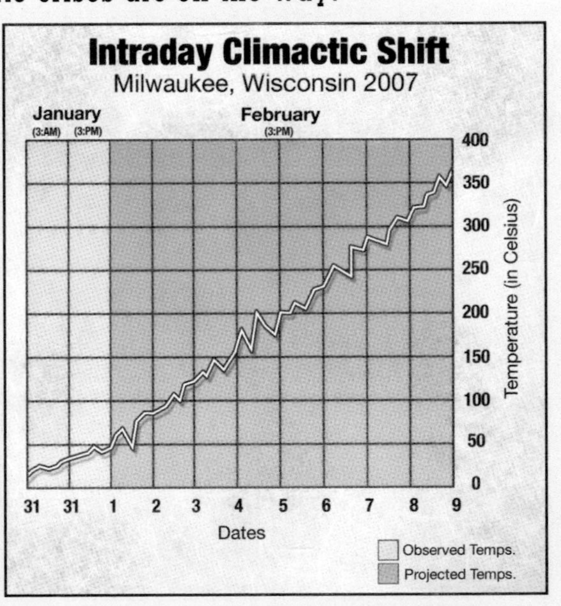

ronment up to 10,000 times more than carbon dioxide emissions. So the lesson is simple: Question everything . . . unless the Swiss say it.

Remember, environmentalists believed another ice age was right around the corner because temperatures had trended down from around 1940 through 1975. At that exact same time, CO_2 emissions were skyrocketing. Put another way, as CO_2 emissions went up, temperatures went down. But that fact, much like the musical career of Leif Garrett, never gets acknowledged today. That's not to say those 30 years make a global climate trend—but maybe, just maybe, the last 30 don't either.

To fight this pathetic record of ineptitude, the media, along with some members of the scientific community, just turn up the heat. They say they are *more* sure, they make *more* colorful statements about their certainty, and they get *more* violent with their language toward those who dare to question them.

Early in 2007, the *Houston Chronicle* ran a story with the headline "Scientists fear they've oversold global warming." Well, if that's true, then it didn't take long for the scientific community to continue to get over their fear. The very next day, Andrew Weaver, a coauthor of the UN climate report, said his findings aren't ". . . a smoking gun, but a barrage of smoking intergalactic missiles." Who talks like that?

A.D.D. MOMENT It took only a week before an article appeared referring to the "barrage of intergalactic missiles" report and going even farther. It was entitled "Experts: Latest climate report too rosy."

NO TO KYOTO

If science has occasional problems, the media have more, and the government has an unlimited supply. So far, the major solution that we've been pitched to fix global warming is the Kyoto Protocol, an embarrassment even by government standards.

To overly simplify the concept, Kyoto is basically a worldwide treaty created in the late 1990s that sets caps on each country's carbon dioxide emissions.

Even if we pretend for a second that every single thing global-warming alarmists claim is true (which it's not) and the Kyoto Protocol's guidelines were fully implemented (they're not even close), the effect on the climate would still be immeasurably small.

But let's look closer anyway, since Kyoto is the poster child

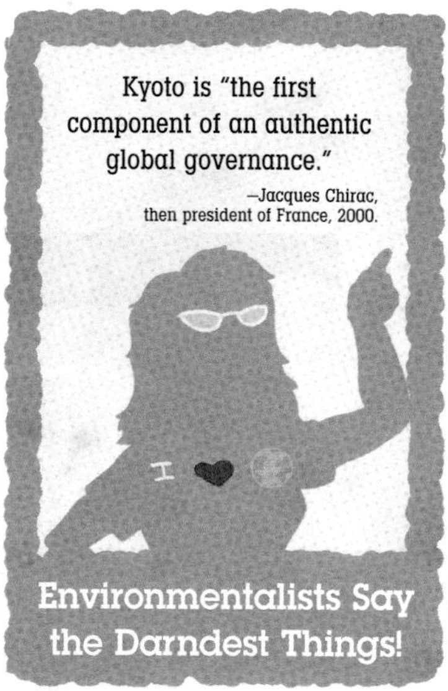
Kyoto is "the first component of an authentic global governance."
—Jacques Chirac, then president of France, 2000.
Environmentalists Say the Darndest Things!

for climate-change proposals. It's been reported that 13 of the original 15 EU nations will miss their targets, along with Canada and Japan (isn't Kyoto a city *in* Japan?). Russia will hit them, but only because they have to decrease their emissions from the days of the Soviet empire—meaning they essentially didn't have to do anything. England has a similar story. The British deregulated their electricity industry and eliminated coal subsidies, thereby making natural gas competitive in price for the first time. People started using more of it, and, since it burns cleaner, England's emissions went down without even a hint of personal virtue involved.

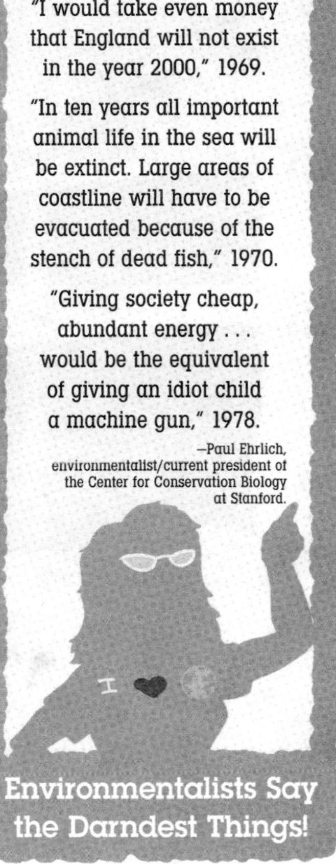

"I would take even money that England will not exist in the year 2000," 1969.
"In ten years all important animal life in the sea will be extinct. Large areas of coastline will have to be evacuated because of the stench of dead fish," 1970.
"Giving society cheap, abundant energy . . . would be the equivalent of giving an idiot child a machine gun," 1978.
—Paul Ehrlich, environmentalist/current president of the Center for Conservation Biology at Stanford.
I
Environmentalists Say the Darndest Things!

The rest of the EU is just comical:

- 64 percent of EU-25 countries *increased* their greenhouse gas output between 2003 and 2004 (the last year data was available).
- The emissions of the EU-15 have *risen* since 1999.
- The EU is only slightly more than *one-tenth* of the way to its Kyoto goals! Yay!

In fact, when Kyoto was opened for signature, the EU had already instantly achieved half of its goal, primarily because of economic changes along with a convenient backdating program. See, even though it was 1997, they used *1990* as the benchmark year from which countries had to reduce emissions. Since 1997, they have essentially made no progress whatsoever, and unless additional measures are enacted (and actually followed), post-Kyoto emissions will actually *increase*.

The U.S. Senate already voted down any treaty like Kyoto by a razor-thin margin of 95 to 0. Maybe that's because it's basically just a wealth-shifting program that holds our country to the highest possible standard while holding China to *no* standard.

A.D.D. MOMENT

Then you have China. The Chinese are building one or two new coal plants every week and are now the world's largest emitter of CO_2, yet they are completely exempt from Kyoto.

Developing nations argue that we *should* be held to a higher standard. After all, we were free to develop economically without these kinds of restrictions; they should be able to do the same. In other words, we did the damage, we should pay the price.

Really? Well, how did you get this technology in the first place? How is it cheap and efficient enough for you to afford? What's that? It's because countries like the United States dumped our money into developing it? Oh, that's right! I almost forgot, we actually spent our time and energy innovating instead of shutting down newspapers and running over protesters with tanks.

This argument shows just how ridiculous the implementation of this sort of agreement is. Everyone *always* thinks *they're* getting screwed. When it really comes down to it, do you think China is actually going to spend billions of dollars conserving energy in hopes of offsetting environmental problems (many outside their borders) that may occur decades in the future? Or do you think maybe they'll spend it on something that will immediately affect their economy? (Trick question. The correct answer is that they'll spend it on executing dissidents and buying big missiles to point at us.)

A SURPRISINGLY CONVENIENT TRUTH

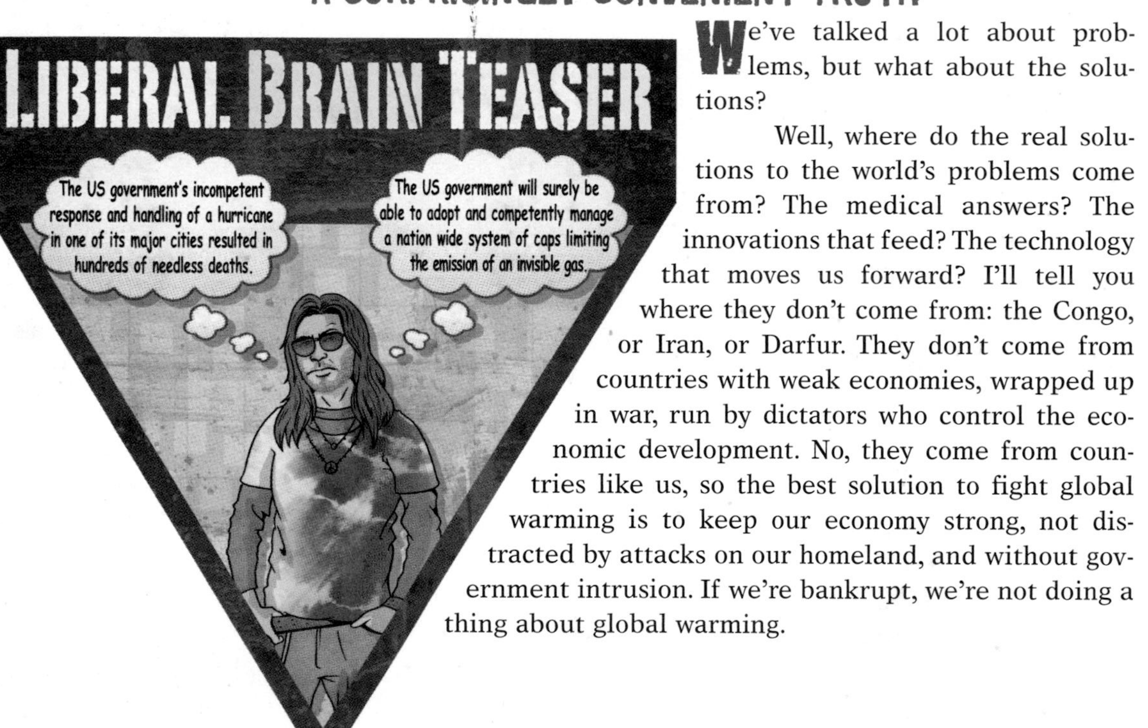

LIBERAL BRAIN TEASER
The US government's incompetent response and handling of a hurricane in one of its major cities resulted in hundreds of needless deaths.
The US government will surely be able to adopt and competently manage a nation wide system of caps limiting the emission of an invisible gas.

We've talked a lot about problems, but what about the solutions?

Well, where do the real solutions to the world's problems come from? The medical answers? The innovations that feed? The technology that moves us forward? I'll tell you where they don't come from: the Congo, or Iran, or Darfur. They don't come from countries with weak economies, wrapped up in war, run by dictators who control the economic development. No, they come from countries like us, so the best solution to fight global warming is to keep our economy strong, not distracted by attacks on our homeland, and without government intrusion. If we're bankrupt, we're not doing a thing about global warming.

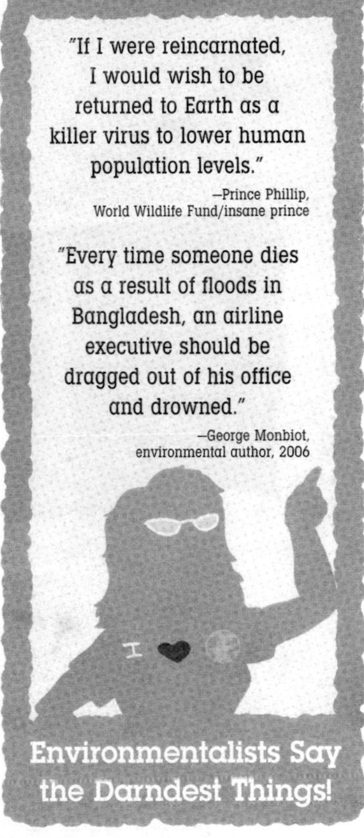

"If I were reincarnated, I would wish to be returned to Earth as a killer virus to lower human population levels."
—Prince Phillip, World Wildlife Fund/insane prince
"Every time someone dies as a result of floods in Bangladesh, an airline executive should be dragged out of his office and drowned."
—George Monbiot, environmental author, 2006
I ❤
Environmentalists Say the Darndest Things!

Let's look at hurricanes for a moment. What do we really know about them? One thing we do know is that *with or without* manmade CO_2 emissions, hurricanes will occur, and some of them will be devastating. People who give slide shows for a living promote the idea that continuing to drive your SUV will either result in more of these storms or make them more powerful. Unfortunately, this theory has become so widespread that it's now part of the so-called consensus that thou shalt not question. But, uncertainty aside, the science itself is, in many ways, irrelevant to what we should do about it.

Hurricane Katrina was tied directly to global warming in *An Inconvenient Truth* (although Al Gore was subtle about it. The movie's promotional photo featured a hurricane emanating out of a smokestack.) Katrina was obviously one of the largest natural disasters this nation has ever faced, but neither the power of the storm nor global warming was to blame. No, the real reason Katrina was so disastrous lies in the fact that it hit a city designed by morons: New Orleans was built in a bowl.

About a year before Katrina hit, we did a radio show about the tragedy that *could* occur in New Orleans if a powerful storm struck and the levees were breached. I wasn't clairvoyant; the information had been available for decades. The combination of the lack of preventive action, people deciding not to leave, and various government entities alternating between breaking and, perhaps worse, *making* promises was what turned Katrina from a hurricane into an event that is worthy of an episode of *Mega Disasters*.

Immediately following Katrina, another storm also reached Category 5 status: Hurricane Rita. It too made landfall but only directly killed seven people. That is far more typical of a powerful hurricane striking America.

Global warming didn't destroy New Orleans; geography, stupidity, and long-term government incompetence did.

Over and over again, America has weathered natural disasters as no other country has done, because we have better buildings, better detection technology, better communication systems to spread the word, and better response teams (despite popular misconception) than anyone else in the world. Why? Money.

In 1998, Hurricane Mitch slammed into Honduras, killing about 7,000 people and another 4,000 in Nicaragua (it would later go on to kill two people in the United States) In 2004, Hurricane Jeanne killed more than 3,000 in Haiti (then five people in the United States). True, these storms hit America with less force, but with the noted and explainable exception of Katrina, no hurricane of any strength has hit the United States and killed more than 100 people since 1972.

LOGICALLY TECHNOLOGICAL

When you hear alarmists rant about the imminent demise of the universe, you almost always hear them predict a lot about what the future will look like. But to most of us, the future isn't quite as dramatic, or frightening, as something happening right now. A small meteor that may slam into Canada next week is far more interesting than a huge asteroid that might wipe out the entire planet 290 years from now. So, to add the appropriate amount of urgency and drama, environmentalists must say that weather events such as droughts, floods, hurricanes, and extreme temperatures are getting worse and worse *right now*.

If that is true, then there should literally be no argument about how to move forward. The key to protecting us from the sometimes temperamental Mother Nature is not trying to control the weather; it's improving our society and simply preparing for inevitable changes. As our technology has improved and nations have become wealthier, the number of people killed as a result of extreme weather worldwide has decreased from 485,200 per year in the 1920s to 19,400 per year from 2000 to 2004. That's a decrease of 96 percent. And remember, there are a lot *more* people on the planet now, so if you look at death rates per million, you see a decrease of an astounding

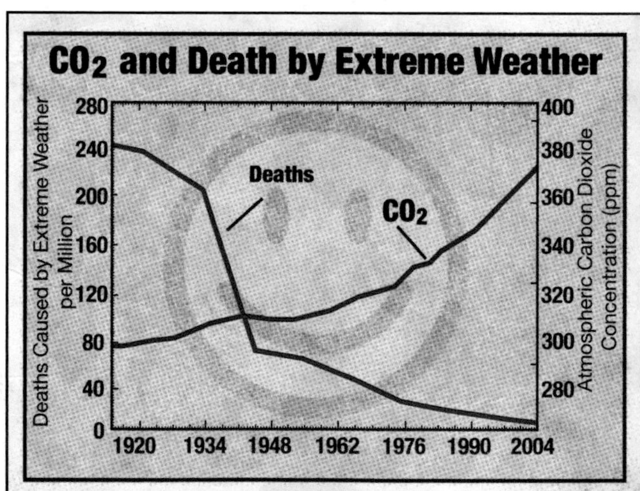

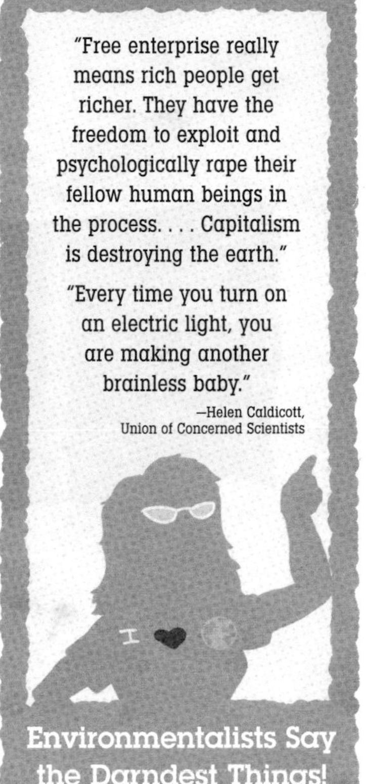

98.7 percent. All this while CO_2 emissions and temperatures have gone through the roof and extreme weather has supposedly worsened.

The tangible and measurable results are quite obvious to anyone who can turn on a computer, let alone produce their very own PowerPoint presentation: We are closer to completely eliminating death caused by weather than we are to destroying the planet because of it.

Armed with this information, what's the better course of action? Should we accept worldwide mandates that hurt our economy and must be followed by governments that can't even agree if the Holocaust happened, all in an effort possibly to reduce hurricane intensity by an estimated one-third of a percent per year; or should we keep our economy strong, continue to innovate, and then share those inevitable technological and economical innovations with the world?

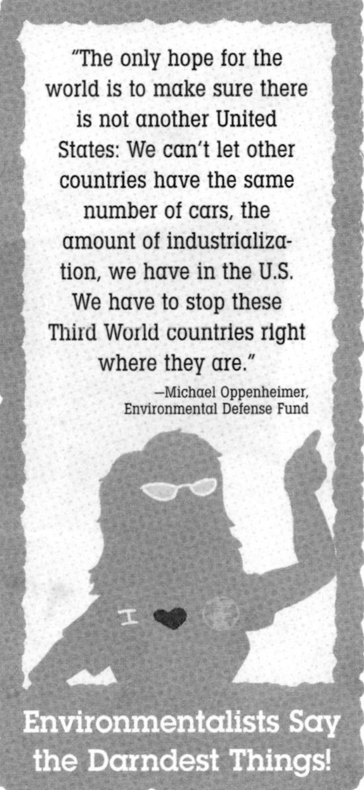

"The only hope for the world is to make sure there is not another United States: We can't let other countries have the same number of cars, the amount of industrialization, we have in the U.S. We have to stop these Third World countries right where they are."
—Michael Oppenheimer, Environmental Defense Fund
I
"Free enterprise really means rich people get richer. They have the freedom to exploit and psychologically rape their fellow human beings in the process. . . . Capitalism is destroying the earth."
"Every time you turn on an electric light, you are making another brainless baby."
—Helen Caldicott, Union of Concerned Scientists
Environmentalists Say the Darndest Things!

Implementing the emissions caps necessary theoretically to lower the temperature two degrees Celsius (which is the low end of the UN IPCC projections) would cost the world between $2.4 trillion and $26.5 trillion. What could we do with that $26.5 trillion instead? Oh, just the usual boring stuff like completely eliminating poverty, educating every child on the planet, and providing access to water and sanitation to everyone on earth for a century. After all that, we'd still have $21.9 trillion left to figure out how to spend.

A.D.D. MOMENT One idea: 109.5 trillion Wendy's Crispy Chicken Nuggets. Just an idea.

It's not just us evil rich countries affected by this environmental alarmism. Eritrea, located right next to beautiful Ethiopia, has announced plans to make its entire coastline an environmentally protected zone. It would specifically protect coral reefs, mangrove forests, and (I kid you not) nesting sites for turtles and 73 species of sea birds. That's their priority? This is a country with a life expectancy of less than 60, a literacy rate of 58.6 percent, and a poverty rate of around 50 percent, and they're worried about a little turtle sex?

I believe it was environmental scholar Richard Cheney who said it best: "Conservation may be a sign of personal virtue, but it is not a sufficient basis for a sound, comprehensive energy policy."

He was, of course, beaten up by every "dot org" in America for saying that, but it's true. The answer isn't for everyone to make sure their lights are turned off when they leave the room; it's not spending trillions on limiting an unmanageable system; and it's not making sure turtles have privacy when they do it.

MY SOLUTION

Let me propose a radical course of action to "solve" global warming: inaction.

I'm so sick of hearing "But shouldn't we at least try?" No—we shouldn't just try, we should try *smart*. When government just "tries," it creates new sets of problems without solving the old ones. Imagine if they had just "tried" to solve global cooling. We'd have far bigger problems on our hands today. The only true answer to this situation is to innovate and adapt.

The innovation part of the equation is both ongoing and virtually unstoppable. Investment in alternative energy reached an estimated $63 billion in 2006, more than double that of just two years earlier. Almost 10 percent of all venture-capital funding in America goes to clean energy, and this investment has already paid dividends.

The cost of generating power from wind has dropped by 60 percent since 1990, and power from the first solar cells in satellites is now 98.7 percent cheaper than when it was introduced. These technologies will be adopted by the world when—and *only* when—they make economic sense, not when we have to depend on countries like Russia and China to be virtuous. Sure, our government can help in the form of tax breaks and incentives, but capitalism is already well on its way to solving this problem itself.

At the same time, we also need to adapt with more obvious solutions. When the heat wave of 2003 hit Europe, nearly 35,000 (mostly elderly) people died. The size and scope of the tragedy gave global-warming theorists an opportunity to spout their views to almost every news camera on the globe. They claimed that events like this justify the EU spending an estimated $1.443 trillion by 2023 to alter its energy industry enough to possibly avert climate change.

Let me propose another option. A hundred years ago, there was nothing you could do about a heat wave except stay away from fat, smelly, sweaty relatives. Now we can do this magic thing called "condition the air"—35,000 air conditioners cost about $2.5 million dollars. Or perhaps you pick a few vacant office buildings that your economy and its double-digit unemployment rates can't support and turn the AC on. Then just fire up a few gasoline-powered school buses, and shuttle old people to the air-conditioned facilities. Repeat every time it gets hot.

In spite of what we want to believe, the earth is not a Lexus that we can climb into, turn the climate control to a comfortable 70 degrees, and leave it there until the end of time. The real climate has millions of variables, and there is still way too much that we don't know. So until we understand it all, the best way we can help is by continuing to increase our investment in clean energy. It's good for our country and the world for other reasons, and if global warming is as awful as some believe, clean energy will help solve that too.

> **A.D.D. MOMENT**
>
> **One relatively easy solution** for many of our power-related problems is nuclear energy. It's clean, it has a stronger-than-you-think history of safe use, and it is already economically viable. The two problems are (1) The same people who complain about fossil fuels have already succeeded in surrounding the industry with so much red tape that we haven't built a new nuclear plant in decades; and (2) while nuclear energy is fantastic for America and a handful of other countries, I don't want any new members to the club. I think I'd rather deal with a few degrees of warming than give nuclear power to a country like Iran, which will use the technology to give "global warming" a whole new meaning. (Think entire earth on fire.)

If you disagree, consider the historical equivalent of what is happening right now. Today's politicians are trying to fix what they believe will be the main environmental issue in the year 2100. Back in 1900, the "environmentalists" of the day were wrestling with the disposal of manure left in the streets from all the horses carting people around our cities. How do you think the Congress of the early 1900s would have done figuring out how to solve the major environmental and scientific issues of today?

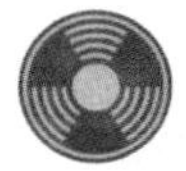

Chapter 2

Marriage, Porn, Adultery, and Divorce: The Circle of Life

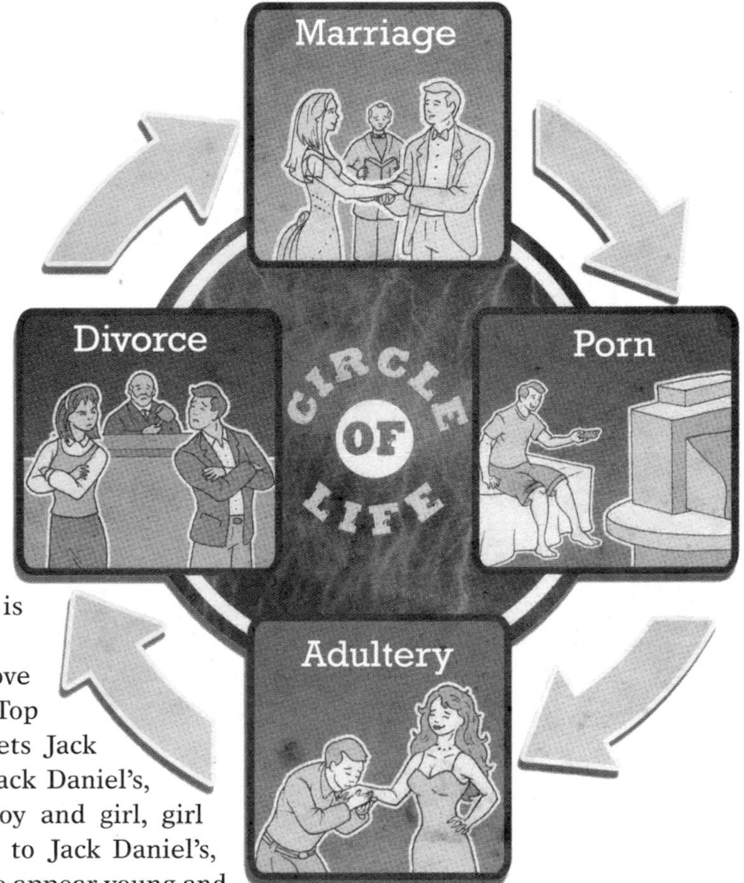

IN THE BEGINNING . . .

When it comes to love, mine is an age-old story:

Boy meets girl, boy falls in love with girl, boy becomes big-time Top 40 DJ, boy marries girl, boy meets Jack Daniel's, boy falls in love with Jack Daniel's, Jack Daniel's comes between boy and girl, girl divorces boy, boy becomes slave to Jack Daniel's, boy gets fat and grows long hair to appear young and less fat, boy fools no one, boy hits rock bottom (fall broken by fatness and ridiculous hair), boy breaks up with Jack Daniel's, boy begins to straighten out, boy gets haircut and loses weight (kind of), boy meets new girl, boy falls in love with girl, girl falls in love with boy (even boy is amazed), boy marries new girl, boy trades Top 40 for talk radio, boy does hilarious impression of new girl's voice to the delight of millions, boy and girl live happily ever after.

I know, I know—you've heard it a million times before. But that doesn't mean I don't have a unique perspective on affairs of the heart. See, I've had my fair share of experience with women (and not just with the likes of Sara Lee, Little Debbie, and Dolly Madison), and I've made every mistake a guy can make. I've been married, I've screwed up, and I've been "unmarried." In effect, I've made my way around the entire "circle of life."

I may not know where every detour, speed bump, or radar trap is along the way, but I hope I can make your trip easier by describing the ones I *do* know about. Buckle up—it's going to be a bumpy ride . . .

MARRIAGE

Finding love is hard, and staying in love is even harder. (Unless you're Bill or Hillary Clinton and obviously incapable of loving anything except the sound of your own voice and your misguided views about, well, just about everything.)

If you do manage to navigate the treacherous waters of dating (which I won't go into here since I've already devoted an important chapter to it) and find yourself actually married to someone, congratulations! The amount of deception that goes into duping another person into spending all of eternity with you is astounding—and you should be proud of your accomplishment. (I've found that this pride can help take the sting out of the fact that you had to buy her a ring that cost more than a fleet of plasma TVs.)

That's certainly the way I feel about my marriage to Tania. It's as if I used false advertising to lure her into a purchase, and now she's lost the receipt, so she's stuck—sucker! But I couldn't be happier about that. I honestly believe with all my heart that I wouldn't be alive today if not for her. She's lent a stability and strength to my life that are impossible to overstate. I don't like doing things without her—we're not

Occupations That Women Find Less Appealing Than Top 40 DJs

5. Ruler of a Middle Eastern theocracy
4. Clown
3. Rapist
2. Other top 40 radio professionals, regardless of position
1. **Cable news host**

co-dependent . . . we're *in love*. I am less than half the man when I'm not with her.

Tania and I are truly a partnership, and our marriage *works* because we *work* at it together. But that simple concept wasn't always so clear to me. I used to believe that marriage was the end of the *circle*—that the work of a relationship ends once you exchange your vows. But in reality, it's just the beginning. That's probably one big reason my first marriage didn't have a chance. Well, that and . . .

"Hello, My name is Glenn . . ."

To truly understand how great my second marriage is, you have to understand how badly I screwed up my first. In case there's anyone left on earth who *doesn't know* that I'm a recovering alcoholic, let me get you caught up quickly: I used to drink. *A lot*.

There's a good chance that I singlehandedly put the children of Brown-Forman (proud maker of Jack Daniel's Tennessee Whiskey) shareholders through college during the late '80s and early '90s.

A.D.D. MOMENT

Even if you haven't yet traveled the full *circle*, you probably have enough sense to realize that a long-term relationship with a bottomless tumbler of Jack with a "twist" of Coke isn't exactly a recipe for a successful marriage. But I didn't realize that—and my first marriage fell apart.

I was a bad husband (and a worse father) for longer than I care to think about. But here's the key: I *do* think about it. Every day. That's the best way I know to make sure I never fall into the same traps again. Looking back, I realize that I was young, foolish, and weak; there were issues from my family's past that I should have dealt with before even thinking of starting a family of my own, but that's not the way it played out.

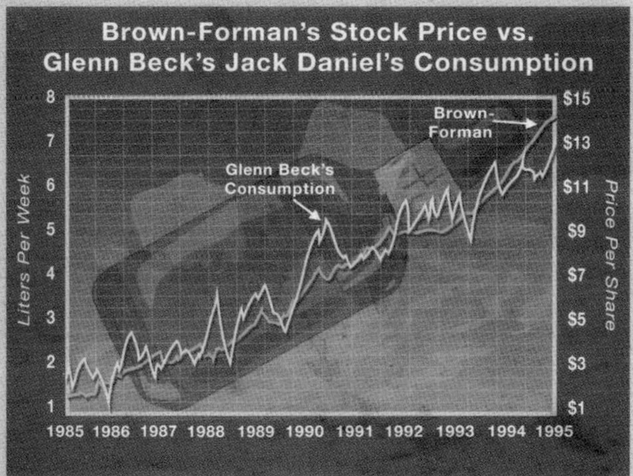

Brown-Forman stock was up over 581 percent from 1985 to 1995—you're welcome.

Fortunately, even though my first marriage had an ending, it was a relatively happy one. My ex and I have made our peace (I'm forever grateful), and I have a tremendously close relationship with my two daughters from that marriage. I ended up with better than I deserve, and I know it.

I tell you all of this because that experience is what helped me to have a second marriage that is nothing less than a gift from God. So, if I may be so bold, when it comes to having a successful marriage, here's . . .

MY SOLUTION

You need help.

Tania and I met at two radio promotion events (I was in Top 40 back then—if you think I'm annoying now, you should have heard me trying to be funny about Huey Lewis and the News) before we ever dated or really even talked.

I was suffering from one of my occasional bouts of sobriety, and I was *struggling*. One day, I told God that I just couldn't handle it anymore. If he wanted me to stay sober, then he'd better throw a roadblock up in my path, or else, that Friday, I was going to have the "happiest" of hours courtesy of Mr. Jack Daniel.

God pretty much kept to himself that whole week, and when Friday came, I kept my promise and headed over to my version of the Regal Beagle. I walked up to the bar, ordered a Jack and Coke, picked it up from the bar, turned around to take that first, glorious sip, and . . . just as I raised the glass to my mouth, the most amazing thing happened: Tania, the woman I'd met just twice before, was standing right there. If she'd been wearing wings and a halo, it wouldn't have been any more obvious. She was my sign, my roadblock. I put the drink back down on the bar and haven't had one since.

How Glenn Spent His Days Before Meeting Tania

Drunk: **92.7%**

Asleep: **4%**

Waiting for liquor store to open: **3.3%**

I knew, from that moment on, that Tania and I would be together forever. There was just one problem: She didn't. See, Tania is smart, way smarter than me (shocker, I know). She understood that unless we shared a common faith, unless we had something deep, meaningful, and spiritual to help guide and bind us, we'd never make it.

Here's a little inside Mormon joke for you: Why any man would want a wife is a mystery. Why any man would want more than one wife is a bigamistery. Thanks, I'll be here all week—try the veal.

A.D.D. MOMENT

That all sounded reasonable to me, but mostly I just wanted to have sex with her, so I would have agreed to almost anything. "You want me to amputate my right index finger right here in front of you with this dull butter knife? Uh, OK, why not? Can we have sex now? No? OK—how about after the bleeding stops?"

But an amazing thing happened as Tania and I went from church to church, "shopping" for a faith: I actually started to enjoy it. The more we looked, the more sense her plan made, and now, years later, our commitment to God has strengthened our commitment to each other. Our faith sustains us, and I'll admit it right now: I'm addicted to it.

I'm not saying that religion is the key to a happy and successful marriage, but I'm not *not* saying it, either. Being dedicated to something bigger than each other has worked for us, but that doesn't mean it's the right answer for you. The key is figuring out what is and then devoting your lives to it. (And, no, drugs, alcohol, porn, and gambling don't count . . . I did plenty of checking during my first marriage.)

PORN

I never thought I'd be writing a letter like this. If it hadn't happened to me, I never would have believed it was possible. But I'm getting ahead of myself. Let me start off by saying: I dig chicks, especially hot ones who aren't wearing much in the way of clothing.

Then again, almost all guys do; it's hard-wired into our DNA. Being attracted to the female form is part of the grand design. I believe God set it up that way so we'd keep making more people. And if we can't have sex for one reason or another, most guys will gladly watch someone else do it.

As I said earlier, I'm no saint; I've seen plenty of porn. Granted, that was back when my day-to-day life made Robert Downey Jr. look like a Boy Scout and way before the Internet porn boom. However—*from what I hear*—it's now amazingly easy to find "adult" content

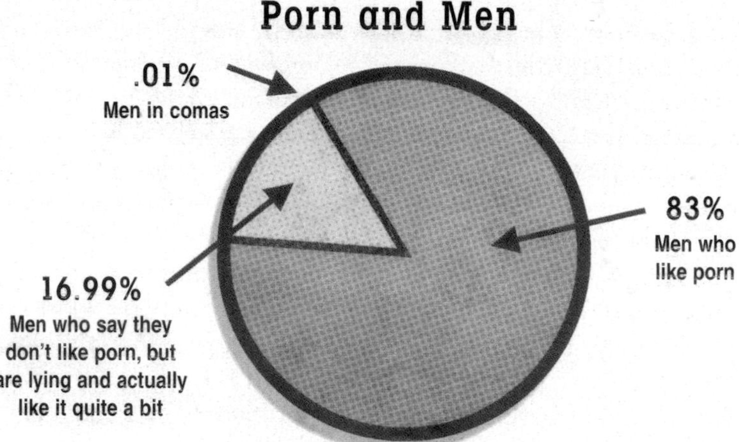

by which at, oh, say 2:00 in the morning, when sleep is elusive, a man can point and click his way down the rabbit hole to far-off lands like Amsterdam or Thailand, where good taste and the laws of physics don't seem to apply. I've heard that you can see things online that would make Bill Clinton *and* R. Kelly blush.

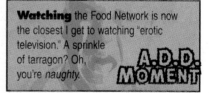

> **Watching** the Food Network is now the closest I get to watching "erotic television." A sprinkle of tarragon? Oh, you're *naughty*. **A.D.D. MOMENT**

The porn industry generates billions of dollars every year. One study pins the number at as much as $97 billion worldwide and $13 billion here in the United States. If that's true (and these companies don't exactly file SEC statements, so it's not that easy to audit), porn earns more each year than—ready to have your mind blown?—Microsoft, Google, Amazon, eBay, Yahoo, Apple, Netflix, and Earthlink *combined*. Mind still not blown? Based only on U.S. earnings, porn makes more than Major League Baseball, the NHL, and the NFL, plus the combined revenues of ABC, CBS, and NBC.

A.D.D MOMENT In a recent reality series on Showtime, two of the "feature starlets" from Vivid Video—the largest mainstream porn producer in the United States—are talking about sharing an apartment . . . you know, becoming roommates to save money. Hmmm . . . if having sex with random strangers doesn't pay well enough for you to live without a roommate, maybe you're in the wrong line of work. I'm just sayin'. . .

Now, I know what you're thinking—"How can I get my hands on some of that sweet porn profit?" Stop! Just because $3,075.64 is being spent on porn *each and every sec-*

ond doesn't mean that it's a good thing. I know, for an avowed capitalist like me, it's very hard to believe . . . but I do.

Just because porn is ready, willing, and able to send you through the looking glass to the darkest side of yourself (for an extremely reasonable price . . . so I hear), that doesn't mean that you should take the trip. In the immortal words of the woman voted "Least Likely to Be Referenced in a Passage about Hot Chicks," you've got to "Just Say No" to porn.

If you'll pardon the crude imagery, porn is a slippery slope. I've had guys tell me, "Hey, what's the big deal? Porn is something that *my wife* and I enjoy together." Well, that is a great big load of crap. When I used to look at porn, the *last thing* I wanted was for my wife to know what I was doing. But even if your wife does watch porn with you, how do you think she'd feel about the unlimited porn-on-demand package you bought at some seedy hotel on your last business trip (you didn't actually think she'd believe that a movie starring Reese Witherspoon cost $24.99, did you?)? Oh, you didn't even tell her about that little purchase?

Of course not, because porn breeds secrets—and secrets destroy marriages. We don't learn anything from pornography—it's sexual miseducation and reinforces the absolute worst notions that exist about men, women, and how we express ourselves in that *wink, wink* way (yes, that's a medical term).

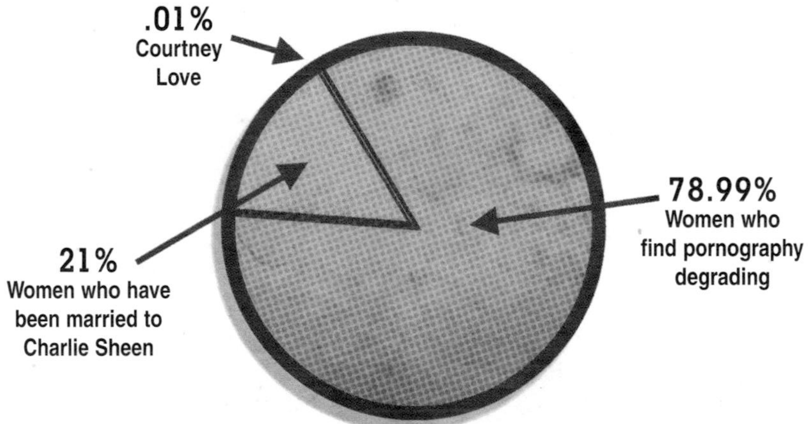

But porn is dangerous in another way as well: respect for women. Or I guess I should say *lack* of respect. Guys are always talking tough about protecting their mothers and sisters and daughters, but who do you think the women are on IFeelNaughty.com? They're someone's sister, daughter, and, yes—even though it's a total buzz kill—often someone's mother.

If we're going to protect, respect, and cherish the women in our lives, paying $39.99 that will be automatically billed to our credit cards as "FunTime Industries" so we can see "bad girls who get what they deserve" while dressed as characters from *The Wizard of Oz* (hypothetically speaking, of course) is not the way to do it. It's not only destructive; it's hypocritical as well.

Porn is one of this life's most readily available distractions; it celebrates our basest instincts and turns classless women like Paris Hilton into celebrities. Believe me, when I can't sleep, I sometimes think about taking a trip down the rabbit hole myself . . . but I don't. It may not sound like much, but I can tell you that self-control does have its own rewards, not the least of which is a happy, healthy marriage.

A.D.D. MOMENT Plus, your email inbox is a lot less scary. Even though it seems like a really great deal, I don't want to read a message about the "Maximizer" that sells for just $69.69 from some Web store in Bangkok.

I hate to be the one to break it to you ladies, but a recent study determined that men who buy and watch pornography are more likely to cheat on you (shocker!). And that brings us to the third stage in our circle . . .

ADULTERY

Is looking at porn the same thing as reenacting it with that hottie from marketing down the hall? Of course not. But turning your attention outside your marriage is always a bad idea.

Unlike a lot of other things that society has only recently decided are a bad idea (i.e., smoking on airplanes, carbs, fossil fuels, and sitcoms starring former cast members of *Friends*), adultery has been frowned

upon since the thrilling days of yesteryear when "Thou shalt not covet thy neighbor's wife" was the hot new catch phrase. Having moments of weakness and confusion in a marriage is natural—anyone who tells you otherwise is breaking another classic rule: "Thou shalt not lie"—but betraying your spouse's trust is something I believe you'll always regret. (And my lawyer agrees.)

If you really must pursue interests outside your marriage, maybe you should consider the final stop on our "circle of life" tour . . .

DIVORCE

Family is fundamental throughout nature; it's a unifying system that lends order to the world around us. But it's under attack. The cynics who run rampant through our popular culture would like you to believe that marriage and the traditional family don't work anymore, that the chances of staying married are about the same as a coin toss, 50/50. You've heard that stat, right? "Fifty percent of all marriages end in divorce." Well, I've got good news: The cynics are wrong, because for most people, that stat is a lie.

The "50 percent divorce rate" gets quoted a lot because it's sensational and shocking. Fortunately, it's not really true unless you meet very specific criteria. According to the annual "State of Our Unions" marriage study, here are some of the factors that decrease your risk of divorce within the first ten years of marriage:

- *Annual income.* If you make more than \$50,000 a year, your odds of divorce are 30 percent lower than those making less than \$25,000 a year.
- *Waiting for marriage.* If you wait until you're

25 years old to marry, your odds of divorcing are 24 percent less than someone who marries at age 18 or younger.

- *Waiting for children.* If you wait until you've been married for at least seven months before having kids, your odds of divorce decrease 24 percent versus a couple having a child before marriage.
- *Family history.* If your parents are married, you're 14 percent more likely to stay together than if your parents have divorced.
- *Religion.* If you practice a faith, you're 14 percent more likely to stay married than if you don't.
- *Education.* If you attended college, even for a day, your odds of divorce decrease 13 percent as opposed to a high school dropout.

This wasn't in the official study, but if you're an idiot named Glenn who's already made a shambles of your life once and were somehow given another chance with a woman who pities you enough to marry you, then your chances of divorce are an absolute zero percent.

The study summarizes all of these statistics pretty nicely (especially that last part) by saying: "If you are a reasonably well-educated person with a decent income, come from an intact family, are religious, and marry after age 25, without having a baby first, your chances of divorce are very low indeed." Even if you just meet a few of the criteria, your odds of divorce are still a lot lower than the nationally advertised 50 percent rate—but you never hear that, because it doesn't sell as many newspapers or magazines. Let's just hope it sells books!

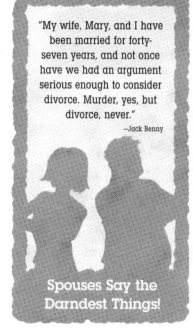

"My wife, Mary, and I have been married for forty-seven years, and not once have we had an argument serious enough to consider divorce. Murder, yes, but divorce, never."

—Jack Benny

Spouses Say the Darndest Things!

That's Great, I Still Want a Divorce

Nobody wants to restart their life after their relationship crashes. But sometimes it's the only thing that can get your life up and running again. (I'm writing this on a new computer, so please forgive the forced metaphor.)

America is a young and aggressive country—we're quick to let go of old traditions in the pursuit of the next big thing. That attitude applies to just about everything from fashion to music to, yes, even marriage. That's a shame—there's something to be said

for perseverance and loyalty to both principles and *people*.

At this point in my life, I don't believe in divorce. I know that's easy for me to say now, but it comes from the understanding that if we all went into marriages with clearer heads, I don't think we'd be looking to get out of them quite so often. Divorce itself isn't a problem; bad marriages are. That's why the only way to "solve" divorce is to make sure that a marriage has every chance to succeed. So, instead of a solution, let me just say this: If you have kids, divorce is going to hurt them the most—I've seen it firsthand. Even under the friendliest of splits, divorce makes raising children difficult, to say the least (just ask Alec Baldwin).

Think about that before you call a lawyer and start divvying up the silverware.

Fun Divorce Facts!

57 percent of the attorneys in the American Academy of Matrimonial Lawyers reported seeing an increase in prenups over the last five years.

But there is a big *but* (and it's not just on Rosie O'Donnell). Raising children in an abusive environment is an even worse alternative. While we can all agree that physical abuse is never acceptable, I've spoken to women who would've preferred that to the years of psychological abuse they lived with during their marriages.

No one should be living under abusive conditions, and in that case, I do support the decision to get divorced, and maybe even . . .

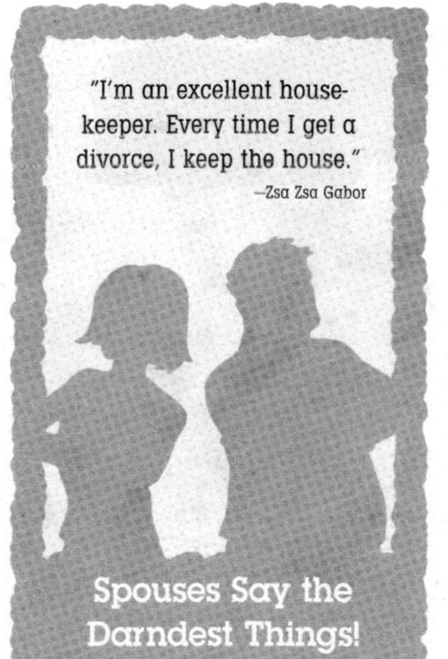

"I'm an excellent housekeeper. Every time I get a divorce, I keep the house."
—Zsa Zsa Gabor
Spouses Say the Darndest Things!

START THE WHOLE CYCLE ALL OVER AGAIN

I wish the issues surrounding the beginning and ending of relationships were as easy to solve as, say, global warming. Al Gore and China's coal plants are easy. The human heart? Not so much. But if we use our heads while following our hearts (and maybe get a little help from our faith), I think we may just have a chance. After all, I tricked not just one but *two* women into marrying me!

Chapter 3

Radical Islam: Politically Incorrect

SARAH PEAKE, a Massachusetts selectwoman, was sitting in a Provincetown meeting in November 2005, and something was bothering her. It wasn't the bad coffee, the stale pastries, or her fellow council members droning on and on. What was bothering Ms. Peake on this particular day was a painting that depicted the Pilgrims voting on the Mayflower Compact hanging on the wall.

There were no women in it. And (gasp) the only Native American in the painting did not have a ballot in his hand!

The thought that history would be represented in such a sexist, racist way (even though it was historically accurate) infuriated Ms. Peake, and she asked that the painting be removed. The council voted, and—this being Massachusetts—three out of four people said they agreed with Ms. Peake. The painting came down.

Was this political correctness gone haywire? Absolutely. But it's literally just the tip of the iceberg in terms of what we'll do to keep people comfortable and appeased, no matter the consequences.

This politically correct, don't-offend-anyone mentality has turned into the Islamic extremists' most powerful weapon.

Islam: Let Me Be Clear

Because I mention *Islam* and *extremist* in the same sentence, let me stop right here. My stance on Islam has been so twisted and mangled and misrepresented that my wife probably even thinks I'm an intolerant hatemonger. So let me be clear, once and for all:

1. I have read the Koran and can tell you that I unequivocally believe that Islam is a religion of peace. The overwhelming majority (I believe at least 90 percent) of all Muslims are good, peace-loving people.
2. Immediately after Septemer 11, 2001, listeners began calling into my radio show demanding guilt-by-association for average Muslims. I begged them not to overreact and explained that the people they wanted to vilify were likely just as shocked and saddened by what happened as they were.
3. Because I personally witnessed how quickly fear can make good, rational people overreact, I have spent years begging moderate Muslims to stand up and denounce the monsters who have perverted their religion.
4. Although some have spoken out, it's clear to me that the radicals' plan to use fear and intimidation is working. They have shown that they are more than willing to kill anyone, including other Muslims, who don't share their beliefs, and that has left many moderate Muslims living in fear.
5. Muslims are *not* the enemy; extremists who want to destroy democracy and create Islamist states all over the world are the enemy.

2+2 = WHATEVER YOU WANT

Political correctness usually goes only so far as to be a minor annoyance, like taking baby Jesus out of a nativity scene or, as in the case above, completely ignoring historical facts for the sake of someone's precious feelings. Well, I have feelings too, and they're telling me our society is slowly going insane.

Have you ever noticed the fuzzy logic that goes on when Islam is involved? I'm not a Muslim theologist, but I am a thinker, and the incidents that have happened over the last few years don't seem to be all that equitable:

- Jesus figure soaked in urine . . . *OK*
- Koran in the toilet . . . *not OK*
- Elephant poop on the Virgin Mary . . . *OK*
- Newspaper cartoon of Mohammed . . . *not OK*
- Calling president of the United States a terrorist . . . *OK*
- Suggesting that some Muslims might be terrorists . . . *not OK*

Do you really think that Islamic extremists care about our stupid little debates over how to avoid hurt feelings? Of course not. They welcome this walk-on-eggshells atmosphere we've created because it's an integral part of how they intend to get close enough to kill us.

Islamic extremists understand that our greatest strength—our freedoms—is also our greatest weakness.

We hold our freedoms, and the document that provides for them—the U.S. Constitution—above almost everything else. But—news flash—the radical Islamists don't. They're disgusted by Western values such as freedom, democracy, or the thought of women being equal to men because their lives are governed by their religion, which has very strict notions of how society should be structured. (Although I have to admit that some of those notions, such as banning television shows from featuring "Surprise! I have four children with three different women and a cocker spaniel!" aren't half bad.)

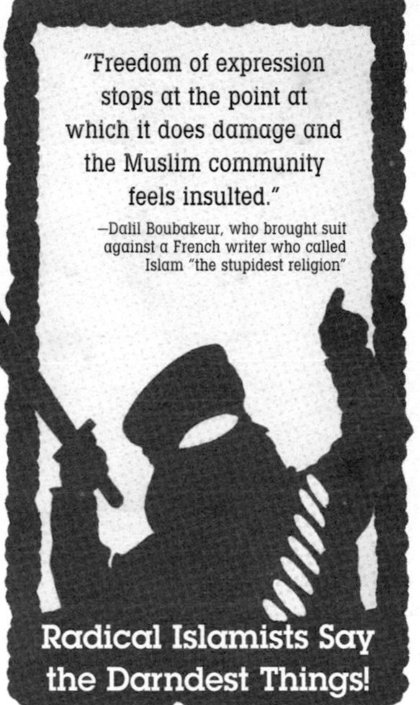

"Freedom of expression stops at the point at which it does damage and the Muslim community feels insulted."
—Dalil Boubakeur, who brought suit against a French writer who called Islam "the stupidest religion"
Radical Islamists Say the Darndest Things!

Most Muslims have a private spiritual life and are happy to live in a country where they can practice their faith freely and openly. But extremists don't want a "private spiritual life"; they want a political system that makes faith a very public, state-oriented system. I didn't get it at first, but now I do. It's about *politics*, not religion. In the world of Islamic extremism, there is no separation of mosque and state because their church *is* their state; their religious leaders *are* their political leaders. And those leaders are happy to give you a simple choice: Live under Islamic rule, or die.

MY SHARIA MORE

A lot of people try to make the motivation behind radical Islamists extremely complicated, but it's not. They simply believe that Islamic law surpasses every other law in society—including our precious little Constitution—and they believe that everybody in the world should live under it.

The basis of Islamic law is called Sharia, which is not an actual set of laws but rather a system of making them based on the interpretations of religious leaders. But these aren't the Roman Catholic types of interpretations such as "Eat fish on Fridays" or Scientologist-type interpretations such as "You must be an action movie star." These are pronouncements that encompass every aspect of life: marriage, divorce, eating, drinking, justice, finance, and every other thing you can think of.

Although it can be interpreted in many different ways, restriction and punishment are common elements of Sharia as followed by extremists:

- An eye for an eye.
- Drinkers and gamblers must be whipped.
- Homosexuals must be put to death.
- Adulterers must be stoned to death.
- Men can hit their women if they want to.
- If you say something negative about Islam, you can be put to death.

Like Elvis bringing rock 'n' roll into the mainstream, the Taliban (or, more accurately, the collapse of the Taliban) helped shed light on how extreme Sharia law can be. They banned kite flying, prevented women from going to school, and outlawed music—sorry, Elvis, that means you too.

A.D.D. MOMENT It also would mean banning rap, opera, and that lady who sings "My Humps"—so it's not *all* bad.

They also mandated that women have a male escort when leaving the house and that anyone who converted from Islam to

Sharia in America

I had the "pleasure" of speaking with Jesse—or "Muhammed," as he wanted to be called—from a New York–based group called the Islamic Thinkers Society. He told me that "the solution to America's ills and afflictions is the Sharia law. It is an answer to all humanity." He also told me they were a "moderate" organization.

Uh-huh. Here's the picture I found on the front page of the Islamic Thinkers Society website. I may not be a "thinker" like them, but that sure looks to me like a big Islamic flag flying over the White House.

another religion must be executed. But at least you got to pick: Islamic fundamentalism or death. Who knew the Taliban was prochoice?

Maybe Islamic extremists are so strict with their rules because they're constantly denied any pleasure. I mean, think about being on a lifelong diet that deprives you of just-baked chocolate-chip cookies. Wouldn't that drive you crazy after, like, five hours? I'd probably go start making insane rules and mandating that everyone else follow them too. Personal choices can often lead to happiness, but having decisions forced on you leads to nothing but widespread misery.

A.D.D. MOMENT

SWEET DREAMS . . .

The infiltration of radicals into America is a slow, gradual process. While most of us don't see it, or we choose to ignore it, the reality of the situation quickly becomes clear when jetliners plummet out of the sky at 600 miles per hour. Unfortunately, if you haven't noticed, just a few years after the biggest terrorist attack ever to hit American soil, we all seem to be asleep again.

So, to wake us up, I'd like to introduce to you Exhibit A on what happens when a whole bunch of people take Ambien all at once: Western Europe.

An estimated 25 million Muslims currently live in Western Europe, and there is a great—if not well publicized—struggle happening over how to integrate them into Western culture. But there's one big problem: They're *not* integrating, and they aren't even being asked to. By using words such as *diversity* and *multiculturalism* and lodging charges of *racism* and *hatemongerism* (OK, I made that one up) over the heads of anyone who disagrees, European elites are allowing some Muslims to make their own laws, even if they trump their own.

Not all cultures are created equal. If our Founding Fathers believed they were, we'd still have a 4:00 P.M. teatime.

A.D.D. MOMENT

These Muslim fundamentalists take advantage of their freedoms in those countries by creating communities within communities and insisting they be governed by Sharia law. Their argument is intuitively simple: "Hey, if this is a free society, then I should be able to practice my religion the way I'm used to."

That's a cute little defense, but Jeffrey Dahmer was "used to" chopping up people and then eating them. Are you saying that we were supposed to let him keep doing it? Of course not. Freedom of religion, speech, and everything else always has one major caveat: They're all subject to the laws of the land. You can practice any religion you want; you can even make up your own, but as soon as your new Church of Vampireology starts mandating that you drink the blood of 26-year-old virgins, we have a problem. Your freedoms are always, *always* secondary to the rule of law—except when it comes to radical Islam, where Sharia trumps all.

But in Europe, large Muslim communities, emboldened by their increasing numbers, are demanding that tenets of Sharia law be allowed to rule. The calls for Sharia are growing louder in countries such as Germany, Italy, Ireland, and Britain, and the European Union has actually proposed that the laws of non-EU countries should be applicable in divorce cases within their countries. That means Sharia could become legitimate civil law for Muslims in Europe, or, at the very least, Muslim women may end up without rights—even if they live in a so-called democratic country.

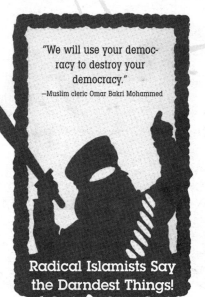

"We will use your democracy to destroy your democracy."
—Muslim cleric Omar Bakri Mohammed

Radical Islamists Say the Darndest Things!

The EU has also recently called for a name change when talking about terrorist acts performed by radical Muslims. Instead of *Islamic terrorists,* the acceptable term is now *terrorists who abusively invoke Islam.* See the difference? Other than length? Me neither—but it makes people feel better, and that's apparently what we're after.

ISLAMISTS IN THE 'HOOD

It's a great concept: Extremists use our political correctness to set up their own little enclaves within European cities and then create "no go" zones for Western leaders and, in turn, Western law. When the home secretary of England made a visit to a predominantly Muslim community to speak last year, he was met with a heckler who asked, "How dare you come to a Muslim area?"

This isn't exactly a new phenomenon. The emergence of Islamic communities was encouraged way back in 1980, when the Islamic Council of Europe published the book *Muslim Communities in Non-Muslim States,* which outlined a strategic plan on how to avoid being assimilated into another culture.

Here's how it works: (1) Concentrate yourselves in large numbers within the community; (2) set up schools and mosques; and (3) avoid being ruled by the majority. The ultimate goal is to gain large enough numbers so that you can eventually take over and spread Islamic rule.

Extremist Communities Invites You To
"Ramadan in July" Neighborhood Barbecue!
Who: All Extremist Community Members!
When: July 4th Weekend!
See All Sorts of Fireworks (haha!!!)
Where: At Community Pool!
Men: Bring The Swimsuits!
PLEASE! NO RAPES ON THE POOL DECK!
Women: Burkas or Die!
What: All-You-Can-Eat-BBQ! Explosive Taste!
No Pork!
No drinking alcohol, unless you're actively training for a terrorist attack— then it's okay.
Activities include: Going Back And Forth On The Monkey Bars While We Videotape You, Tetherball, Badminton, Shooting Gun Pointlessly Into Sky, Infidel Lawn Jarts, Suicide Water Balloons!
RSVP by martyring youngest son at nearest Quiznos.

Dr. Patrick Sookhdeo, director of the Institute for the Study of Islam and Christianity, says, *"In a decade, you will see parts of English cities which are controlled by Muslim clerics and which follow, not the common law, but aspects of Muslim Sharia law . . . the fundamental rule [of Islam in Europe is to] never dilute your presence. Do not integrate."*

In the meantime, cities in Europe (particularly London and Paris) are seeing the problems with large pockets of fundamentalist Muslims creating their own communities. Churches are being burned down; street riots are almost common; Jewish students are being attacked; schools are being forced to stop teaching about the Holocaust because it may be "offensive"; halal meat is served in prisons, schools, and hospitals; and some districts in the London area have been forced to change their names if they sound "too Christian." The Sharia Law Council for the U.K. has pressured the country into providing mortgages and pensions under Sharia principles, and in December 2004, the National Audit Office agreed to overhaul the tax system because Muslims with more than one wife were being "unfairly" penalized.

A.D.D. MOMENT Like having more than one wife isn't already punishment enough.

The U.K. Islamic Mission summed up the overall idea pretty well: "establish Islamic social order in the United Kingdom in order to seek the pleasure of Allah." So long as the British stay asleep, "Islamic social order" is exactly what will happen.

French Fried

I could write an entire book about all of the problems that the Frenchy-French have, not the least of which is the fact that the entire country smokes like a coal-fired power plant. But since I only have a chapter, let's focus on the fact that over the last 20 years, France essentially has allowed the establishment of a separate Muslim state within its borders.

Hey, Simon & Schuster, if you're reading this, consider that part about the Frenchy-French to be my next book proposal.

A.D.D. MOMENT

Many Muslims in France think of themselves as Muslim, not French. According to the BBC, *"Ten years ago these [rioting] youths were seen as French 'Arabs.' Now most are commonly referred to, and define themselves, as 'Muslims.'"*

Scattered throughout France are hundreds of Muslim "ghettos," where poor, unemployed, angry young men live under a commitment to Islam, not democracy. In 1991, there were 106 of these "no go" zones, or "hot spots" as the Frenchy-French authorities call them. By 2002, when they conveniently stopped counting, there were 818. The violence in some of these places is so out of control that the police often refuse to intervene. Unfortunately, that only helps to further segregate these enclaves from the rest of society.

"The heart of the matter is that no Islamic state can be legitimate in the eyes of its subjects without obeying the main teachings of the Sharia. A secular government might coerce obedience, but Muslims will not abandon their belief that state affairs should be supervised by the just teachings of the holy law."

—Mohamed Elhachmi Hamdi, editor in chief, *Al-Mustakillah*

Radical Islamists Say the Darndest Things!

This boiling cauldron of anger and radicalized youths exploded in late 2005, when riots broke out.

In an effort to stop the attacks and distance them from Islam, France's most influential Islamic group issued a religious edict, or fatwa, condemning the violence. "It is formally forbidden for any Muslim seeking divine grace and satisfaction to participate in any action that blindly hits private or public property or could constitute an attack on someone's life," the fatwa said, citing the Koran and the teachings of Muhammad.

Nine thousand burned police cars later, it looked as if nobody was listening.

WE DON'T NEED NO EDUCATION

Segregation has spilled over into European schools, where previously unthinkable exceptions are now being made.

The French Ministry of Education investigated 61 schools and found Muslim students refusing to dance, participate in sports, eat food that wasn't halal (prepared by Sharia law), draw a right angle (it looks like part of a Christian cross), or swim (they'd be polluted by infidels' water). Some Muslim students also refused to learn English or read certain books that offended them, and in some schools, these students were even given separate toilets and showers so they wouldn't have to mix with the "impure."

"We do not want to assimilate. Assimilation is cultural rape."
—Dyab Abu Jahjah, Arab European League founder
Radical Islamists Say the Darndest Things!

A report titled *Towards Greater Understanding—Meeting the Needs of Muslim Pupils in State Schools* was published earlier this year by the Muslim Council of Britain. It demanded that all "un-Islamic" activities be banned in school, including swimming lessons during Ramadan, opposite-sex contact sports, and Muslim students drawing people in art classes. It also encouraged a religious curriculum, including teachings about Islam, as long as Muslims could opt out of any lessons regarding Christianity or Judaism.

Europe, a mind is a terrible thing to waste. I guess I can only hope that your fall from grace (I use the term *grace* loosely) will serve as a wakeup call for those of us with enough time to change our course.

NOT IN MY BACKYARD

We've all heard the song "God Bless America," but most of us don't realize that there's actually a verse before the one we all know. It goes like this: "While the storm clouds gather far across the sea, let us swear allegiance to a land that's free."

Well, the storm clouds are gathering, all right. France is literally teetering on the edge, and our biggest ally, England, is about to be turned inside out as well. If you think those clouds won't make their way across the Atlantic, you're dead wrong—they're already here; you just need to know where to look.

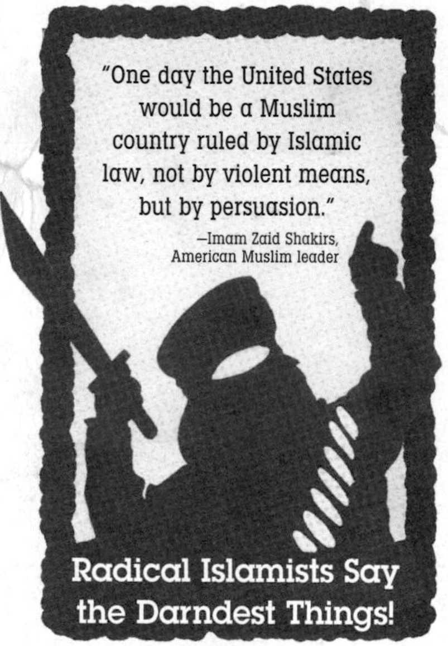

"One day the United States would be a Muslim country ruled by Islamic law, not by violent means, but by persuasion."
—Imam Zaid Shakirs, American Muslim leader
Radical Islamists Say the Darndest Things!

The U.S. prison system, full of people looking for hope and purpose and redemption—and with a lot of time on their hands—is a feeding ground for radicals seeking to marginalize moderate Muslims and convert those of other faiths. Warith Deen Umar, the former chief Muslim chaplain in the New York State Department of Correctional Services, was banned from setting foot in state prisons in 2003 when the *Wall Street Journal* reported that he said the 9/11 terrorists should be remembered as martyrs. Umar believes terrorism is accepted by the Koran. "Even Muslims who say they are against terrorism secretly admire and applaud [the 9/11 hijackers]. . . . This is the sort of teaching they don't want in prison," he said. "But this is what I'm doing."

New York Senator Chuck Schumer's office wrote that "Umar has wielded tremendous influence over the 45 or so clerics or imams that currently preach within New York's prison system, almost all of whom subscribe to his brand of Wahhabi extremism."

Glenn Beck/Chuck Schumer Agreement Rate

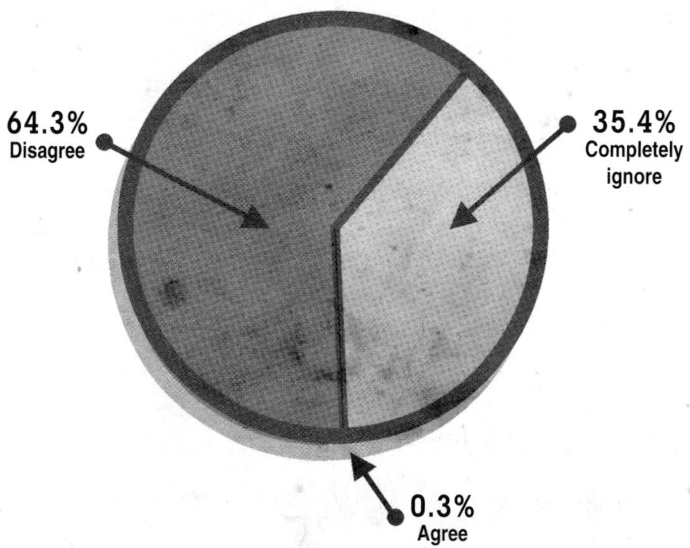

Schumer himself went even further. In a letter to the head of the State Department of Corrections, he advocated the immediate firing of all imams hired under Umar's tenure: "These imams represent a clear and present danger to the safety and security of New York State's prison system and indeed our entire country. . . . I urge you to dismiss all imams hired under Mr. Umar's supervision and to reconstitute the Muslim leadership inside New York State's prisons to ensure that it reflects a more moderate brand of Islam that represents the diversity of belief within the Sunni, Shia and Sufi sects that make up the Muslim community." Unfortunately, it doesn't look as if the Department of Corrections listened—maybe it'll take one of these prisoners doing something drastic before they start to pay attention.

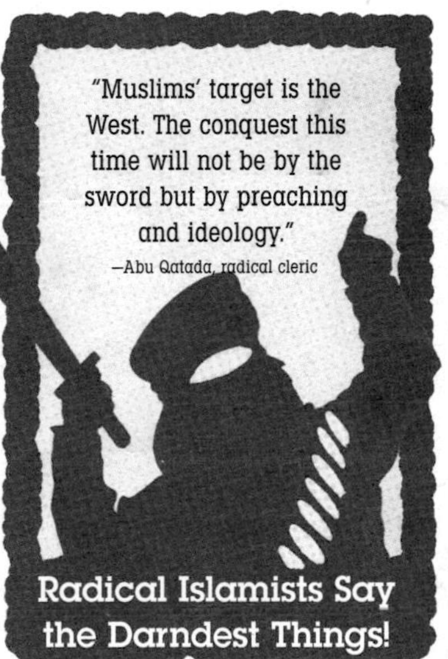

"Muslims' target is the West. The conquest this time will not be by the sword but by preaching and ideology."
—Abu Qatada, radical cleric
Radical Islamists Say the Darndest Things!

This isn't just a New York problem; it's happening in prisons all across the country, and law enforcement is worried about it. FBI Director Robert Mueller told the Senate Intelligence Committee, "Prisons continue to be fertile ground for extremists who exploit both a prisoner's conversion to Islam while still in prison, as well as their socio-economic status and placement in the community upon their release."

It's right out of a twisted math book: Thousands of Young Men + Thousands of Spare Hours + Dozens of Radical Clerics Teaching Them = Bad News for America.

DESERT HEAT

When you think of Phoenix, you probably think about sand. And heat. And its NBA team that's never won an NBA championship (OK, someone gave me that one). But Muslim extremists just think of it as home. For more than twenty years now, they've been slowly migrating to the Phoenix area and opening schools and mosques that preach hate.

Right after 9/11, a big "What did you know and when did you know it?" controversy broke out after an FBI memo surfaced in which it was clear that the government had knowledge of terrorists training with planes. That memo's title? "The Phoenix Memo," because it was written by the Phoenix branch of the FBI. It read, in part:

"Phoenix has observed an inordinate number of individuals of investigative interest who are attending . . . civil aviation . . . colleges in the State of Arizona." A few people known to be friends of Osama bin Laden were also known to reside there, and at least two of the 9/11 hijackers went to flight school in the area.

The author of that memo, FBI agent Kenneth Williams, later testified in front of Congress that Islamic extremists may flock to Arizona because it reminds them of home, but they stay for the terrorist ties: "These people don't continue to come back to Arizona because they like the sunshine or they like the state. I believe that something was established there, and I think it's been there for a long time."

Later, the 9/11 Commission's report implicated Phoenix even further by referring to a CIA/FBI memo titled "Arizona: Long Range Nexus for Islamic Extremists." I'd love to tell you more about it, but that report is still highly classified.

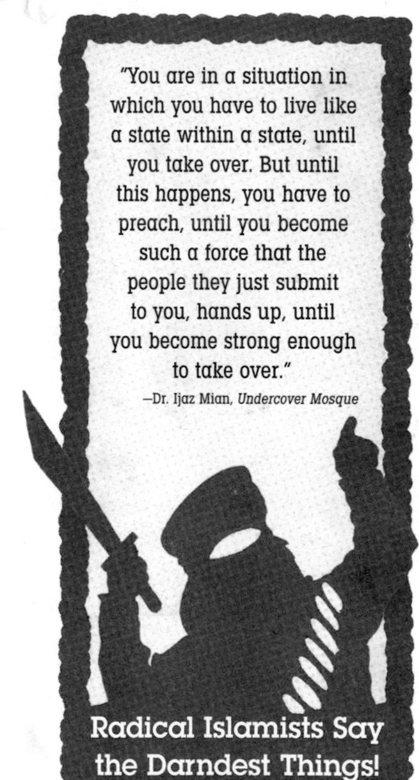

"You are in a situation in which you have to live like a state within a state, until you take over. But until this happens, you have to preach, until you become such a force that the people they just submit to you, hands up, until you become strong enough to take over."
—Dr. Ijaz Mian, *Undercover Mosque*
Radical Islamists Say the Darndest Things!

And then there are the "isolated incidents" that someone far more conspiratorial than I might find interesting. In November 2006, Sisayehiticha Dinssa was stopped by Detroit police and found to be carrying $80,000 in cash and information about cyanide, nuclear power plants, and suitcase bombs, along with newspapers commemorating the 9/11 attacks. He also had a handwritten note that said: "This community is angry. Something is going to happen. We are going to see justice. This is a powder keg waiting to go off." Dinssa was flying to Phoenix.

Or what about "the Flying Imams" who were detained after acting suspiciously like the 9/11 hijackers? Yeah, they were heading to Phoenix too. Maybe that's part of the reason Phoenix's Sky Harbor Airport is the first airport in the country to test the new "backscatter" security machines that critics say reveal a lot more than just weapons.

But it's not just a small amount of anecdotal evidence that points to Arizona as a hot spot. Most people associate Steve Jobs with the creation of Apple, even though Steve Wozniak was also a founder. Well,

Attn: [redacted]
Level 4 access

Arizona: Long Range Nexus for Islamic Extremists
Transcript of meeting between undercover CIA/FBI agents
Topic: Phoenix, Arizona

CIA: Hey, you know what I've noticed lately about Phoenix?
FBI: The heat?
CIA: No, the heat doesn't bother me. You know why?
FBI: Because it's a dry heat?
CIA: Exactly.
FBI: So what have you noticed?
CIA: All the Islamic extremists.
FBI: Yeah, what should we do about that? Should we tell people?
CIA: Nah, the details will freak everyone out.
FBI: Then what should we do?
CIA: Let's just title the transcript of this conversation something scary. Maybe even add "nexus" to it—no one knows what that really means.
FBI: Right. Then, later we can say "I told you so!"
CIA: Exactly. Wanna play golf?
FBI: Nah, it's too hot.
CIA: Yeah, but it's a dry heat.

(end transcript)

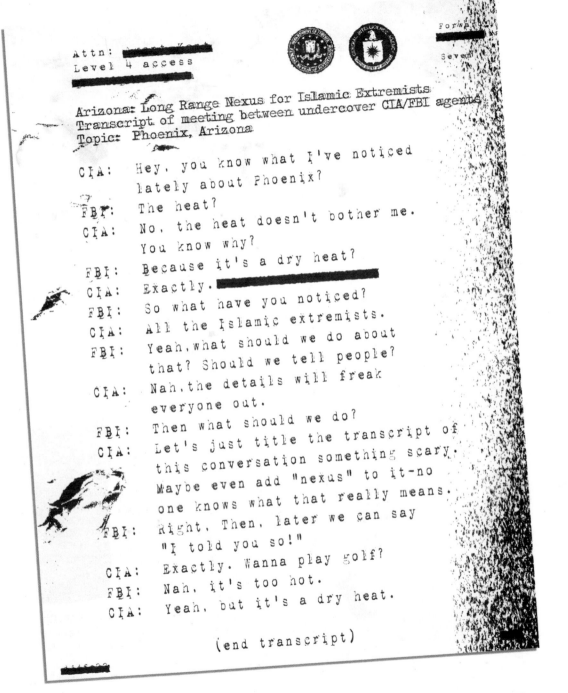

there's a similar dynamic with our good buddies at Al Qaeda. Osama bin Laden may get all the publicity, but Wa'el Jelaidan was a founding member. He was also the president of the Tucson Islamic Center in the mid-'80s.

IF YOU SEE SOMETHING, SAY NOTHING

Our government implores citizens to speak out when they see suspicious behavior. But when that behavior involves sensitive subjects such as Islam, the "good citizen" is often dragged through the media as a hateful, racist, phobic bigot. How likely would you be to put your reputation on the line if you saw a few suspicious things at the airport but really had nothing more than "just a gut feeling" that something was wrong?

Right after 9/11, a woman in a Florida diner became suspicious of some Muslim men huddled together, looking as if they were up to no good, so she called the police. It turns out she was wrong, but our open-minded and compassionate media proceeded to drag the woman through the mud, commenting on her hairstyle and her accent. She was depicted as a backwoods, racist hillbilly.

And then there is the infamous "Flying Imams" incident I touched on earlier. I don't know about you, but if I get on an airplane and six fidgeting Muslims are griping about the United States at the gate, praying to Allah immediately before takeoff, asking for seatbelt extenders when none is needed, and playing musical chairs once they board, I'm going to need a drink and a new pair of underwear.

But the nervous passengers who turned them in were tarred and feathered in the media after the imams cried discrimination and said this proved America's racism and lack of understanding of Islam.

How can you ask people to be the first line of defense against terrorism when every time they put up a red flag, they end up vilified? Are you only allowed to sound alarm bells if you're 100 percent sure what's going on? We're told to alert authorities if we see something suspicious, but if we're wrong about it, then we're the ones who wind up under suspicion of racism.

I'm thankful there are still people willing to take the chance. Remember the New Jersey Circuit City employee who foiled the "Fort Dix Six" terror plot? He noticed that the video he was transferring to DVD depicted jihad training, and by speaking up, he may

How did three of the Fort Dix suspects get into the country again? Ohhhh, that's right, across the unprotected border from Mexico. But who needs a fence, right? I mean, three little terrorists shouldn't spoil the fun for everyone.

A.D.D. MOMENT

have saved thousands of lives. But I think we all know what would have happened if he'd been wrong. Hello, ACLU.

ALWAYS PLAN AHEAD

In 2002, author Anis Shorrosh laid out what he said was radical Islam's "Twenty Point Plan" for undermining America. See how many of these sound familiar to you:

- Terminate America's freedom of speech with statewide and nationwide hate-crime bills.
- Yell "foul, out-of-context, personal interpretation, hate crime, Zionist, un-American, inaccurate interpretation of the Koran" anytime Islam is criticized or the Koran is analyzed in the public arena.
- Accelerate Islamic demographic growth via massive immigration, marriage, and prison conversions.
- Use the American educational system to teach loyalty to the Koran and spread dislike of Jews, evangelical Christians, and democracy.
- Appeal to compassionate and sensitive Americans for sympathy and tolerance toward Muslims in America who are portrayed as mainly immigrants from oppressed countries.
- Use riots and demonstrations inside prisons to demand Islamic Sharia as the way of life.
- Open charities throughout the United States, but use the funds to support Islamic terrorism.
- Send intimidating messages and messengers to the outspoken individuals who are critical of Islam and seek to eliminate them.

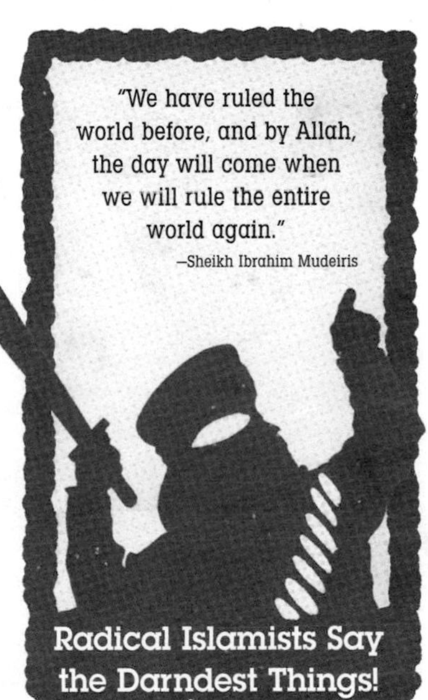

"We have ruled the world before, and by Allah, the day will come when we will rule the entire world again."
—Sheikh Ibrahim Mudeiris
Radical Islamists Say the Darndest Things!

But even more chilling is the supposed Al Qaeda "Master Plan." In his book *Al-Zarqawi—Al Qaeda's Second Generation*, Jordanian journalist Fouad Hussein lays out what he describes as a seven-phase, 20-year plan to establish an Islamic caliphate.

Phase One: "The Awakening" Wake up Muslims around the world by provoking the United States to attack the Islamic world. Check. 9/11, with its resulting wars in Afghanistan and Iraq was a pretty good start for this phase. Hussein wrote that Al Qaeda considered it to be "very successful" and believes that its message is now being heard "everywhere."

Phase Two: "Opening Eyes" This is likely the phase we are currently in. The idea is to turn the Islamic community into a "movement" by recruiting young men and making Iraq the central base of operations.

Phase Three: "Arising and Standing Up" Attacks on Syria, Turkey, Israel, and possibly Jordan highlight this stage, which is hoped to make Al Qaeda "a more recognized organization."

Phase Four: "Take Over" With many Middle East countries facing terrorist attacks, Al Qaeda's hope is to begin collapsing the governments of hated Arabic countries. Simultaneously, terrorists intend to attack oil infrastructure and suppliers and cripple the U.S. economy through cyber-terrorism.

Phase Five: "Caliphate" With weakened or toppled governments and a decreased willingness of Western governments to intervene, an Islamic state can be created to bring about "a new world order."

Phase Six: "Total Confrontation" A "fight between the believers and the nonbelievers" will be initiated by the new Islamic army. Although it's not included in Hussein's book, I really believe that extremists will begin to specifically target our children. Schools and school buses are not only easy targets, but the result of any attack on them would be nothing short of catastrophic. It would turn us into a nation of irrational nut-jobs who would do insane things like torch mosques—and that's exactly what they want.

This is yet another way that our political correctness is killing us. If we were able to talk openly about this kind of stuff, it would reduce the chance of a severe overreaction happening. Unfortunately, we can't—at least without being called a racist or an Islamophobe.

Phase Seven: "Definitive Victory" With "one and a half billion Muslims" fighting, the Islamic army will defeat all others within two years, and the caliphate will stand.

Whether or not the details of the plan are correct isn't the issue. The fact is that we know the *goal* is accurate because we've heard it from extremists over and over again throughout the Middle East. Can it work? Well, you can already see how Americans' attitudes have changed since 9/11 and the war in Iraq—we just don't want to deal with this stuff anymore. But while we put on our blinders and retreat, the terrorists are methodically plodding along, continuing with their long-term plan for our annihilation. If we don't wake up, then the answer is yes, it *can* work.

MY SOLUTION

When you combine everything happening around the world these days with the unbelievably specific plans of our enemies, things start to seem overwhelming. But it's not too late; this is a war we can win. Al Qaeda may need seven phases to establish their caliphate, but I only need four to prevent it.

Phase One: "Calling Evil by Its Name"

No one can be silent anymore. We all, Muslim and non-Muslim alike, must speak up and say "Enough" if we don't want our history, our culture, and likely our entire civilization to be completely destroyed.

Women need to take the lead on this. Where's the National Organization for Women speaking out against the fact that women in extremist societies are tortured, discriminated against, forced into arranged marriages, and not allowed access to education? Aren't they supposed to advocate and defend women's rights? Every woman in America, regardless of her religious beliefs, should stand up against this cruelty, and the rest of us need to encourage and empower women to do so.

I love the people who say, "Oh, Glenn, let's just talk to them. If we try to understand them, then they won't be so angry with us." Are you serious? You cannot debate Muslim extremists! They're simply not interested in chitchat. The second you question motives or ask honest questions about Islam, you are automatically labeled a racist Islamophobe and compared to the Nazis. French writer Michel Houellebecq called Islam "the stupidest religion" and ended up in court. Theo van Gogh made a 10-minute film about Islamic extremists and ended up dead.

Ayaan Hirsi Ali, the former Muslim who fled Somalia and an arranged marriage and was targeted for death by Theo van Gogh's killer, appeared on my show recently. I asked her, as a woman who has seen up close the transformation from moderation to

extremism and experienced the hate that accompanies it, what she thought people need to hear, and her answer was chilling: "For those people who say it's a small problem, I want to tell them it starts small but it grows. When I was living in Africa . . . the first veils . . . were remarkable. Now a country like mine in Somalia is entirely in the hands of people who want to introduce Sharia or Islamic law, which was just unfathomable 20 years ago."

Dr. Zuhdi Jasser of the American Islamic Forum for Democracy is fighting to save his country and his Muslim faith by speaking out. He rightly believes that the bulk of the fight will have to be undertaken by Muslims themselves: "We have to start understanding as a community that the only way to defeat this is to get back the moral courage of Islam, to declare that the Islamists are our enemies and that we are Americans first and Muslims second. What gives us our freedom to be Muslims is our country."

But Dr. Jasser is also a target. He was recently called a "dog" in an editorial cartoon in the *Arizona Muslim Voice.* He fired back at the publication, saying, "It reeks of the tired and pathetic technique to vilify and demonize those who threaten their control the most rather than to deal with the core issues they raise."

Phase Two: "Reinstate the First Amendment"

Free speech must reign; political correctness must die. It might seem like a trivial point when talking about extremism, but our country is headed down a very dangerous path if we keep letting special-interest groups—whether they are based on religion or not—become more important than the laws of the land.

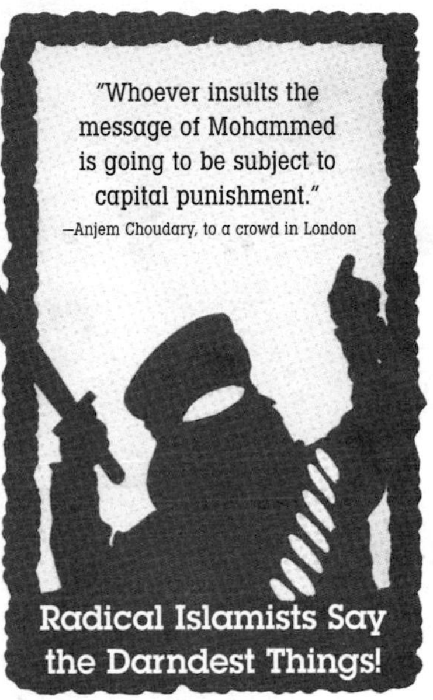

"Whoever insults the message of Mohammed is going to be subject to capital punishment."
—Anjem Choudary, to a crowd in London
Radical Islamists Say the Darndest Things!

In its *Cantwell* decision, the U.S. Supreme Court wrote: "The [First] Amendment embraces two concepts . . . freedom to believe and freedom to act. The first is absolute but . . . the second cannot be. Conduct remains subject to regulation for the protection of society."

Slippery slope has become a cliché, but that's because it's absolutely true. Giving in to one group that's offended by teaching the Holocaust or another group that wants to start a private community may not seem like a big deal, but all of those concessions begin to multiply, and you end up reliving Ayaan Hirsi Ali's experience.

Phase Three: "Borders—More Than a Bookstore"

Our current way of handling our borders, essentially hoping that the people who cross them are innocent workers instead of terrorists, is going to get us all killed. It may be a guy smuggling in a nuke or a couple hundred extremists coming in over the decades to preach Western hatred and Islamism—but either way, you simply cannot have a country without secure borders.

A.D.D. MOMENT

Does anyone remember Al Qaeda's attempted bombing of LAX that we foiled right before New Year's Day, 2000? How did the terrorist, Ahmed Ressam, get into the United States? He crossed the border. The U.S.-*Canadian* border. Maybe we should start taking *both* borders seriously.

Phase Four: "Exposure"

A recent report for Congress highlighted how important the Internet has become for Islamic extremists: These groups "have come to value the Internet so much for its ability to spread their message that some have said the keyboard is as important as a Kalashnikov rifle."

The report went on to talk about how extremists are able to come together online in ways that often later translate into the physical world. Remember the plot in the summer of 2006 to simultaneously bomb airplanes headed from the United Kingdom to the United States? London Police Chief Ian Blair said that the Internet helped the suspects go "from what would appear to be ordinary lives in a matter of some weeks and months, not years, to a position where they were allegedly prepared to commit suicide and murder thousands of people."

But the power of the Internet shouldn't be used only by extremists who want to expose their views to the masses. We can use it to expose *them* to the masses.

The mainstream media outlets really have no interest in showing us what extremists say or do or how clearly they state their threats against us. That's why it's up to all of us—the ones who understand what's happening—to spread the word, and the Internet is a great way to do that.

The most important thing we can all do is be aware. Lots of stuff goes unnoticed by the average American because we are all busy living our lives, and we don't think small changes will affect us. If you have learned anything from this chapter, I hope it's that the little things *do* affect us. When it comes to Islamic extremism, we *should* sweat the small stuff.

So, let's please *stop it* with the political correctness. What ties people like Selectwoman Peake in Massachusetts together with radical Islamists who want to change school curriculums is their insistence on revisionist history. Just because something happened that we don't like or agree with doesn't mean it didn't happen.

There's a lot of stuff in our history we'd like to forget: the Holocaust, slavery, New Coke. But we are better off having lived through it and learned from it than pretending these things didn't exist just because some aspect of them offends us. Remember, we are still a free society, living under the Constitution. You may not like what I have to say, but (so far) I have the right to say it without being killed.

There are two fronts that must be defended in the war with Islamic extremists: our homeland and our freedoms.

If we don't vigilantly defend both of them, we will end up with neither.

Chapter 4

Body Image: The NEW Hotness

SOMEWHERE BEYOND my pink cashmere sweaters, my obsession with Yankee Candle, and, of course, my occasional (and by occasional I mean frequent) bouts of weeping, I'm all guy—no more or less evolved than the workers who shout at women from construction sites.

Unlike those masters of chivalry, I may be able to hold my tongue, but I still find it hard to avert my eyes. A hot woman is a hot woman, and no red-blooded American male can be expected *not* to look. Just like the porn thing, it's hard-wired into our DNA. I have a theory that God himself built men this way by putting magnets in our eyes and iron plates in women's behinds. It's pure biology, beyond our control. I bet that even the pope has moments when he thinks to himself, "Don't look at her butt. *Don't* look at her butt. Inappropriate, inappropriate."

Basically, I'm a hypocrite when it comes to women. I don't mean to be, I try hard *not* to be, but I am nonetheless. As much as I hate the idea that one day some guy will look at one of my three daughters as if she were a 28-ounce porterhouse, I can't help but do that myself to other women. It's not that I don't understand that once upon a time those (unbelievably hot) women were someone's little girls; it's just, well, it's those damn eye magnets—I can't stop it.

And that's exactly the problem. We've become a society that completely revolves around sex. Sex sells magazines; sex gets ratings; sex sells products on billboards, on the Internet, and on television (except on my show). In fact, you probably just reread that last sentence twice because I used the word *sex* multiple times. It's an adage as old as advertising itself: Sex sells. And nothing sells sex better than an impossibly gorgeous woman.

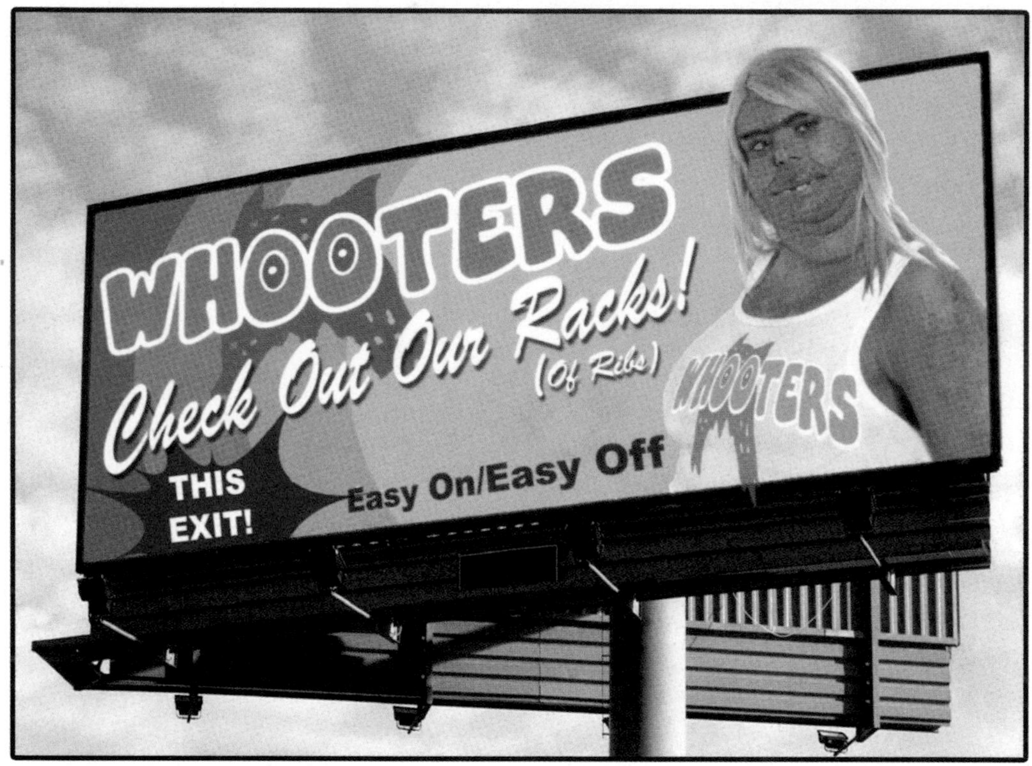

Before Photoshop.

THE MESSAGE AND THE MADNESS

You can find plenty of hot women hawking plenty of products, but it's what you *won't find* that's ultimately more important: an ounce of body fat on any of them.

That's not reality, that's technology. Whatever fat or flaws these women have are conveniently Photoshopped or airbrushed out well before their pictures ever appear on a 50-foot highway billboard.

That's not something we usually pause to think about before hitting the TiVo slo-mo button, but it should be, especially when our kids are around. Think about it—from the day our children stop using a sippy cup, they're bombarded with images that project a nearly unattainable physical ideal.

When was the last time you saw a zit on Scarlett Johansson's forehead? How about

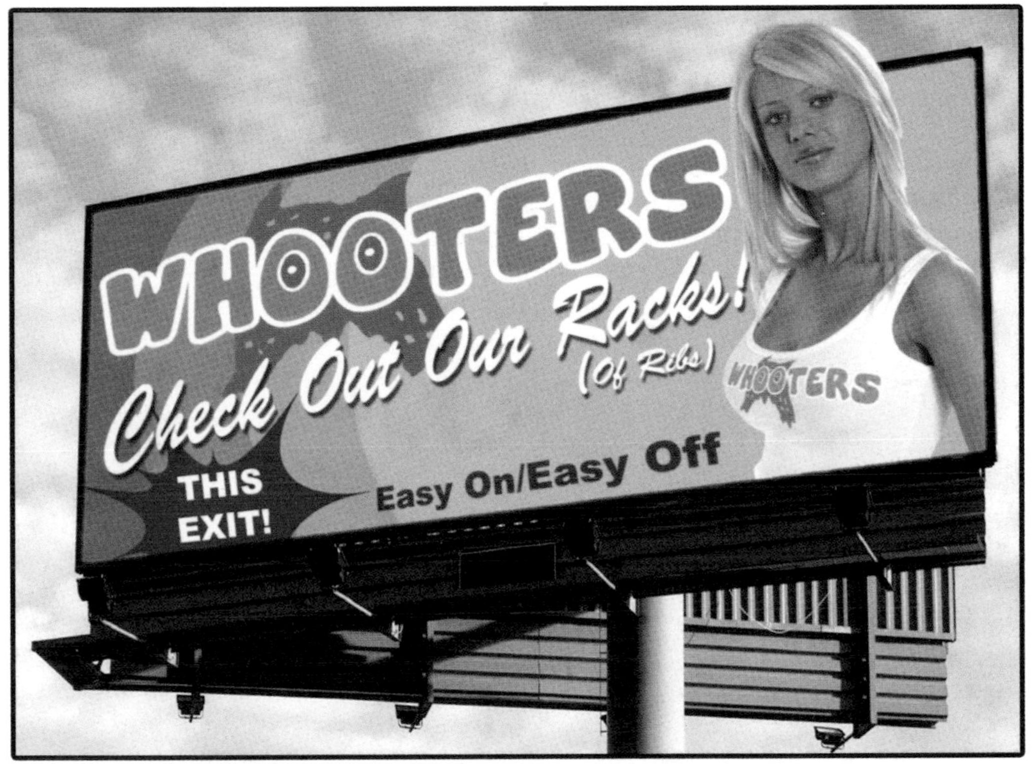

After Photoshop.

crow's feet around Madonna's eyes? Cellulite on Charlize Theron? I'll answer for you: Never. Not because they don't have those imperfections (except for Charlize; she's pretty much perfect) but because they don't have them in *public.* A few mouse clicks here, some makeup and lighting adjustments there, and—poof!—the effects of aging and eating disappear.

And that's exactly the problem. Those images may not seem dangerous right now, but they form the foundation upon which our children's self-esteem and body image will be based. It's not rocket science. The shakier that foundation, the more likely it is that their entire house will collapse later in life.

How am I supposed to convince my teenage daughter that it's OK to have a little acne when no teenage celebrity has any? When they're horrified by cellulite, what famously hot movie star can I point to and say, "Look at her—she *must* have cellulite because she's always wearing slacks!" How can I convince my kids that eating a bowl of ice cream isn't a death sentence when so many of their friends believe that it is? I'm just one man—there's no way I can fight an entire culture . . . but that doesn't mean I won't try.

REQUIRED READING: FROM OUR RACK TO YOURS

Between 8 million and 10 million women in this country suffer from some sort of eating disorder. Even though no fancy study has wasted money confirming it yet, I'm going to go out on a limb and say that most of them are reading magazines with articles like "The Look That Keeps Him Hot for You" just before they head to the bathroom to barf up their lunch.

Think I'm exaggerating? Yeah, not so much. That's an actual article title from a recent issue of *Cosmo.* Go ahead, Google it, I dare you. I don't often use the word *hate,* but I think it applies here. I *hate* fashion magazines.

Here's something a fancy study *did* confirm: The more fashion magazines a girl is exposed to, the more likely she is to suffer from poor body image. I could've told you that for free.

Strictly for research purposes, of course, I had one of my staffers pick up a copy of *Cosmopolitan* magazine. (I wouldn't be caught dead with a *Cosmo*, because if I were caught dead with a *Cosmo,* I'd be dead and would have no way to explain it.) Among such features as "Smooth Sexy Legs: Five Simple Steps," "Outfits That Add Five Pounds," and "Clothes That Flatter Your Butt" are ads. Lots and lots of ads. You have your clothing and fashion ads, ads for beauty products (perfumes, moisturizers, and things that I don't know what they do but look like they'd probably hurt), and, of course, ads for diet and weight-loss products. But that makes sense, since finding clothes that "Flatter Your Butt" means you gotta get rid of the junk in the trunk.

"But Glenn," you ask, "don't these magazines also include articles designed to *boost* a woman's self-esteem?" Why, yes, great question, they do. But one write-up about being "Sexy at Any Size!" hardly balances the dozens of ads, columns, articles, and, most important, pictures that are designed to inspire a futile goal: perfection.

While tabloids aren't quite in the same category as the *Vogue*s and *Glamour*s of the world, these IQ-draining magazines aren't exactly innocent. I saw a recent issue (a friend gave it to me, I swear)

Sexy at *any* size? Really? I know this is a body-image chapter and all, but that's just plain misleading.

with a two-page spread featuring a circled area of cellulite on Mischa Barton's backside. The idea was to make "real women" feel "normal." Uh-huh. You can polish it any way you want, but bull crap is never going to turn into gold, and spin is never going to become reality. How are "real women" supposed to reconcile what is clearly being highlighted as undesirable with the reflections they see staring back at them in the mirror?

Here's what tabloid publisher Louisa Hatfield told Australia's newspaper *The Age* in 2006: "Women are obsessed with body image. They think about their body image more than they think about their children. They think about it even more than men think about sex—which is about a million times a day, isn't it?"

Actually, Louisa, guys think about sex 1.37 million times a day, but who's counting?

A.D.D. MOMENT

Cha-ching! (That's the sound of the cash registers going off inside the offices of fashion magazines and tabloids everywhere.) Anything people are obsessed with (their homes, their kids, their cars, their pets) has a corresponding industry to cash in on it. Body image is no different.

CUT IT OUT! (NO, SERIOUSLY)

If diets and "Hollywood-approved" weight-loss drinks won't cut it, then some doctor will. Literally. Oh, did I forget to mention how many plastic surgery ads those magazines have?

Cosmetic surgery is a now $15-billion-a-year industry in America. The number of procedures, from liposuction to "foot facelifts," has increased more than 800 percent in the past 15 years alone. Allow me to repeat that for you: 800 percent! But that probably doesn't come as much of a surprise if you've turned on the television lately. From *Dr. 90210* to *The Real Housewives of Orange County*, plastic surgery has become almost routine.

A.D.D. MOMENT If you're thinking about plastic surgery, head on over to awfulplasticsurgery.com, and have yourself a gander.

"Oh, Glenn," you must be saying, "that stuff is just for celebrities and the very rich. *Real* people don't do that."

First, stop interrupting me. Second, oh yeah? Two-thirds of the Americans who choose to get a little *nip* here and a bit of a *tuck* there make less than $50,000 a year. That doesn't sound like the caviar jet-set to me.

But more shocking than these people's income (or lack thereof) is their age. Of the millions of cosmetic procedures performed each year, hundreds of thousands of patients are between 13 and 19 years old. Instead of getting a set of keys for a new car at graduation, more and more girls are asking for a set of something else. And apparently, parents are actually saying yes. Who are these people? What father in his right mind wants to give his daughter something that will make *more* men drool over her?

THE MEASUREMENT MODEL: BUILT LIKE A RULER

Image is everything. That clever little marketing catch phrase has never been truer than it is right now. Without image, and the importance we place on it, there would be no industry built around selling its ideal. In other words, no image, no fashion industry; no fashion industry, no models; no models, no pictures; no pictures, no magazines; no magazines, no unrealistic standards. It's a vicious cycle. The more we focus on *image,* the worse the *body image* problem becomes—simple logic applies.

It does not apply, however, to the models featured in the photo spreads.

The average American model is 5'11" and 120 pounds. Slap a size zero dress on a telephone pole, and you start to get a sense of what that's like. On the other hand, the average American *woman* is 5'4" and weighs 163 pounds. You bought the book, so I'll do the math. That's seven inches shorter and 43 pounds heavier than the cover girls.

Let's say *your* 15-year-old daughter is better than average; she's 5'6" and weighs 125 pounds. By the new global standard of who's a fatty and who's not (or as the Ph.D.'s like to call it, "body mass index") she's a 20.2. That's firmly in the "healthy weight" range.

Unfortunately, that still makes her five inches shorter and a few pounds heavier than the women the fashion police suggest she model herself after. Apparently, "better than average" isn't good enough anymore.

After three runway models died of self-inflicted starvation, the fashion industry wasted no time imposing a public relations–driven guideline that any model walking the runways—from Madrid to Milan—could have no less than an 18.5 BMI. Sounds great, right? Sure, until we do a little reverse math on that number.

In order for a five-foot-four-inch woman to achieve that same BMI, she'd have to weigh—ready for this?—108 pounds. Considering that's a full 55 pounds less than average, most women will never have to worry about the fashion industry's little foray into self-regulation.

But someone who did have to worry about it was Victoria's Secret supermodel

Guys, before you break out the calculator to do some quick math on the wife, let me remind you that research suggests that married men aren't exactly saying no to dessert very often. Studies show that married men are more likely to be obese than single men. Gee, I wonder why that is. Could it be the contractually mandated sex? (By the way, most women are in breach of that contract.) **A.D.D. MOMENT**

Gisele Bundchen. She (reportedly, of course) had to *gain* 14 pounds to walk the catwalk in Milan. For someone who's been trained to keep herself so thin for so long (Gisele first got into modeling at age 13), I bet gaining weight was harder than losing it.

Before you start telling me that I should at least appreciate the fact that the industry has *tried* to help, consider this: The guidelines are just that, voluntary guidelines. When's the last time anything *voluntary* has forced real change? Young, skinny, impressionable girls may make good models, but they hardly make good *role* models.

THE AGING PROSTITOT

Maybe you can't take a ruler and draw a straight line between a celebrity-obsessed, self-indulgent culture and sexed-up outfits for seven-year-olds who want Botox shots before they hit up the next Gymboree party, but it's an evolutionary change that is undeniable.

Remember that foundation we talked about earlier? Yeah, well, if you were wondering what the end result of a shaky one looks like, it's this: a prostitot.

Unfortunately, things don't exactly improve once your little prostitot hits her teenage years. Even though every generation says they have the worst teens ever, today's parents actually do. A 2006 San Diego State University study found that the current crop of college students are—ready for this?—almost twice as narcissistic and image-conscious as they were just 24 years ago.

Some of that is because of the me-me-me culture of Internet sites such as MySpace and Facebook and YouTube, but some of it has also got to be related to the shaky foundation that so many of these teenagers' formative years were built on.

IT'S ALL GREEK TO ME

As our prostitot continues to evolve past her teenage years, she usually reaches a place that only makes her body image worse: college. Here's a purely hypothetical example to show you what I mean.

Let's say there's a small, bucolic private college in the Midwest (we'll call it "DePauw University"—merely for the sake of the story). One of "DePauw's" sororities, let's call it "Delta Zeta," decides to toss out all of the women who don't look like the stereotypical sorority girl you may be familiar with from such vintage films as *Animal House, Porky's, Porky's II (The Next Day), Porky's Revenge,* or *Revenge of the Nerds*. Well, actually, they don't *say* that's the reason, but the sorority's on-campus nickname, "the dog house," doesn't leave much room for doubt.

Anyway, after the girls are sent to the pound, "DePauw" ends up in the middle of a firestorm (again, hypothetically, because this example is *totally* fictional) and has to shut down the sorority house and kick the remaining girls off campus—squarely onto their perfect little butts.

There are two morals to this story. First, it's obvious that looks, not friendship, love, or loyalty, are the only thing that really matters. And second, trying to mold your surroundings to look more like an episode of *The O.C.* doesn't create *positive* self-image; it just means you're *obsessed* with it.

MY SOLUTION

The best present you could possibly give your kids this year isn't made by Sony, Dell, or Apple. It actually costs much less. It's an environment where they aren't being constantly targeted and bombarded by everything I've just described. It's something you build for them, a kind of safety zone where they get to spend real time with the family rather than plopping down in front of a TV or computer and staring at Paris Hilton's "night vision" classics all evening.

I know her grandfather built an empire on hospitality, but I wouldn't invite Paris into my home, and neither should you.

A.D.D. MOMENT OK, fine—when I was single, I would have invited Paris into my house . . . but I wouldn't have felt good about it.

My family has an unwritten rule: if you wouldn't spend time with someone in real life, then don't let them into your living room via the television set either. It seems simple, but these days, we're not just letting those people into our living rooms; we're letting them right into our kids' bedrooms.

Now, I don't mean to sound hypocritical, but every time I hear some crazy cable news pundit (present company excluded, of course) railing against celebrities for causing the poor self-esteem of our children, blood just shoots out of my eyes. Celebrities aren't the problem; parents are the problem. Celebrities only have power because we give it to them—but we've been doing that for ages, and things haven't always been this bad.

A.D.D. MOMENT

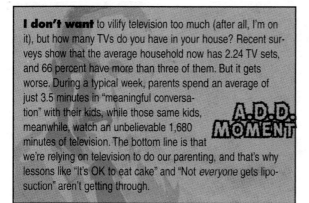

I don't want to vilify television too much (after all, I'm on it), but how many TVs do you have in your house? Recent surveys show that the average household now has 2.24 TV sets, and 66 percent have more than three of them. But it gets worse. During a typical week, parents spend an average of just 3.5 minutes in "meaningful conversation" with their kids, while those same kids, meanwhile, watch an unbelievable 1,680 minutes of television. The bottom line is that we're relying on television to do our parenting, and that's why lessons like "It's OK to eat cake" and "Not *everyone* gets liposuction" aren't getting through.

Back in the 1930s, I'm sure that plenty of kids admired Babe Ruth more than FDR, and the Babe was an alcoholic and an adulterer. But the difference between then and now is *access.* If the Babe were playing today, he'd probably have his own line of bourbon, along with a reality show taking you "behind the scenes" of his adultery. It's not the role models who are the problem; it's the constant and seemingly limitless exposure our children have to them.

Fortunately, that's something we *can* change, because we control the access by controlling the purse strings. Is your eight-year-old part of the underground child-labor market? No? Then someone in your house is giving her the money for the rhinestone Baby Phat tank top.

A.D.D. MOMENT Has anyone else noticed the disturbing trend of putting words on the rears of sweats and shorts? I haven't noticed, because I'd never, ever, ever, ever look there, of course—but a friend of a friend told me that it's particularly trendy these days.

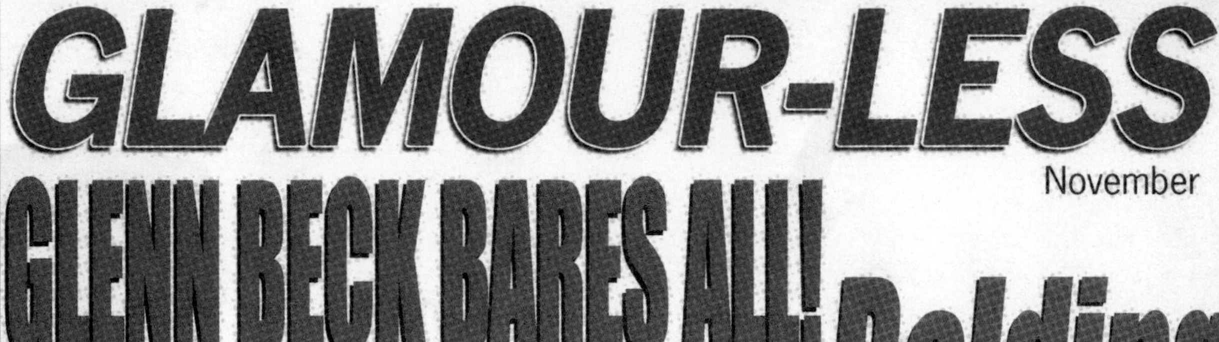
GLAMOUR-LESS
November
GLENN BECK BARES ALL!
Hair Style
He dies the sides of his head gray to help you feel better about yourself! p.92
Balding
The camera may add 15 pounds, but it sure doesn't add any hair!
Man Boobs
His message to teenage girls considering breast enhancement: bigger isn't *always* better!
Double Chin
He never passes a Cinnabon without clearing out the glass warming bin. Even when he's not hungry!
U.S. $3.99
CAN. $4.99
Gut
Despite the overwhelming evidence that it would help, he selflessly avoids exercise at all cost!

998 776 237 2234907653 23 3

My Gift to You

Celebrities are good at complaining about problems but not so good at doing their part to solve them (e.g., every celebrity who sits on a private jet while talking about global warming). That's why I've carefully crafted my image as the exact opposite of what you normally get from fashion magazines. I realize that this might not help my ratings, but I'm so dedicated to fixing the problem of software-enhanced body image that I'm willing to put my real self out there.

I get how hard it is to shop for kids. In the not too distant past, I was out with one of my daughters at a popular retail outlet whose name I shall not repeat here except to say it may or may not rhyme with *Crap*. We were looking for a pair of modestly cut, nondorky back-to-school jeans. Who knew that would be such a problem? Not this guy.

After a little looking around, the fruit of my loins tried on a pair that, well, pretty much showcased the fruit of hers. Honestly, they were borderline lingerie.

I ever so gently suggested that I didn't think they were appropriate, and before she could tell me how old and out of touch I was, the 20-ish salesclerk with the nose ring did it for her. "It's *not* inappropriate," she snarled. "It's how *everyone* is wearing them these days."

Now, in most states, including the one I happened to be in at the time, it is illegal to kill another human being. Consider that a lucky break for my new friend in sales, because that law is the only reason she's still breathing.

I hope my daughter learned something from that whole debacle: Just because the store clerk likes to be led from trend to trend by her nose ring doesn't mean that you have to follow.

But ultimately, the solution comes down to common sense: Have dinner together as a family tonight. Spend time with each other. Talk to each other. As parents, we need to start leading by example. Yes, the magazines, the ads, the plastic surgery—it's all part of the problem, but each time you try to squeeze your fat fanny into a pair of size four True Religion jeans, your daughters learn to pray at the same altar.

There's a bit of dime-store philosophy I picked up along the way somewhere, and it goes like this: "That which you gaze upon you will become." I don't know about you, but I'm pretty happy to have my wife and daughters gaze upon Little Debbie and admire Betty Crocker, as long as we're all doing it together . . . as a family.

Learn the Lingo

If you're going to talk your angel out of becoming a prostitot, you've got to know what you're talking about:

- The part of the panties you can see because the pants are so low? *Whale tail.*
- That tattoo on her back, right over the bum? *Tramp stamp.*

Chapter 5

Blind-Dating: Playing the Powerball of Love

MARRIAGE OFTEN GETS A BAD RAP, but it actually has quite a few benefits. You no longer have to comb your hair, wear pants around the house, or—most important—go on painfully awkward dates (i.e., any date with me).

Of course, the most agonizing type of date out there is the blind variety. It is literally the bane of existence for anyone who's single, yet millions continue to suffer hopelessly through them every year. The evolution of the Internet has only made things worse. Web sites like eHarmony, Match.com, LavaLife, HispanicAmishWidowsSeekingDivorcedCroatians.org, and a host of others are signing up millions of members and making e-fortunes off people's strategically cropped, airbrushed photos and lack of conversation skills.

A.D.D. MOMENT **It goes without saying** that the best part of marriage is getting the privilege of spending the rest of your life—no, make that all of eternity—with the same wonderful, beautiful woman. A wonderful, beautiful, and *understanding* woman who realizes that her husband accidentally calling her Jessica during an act of love doesn't marginalize our amazing relationship. In a way, it's sort of a compliment. Right? Who's with me on that? Nobody?

A.D.D. MOMENT No one is honest in online dating. No one. Alcoholics check off "I drink socially," and three-pack-a-day smokers check the "On occasion" box. Everyone claims to be reading Nietzsche, they're all "easy-going," and of course, "I've never tried this before, so here goes!" is the first line in 90 percent of profiles.

Well, I'm here to end the misery. For just pennies a day, you can help a blind-date sufferer finally get the sweet love he or she deserves. It's true, and I'll show you how (cue Suzanne Somers).

WHY, AMERICA, WHY?

My personal experience with blind dating has led me to the following conclusion: All blind-date participants should actually be blind. That would solve a lot of problems. But until that happens, we're left with a bunch of desperate people who still have their vision and, consequently, their standards.

When you get right down to it, isn't that really the problem? Standards, I mean. After all, the only reason anyone is on a blind date in the first place is that they couldn't attract even the slightest interest from any living human being who has actually ever seen them. What makes you think that someone who's been rejected by hundreds of millions of people is going to look like Jessica Alba or Brad Pitt? I'll tell you what: your standards. I hate to be the one to have to give you the hard truth, but it's time to get rid of them.

We've all heard this line at one time or another: "She's got a fantastic personality!" or "He's got a heart of gold!" Let me translate that for you: On a good day, they look like the love child of Khalid Sheikh Mohammed and Helen Thomas.

The real estate industry uses certain code phrases to market properties (e.g., "Cozy" means "You'll barely fit") that you need to know about to be successful. Blind dating is no different. Someone marketed as having a "fantastic personality" is really "O'Donnell-esque," and someone who "likes to spend time at home" probably has a kid (or five) or is under house arrest. You just need to learn the lingo.

You're probably reading this now and thinking, "But Glenn, looks aren't everything! What about connecting with someone's spiritual side?"

Sure, I'll give that to you. I *did* connect with my wife's spiritual side . . . but not on our first date, maybe not even on our thirty-first date. Tania's spiritual side is what will keep us together for all of eternity, but it's not what *brought* us together. A different side of her was responsible for that; a lesser man would claim it was her backside. Well, in this case, I *am* that lesser man. If she looked like Pete Rose, I don't think we'd have done quite as much "connecting."

Unless you're being set up with the Flying Nun or the ghost of Bing Crosby, save your spiel about spiritual connections for someone else—there's no such thing on a first date.

So, what does all of this mean (other than that

Worst First Date Ideas

- The OTB.
- Donating bone marrow.
- Renewing your driver's license.
- The church you want to marry her in.
- Tour of Neverland Ranch.

I'm an extremely shallow man)? I'm honest. Unfortunately, that quality is missing from the vocabulary of most blind-daters. And let's face it, the folks who *are* honest get no emails.

HONESTY, NOT PHOTOSHOP, IS THE BEST POLICY

Even though websites and technology have helped take some of the "blind" out of blind dating, you still have no idea what to actually expect once you show up. That's because honesty, particularly photographic honesty, is pretty hard to come by.

The rules shouldn't be that complicated. If you're a bald man (or woman), don't put a picture of yourself with hair from a 1987 Whitesnake concert on your Match.com profile. The same goes for height and weight. If 300 pounds is your diet goal weight, you're not "cuddly" or "voluptuous"—you're "gargantuan." And if you're a guy who rounds up his height to 5'2", you're not "compact," you're a shoddier-looking version of Tom Cruise (without the fame, the hot wife, and the cool spaceship religion).

Honesty is such a major problem with blind dating that I'd go so far as to make it federal law. Let's call it the Truth-in-Dating Act. It would require both parties to send their prospective dating partner three unedited, unaltered photos (including at least one full body shot) taken within the previous six months. Certified, notarized. Whatever it takes.

But the Truth-in-Dating Act isn't so shallow as to be exclusively about looks. Net worth matters as well. Since a guy saying "I'm in sales" often really means "I'm in debt," all men must come to the first date with their complete financial records and a recent W-2 form, along with indisputable proof that they do not currently live in their parents' basement.

Women, on the other hand, must provide medical records to prove that (a) all of their lady parts have always been lady parts, and (b) they're not completely and utterly insane.

The Real Story

Matt meets a girl online. She's very cute. Lots of email is exchanged. She makes plans to visit him for a weekend. At the airport, a ginormous girl steps off the plane and approaches Matt. She doesn't look anything like the photos. Matt questions her. She tells him she used her friend's photos, "But now that you know the real me, it doesn't matter!" Things went downhill from there.

The above is a recap of approximately 98.7 percent of the long-distance dates that originated on the Internet. Consider yourself warned.

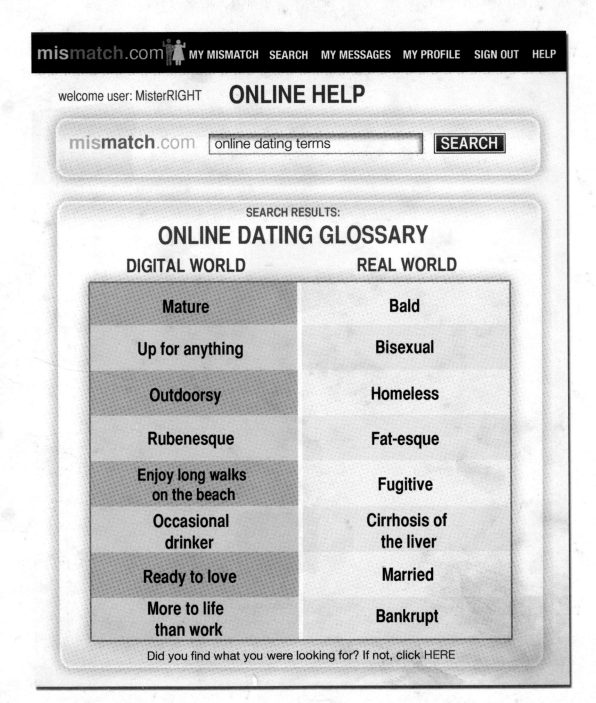

mismatch.com MY MISMATCH SEARCH MY MESSAGES MY PROFILE SIGN OUT HELP

welcome user: MisterRIGHT

ONLINE HELP

mismatch.com online dating terms SEARCH

SEARCH RESULTS:

ONLINE DATING GLOSSARY

DIGITAL WORLD	REAL WORLD
Mature	Bald
Up for anything	Bisexual
Outdoorsy	Homeless
Rubenesque	Fat-esque
Enjoy long walks on the beach	Fugitive
Occasional drinker	Cirrhosis of the liver
Ready to love	Married
More to life than work	Bankrupt

Did you find what you were looking for? If not, click HERE

Any fraud would be dealt with swiftly and mercilessly. Both your fake and real pictures would be posted side-by-side on a free, public website for everyone to enjoy. The conned dater could also post a short summary of the deceit and include any emails from you describing yourself ("I wouldn't say I have six-pack abs, but—well, you know, let's just say I work out").

That would hopefully prevent a prospective dater from seeing this: ↓

Blind-Date-Photograph Warning Signs

- Closeup of one eye and part of a nose. *Hiding morbid obesity.*
- Wearing motorcycle helmet. *Hiding male pattern baldness.*
- Standing with two hot women. *Desperate to show he's been near pretty girls before.*
- Sitting on bed with three cats. *Crazy cat lady. Stay away!*

Digital World

When they'd really be getting this: →

Real World

Actually, I'm not sure which one would be more of a letdown.

THE RULES

You've probably heard of the book *The Rules*, which purportedly reveals the surefire methods that women can use to hook men. Rules such as:

- Don't accept a Saturday night date after Wednesday. (I don't know what that means.)
- Don't talk to a man first. (And never, ever ask him to dance.)
- Don't call him, and rarely return his calls. (Apparently, every girl I met in high school read this stupid book.)

Well, blind dating has rules as well.

For Men

1. Treat the date as if you're hosting your own interview show. Women always say men lose points whenever they "talk too much about themselves," so shut your pie hole and let her do the talking. Obviously, you should avoid politics at all cost. Her reaction to "I really hope Cheney runs in '08" may not be exactly what you hope for.
2. Don't step in poop. It sounds simple, but I've found that almost anything is forgivable on a first date except stepping in dog poop. Trying to remove said poop by wiping your shoe on the front steps of your date's home does not—I repeat, not—make things better. Trust me, this is one of those "things I wish I had read first" rules: If you step in poop, excuse yourself from wherever you are and never, ever come back.
3. Floss before, not during, the date. I've found that women don't appreciate you flossing at the dinner table with a matchbook, business card, piece of cutlery, or strand of their hair as much as you'd think. Again, just one of those things I wish I had read first; consider yourself fortunate.

For Women

1. Cleavage is like bacon: The more, the better. It doesn't matter what you look like; if you show your blind date a little cleavage, you can pretty much guarantee a second date . . . along with no eye contact whatsoever. Bottom line: Guys are not complicated. We're easily bordering on simian. Women should pity us, really.

A.D.D. MOMENT Yes, I know this section is crass, but I'm targeting the typical online dater here. If you're unlike 97.3 percent of normal online daters and you're looking for something a little more emotionally rewarding from your dating experience (or if you're my wife and want to kill me), please substitute the word *intellect* for *cleavage* in this section. Also, please substitute *disrespect* for *eye contact*.

2. Erase the past. We get it; you've had boyfriends before us. But here's the thing, and I'll try to put this as gently as possible: we don't care. We don't want to hear about your "ex Larry who laughed like a llama" or the last guy you dated who made you pay for dinner. Maybe you didn't get the memo, but it's over. That's why you're on this desperation date with us, remember?
3. If you want us to kiss you at the end of the date, please—I beg you—let us know! I speak unilaterally for all men when I say we're absolutely clueless. We'll always assume you're not interested unless you give us extraordinarily overt hints, such as touching us on the leg, playing with your hair, or not interrupting the date to take a call from your ex-boyfriend.

MY SOLUTION: LOVE AT SECOND SIGHT

I never understand women who say, "I wasn't attracted to him at first, but then I got to know him, and—*I learned to love him*." Come again? You *learned* to love him? What could that possibly mean other than "He was a 90-year-old, wheelchair-bound deaf-mute . . . but once I found out he was worth billions, he turned into Jake Gyllenhaal."

Of course, guys aren't as superficial as women. They're *more* superficial. That's why it's in everyone's best interests if all blind dates are mandated to use the "Two-Minute Drill."

Get your mind out of the gutter—it's not what you're thinking. The Two-Minute Drill is a very simple idea that would completely take all embarrassment and awkwardness out of a blind date. Who's not in favor of that? Here's how it works:

1. The daters meet at a prearranged, neutral, public setting. Bars and restaurants are off limits; think more like a park, shopping mall, or busy wheat field—places where people can size each other up from a distance and easily disappear if necessary.
2. The daters slowly approach each other and close to within five feet. Each party (respectively) then flexes his or her muscles and/or bends down, pretending to pick something up. The other party observes.
3. No words are allowed to be spoken. This is a very important rule.

mismatch.com MY MATCH SEARCH MY MESSAGES MY PROFILE SIGN OUT HELP

welcome user: hogheaven267

<< prev photos next>>

MisterRIGHT93

"A Whiter Shade of Pale"

43-year-old man New York, NY, U.S.A. Seeking women 19-35, or anybody with low standards

Online Now!

ABOUT ME

Relationships:	Not enough
Have kids:	Yes
Want kids:	I like babymaking...
Ethnicity:	Any; the less you can understand me, the better
Body type:	Teletubbie-ish; tubular
Height:	6'2"
Religion:	Mormon—or should I say, I'm MORE-MAN than you'll ever know
Smoke:	I'm smokin' hot, does that count?
Drink:	I was like Courtney Love in the mid '90's
For fun:	Making fun of Nancy Pelosi, wearing multi-colored shirts, eating McGriddles while watching *24*, eating McGriddles while watching *24* and wearing multi-colored shirts
My job:	Building media empire, hearing myself talk
My education:	Some junior high school; proficient in emailing
Favorite hot spots:	Arby's and Euro Disney
Favorite things:	Pants with elastic waistbands
Last read:	*The Real America*
Hair:	Salt and pepper and pepper without the pepper, salt and salt
Eyes:	Blue, occasionally crazy
Best feature:	My soft, comfy belly
Body art:	Tattoo of Jeane Kirkpatrick on left bumcheek
Sports and exercise:	Competitive eating
Languages:	Broken English
Turn-offs:	Recycling, hippies
Turn-ons:	Capitalism, Condoleezza Rice

Want to flirt?

4. Like in a "rock, paper, scissors" game, the daters hold out clenched fists and after three shakes, reveal either a "thumbs up" or "thumbs down" simultaneously.
5. If either party shows a "thumbs down," the date ends immediately; the parties scatter. No monies have been exchanged, no valuable time wasted.

Frankly, blind dating never worked out for me. From the awkward silence, to the restraining orders, to the chilling effect of my "irrational" opinions on the conversation, it was all bad. That doesn't mean it can't work for you—especially if you follow the guidelines in this chapter. And honestly, if you can get a complete stranger to stand in the middle of a wheat field and play a twisted version of "rock, paper, scissors" with you, that person is probably the One.

Every day, I count my blessings that my dating experience worked out the way it did. After all, if it had gone any other way, I may never have met my beautiful, loving, and *understanding* wife—the woman who puts up with me, takes care of me, and mothers like no other.

I love you, Gina.

Chapter 6

The Income Gap: The Rich Get Richer, Good for Them

"Today, under George W. Bush, there are two Americas, not one: One America that does the work, another America that reaps the reward. One America that pays the taxes, another America that gets the tax breaks. One America that will do anything to leave its children a better life, another America that never has to do a thing because its children are already set for life."

–John Edwards, 2004.

AS JOHN EDWARDS was making that speech and laying out his optimistic picture of America during the 2004 presidential campaign, he was also doing something else: purchasing 102 acres of land in Orange County, North Carolina.

After losing the election, Edwards had plenty of free time to figure out what kind of house to build on that property—and he chose well. The main residence has five bedrooms and six and a half baths, and it connects (via covered walkway) to a gigantic recreational facility known as the Barn, which features an indoor pool; basketball, squash, and handball courts; and its own stage. In total, the estate contains more than 28,000 square feet and cost a million dollars more than any other home in the entire county. It also happens to sit directly across the street from a trailer park.

I think John picked the right America to live in.

Meanwhile, Edwards visited the "other America"—the lawn of a woman who lost her house to Hurricane Katrina—to launch his 2008 presidential campaign.

John Edwards might be one of the globe's largest emitters of the phrase *income inequality* (and arguably the most hypocritical), but he's certainly not the only one. That phrase is an all-time favorite of politicians, right on the heels of the *wealthiest one percent, gender gap,* and *My secretary stays in my hotel room when I travel to save the*

A.D.D. MOMENT

The people Edwards refers to obviously represent a small percentage of the U.S. population. Can you imagine vilifying any other minority group like that? Most wealthy people have worked hard to leave their children "set for life," and someone should tell Edwards that those who make more than $100,000 a year pay 82 percent of this nation's taxes. How can you possibly describe them as the "America that gets the tax breaks"? I think rich people need some organization to fight for their minority rights! Maybe they could buy one.

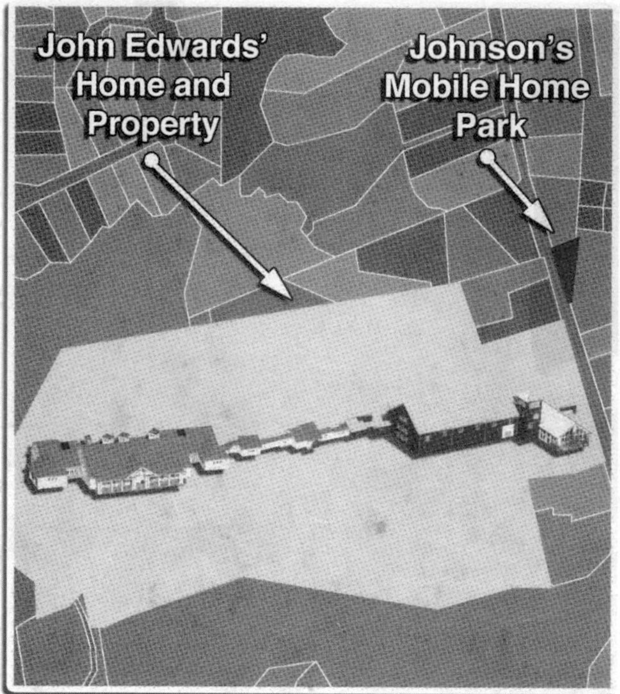

You've got to love how John Edwards, a guy who has campaigned on poverty and global warming, clear-cuts acres of thick forest to build not only an energy-guzzling mansion but also his own personal soccer field. Maybe he should start giving speeches on "The Two John Edwardses." That would be entertaining.

taxpayers money, and it's not hard to see why. After all, *income inequality* creates great mental imagery of evil rich bastards rolling in piles of cash while the poor suffer as a result of their unending greed.

Let me be completely clear about something: I *don't care* about income inequality. I *don't care* if some people make a lot more money than other people. In fact, I want that to happen because it motivates people to push themselves harder. It's a function of capitalism, and I like capitalism.

I *do care* that people are able to meet their basic needs such as food, drink, and shelter. If life is a stock market, I'm bearish on starving people to death. I *also care* about people having every opportunity to succeed financially if they work hard. No one should ever face an uphill battle simply because of race, gender, or anything else other than merit.

If you could really get inside John Edwards's heart of hearts, I bet that even he would admit that he doesn't *really* *believe* that every person should have an *equal* chance to succeed. I would bet that he wants *his* kids to have a better opportunity than *your* kids. That may sound cold, but if that's not true, then why wouldn't he buy a small home, send his kids to community college, and give the rest to that "other America" he spends so much time talking about?

The place where income inequality doesn't exist (at least in theory) is a little town called Communism. The bad news is that this town usually murders millions of its own citizens. But that seems like a small price to pay for the good news: *income equality*! (Note: Top politicians don't count. They can make as much as they want.) The people who work hard and affect society for the better make the exact same amount as the lazy moron who doesn't even show up to work half the time. Sounds fantastic!

A.D.D. MOMENT

Is John Edwards working so hard to save all of his money for a blowout funeral featuring the Rolling Stones (who at that time will be approximately 214 years old and still touring)? No. He's working hard now so that his kids can go to the colleges they want and have the best possible chance at success.

But politicians can't say things like that. They have to shed a tear (at least in public) anytime they see something as unequal. Maybe it's time to go back and review what equality really is supposed to mean in America.

It all starts with a little memo called the Declaration of Independence. Here's how most people read what I believe is one of the most important phrases in the history of the world:

that all men are created EQUAL,

But I happen to put the emphasis on a different word, and it changes everything:

that all men are CREATED equal,

That's right, Jack. Every man is *created* equal. It's what you do with it from there that makes the difference. We are all free agents in life. We make our own decisions. We control our own destiny.

ALL IN THE FAMILY

Stop and think about the families you know who have a few working-age children. Does every child in the same family earn the same amount of money? No? Well, that doesn't make sense. They ostensibly have the same genes, the same parents, the same upbringing, and the same opportunities.

If the politicians who say that economic differences are caused by the evil system lining up to crush our spirits are right, then you'd think that all siblings would earn the same salary. But they don't. Alec Baldwin makes millions, while his brother William, who entered the same field at around the same time, makes as much as an armless tennis pro. Is that because of the unfairness of our system? Of course not; it's because different people have different levels of talent, make different choices, and have different ideas about success.

Think about two brothers who decide early on that their mission in life will be to help other people: One brother becomes a doctor, and the other goes into the Peace Corps. Although their focus in life might be exactly the same, their tax returns are going to be a lot different. In fact, when examining income inequality in America, *"sibling differences represent about three-quarters of the all differences between individuals,"* according to research about family structure in the groundbreaking book *The Pecking Order*. The majority of our differences in income lie *within* families, not *between* them.

IN TRUST FUNDS WE TRUST?

Politicians (most of them with names followed by a *D*) and their vision of modern-day robber barons living off trust funds by exploiting the poor are simply not backed up by the facts.

In 1916, the wealthiest one percent lived almost solely on inheritance and previously made wealth. Their huge stashes of old money continually churned out new money at such an amazing rate that the wealthiest people earned only about one-fifth of their income from actual work. Today that number has tripled to 60 percent.

But politicians have never been ones to embrace stats that don't fit their platform. They still love to paint the picture of an elite ruling class crushing the poor, while the reality is that advances in our quality of life have been widespread and impressive:

- Between 1979 and 2004, the number of American households earning less than an inflation-adjusted $75,000 per year decreased by 10.1 percent, while those earning more than $75,000 increased by the same amount. Translation: More people are earning more money.
- In that same time period, the median size of a newly built home increased from 1,485 square feet to 2,140 square feet. Close to 40 percent

of all new homes are now built with four or more bedrooms, and 90 percent have central air.

- Between 1997 and 2003, the number of people with computers at home rose by 68 percent, and 206 percent more people had obtained Internet access.
- The inflation-adjusted net worth of the median family rose by 31 percent from midway through Bill Clinton's term to midway through George W. Bush's. Shockingly, a full 54 percent of Americans hold no credit-card debt. (However, if it's just the small detail of a missing Social Security number holding you back, then I'm sure Bank of America will help you out.)

Anyone who's ever had a savings account knows that it's easier to make money when you have money. That's one of the reasons people try so hard to get rich in the first place. So what does it matter if life is getting better for some people faster than others, as long as it's getting better?

A.D.D. MOMENT

The New York Times reported: *"Income inequality grew significantly in 2005, with the top one percent of Americans—those with incomes that year of more than $348,000—receiving their largest share of national income since 1928."*

I know this is going to come as a shock, but the *New York Times* analysis wasn't exactly fair. They tried to make their cute little point by using income-tax returns, but tax law changes over the past few decades have made year-to-year analysis virtually irrelevant (unless, of course, you're just trying to find statistics to justify your biased perception in the first place).

Thousands of *businesses* now report their income on *individual returns*, corporate bigwigs are taking more of their stock options as salaries instead of paying capital gains tax, and when tax rates are lowered, the rich don't feel as if they're getting raped as badly, so they wind up reporting more of their income. In other words, much of the income was there all along; it just wasn't showing up on *individual* income-tax returns. Although this doesn't fit into the dark, gloomy prism that the *Times* likes to see the world through, well-researched papers actually show that incomes of the wealthiest people aren't really growing at all.

By the way, there wasn't even a passing mention of any of this in the *Times* article. They probably needed that space in the paper to tell some more terrorist groups exactly how we're monitoring their communications or where our troops are going to strike next.

THE MYTH OF AMERICA AS THE LAND OF OPPORTUNITY

The vision of income inequality does encourage one very serious condition: It makes people believe they *can't* make it.

A study from American University called "Understanding Mobility in America" attempted to do just that. It concluded that people who grow up wealthy wind up having a better chance at staying wealthy. What a revelation! Did the same study "uncover" that people who grow up in America have a much better chance of turning out American?

Apparently, if you grow up rich, there's a 22 percent chance that you'll stay that way. Surely, that statistic proves the United States produces an abnormally large number of stupid rich kids, but that's not where the geniuses at the university named after America went. Instead, they focused on the finding that a person born poor has only a one percent chance of eventually being in the top five percent of wage earners. One analyst then went on to say that this debunks "the myth of America as the land of opportunity."

A.D.D. MOMENT America isn't the land of opportunity? Really? Have you taken a stroll on the beautiful shores of the Rio Grande lately? Those people aren't running over here in the dead of night because they want to visit Knott's Berry Farm. By the way, this study didn't even look at immigrants at all, which—if I remember my history correctly—was how the phrase *land of opportunity* started in the first place.

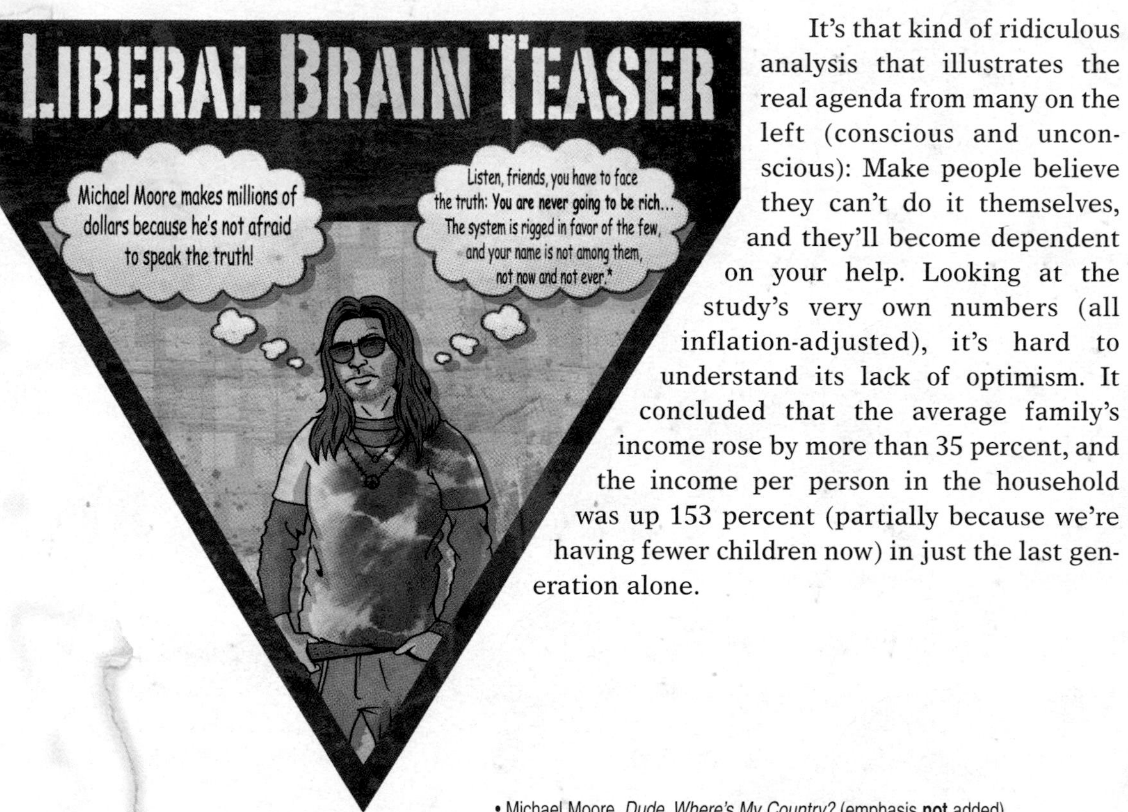

LIBERAL BRAIN TEASER
Michael Moore makes millions of dollars because he's not afraid to speak the truth!
Listen, friends, you have to face the truth: **You are never going to be rich...** The system is rigged in favor of the few, and your name is not among them, not now and not ever.*

It's that kind of ridiculous analysis that illustrates the real agenda from many on the left (conscious and unconscious): Make people believe they can't do it themselves, and they'll become dependent on your help. Looking at the study's very own numbers (all inflation-adjusted), it's hard to understand its lack of optimism. It concluded that the average family's income rose by more than 35 percent, and the income per person in the household was up 153 percent (partially because we're having fewer children now) in just the last generation alone.

• Michael Moore, *Dude, Where's My Country?* (emphasis **not** added)

In fact, those who make the least amount of money (the bottom fifth of all earners) now have an almost 60 percent chance that their children will leave that group. Of those people, almost 60 percent move up more than one quintile. The land of opportunity is alive and well.

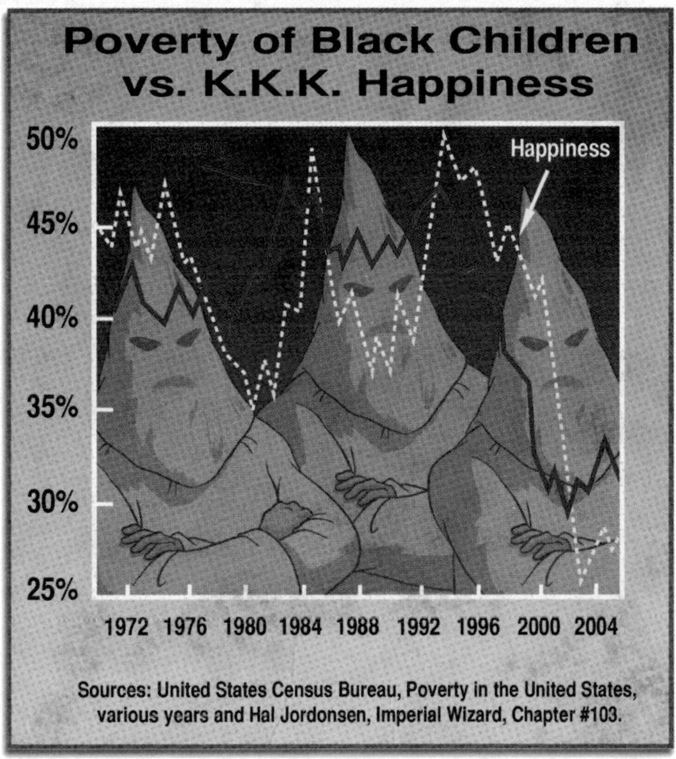

Sources: United States Census Bureau, Poverty in the United States, various years and Hal Jordonsen, Imperial Wizard, Chapter #103.

MY SOLUTION

The problem isn't income inequality; the opportunity to rise is as ample as the opportunity to bed Paris Hilton. The real problem is figuring out how to maintain, and ultimately improve, the situation, and there are pragmatic ways to do so. But, as politically incorrect as it is, maybe the right approach isn't to try to find problems with the financial health of *America* and instead try to examine the financial health of the *poor family* in America. Here are the unpleasant facts:

- About two-thirds of "poor" children reside in single-parent homes.
- Poor mothers who married before their baby was six months old were half as likely to be raising the child in poverty five years later.
- Married men drink less, take drugs at a lower rate, and earn between 10 and 40 percent more than single men with similar résumés.
- 92 percent of children who live in families that make more than $75,000 per year live with two parents; 80 percent of those who live in families that make less than $15,000 do not.
- Kids who don't live with two biological parents are more than five times as likely to be poor and twice as likely to drop out of high school and have behavioral problems.
- Those who marry and never divorce end up more than four times richer than those who never marry.

What does all of this mean? Number crunchers say that if the nuclear family hadn't collapsed as it has over the last generation, the poverty rate would be 26 percent lower for white children and 38 percent lower for black children. Another estimate found that if poor mothers married their children's dads, almost three-quarters would immediately be lifted out of poverty. Not only is this an inarguable case for encouraging marriage in society, but it's a good bullet-point list to have handy for that hesitant girlfriend you just proposed to on the big screen at a baseball game.

Just as important, we've got to stop telling people they can't do it. I've come to realize that one of the main keys to success in the capitalist system is simply to believe in it. In other words, if you want to beat 'em, join 'em. When you think success is possible, you spend more time thinking about how to achieve it and less time complaining about all of the system's imperfections.

If you can't find a way to embrace our system instead of whining like a toddler who wants animal crackers, try renting an apartment in China for a couple of years. They have a much different system, and perhaps you'll flourish in it. Although my guess is that you'll be back on Air Beijing in a week, begging for the unjust American lifestyle you now hold in such disdain.

We also have to stop giving out 14th-place trophies. For whatever reason, we've adopted the idea that the best thing we can do for our kids is to remove all conflict and struggle from their lives. We're so concerned with people's feelings that we shield them from the truth. When you finish 14th, you don't deserve a trophy.

What you do deserve—and what you need—is a lesson in how the real world works. When you don't perform, you get nothing. The phrase is "To the victor go the spoils" not "Spoil those who aren't the victor." If we continue to shelter our kids the way we do, we'll have a generation of adults who can't handle the financial, emotional, and political struggles of everyday life.

14th PLACE
Awarded to: Jimmy
For Achieving: Nothing
Key Statistics: On Time for Most Games, Most Career Errors, Occassionally Remembered Rules, Moderately Believable Fake Injury, Diffused Father's Rage Before He Murdered Umpire.
Pleasant Prairie Little League

It's the struggle that makes us strong. If we understand up front that everything isn't going to be handed to us, that struggle becomes a blessing. Many of the greatest people in history had a bad lot in life, and most of them were great *because* of that lot. Need I remind you that Jesus was born in a manger?

Now, if you'll excuse me, I'm going to play some squash over at John Edwards's house.

Chapter 7

America's Oil Dependence: The Peak of Stupidity

SOMEDAY WE WILL RUN OUT OF OIL.

Yeah, I know, that's not exactly the happy beginning to a chapter you were hoping for, but it's an indisputable fact. You *are* going to die someday (why don't you have a will yet?); the Social Security system *will* go bankrupt (why haven't we fixed it yet?); Rosie O'Donnell *will* keep saying idiotic things (why do we still listen?); and this country *will* run out of oil.

Those things all may be inevitable, but there are things we can be doing *now* to minimize their impact. Take death, for instance. Every single person on this earth will die someday, but how many of us have taken the time to create a legal will? How many of us have bought our burial plots or prepaid our funeral expenses?

Don't feel bad if those things are still on your to-do list. You're not alone. Most people just feel it's too far away to take seriously; we believe there will be plenty of time to figure it all out later. Plus, who wants to pay for a funeral *now* or a will *now,* when there are other things (far more fun things) to spend our time and money on? And—let's just be real honest—we won't even be alive when our children and grandchildren benefit from all of our foresight and hard work . . . so is it even worth it?

Of course it is. We want our next generation to live in a world that's *better* than the one we had. We want there to be peace, fewer wars, less terrorism, and a cleaner environment. Yet, inexplicably, we refuse to make the difficult decisions that would make those dreams possible.

The impending energy crisis will affect every single one of us. Depending on how bad it gets, gasoline will be rationed, severe rolling blackouts will be common, food prices will skyrocket, and the economy will begin a long fall. But all of that is only the beginning. It's really the *next* generation that will pay the ultimate price for our apathy: wars on an unprecedented scale, massive unemployment, food shortages, and long, cold winters without heat. Oxford-educated oil geologist (and fellow end-of-oil alarmist) Jeremy Leggett describes it this way, "The price of houses will collapse. Stock markets will crash. Within a short period, human wealth—little more than a pile of paper at the best of times, even with the confidence about the future high among traders—will shrivel . . . Once affluent cities with street cafés will have queues at soup kitchens and armies of beggars. The crime rate will soar. The earth has always been a dangerous place, but now it will become a tinderbox."

Hold on a second. Forget about endless human suffering, is this guy insinuating that I won't be able to get biscotti at my favorite Manhattan café anymore? Well, now he's got my attention.

"Glenn, I already bought your stupid book. Stop trying to scare me!"

I know that's what it seems like I'm doing, but trust me, I haven't suddenly turned into Al Gore. There's already a long list of issues that people hate me for; I'm not exactly shopping around for another.

- Radical Islam? I'm a hatemonger.
- Iran? I'm a fearmonger and sometimes also a fear/warmonger combination.
- Illegal immigration? I must hate Hispanics. (Sometimes also abbreviated as *racist* or *bigot.*)

Things That Will Kill Us before Oil

I've always believed that a spoonful of sugar makes the medicine go down. Sure, this chapter may be full of doom and gloom, but there is good news: Lots of things may kill us well before the oil ever runs dry! To give you some hope that peak oil may never even matter, I'm going to share a few of those other threats with you throughout this chapter in the form of actual quotes from my television show.

#13: Political Correctness

"Here's the point tonight: Political correctness is going to lead us all to a place where we're down on our knees and somebody is standing behind us with a machete. . . . Political correctness is going to kill us."

☢ Global warming? I'm a "fascist" (thanks, RFK, Jr.!) who believes that penguins should be on a different type of list: a menu.

A.D.D. MOMENT Actually, the last part is true—penguins always seem to get a free pass. I bet that's because they're so darn delicious.

Things That Will Kill Us before Oil

#22: Iranian president Ahmadinejad (since I can't pronounce it, I just call him President Tom)

"President Tom is the head of the snake. This is the guy who will be responsible for the deaths of me and you if we don't wake up soon."

You get the point. When I really believe in something, I'm willing to stake what little is left of my reputation and credibility on it. Peak oil is no different.

Along with the fight against radical Islam, our impending energy crisis is one of the defining issues of our generation. That means it's up to us, right now, to make a decision: Do we fight, or do we continue to live in denial? If the right answer seems obvious, then keep reading, because generation after generation has made the wrong choice.

THE OIL OCTOPUS

So many people talk about the oil monkey that I feel it's time to change things up. When's the last time you had a monkey *or* an octopus on your back? See what I mean? Neither of them makes any sense, so let's go with octopus. It's got 200 percent more appendages than a monkey.

But I guess the actual animal doesn't matter as much as the fact that it's been attached to us for decades now. How did we get addicted in the first place? After all, in 1859, the United States produced a grand total of 2,000 barrels of crude oil. One hundred forty-eight years later—literally a blip on the timeline of life—we produce 1.9 *billion* barrels a year, and that isn't near enough. To quench our thirst, we still need to import *another* 3.7 billion barrels. Put your abacus away; that's a grand total of 5.6 billion barrels.

Does anyone actually know how to use an abacus anymore? If so, I'd like to meet that person. Then I'd like to give him a calculator.

From 2,000 to 5.6 billion barrels. How did that happen? The answer is 148 years full of greed, money, false starts, and false promises.

A 12-STEP PROGRAM

Ask anyone who's ever been addicted to something which is easier, getting hooked or getting clean? Cigarettes, alcohol, crack, gambling, porn, or oil—it doesn't matter. Once something becomes intertwined with your everyday life, it's almost impossible to go without it. And that's exactly what's happened with oil, a substance that's gone from fueling a few lanterns to being the primary source of energy for every single thing we consume, every day.

One of the reasons for that is that it's so remarkably effective. One gallon of gasoline contains the equivalent of about 500 hours of human labor. Think about that—500 hours contained in a little milk jug's worth of gasoline. And I'm not talking about work in some abstract, high school physics class way; I mean actual *work.*

Think about it this way: A Category 3 hurricane just blew through your town, and there are tree branches down all over your property. You can get out your chainsaw, fill it with gas, and cut up all the downed trees in about 30 minutes, or you can find your rusty hand saw and get to work.

I'd choose option three, call a landscaper, but that's another story. Let me describe the concept of work in a language I understand a lot better than yard work: cars.

Land Rover's 2007 Range Rover (a sweet ride) can go about 14 miles in 14 minutes on one gallon of gasoline. Environmentalists are always complaining about how bad that is, but it's actually pretty impressive. Imagine how long it would take you to *push* a Range Rover 14 miles. A lot longer than 14 minutes.

The lesson here is that manual labor is bad; internal combustion engines are good. But I guess another, maybe even more important lesson is that oil and gas are far more efficient than we'll ever be—and that's why we use so damn much of them.

HOW BAD IS IT?

Like a doctor who has to give a patient bad news about a medical condition, I'm just going to give it to you straight: It's bad. Very, very bad. In fact, it's terminal.

It may not be a widely advertised fact, but U.S. oil production peaked way back in 1970. Now attention has shifted to another, more important peak: the global one. Even the most optimistic among us believe that peak will happen within the next 25 years. Many of the, let's

A.D.D. MOMENT

The worldwide peak of oil is actually called Hubbert's Peak, after the guy who accurately predicted it 14 years before it happened. Since "Beck's Peak" would sound pretty cool in the history books, I'd like to go on record right now: World oil production will peak in 2010. (You heard it here first.)

call them "less optimistic" people, believe it will happen within the next five years. Some even believe that it's *already* happened.

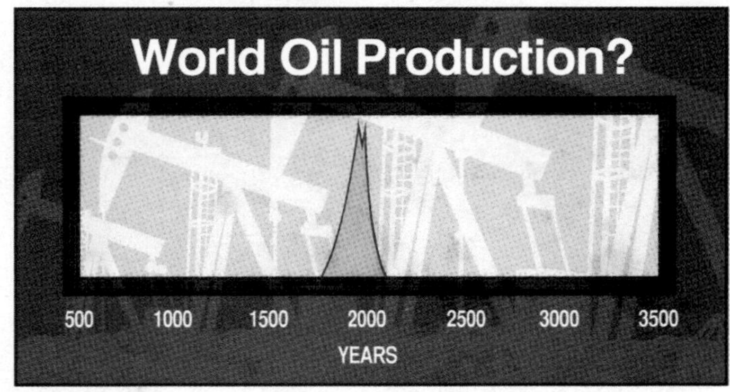

But the exact year that oil peaks isn't a big deal. There will still be years and years of oil left and maybe even more years of reserves still to be found. But it *does* mean that the world will never again increase its production.

Meanwhile, consumption is increasing year after year with no end in sight. The U.S. Energy Information Administration predicts that the world will consume 118 million barrels a day in 2030 (about 39 percent more than the 85 million barrels we currently use). Now, I'm no economist, but I am a thinker. Rising demand combined with decreasing supply usually means—say it with me—higher prices! In this case, much, much, (much) higher prices.

But that's where the typical rules of economics start to derail. Normally, higher prices mean that demand decreases and everything balances out again. But oil doesn't act "normally" because it's not a discretionary purchase. We *have* to be warm, and we *have* to get to work (unless we live in an igloo and work at home). Think about it more like tap water. If water prices increased by 25 percent, you might try to conserve more, but you still have to shower, wash the dishes, and do your laundry. Conservation can go only so far.

One study recently concluded that if gas prices went from three dollars to four dollars a gallon (a 33 percent increase) and stayed there for an entire year, Americans would cut their demand by just 5 percent. Prices would need to stay high for at least five years before people start to really change their behavior. That's why temporary shocks to the system (such as Hurricane Katrina, the Iraq invasion, or even the oil embargo in the 1970s) never result in any lasting changes.

If we want real, long-term change, we need prices to go up and stay there, but more on that later. What keeps me up at night these days is the *psychological* impact of peak oil. This country is like the guy in the bar who everyone knows is an alcoholic, except for him. We're in denial. But the benefit of that denial—that ignorance, if you will—is

Gas Station Humor

Whenever gas prices go up fast, some stand-up-comedian gas station owner decides to put up the typical joke on his sign.

Well, I say it's time for some new material. Unfortunately, these guys probably don't own gas stations because of their cutting-edge creativity, so I thought we'd help them out with a few ideas.

How about organ donation?

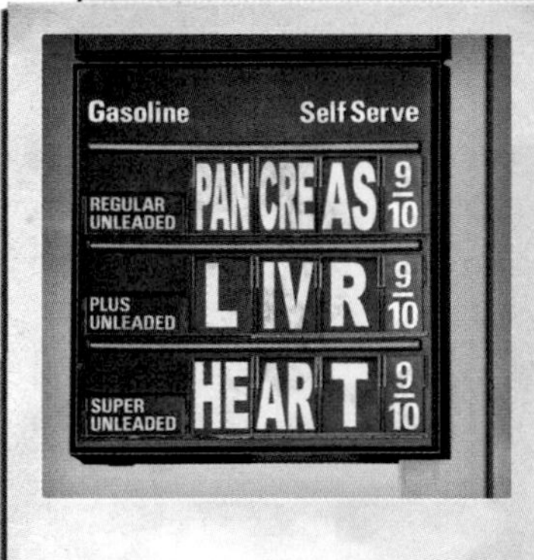

The senses?

What about a no-holds-barred wild evening?

bliss. When you don't admit you have a problem, you don't have to worry about fixing it.

What happens when the entire country wakes up from that denial all at once? What happens when the front page of the *New York Times* declares, "Experts Agree: World Oil Production Has Peaked"?

I'll tell you exactly what happens: absolute panic and complete chaos.

Things That Will Kill Us before Oil

#37: Hugo Chavez

"Venezuelan President Hugo Chavez. He doesn't believe in the apocalypse like the nut jobs do in Iran. But I'm telling you now, he is willing to align with them, because he wants to destroy us as well. Let's not forget he also controls CITGO."

SCARING THE BAT CRAP OUT OF YOU

The end of oil is a long way off. I get that. You don't want to think about the oil change you need for your car next month, let alone the *end* of oil in some future decade. So let's bring this back to the present day. Since U.S. oil production has already peaked, we're left relying on the term you've heard politicians use as campaign slogans for years: *dependence on foreign oil.*

But who really cares? We rely on foreign countries for lots of things, right? We depend on China for little cocktail umbrellas, and we're definitely dependent on France for champagne and skinny cigarette-smoking jerks. Why is this any different? Well, aside from the obvious reasons (i.e., cocktail umbrellas, champagne, and French guys don't provide the entire basis for our civilization), the main problem is that, generally speaking, the more oil they have, the more they hate us.

Take Ireland. That's a country you really don't think of in any sort of World War III context, right? I mean, I really don't see the Irish starting a secret nuclear program anytime soon. Well, guess what? Their oil reserve is somewhere in the neighborhood of zero barrels. And in case you haven't noticed, friendly countries such as Switzerland and Australia aren't exactly known for their massive oil fields either.

So that leaves most of the oil with the countries that always seem to be in the middle of our nightmares, countries such as: Saudi Arabia, Iran, Venezuela, Russia, and Nigeria. I know, I know, what could possibly go wrong?

If peak oil is like being diagnosed with terminal cancer, then our dependence on foreign oil is like an undiagnosed heart condition. Both will eventually kill you, but the heart condition can do it fast and without warning or mercy. Well, our foreign oil suppliers can kill our economy just as fast—that's why it's so important to know exactly who our dealers really are.

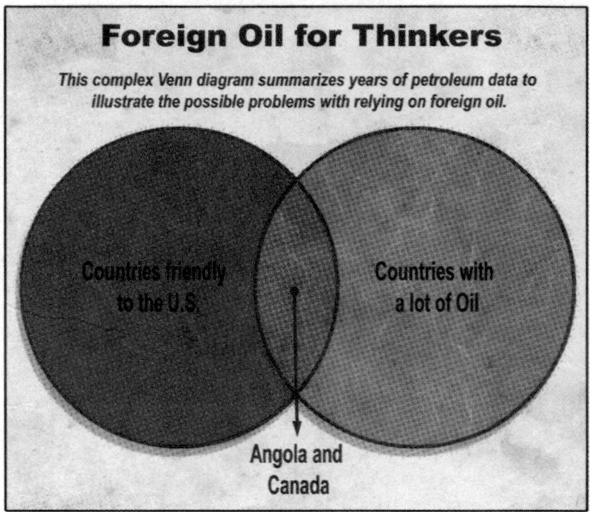

Let's start at the top of the list. If you had to bet your life on which country we import the most oil from, what would you pick? Saudi Arabia? Sorry, it's actually number three. Venezuela? Nope, it's fourth. The two countries we import the most oil from are—drum roll, please—Canada and Mexico. Surprised? You're not the only one; I couldn't believe it.

That Mexico is number two is especially shocking. I knew it exported lots of *pico de gallo* and illegal, low-wage workers, but oil? Yes, oil—and lots of it. In 2005, we imported 568 million barrels from Mexico, about 15 percent of our worldwide total. By way of comparison, Canada, our leading supplier, sold us 596 million barrels, so Mexico wasn't far behind.

But here's the problem: Mexico's oil may be running out a lot faster than anyone thinks. Its largest oil field, Cantarell (which is the second-largest oil field in the world), is responsible for 60 percent of Mexico's oil production . . . but maybe not for long. New reports suggest that the field is in the midst of a major decline, and Mexico's own government issued a report concluding that a worst-case scenario could be a 71 percent drop in production by the end of 2008.

That creates two big problems for us. First, it would mean that we'd have to replace the Mexican oil with oil from another country—likely a Middle East creepocracy, thereby making us even more reliant on countries that don't exactly see eye to eye with our Bill of Rights. But a second, less obvious problem is that oil revenues fund about a third of Mexico's entire federal budget. Take most of that revenue away, and the Mexican economy will implode. If you think there's a problem with undocumented workers coming here now, just wait.

While we're on the subject of crackpot theories, let me give you another one. Everyone knows that Iran wants a nuclear program, but what many people don't know is that the six members of the Gulf Cooperation Council—Bahrain, Kuwait, Oman, Qatar, Saudi Arabia, and the United Arab Emirates—all want one as well. So do

Egypt and Yemen. In fact, you're hard pressed to find a country in the Middle East that *doesn't* want to start a nuclear program. But the question has always been why. If all of those countries are floating on oil, why are they so interested in a nuclear program and all the scrutiny that comes with it?

The crackpot answer is frightening: Those countries understand, better than anyone, that the end of oil is coming. They've already faced the reality that we haven't, and they're starting to adapt. After all, these countries can't exactly come out and say, "Attention! We are starting a nuclear-fuel program because we have just 20 years of oil left." That wouldn't be good for business.

A.D.D. MOMENT

Everyone is always wondering why the highest levels of our government don't take illegal immigration more seriously, why they won't just build a fence along the entire border. Well, I lay out my whole theory in the illegal immigration chapter, but I think a big part of it may have to do with oil. Would anyone *really* be shocked if an understanding exists between our governments that we keep the borders porous and they keep the oil pouring? I'm not saying I believe that, but I'm not *not* saying it either.

Consider the poster child for a seemingly unnecessary nuclear program: Iran. It exports about 2.5 million barrels of oil a day right now, but some experts believe that'll be down to just 1.4 million in three years. That would be an enormous 44 percent decrease. But if Iran can begin a transition of some of its oil- and gas-powered electrical plants to nuclear power, that would free up a lot more oil to be exported. Considering that oil provides Iran's government with 90 percent of its revenue, it's really not that far-fetched to think Iran would want to keep those exports flowing, at any cost.

But what scares me the most isn't a major OPEC country slowly running out of oil or a natural disaster temporarily ravaging a major port; it's a coordinated, international terrorist attack. Not long ago, at the World Economic Forum, a group of experts war-gamed a scenario involving three separate but simultaneous terror attacks against oil interests. Although none of the attacks was crippling, oil prices jumped overnight to $120 a barrel, and gasoline skyrocketed to $5 a gallon.

Sometimes it doesn't even take an actual attack, just the rumor of one. In March 2007, a rumor that Iran had fired a missile at a U.S. warship in the Persian Gulf caused oil prices to jump five dollars a barrel (more than seven percent) in just seven minutes. Now, imagine what would hap-

Things That Will Kill Us before Oil

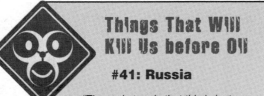

#41: Russia

"The real story is that this is just more irrefutable proof that Russia is maneuvering to reestablish their beloved Byzantine Empire."

pen if the rumor turned out to be true, or if terrorists targeted the world's largest oil field (Ghawar in Saudi Arabia), which is responsible for over 6 percent of the world's production? One hundred twenty dollars a barrel would seem like a bargain.

As with almost everything else that's terror-related, most experts say that a major attack against oil interests isn't a question of *if,* it's a question of *when.*

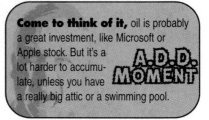

Come to think of it, oil is probably a great investment, like Microsoft or Apple stock. But it's a lot harder to accumulate, unless you have a really big attic or a swimming pool. **A.D.D. MOMENT**

GETTING THE OCTOPUS OFF OUR BACK

It's not exactly breaking news that we're running out of oil. We've been talking (key word: *talking*) about what to do for the better part of four decades now. As I said before, U.S. oil production peaked in 1970, but with so much foreign oil still flowing, that little headline didn't do much to get people to take the issue seriously.

In fact, the event that finally got us to start having a conversation about our addiction came in 1973, when our dealers (OPEC) cut us off. They didn't appreciate the fact that we were supporting Israel in a war against Egypt, so they used their greatest weapon—oil—against us. And what a weapon it was. In just more than three months, the price went from $3 a barrel to $11. Panic set in; mission accomplished.

But sometimes progress is a byproduct of panic; sometimes change can only come through crisis. And so it was in 1974, as the 267 percent price increase propelled our oil addiction to the front pages and, in response, President Nixon launched Project Independence: "Let this be our national goal: At the end of this decade, in the year 1980, the United States will not be dependent on any other country for the energy we need to provide our jobs, to heat our homes, and to keep our transportation moving."

It was a bold statement, and a noble cause, but it was doomed from the start. OPEC lifted their embargo in March 1974, and, not surprisingly, ending our foreign dependence just didn't seem like such a priority anymore.

Enter Gerald Ford. The next year, he signed the 1975 Energy Policy and Conservation Act and decided that Nixon's deadline of 1980 for independence was completely unrealistic. So he pushed it back five years. The new date was 1985 (and you can take that to the bank).

Like Nixon, President Ford didn't stick around long enough to make sure his goal was met, so that left things up to Jimmy Carter. Normally, that would be a bad thing.

I mean, I don't want Jimmy Carter responsible for my omelet, let alone solving our energy crisis, but, in this case, could Jimmy Carter actually be the right guy?

Faced with another crisis (this time a result of the shah of Iran fleeing into exile along with the outbreak of the Iran-Iraq war), Carter got serious. Oil had gone from $14 a barrel in 1978 to $37 in 1981, and people seemed finally to realize that it wasn't smart to base our entire way of life on the emotional swings of some Middle East nut-tatorship.

On July 15, 1979, Carter tried to tap into that realization by going on national television and delivering a speech called "Crisis of Confidence": "Beginning this moment, this nation will never again use more foreign oil than we did in 1977—never. From now on, every new addition to our demand for energy will be met from our own production and our own conservation. The generation-long growth in our dependence on foreign oil will be stopped dead in its tracks right now and then reversed as we move through the 1980s, for I am tonight setting the further goal of cutting our dependence on foreign oil by one-half by the end of the next decade—a saving of over 4.5 million barrels of imported oil per day."

Yeah, not so much. But at least Carter *tried.* In 1980, Congress passed Carter's Energy Security Act, which authorized the creation of something called Synthetic Fuels Corporation (SFC), a company tasked with creating 2 million barrels a day of synthetic oil within seven years.

To help it along, Congress had provided up to $88 billion in loans and incentives (that's $223 billion in today's dollars), and the program received lots of media attention (and scrutiny). But no amount of money was going to help, because OPEC, acting like a big-box retailer trying to crush an annoying little upstart, took notice and responded.

During the time that SFC was in business, OPEC lowered the price of oil from $37 a barrel back down to less than $14. Given that synthetic fuel cost a lot more than that to produce (a *lot* more), the program didn't seem so interesting, or necessary, anymore. And back to sleep we all went.

Six years later, President Reagan shut the company down. Energy Secretary John Harrington said that oil prices had just dropped too low to make it a viable business. Congratulations, OPEC, mission accomplished.

The Reagan, Bush, and Clinton years all involved a lot of lip service about energy independence and national security, but those three administrations all pretty much ended the way they started: no new energy sources and increased dependence on foreign oil.

And that brings us to George W. Bush. Although 9/11 (with its 15 Saudi hijackers), made it clear just how suicidal it is to rely on countries such as Saudi Arabia for our energy, President Bush actually seemed to understand that lesson well before the towers fell. Earlier that year, California had suffered rolling blackouts, prompting the president to deal with the energy crisis. In May 2001, he said, "What people need to hear loud and clear is that we're running out of energy in America. We can do a better job in conservation, but we darn sure have to do a better job of finding more supply. . . . We can't conserve our way to energy independence."

A sitting president of the United States had just plainly told his country that it's running out of energy. That's virtually unprecedented, and it should've served as a wakeup call about just how dire the situation had become. But, of course, it didn't, and we hit the snooze button *again.*

Just weeks before the president's alarmingly honest remark, another high-ranking official made a frightening remark of his own that received virtually no attention. This time, it was Lee R. Raymond, chairman and CEO of ExxonMobil (and a guy who probably knows a thing or two about oil): "The idea that this country can ever again be energy-independent is outmoded and probably was even in the era of Richard Nixon."

If you put President Bush's comment together with Mr. Raymond's, it would probably sound something like this: "What people need to hear loud and clear is that we're running out of energy in America and there's no way we'll ever recover in time to prevent that from happening." Are you starting to see why I spent my last summer vacation learning how to can my own vegetables?

But let's say that Mr. Raymond was wrong, that we *can* still become energy-independent. How do we even get started? High oil prices alone don't seem to matter (they've more than doubled since President Bush took office and at one point had gone up more than 170 percent), and the dangers of Middle East dependence couldn't be clearer. Yet nothing of any consequence is really happening. How will that ever change?

Things That Will Kill Us before Oil

#63: World War III

"It's World War III, but I'm telling you, I think Jesus could come out of the sky at any time. He could be making a glorious appearance, you know, in the next 15 minutes."

THE NEXT COLOR OF GOLD

Many people believe that we only have to look to the past for the solution. One example that is frequently cited involves the transition from whale oil to kerosene in the 1800s. According to the story, whales were becoming extremely scarce, forcing the supply of whale oil to decrease and prices to skyrocket. Enter kerosene, a cheap, clean, plentiful alternative. The pretty whales were saved from extinction, and the country was saved from darkness—just in the nick of time and all thanks to American innovation.

The only problem with that anecdote is that the passage of 150 years has caused one big fact to be left out. Well before people were concerned about how many whales were left, another fuel had already become popular: camphene, an alcohol derivative. But at just the same time as petroleum was discovered in Pennsylvania, making kerosene cheap and plentiful, a huge alcohol tax was also going into effect. That drove the price of camphene through the roof, making kerosene the perfect substitute. The rest, as they say, is history.

The modern-day lesson is that it wasn't some silver-bullet new technology that saved us from the brink of darkness; alternatives were already in place. Besides camphene and whale oil, there were several other products available, each with its own pros and cons. Eventually, kerosene won out because it was the best and (thanks to the government's tax policy) cheapest product.

Today we need those same alternatives to become viable products so that, over time, society can decide which one will be the anointed successor to oil. But we also need private corporations to do what they do best: think selfishly, and let greed and profits force us into a new direction. That's exactly what happened earlier this century as our initial flirtation with oil quickly turned into an obsession.

A STREETCAR NAMED CORRUPTION

Back in 1914, electric streetcars were responsible for 100 percent of mass transportation within U.S. cities. But a consortium of companies representing three different industries (automobiles, oil, and tires) decided that a lot of money could be made if buses, not streetcars, became the standard—and they decided to act.

In 1936, those companies formed National City Lines (NCL), a holding company tasked with furthering the city bus agenda. And further the agenda it did. Over the next few decades, buses replaced streetcars in almost every major city, including New York and Los Angeles. People disagree about whether NCL was completely responsible (some argue that it bought up streetcar systems across the country and systematically dismantled them, while others say that never happened), but what no one can deny is that by 1950, the streetcar was virtually obsolete.

No matter how much influence NCL actually had, the mere fact that companies from completely different industries came together to serve their common interests by influencing change is inspiring for the situation we find ourselves in now. Far better than any government agency, private industry can lead us through another transformation, but it needs the right incentives. Remember, for better or worse, American companies are in business to make money, not to solve social problems (that's Bono's job). We have to make alternative energy *profitable*, not just fashionable.

But there is one golden rule: Whatever incentives are offered have to be completely isolated from the price of oil. John D. Rockefeller, owner of Standard Oil, admitted that he used to lower his oil prices and put his competitors out of business anytime they mounted a serious challenge to him. It was also falling oil prices that doomed SFC, a massively funded operation. The only way to avoid falling into that same trap again is by making sure that new technologies and alternatives are profitable whether oil costs $40 or $140 a barrel.

Things That Will Kill Us before Oil

#77: Iran

"So here's what I know tonight: There is a possible apocalyptic war on the horizon, and it will be centered around President Tom and his boss, the Ayatollah Khamenei . . . it doesn't matter if I don't believe that it's the apocalypse; it doesn't matter if you don't. The important thing is these people do, and they're dead serious. A year ago, [they] said the end of the world would happen within three years."

THE SOLUTION

If you want the real, honest answer, you're in luck, because it's very simple: I think we're all screwed. But since you paid for the book, I'll humor you.

Let's start by talking about what is not the answer: wind, wave, solar, geothermal, hydrogen, ethanol, cellulosic ethanol, nuclear, biodiesel, biobutanol, natural gas, tar sands, solar satellites, oil shale, asteroid mining, turkey waste, garbage, or black holes.

All of those technologies have their supporters (yes, even black holes), but none of them, on its own, is ready to replace oil—especially when it comes to transportation. I know that's surprising, considering how much press and publicity some of them have gotten (especially hydrogen and ethanol), so let me explain exactly what I mean.

Take ethanol. Although Big Corn is a pretty powerful lobby and did a great job working itself into State of the Union addresses, there are two big problems with ethanol that you won't find on the front page of its marketing brochure.

What we really need right now is a new MacGyver. Pincushion, tomato, rubber band, staple, bandanna . . . oil problem solved

A.D.D. MOMENT

First, if you are really talking about producing ethanol in quantities large enough to replace a material amount of our oil, then you're talking about a lot of corn. A *lot* of corn. According to some estimates, it may take as many as 11 acres of farmland to produce enough ethanol to power just one car for one year. To reach President Bush's goal of producing 35 billion gallons of ethanol a year (which would replace just 15 percent of our gas consumption), experts say we'd have to turn an area the size of Kansas and Iowa into farmland. To fuel every American car with 100 percent ethanol, approximately 97 percent of the United States would need to be covered with corn fields.

That's obviously completely impossible, but don't forget that even at the lower levels our politicians support, we still need farmland to—well, to farm. That means growers would quickly begin to reach a "food versus fuel" decision on what to do with their land. A recent study concluded that since our cattle, pork, and poultry are all based on corn feed, prices for those foods could rise 60 to 70 percent over the next two years as more and more corn is devoted to energy instead.

The second unadvertised problem with corn-based ethanol is that it requires massive amounts of energy to create. Take a wild guess where that energy comes from. Yeah, oil. According to David Pimentel, a professor at the College of Agriculture at Cornell University, it takes about 1.29 gallons of gasoline to produce one gallon of ethanol. That's like trying to get rich by spending $1.29 to buy a one-dollar bill.

I'm not trying to bash corn ethanol; I'm just trying to show you that *every* alternative has warts; every so-called miracle technology has pros *and* cons. But let me break out of the Democratic mode of only telling you what's *not* going to work and tell you what will.

Short Term

The bottom line is that we need to buy time. Promising technologies are out there, but nothing will happen overnight. To buy that time, we need to start taking advantage of our massive coal reserves by building coal-to-oil synthetic fuel plants—and we need to build them now. By some estimates, we have 100 to 250 years of coal reserves—we're literally the Saudi Arabia of coal—and it's time we start leveraging that.

When the rest of the world became a tad upset with him, Adolf Hitler was forced to use coal-to-oil technology to fuel his war machine. You can read more about those amazing plants in this book dedicated to his brilliance.

The problem with the technology has always been that it costs somewhere in the neighborhood of $45 to make a barrel of synthetic oil from coal, and historically speaking, that's been expensive compared to regular oil. But not anymore. With current prices well more than $45 (and likely to be much higher once the world wakes up to its future), the time to start using our coal is now.

A.D.D. MOMENT

If you're some environmentalist who mistook this for Al Gore's book, then (a) I'm sorry, but no refunds, and (b) stop having a heart attack. CO_2 can be pumped into natural ground reserves, so your precious little atmosphere will be just fine.

Long Term

There are many promising technologies in the works and so many others right over the horizon. I'm not going to bore you with the details of things such as biomass fuels, but trust me, if we can buy ourselves time—and that's a big *if*—I honestly believe that American ingenuity will once again save us from the brink. But remember, we need to make sure companies are interested in new technologies *regardless* of the price of oil. No company will invest the billions necessary to bring alternatives to the market if it thinks that OPEC can snap its fingers and put it out of business by driving down the price of oil a few months later.

Even though I'm a big believer in American capitalism, I do want to offer a warning alongside that healthy dose of optimism. A lot of really smart people, including noted economist Philip Verleger, believe that the massive decline in oil prices in the 1980s (oil was $30 a barrel in November 1985 and $10 a barrel in July 1986) is what ultimately caused the Soviet Union to collapse. The theory goes that the Soviet economy was so reliant on oil money that it just couldn't adapt when that revenue started to dry up. Does anyone really think that we're immune from experiencing that same fate? When the oil dries up, what happens to our "petroleum-based economy"?

It's not easy to ask that question, and it's even harder to answer it. But, as with the other great enemies that threaten our way of life, it's time to start having open, honest conversations about it. When the end of oil comes, it won't matter if you're rich or poor or if that car sitting in your driveway is a Prius or a Range Rover—with an empty gas tank, all you've got is a zero-emissions driveway decoration.

Chapter 8

Education through Indoctrination

BELIEVE IT OR NOT, I am technically *not* a genius. I know, you're shocked. As far as formal education goes, I went from high school right into radio and never looked back.

Along the way, I learned many things—things that are probably not included in a textbook but important life lessons nonetheless. For example, Jack Daniel's isn't actually part of the official food pyramid, my fashion sense isn't universally appreciated, and people don't enjoy working for a guy who fires them for bringing him the wrong type of pen. But one thing *is* still as true today as it was when I first decided to avoid higher education more than 20 years ago: Colleges and universities are overrun with activist liberal professors.

Elect Gore (Again)!

84 percent of college professors voted for Al Gore in 2000; 9 percent voted for George W. Bush.

I'm not entirely sure how it got that way, but the extraordinarily high concentration of liberals who've decided to teach has resulted in college campuses turning into self-contained socialist enclaves, complete with used bookstores, organic produce, and nearby movie theaters showing foreign films. They're places where you're free to express *one* opinion—and it had better be the same as your professor's.

Can someone please tell me what the allure of foreign films is? Isn't the whole point of going to the movies that you *don't* have to read?

A.D.D. MOMENT

Let me stop for a second to clarify or, more accurately, provide a disclaimer: I did attend college—sorta. It was Yale (they apparently have even lower standards than my wife), it was for only one semester, and it was as a nondegree student, meaning that they had no intention of ever acknowledging that I actually went there.

I didn't stay at Yale for a variety of reasons, and although I sometimes regret it (they don't), the silver lining is that the whole experience has made me even more passionate about education and college degrees for my kids.

The other good thing about not staying in college was that I was left with no other option but to educate myself. So, instead of regurgitating the ideas of tweedy intellectuals dressed up as my own, I simply started to read and take in as much information as I possibly could. I wasn't expecting to find answers—I was just hoping to discover more questions and better ways to ask them.

As I searched to understand things such as the meaning of the universe and my place in it, I learned something profound: There is no *one person* who has all the right answers. Life's most challenging and interesting questions can only truly be answered by taking in all the information, from all different points of view. If I read something and it made sense to me, I immediately went out to find a book by someone who thought the first guy was a nut-job. It was only then, after reading and studying both sides of the issue, that I felt free to make up my own mind—and even then, my ideas usually fell somewhere in the middle.

Isn't that what learning and education should really be about? Discourse. Examination. Looking at something from all sides, not just one. These days, it's the opposite.

Liberal-turned-conservative David Horowitz highlighted the bias on college campuses when he attempted to place *paid* advertisements in college papers. The ads eloquently and intelligently challenged the idea of "reparations" for slavery. Most papers rejected him outright. A few did publish the ad, and those papers found themselves in hot water with professors, administrators, and students—to the point where many of the papers themselves were confiscated and destroyed.

"Oh, the Humanity!"

I have four kids. I assume they're each going to want to spend (at least) four years in college. So, let's see, that's 16 years of college times an overage of, ohhh, let's say $35,000 a year to be conservative (my youngest two kids are under three years old), yields a total of—wait, that can't be right. There's no way. $560,000? Five hundred and sixty *thousand dollars*? What in the name of all that—

My personal nightmare: My daughter attends a college party one night, and someone comes up to her and asks her to experiment with a "Hillary in 2008" button. Will she know enough to *just say no?* I hope so. But what if she doesn't? *What if she becomes a liberal?*

I can honestly tell you that I'd be fine with it. Really. No, I'm not joking.

See, my daughter and I have made a deal. I'll (grudgingly) pay for her college education, and all I ask in return is that she talks to me about what she's learning. I listen to her point of view, and she listens to mine. Who knows—maybe she'll change my mind about a thing or two, or maybe ol' Dad will give her something to think about as well. It doesn't really matter that she agrees with me, but it does matter that she keeps an open mind and remains tolerant of those who challenge her.

If only most college professors felt the same way.

A.D.D. MOMENT

College Pledge

I ________________, son/daughter of __________________,

being of sound body and mind, do hereby resolve to attend college in a truly open minded fashion.

Heretofore, I agree to the following provisions:

I. I will not conform to what I will soon perceive as trendy and original, just to coincide with my peers and professors.

II. I realize that what I will receive on campus will be a constant stream of unquestioned liberal ideals, presented as fact, and I recognize that I am the only barrier between those statements and the truth.

III. I understand that my parents should not be forced to pay for my indoctrination to the liberal cause of the day and that, as a token of my gratitude for tuition, I promise to honestly question the ramblings of former activists posing as educators.

IV. I hereby state that I am intelligent enough to realize that fighting against the establishment in college may often times mean agreeing with my parents and I will not be embarrassed to do so, even if they dress poorly, humiliate me, or just seem generally pathetic.

V. I promise that if, after a period of honest questioning, I still find myself being drawn to the dark side of the force, I will take action by initiating a conversation with my parents about each position in question.
   a. The meeting will last a minimum of one hour.
   b. In this meeting, I will provide my full attention and will carefully consider my parents' viewpoint.
   c. I will not disregard my parents as out of the loop, old, or mindlessly controlled by the establishment.

VI. If, after this careful consideration of my parents' wise thoughts and beliefs, I still think they are incorrect, my parents will happily recognize my independence as a thoughtful individual and we will simply agree to disagree, with no hard feelings or lingering anger.

At this time I will also forfeit any and all monetary payments made on my behalf regarding tuition, sustenance, entertainment, travel, etc.

We the undersigned do hereby declare this document to be a binding agreement throughout the universe for all eternity.

Child ______________________________ Date ________

Parent ______________________________ Date ________

Parent ______________________________ Date ________

Why? Because they dared to *present a counterargument to a very debatable topic*. What's happening on our college campuses when ideas cannot be expressed, much less discussed? Isn't that one of the reasons you go to school in the first place?

Do I sound cranky (I mean more so than usual)? Good, because I am, and if you're a parent, then you should be too. Our children's education is being hijacked, and there's almost nothing we can do about it.

TENURE-ITIS

Worse than these liberal activists winding up as teachers is the fact that many are protected by an archaic tenure system that pretty much guarantees they can't be fired. It also pretty much guarantees that they can teach almost *anything* they want *any way* they want. That means that an environmental science professor could teach the "dangers" of global warming by showing *An Inconvenient Truth* without ever having to mention that much of the science is up for debate (or screening Glenn Beck's award-winning* documentary *Exposed: The Climate of Fear* as a counterbalance).

That has the benefit of empowering these renegade "educators" to increase their activism without risk while simultaneously lowering the standard of our children's education. Can you imagine other professions adopting a similar tenure system? Would you like to be operated on by a surgeon who's in it for life, no matter how he performs, or represented by a politician who doesn't have to worry about being reelected? When you take competition and performance out of the equation, you reduce quality—it doesn't get any simpler than that.

The idea of tenure originated in the late nineteenth century and was based on a German model that dates back even farther.

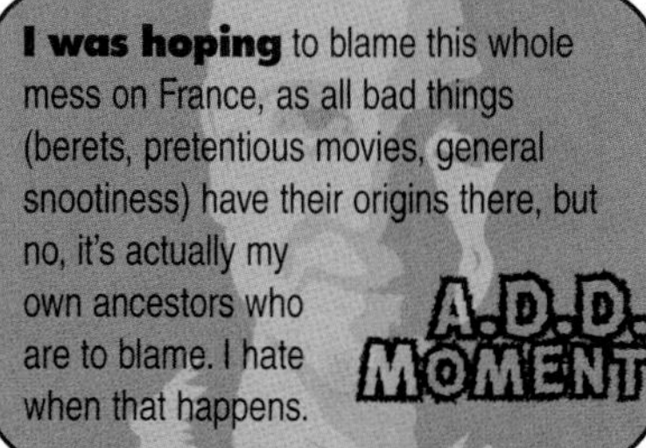

I was hoping to blame this whole mess on France, as all bad things (berets, pretentious movies, general snootiness) have their origins there, but no, it's actually my own ancestors who are to blame. I hate when that happens.
A.D.D. MOMENT

Back then, most universities were underwritten by wealthy industrialists whose politics were often in direct contradiction to the more liberal, populist professors who taught there. In theory, tenure seems like a noble idea with good intentions (like socialism and eating pie for dessert after every meal . . . *every meal*). But you do remember what road is paved with good intentions, don't you?

Tenure, like labor unions and Harry Belafonte, had a time and a purpose. But as those things have gotten older, they've had to fight to stay relevant. And they're not winning.

*The Fine Print: Exact awards have not yet been announced.

Yes, educators should be free to teach without political or philosophical restraints—that's a good idea. However, the last time I checked my calendar, it wasn't the late nineteenth century anymore. It's a whole new world, and the old concerns of the oppressive Carnegies and Rockefellers squelching academic freedom simply don't apply. Barbers are no longer also "doctors," "separate but equal" is a bad memory, and the safeguarding of our "morality" through Prohibition is in our past—and for good reason. Those ideas were ill conceived to begin with, and we've evolved beyond the limited scope of the thinking that was in vogue when they were established.

Do I think a professor should be fired for saying America is evil or communism is a great idea? No, not at all. I think the professor is wrong on both counts, but presenting those ideas should inspire others to stand up and say, "I think you're wrong, and here's why." That's when the whole education thing we're paying all that money for actually happens.

"Oh, the Humanity!"

Most college professors are forced to work for a grueling nine months a year, often teaching three or four days a week for upward of three hours each day!

Vote Howard Dean!

How did college faculties get so crammed with liberal thinkers in the first place? Well, it seems to be a case of self-selection. A recent study shows that 72 percent of college professors identify themselves as "liberal" compared with just 15 percent who claim to be "conservative." And if you look at the "elite" schools—places such as Harvard and, yes, Yale—87 percent say they're liberal.

Think about how unbelievably high 87 percent is. Just 82 percent of people believe that God exists. So, on a percentage basis, there are more people who don't believe in any form of God than there are politically conservative professors in this country's elite colleges.

Are you still wondering why this problem is included in the book?

MY SOLUTION

This is actually one of the chapters where I *don't* have to write my way out of giving you any kind of real solution, because I *actually* have an answer. It all starts with getting rid of the tenure system.

It's not going to be easy—those who are served by tenure will protect and defend

People Who Are Horrible and Also Happen to Teach

1. Xavier University's PETER KIRSTEIN. He's the history professor who sent an angry e-mail message to an Air Force Academy cadet denouncing the "baby-killing tactics" of the U.S. Air Force and calling him a "disgrace" to his country. Xavier didn't listen to the thousands of complaints that were sent in demanding his firing; otherwise, ol' Pete may not have become so popular on the speaking circuit. Whew—that was a close one!
2. DR. ONEIDA MERANTO of the Metropolitan State College of Denver. She suggested that Republicans were incapable of thinking critically and threatened her students by saying that if there were any Republicans in her class, they should drop it immediately because there was no way they'd succeed. Oh, and this was during her first lecture of the first class of the year.
3. WARD CHURCHILL. Remember him? He's the University of Colorado at Boulder *tenured* ethnic studies professor who exercised his "academic freedom" by writing that many of the people who died in the World Trade Center bombings may not have been that innocent, labeling them as "technocrats" and "Little Eichmanns." Yikes—someone doesn't sound so "Rocky Mountain high"!

E. Smurfs

F. Superman

25. Select the Person Worse Than Ward Churchill

A. Osama bin Laden

B. The guy who told me how "The Sixth Sense" ended as I was waiting in line at the movie theater

C. People who use "party" as a verb, regardless of age

D. Anyone who watches "Two and a Half Men"

E. Satan

F. All of the above

26. Pick your favori olor

reen

it at all costs—but it's going to be awfully hard ever to achieve balanced education for our kids if none of the current professors can be fired.

A.D.D. MOMENT The first rule of tenure is you do not talk about tenure.

The one thing going for us is that most colleges are *businesses,* and—just as with grocery stores or muffler shops—if you don't like the service, the best response is to take your business (and your money) elsewhere. When working with your children to find the schools that are best for them, look for institutions that hold their faculty to the highest standards. If you're lucky enough to find one that doesn't play by the tenure game, reward it with your tuition dollars (in the process, you'll be rewarding your child with an education where competition raises the bar for teachers).

Competition is what fuels the marketplace—it forces companies to cut costs and increase service, all in an effort to attract more of our dollars. *People vote with their dollars.* It's a bedrock principle of capitalism, and I'm always shocked when I don't see it used as often as possible. The ultimate marketplace, whether it's for ideas or laundry detergent, is where good "products" succeed and bad ones fail.

If you think that this crude capitalist model shouldn't apply to ivy-covered halls where lofty ideas are pondered over steaming mugs of herbal tea, think again. *Every* company—yes, even a college—has a bottom line. Whether it's Wal-Mart or Harvard, it's money that matters, and liberal professors, like Wal-Mart greeters, won't work for free any sooner than you or I will.

I can appreciate that institutions of higher learning are not exactly places that welcome change, so while we're working on the big picture, let's also pressure colleges and universities in smaller ways. Keep track of your kids' classes, and make sure they let you know what they're being taught—and by *whom.* Stay involved—protect the investment you've made both in your child's education and *your child.* You've done all you can for the first 18 years—don't let four years at the hands of some bleeding-heart activist undo all your hard work. After all, your child may be the one taking the classes, but you're writing the checks.

INSTITUTIONS OF LEFTIST LEARNING

Unless you want your child moving to Africa to save the Sooty Tern seabird after graduation, these are some schools you may want to avoid applying to.

3. **Warren Wilson College** The *Princeton Review* quoted a Warren Wilson student as saying, "Politically, Warren Wilson 'consists of various facets of the left wing: the Democrats, the Greens, and the anarchists. No Republican has ever set foot on this campus. Ever. If they did, they'd probably be pelted to death with hand-rolled cigarette butts.' "

   Wow, sign me up! One other interesting fact is that Warren Wilson College is one of just a handful of U.S. colleges that require their students to work for them during their time at the school. Hmm, what kind of system teaches that everyone should work for the common good instead of individual profit? Oh, that's right, it's socialism!

2. **New College of Florida** What sets this school apart from most is its use of "narrative evaluations." That's a nice way of saying that traditional letter grades are replaced by heartwarming pep talks at the end of each semester detailing what each student needs to improve on.

   Aww, that's so cute. Here's my narrative evaluation of this idea: "Thanks

The Liberal College Professor

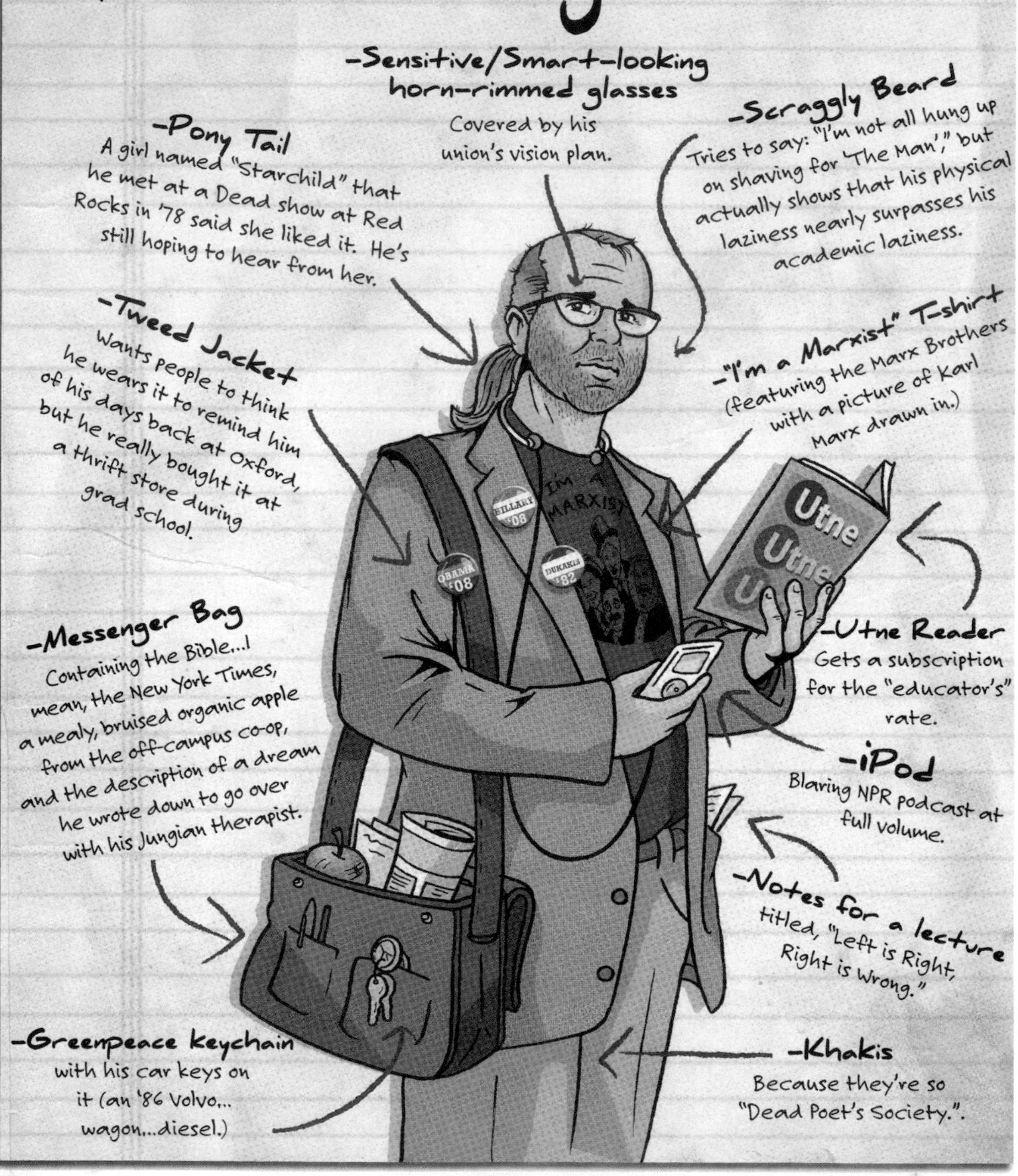

for trying so hard and everything, but this is quite possibly the most idiotic idea I've ever heard. Your school should be shut down immediately, and all former students should be made to go back and attend a real college that uses real grades."

1. **Mills College** According to the *Princeton Review,* "if you aren't a leftist-socialist-Nader voter . . . you are often dismissed as someone of no consequence and possibly a racist, classist, elitist." Well, I can certainly understand why they'd be in such awe of Nader—I mean, he's won all of those elections, right? Wait—he hasn't won *any* elections yet? Maybe he should run to be president of Mills. Nah, he'd probably still lose.

I told you earlier about the study in which 87 percent of professors at elite U.S. colleges are self-proclaimed liberals, but that statistic is only frightening if those political views seep into their teachings. So, do they?

Yes. According to a survey commissioned by the American Council of Trustees and Alumni conducted at the University of Connecticut, almost half of students said that their professors use the classroom to present their personal political views or "frequently comment on politics in class even though it has nothing to do with the course," while almost a third said that they feel they "have to agree with the professor's political or social views in order to get a good grade."

So, not only are political views (which we've already established are primarily liberal) making their way into classrooms, but many students are actually feeling pressured to *agree* with them. What a great system! Why don't professors just use thumbscrews and put students in tiger cages until they give up, fall in line, and buy Jerry Brown T-shirts?

Answers are great for math problems and spelling tests, but when it comes to being able to turn academic philosophies into a dynamic system for living a rich and productive life, I'm afraid that our children will be better served by the ability to ask meaningful questions than they will by the answers that some aging hippie gave them during freshman year.

Remember, professors aren't there to teach people *what* to think; they're there to teach them *how* to think. It's time someone taught *them* that.

Class dismissed.

Hate U Class Syllabus: Psychology 101

Mon-Wed-Fri; 2p–4p; 3 credits.
Carter Hall

Professor Tuttle will introduce the class to the principles of modern psychology: George Bush sucks, and Cheney is a terrorist. Students will learn about Freud, Jung, and Bush being Hitler. The fundamentals of psychology coupled with the fact that the United States is an imperialist aggressor nation run by Zionists will give students a well-rounded introduction to their field.

Chapter 9

Political Games: America's on a Losing Streak

AUGUSTA NATIONAL GOLF CLUB, the course where the Masters golf tournament is played each year, is one of the most private, most exclusive golf clubs in the country. There is no application process, and membership is by invitation only—which makes sense when you consider that current and former members include George Shultz, Peter Coors, Jack Welch, Bill Gates, Sam Nunn, William Ford, and Warren Buffett.

Augusta and its fiercely private membership found themselves in the middle of a national controversy back in 2002 and 2003, when Martha Burk, chair of the National Council of Women's Organizations, publicly threatened to boycott the Masters' sponsors and protest outside the club because women were not allowed to be members at Augusta. As the pressure mounted and the tournament drew near, speculation increased about what the club would do. After all, many of the members are CEOs of America's top corporations. Could they really be associated with a club that was publicly being called sexist?

I don't know this for a fact, but I've heard that Martha Burk is a big, *big* fan of mine.

A.D.D. MOMENT

The responsibility to formulate a carefully crafted, politically correct response that would defuse the situation fell to the club's chairman, Hootie Johnson. He wrote, "We will not be bullied, threatened, or intimidated. We do not intend to become a trophy in their display case. There may well come a day when women will be invited to join our membership, but that timetable will be ours, and not at the point of a bayonet."

Not exactly the tone you'd expect. But later, Johnson softened his stance: "Ms.

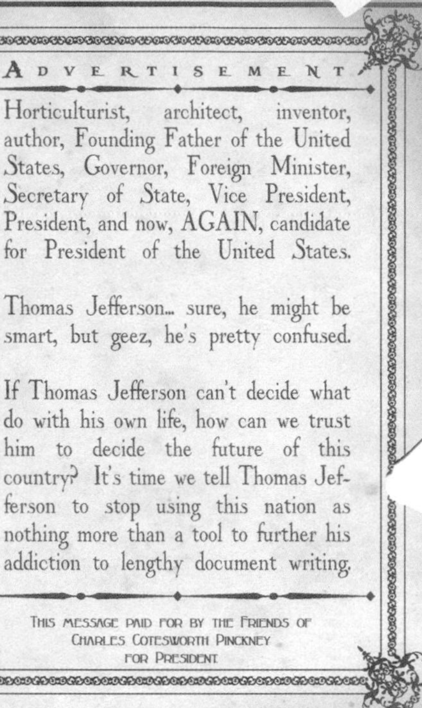
Tuesday, March the Third, Eighteen Hund...

ADVERTISEMENT

Horticulturist, architect, inventor, author, Founding Father of the United States, Governor, Foreign Minister, Secretary of State, Vice President, President, and now, AGAIN, candidate for President of the United States.

Thomas Jefferson... sure, he might be smart, but geez, he's pretty confused.

If Thomas Jefferson can't decide what do with his own life, how can we trust him to decide the future of this country? It's time we tell Thomas Jefferson to stop using this nation as nothing more than a tool to further his addiction to lengthy document writing.

THIS MESSAGE PAID FOR BY THE FRIENDS OF CHARLES COTESWORTH PINCKNEY FOR PRESIDENT

Yesteryear Smear

Campaign attack ads seem to be standard practice these days, but the truth is that they've been around a lot longer than most people realize. As proof, we searched the microfilm archives and dug up a series of newspaper attack ads from the 1804 presidential election between incumbent Thomas Jefferson and challenger Charles Cotesworth Pinckney. Pinckney's first shot is displayed here—the others are spaced throughout this chapter.

Burk has nothing to do with this club. Her threats mean nothing to me."

Then again, maybe not.

But behind closed doors, away from the reporters, Hootie was formulating his real response: No more commercials. If sponsors wanted to pull out, he reasoned, let them; they'd get one sponsor to pay for the whole thing and cut out all commercial time.

It worked. For two straight years, the Masters television broadcast included no commercial time, making it the greatest televised sporting event in history (or so I'm told—I'd rather spend a weekend in Paris with Sean Penn and Martin Sheen than watch a golf tournament).

But the best part of all (at least for Hootie and Augusta) was that Martha Burk became irrelevant, and the protests turned into a joke. She'd lost all her leverage and, consequently, all her power.

A.D.D. MOMENT

I'm convinced that if a group of albino Wiccans somehow raised a boatload of cash, we'd honestly be choosing candidates based on who has the best magic potion solution for the day's biggest issues. At a minimum, there would be earmarks for a "9/11 Albino Wiccan" museum snuck into a spending bill by some congressman.

I tell you this story because it's a great illustration of how politics *doesn't* work. If something similar had happened in Washington, the politicians would have completely caved to the special-interest pressure, issued apologies, and replaced all male members of their staffs with women.

Regardless of how you feel about Augusta's policies, it was their members' decision to make. There wasn't any effort to hide what they believed. The decision about whether it was right or wrong was left to us to make, and we had all the information we needed right in front of us. If politicians could somehow find that sort of strength in *their* convictions, then maybe our government would finally run as smoothly, and be as entertaining, as a commercial-free Masters Tournament.

Unfortunately, that's a big, fat, 1300-pound-guy-lifted-out-of-his-bed-by-a-crane-sized *if.* Those groups control a lot of money; money wins votes; and votes determine power. I think it's pretty safe to say that politicians like power.

The reason this chapter is in the book is that it's the foundation for almost every other problem we cover. Our politicians wield the power to change, the power to lead, the power to solve, and the power to bridge our divisions. Unfortunately, they spend the most time using their power to accumulate even *more* power.

To them, our nation is like a giant Monopoly board, and they spend their turns trying to figure out how many properties they can acquire without winding up in jail. (Obviously, many of them aren't very good at it.)

PARTY BEFORE PRINCIPLES

One of the things that always amaze me about politicians is how venomous they can be toward each other and then seemingly still be friends afterward. "I know he said that the terrorists would win if I'm elected and that I was behind the 9/11 attacks, but he really fought a great campaign; my hat goes off to him."

It's almost as if all the public mud slinging and name calling is, well, just a game.

Attack of the Attack Ads

During the 2006 campaign season, the attack ads were flying from both sides of the aisle, and some of them became unbelievably personal. Remember, a campaign is essentially a long interview process; it should focus on your ability to do the job, not unrelated (and often untrue) personal issues.

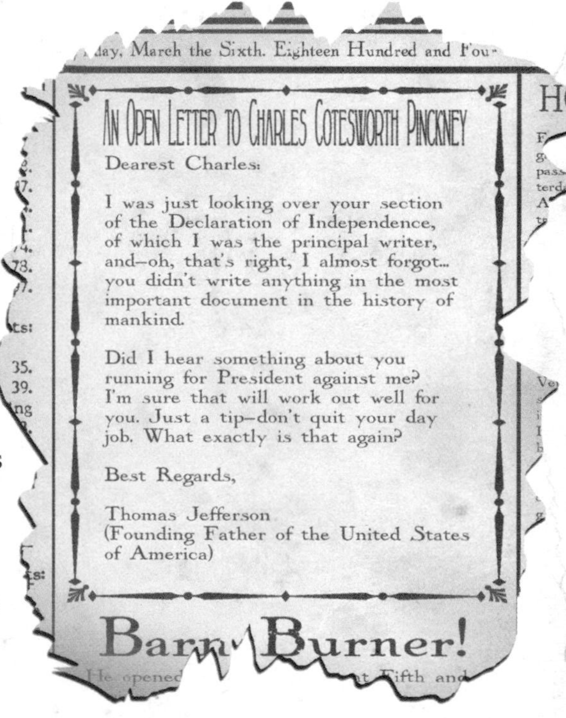

day, March the Sixth. Eighteen Hundred and Fou-

AN OPEN LETTER TO CHARLES COTESWORTH PINCKNEY

Dearest Charles:

I was just looking over your section of the Declaration of Independence, of which I was the principal writer, and—oh, that's right, I almost forgot... you didn't write anything in the most important document in the history of mankind.

Did I hear something about you running for President against me? I'm sure that will work out well for you. Just a tip—don't quit your day job. What exactly is that again?

Best Regards,

Thomas Jefferson
(Founding Father of the United States of America)

Barn Burner!

In the 13th District of North Carolina, Republican Vernon Robinson was running for Congress against the Democratic incumbent, Brad Miller. Here are a few actual lines from a television ad financed by Robinson's campaign:

- "Brad Miller even spent your tax dollars to pay teenage girls to watch pornographic movies with probes connected to their genitalia."
- "Brad Miller spent your money to study the masturbation habits of old men."
- And this, from a radio ad (with mariachi music playing in the background): "If Miller had his way, America would be nothing but one big fiesta for illegal aliens and homosexuals."

Think about the message these ads are really trying to send. If you reelect Brad Miller, this country will turn into a nonstop homosexual, pedophile, illegal alien, and teenage girl party. Would those groups of people even *want* to party together? I think it might be awkward.

This race devolved even further than the "masturbation habits of old men." Robinson actually put out a campaign flyer that seemed to suggest that Miller himself might be a homosexual, since he's middle-aged and childless (he'd been married for 24 years). Pretty bad, right? Well, I bet Robinson must have felt like quite the idiot when Miller's wife was then forced to respond: "It wasn't God's will. I had a disease known as endometriosis. I had a hysterectomy when I was single, at 27. I met Brad after that."

Oops.

The fact that a candidate's wife had to answer questions about her ability to have children should absolutely shock and sicken you. Unfortunately, it probably doesn't—and that's a microcosm of everything that's wrong with politics.

...day, April the Twenty First, Eighteen Hundred and Fo...

An Open Letter to Thomas Jefferson

Dearest Thomas:

Thanks for writing. I'm glad you kept your letter short because when you blather on and on (like you did in your part of that Declaration thingy) I tend to drift off. You can be quite a bore!

Anyway, I just wanted to reminisce about that time, in 1775, when we went out to risk our lives and fight for freedom. What great memories. Those were great times to be a part of. Wait, what's that? You were too busy doodling? Oh, my bad.

Yours faithfully,

Charles Cotesworth Pinckney
(Soldier who went through hell on earth for this country while you played "spin the candle" with the maids.)

Monday, May the Ninth, Eighteen Hundred and Four

AN OPEN LETTER TO CHARLES COTESWORTH PINCKNEY

Poor Charles:

I know of your exploits on the battlefield, they are well documented. Like, for instance, that time you raped and killed a family in Jamestown. Thought you'd destroyed the evidence on that little escapade, didn't you?

May I be so bold as to suggest a new campaign strategy for you? Murder me. Your biggest political weakness is the fact that I am alive.

Best Regards,

Thomas Jefferson

Mr. Robinson, incidentally, was not elected.

Not to be outdone by those ads, Democrat Michael Arcuri and Republican Ray Meier, running for New York's 24th Congressional District, upped the ante ever more. An anti-Arcuri campaign ad featured the silhouette of a stripper next to video of Arcuri. The narrator ominously said, "The phone number to an adult fantasy hotline appeared on Michael Arcuri's New York City hotel room bill . . . while he was there on official business. . . . Who calls a fantasy hotline and then bills taxpayers? Michael Arcuri."

"Bad call!" the stripper adds in a sultry voice.

There's only one problem: Arcuri had already proven that the phone-sex allegation wasn't true. His coworker had used his hotel room phone and inadvertently dialed a 1-800 prefix instead of a 212 prefix when trying to reach the state's Department of Criminal Justice Services. It was just a coincidence that the rest of the digits were exactly the same. According to phone records that Arcuri produced, the first call lasted just moments and was immediately followed by the second call.

Does the truth even matter anymore? (That's a rhetorical question.)

To his credit, Arcuri's opponent said the ad, which was created by the National Republican Congressional Committee, was "way over the line." Incidentally, both candidates say they are friends. As I said before, it all sure seems like one big game.

Expedient Hypocrisy

One of the Democrats' constant complaints when they were the minority was that the GOP held votes open longer than necessary in order to round up additional votes on the House floor.

Here's what Congressman Steny Hoyer (D-Maryland) said on July 8, 2004 (emphasis added): "House Republican leaders proved once again today that they will stop at virtually nothing to win a vote, even if that means *running roughshod over the most basic principles of democracy* such as letting members vote their conscience and calling the vote after the allotted time has elapsed. They ought to be ashamed of themselves, but when it comes to holding votes open and twisting the arms of their own members they clearly have no shame. These *back-alley tactics* have no place in the greatest deliberative body in the world. They might be the lifeblood of the *tin-horn dictator,* but not a world leader. It's an *embarrassment.*"

Those are some pretty harsh words (but don't worry, I'm sure they're all still friends).

Now, fast-forward to March 2007, after Steny Hoyer became House majority leader. During the buildup to what was expected to be a close vote on an important Iraq war-spending bill, Hoyer was asked if he would keep to the allotted time. He paused and then replied that many votes can run long for "various reasons." So there are "various reasons" to run "roughshod over the most basic principles of democracy?" Sounds like something a "tin-horned dictator" would say.

Quid Pro Quo

When Representative Mike Rogers (R-Michigan) offered a procedural motion to eliminate a $23 million earmark for the National Drug Intelligence Center (NDIC), he knew that he wouldn't exactly be making friends with John Murtha (D-Pennsylvania), the Appropriations Defense Subcommittee chairman whose district includes the NDIC.

But what happened next shows you just how convoluted, elitist, and unbelievably out of touch politicians have become. Murtha approached Rogers on the House floor and told him "in a loud voice" that there would be consequences and that he would "not get any earmarks now and forever" for his district.

That threat not only violated House ethics rules but also broke the highly publicized promise that the new Democrat-controlled Congress made to reform the earmark process. Republicans asked that Murtha be reprimanded for his actions, which put Democrats in the unenviable position of either voting against one of their own or violating a major campaign promise.

Wednesday, May the Twenty Third, Eighteen Hundred and

An Open Letter to Thomas Jefferson

Bastard Thomas:

Thanks for the campaign advice, maybe I'll take you up on that. Say hello to your love slave for me.

Yours faithfully,

Charles Cotesworth Pinckney

Which did they choose? Take a wild guess. The reprimand motion never even made it to the Ethics Committee.

The Flip-Flop

On March 22, 2007, Democrats proposed a bill that would require pulling our troops out of Iraq 120 days after the bill was enacted.

I have no problem with a bill like that coming up for a vote, as long as its supporters *truly believe* in it. Unfortunately, with control of Congress changing hands while the situation in Iraq was deteriorating, figuring out what's passion and what's just politics isn't easy.

Here is what a few of the "firm deadline for withdrawal" supporters had to say *before* the elections:

- *"As far as setting a timeline. . . that's not a wise decision, because it only empowers those who don't want us there."*
  —Senator Harry Reid (D-Nevada), January 31, 2005
- *"A deadline for pulling out will only encourage our enemies to wait us out. It would be a Lebanon 1985, and God only knows where it goes from there."*
  —Senator Joe Biden (D-Delaware), June 21, 2005
- *"I don't believe it's smart to set a date for withdrawal. I don't think you should ever telegraph your intentions to the enemy so they can await you."*
  —Senator Hillary Clinton (D-New York), September 22, 2005
- *"A hard, fast, arbitrary deadline for withdrawal offers our commanders in the field and our diplomats in the region insufficient flexibility to implement that strategy."*
  —Senator Barack Obama (D-Illinois), June 6, 2006

How can they so blatantly flip their opinions and keep a straight face? Because they know that Americans have the attention span of a cheerleader in an algebra class. We've got to start having longer memories and holding these politicians' feet to the fire when they shift opinions for political convenience.

The People's Work

On May 17, 2007, House Minority Leader John Boehner (R-Ohio) released an angry, passion-filled letter to the media. Was it about Iraq? Immigration? Health care? Iran?

No, it was about the ability to offer a motion to recommit and/or to test germaneness on a motion to recommit.

Do you have any idea what that means? Me neither.

Turns out, Democrats had threatened to change procedural rules that had been in effect since Thomas Jefferson wrote them in 1822. Republicans didn't like that idea. So, for weeks, members of both parties spent countless hours issuing reports and press releases and holding meetings on the motion to recommit.

That, of course, is the people's work.

If you are an insomniac who's tried everything from warm milk to Ambien with no luck, I have come up with the ultimate cure. Start Googling "the ability to offer a motion to recommit and/or to test germaneness on a motion to recommit." You'll be asleep in 15 seconds. A.D.D. MOMENT

All Hail the Exalted Cyclops!

I might be going out on a limb here, but I doubt that many politicians would welcome the title of "Kleagle" showing up on their résumés. Unfortunately (for him), Robert Byrd, the Democratic senator from West Virginia, is stuck with it.

In 1942, at the ripe old age of 24, Byrd joined the Ku Klux Klan. Ten years later, he decided to run for Congress. Surprisingly, his KKK membership became an issue.

His campaign claimed that Byrd had only been in the KKK for about a year before realizing it "wasn't for him." Unfortunately, Byrd's own 1947 letter to a grand wizard seemed to indicate otherwise. He wrote: "The Klan is needed today as never before and I am anxious to see its rebirth here in West Virginia and in every state in the nation."

Oopsie.

I'm guessing that if it wasn't 1952 in West Virginia when that little bombshell dropped, his campaign might have been hurt a little more than it was. In fact, given that it *was* West Virginia circa 1952, you can make the case that his campaign was probably responsible for leaking the letter. Needless to say, Byrd won the election.

If George W. Bush, Dick Cheney, and Nancy Pelosi all dropped dead, Robert Byrd would be the new president of the United States. Have a nice day! A.D.D. MOMENT

Forty-five years later, Robert Byrd was again asked about the KKK. You'd think he would have come up with a good response by now, but you'd be wrong. Byrd replied, "Be sure to avoid the Klu Klux Klan. Don't get that albatross around your neck. Once you've made that mistake, you inhibit your operations in the political arena."

The big lesson that Robert Byrd has apparently learned from all of this? The KKK may hurt your political career.

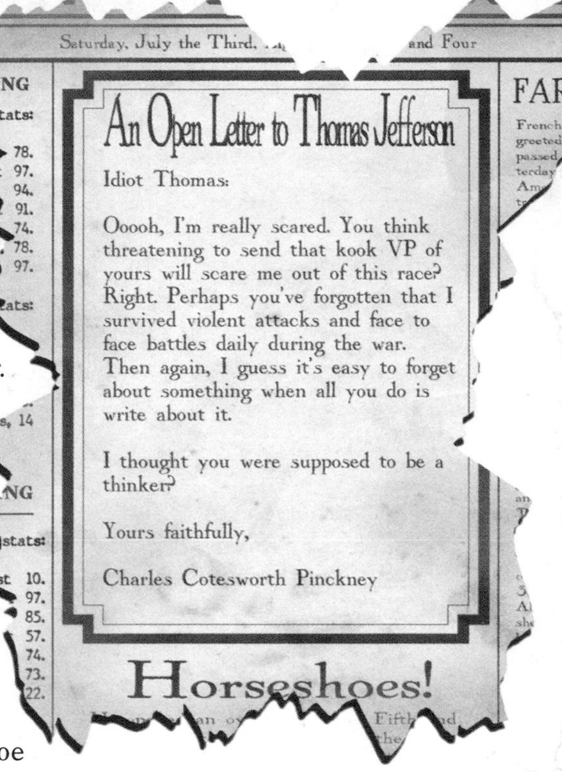
Saturday, July the Third, ... and Four

An Open Letter to Thomas Jefferson

Idiot Thomas:

Ooooh, I'm really scared. You think threatening to send that kook VP of yours will scare me out of this race? Right. Perhaps you've forgotten that I survived violent attacks and face to face battles daily during the war. Then again, I guess it's easy to forget about something when all you do is write about it.

I thought you were supposed to be a thinker?

Yours faithfully,

Charles Cotesworth Pinckney

Horseshoes!

It's My Party

For 18 years, Joe Lieberman (D-Connecticut) served this country as a proud, honest mainstay as a U.S. Senate Democrat. But in 2006, things changed.

Democratic challenger Ned Lamont, running on an antiwar platform, was beating Lieberman in most polls as the primary drew near. Lieberman, sensing a possible loss, foreshadowed his plans if he were to lose. "I'm a loyal Democrat," he said, "but I have loyalties that are greater than those to my party, and that's my loyalty to my state and my country."

A few months later, Lieberman lost the primary and filed to run as a third-party candidate. That's when it became obvious just how many friends 18 years as a loyal Democrat really buys you.

Hillary Clinton had been friends with Joe Lieberman since their days as students at Yale Law, more than 30 years ago. She was a big supporter of him during the primary and endorsed him against Lamont.

The day after Lieberman lost in the primary, she acted as if he were dead to her. She said he should "search his conscience" to decide if running as an Independent was really a good idea and then said, "We have a lot of years in that friendship. Now, the voters of Connecticut have made their decision and I think that decision should be respected."

Hillary then donated $5,000 to Lamont's campaign and declared that she would campaign with him, sponsor a fundraiser for him, and lend him one of her top political strategists. Bill Clinton also issued a statement of support for Lamont. So much for 30 years of friendship.

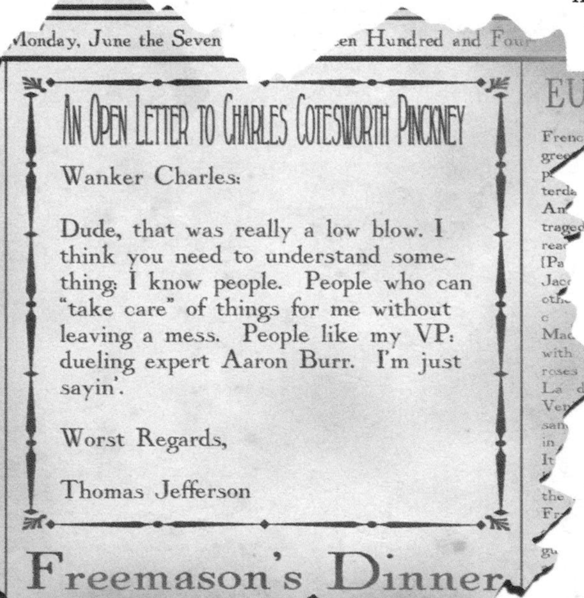
Monday, June the Seven ... en Hundred and Four

An Open Letter to Charles Cotesworth Pinckney

Wanker Charles:

Dude, that was really a low blow. I think you need to understand something: I know people. People who can "take care" of things for me without leaving a mess. People like my VP: dueling expert Aaron Burr. I'm just sayin'.

Worst Regards,

Thomas Jefferson

Freemason's Dinner

Howard Dean, the Democratic Party's national chairman (and someone experienced in losing primaries) didn't mince words. He called on Lieberman to quit the race and said that no Democrat leaders should support him, declaring that they "have an obligation" to support their nominee and—ready for this?—that Lieberman was being "disrespectful of Democrats and disrespectful of the Democratic Party" by staying in the race.

Chris Dodd, Lieberman's longtime friend, close advisor, and a fellow Democratic senator from Connecticut, said, "Joe Lieberman is a good man—and a very good Democrat" in the months before the primary. The day after it, he endorsed Lamont.

You might know this story already, but you may not have considered how significant it really is. It serves as a direct window into the soul of the Washington politician, and it's quite possibly the most transparent example of pure partisan politics that we'll ever see. Both Lieberman and Lamont were the same men the day before the primary, with the same characters and the same positions on the issues.

Those who believed that Lieberman was the best man to help the country before the primary were faced with a simple decision: the nation or the party. Those who changed their minds, in no uncertain terms, chose the party. The people of Connecticut chose differently, and Lieberman was easily reelected as an independent.

MY SOLUTION

As much as I'd like to sit back and blame everything on Washington, we have to realize that politicians are only a reflection of us. Sure, they add about 500 times the amount of "dirtbag" into the mix, but in essence they're divisive because we're divided. If we really want to fix politics, we need to fix ourselves first.

Part of what's dividing us is our own narcissism. We've lost our collective values, and we've put what's best for ourselves above what's best for our country, our neighbors, and, in some cases, even our own families. This narcissism leads to pessimism, which leads to apathy and resentment. How many times have you heard people say, "Well, I'm just not even going to vote anymore—it's pointless." When people disconnect from the process, they stop talking to one another. More important, they stop *listening* to one another.

In America, we *expect* our politicians to be corrupt, ineffective, and dishonest. We *expect* them to be divisive partisans, and that's exactly what we get. Because we expect it, because we empower the same vicious wheel to continue to turn over and over again, we deserve it.

I think the first step to turning the whole thing around is to end the atmosphere of partisan shout fests and get back to having real conversations. We're capable of such great things, but we have to respect one another, and respect comes from listening to one another.

I often like to say that life isn't about left or right, it's about right and wrong. I honestly believe that, but how many others do? Think about the attack ads I mentioned earlier. Do you know *why* political candidates run those ads? The answer is simple, although it's tough to accept: They run them because they work. People may feign disgust, as they feign disgust over constant news coverage of Paris Hilton going to jail, but then they're the first in line when the new issue of *US Weekly* hits the newsstands.

If we want to change things, we have to turn that into *real* disgust. We have to reject the candidates who use gutter politics to get elected, and we have to favor the ones who put principles over party and political games.

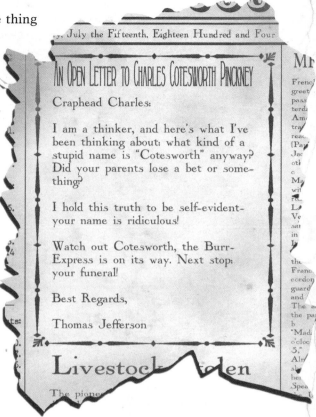

...y, July the Fifteenth, Eighteen Hundred and Four

AN OPEN LETTER TO CHARLES COTESWORTH PINCKNEY

Craphead Charles:

I am a thinker, and here's what I've been thinking about: what kind of a stupid name is "Cotesworth" anyway? Did your parents lose a bet or something?

I hold this truth to be self-evident—your name is ridiculous!

Watch out Cotesworth, the Burr-Express is on its way. Next stop: your funeral!

Best Regards,

Thomas Jefferson

Livestoc... ...en

We the People still have the ultimate voice in this country, and we can change our course by empowering those who not only stand for the truth but will fight for it.

When politicians are forced to care about *every* voter, when they are constantly reminded that they serve at *the will* of the people, when we start to reconnect with our values, politicians will be forced to reconnect with us.

More than two centuries ago, the founding fathers designed our system of government. But they didn't give the most important responsibilities to the executive, legislative, or judicial branches. They gave them to us. We the People. We have the power to change everything; we just have to decide to use it.

America, it's time to go to work.

Chapter 10

Sleepytime! The Weekend Movie Rental

WITH ALL OF THE SERIOUS PROBLEMS facing the world these days, it might seem like a waste of valuable pages to talk about something as trivial as how to agree on a movie to watch. But, as you'll soon see, picking the right movie directly affects the future of the human race.

HOLLYWOOD IS HURTING BIRTH RATES

Here's what Hollywood needs to realize: *movies are an escape.* Life can stink sometimes. At some point, everybody on the planet has to suffer through a crappy job, a bad marriage, or a John Kerry speech. We look to movies as an escape from all that (an escape for pathetic married men like me that we hope leads to sex).

Did you know?
Dakota Fanning once killed a guy in a bar fight.

But, believe me, nobody's escaping anything after watching Al Gore give a two-hour global-warming slide show. It's a well-known fact that any movie featuring footage of melting glaciers is a guaranteed nookie killer, but glaciers aren't alone. There are plenty of other things that Hollywood should ban based solely on their ability to prevent me from sealing the deal:

- Movies that feature cancer-stricken mothers (*Stepmom, The Family Stone*).
- Movies that feature "messages" (*Crash, Happy Feet*).
- Movies that feature George Clooney. (There's no way any woman is going to be in the mood when she's going home with someone who looks like George Peppard after watching two hours of George Clooney.)

The common denominator among these films is obvious: They all make my wife cry and fall asleep. That, in turn, means no sex—which makes *me* cry myself to sleep. What the Hollywood pinheads don't realize is that preventing dudes from having their weekly eight minutes (fine, five minutes) of bliss with their wives (all right, all right, two minutes) makes them directly responsible for the extinction of the human race.

It's all explained in a very simple equation:

Crappy Movies = No Sex = No Babies = End of Mankind.

LASERS AND BONNETS

OK, so choosing the right movie is important, but where do you start?

The first thing you've got to consider is timing. On a Tuesday night, when your wife's in a bad mood because you didn't take out the garbage again (hypothetically, of course), and there's virtually no chance of sealing the deal, you can go nuts. Choose a nice James Bond movie, or, if you're feeling particularly risqué, go for anything featuring the three L's: lasers, ladies, and more lasers. (I simply call these "laser movies" for short.)

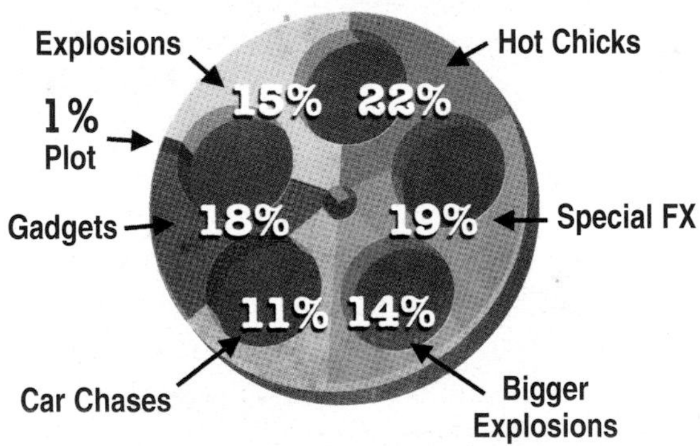

A Friday night, however, is a whole new ballgame. It's no longer about the chores you didn't do; it's about getting lucky. Gentlemen, you know as well as I do what that means: You've got to do—or see—whatever it takes. Unfortunately, "whatever it takes" is almost always the dreaded "bonnet movie."

If laser movies are our meat and potatoes—the food we'd live on if no one harassed us about our diet—then bonnet movies are like spinach and broccoli. We only watch them when we're forced to.

The actual definition of a bonnet movie is very scientific, and I've been refining it for years, but I'll summarize it for you:

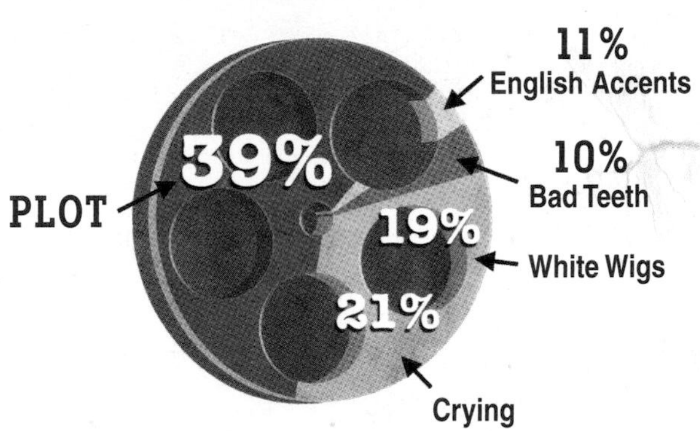

Bon•net mov•ie—*noun*

1. Any film based on the work of Jane Austen.
2. Generally, any movie featuring either Emma Thompson or Kate Winslet in a lead role.
3. Any movie that is muddy, pale, and difficult to understand (kind of like Mickey Rourke).
4. Any movie that features horses, English manor houses, and/or effeminate men with fluffy collars.

Of course, no matter the actors, the key feature of all these movies is that virtually everyone is inexplicably wearing a bonnet.

Bonnet movies are about as sexy as gum disease, which is a pretty apt comparison since they almost always take place in eighteenth- or nineteenth-century Great Britain (they weren't too big on dental hygiene back then—or, come to think of it, ever). The point is that, for some absolutely insane reason that men are not meant ever to understand, chicks dig bonnet movies. And that's why, if it means increasing my odds of having sex, I'd not only take my wife to see a bonnet movie, I'd *wear* a bonnet, put in fake teeth, speak in an English accent, and read really bad poetry to her in a meadow as she calls me Mister Darcy.

Did you know?
Tom Cruise is under your bed right now!

Mercifully, I don't have to do any of that. I can just take her to see *A Little Women's Room with the Remains of the End of Howard's Prejudice,* buy us a tub of popcorn (large, extra butter) and a pack of Goobers (okay, two packs), and reap the benefits.

PLAYING THE ODDS

If you're already in a relationship, you're going to have to suck it up and realize that a large percentage of your moviegoing time will be spent watching bonnet movies. But not all relationships are the same. A budding new romance is far different from a twenty-five-year marriage. Since this can get pretty confusing, let me illustrate the differences with a series of easy-to-understand ratios.

DATING FOR SIX MONTHS OR LESS: Five bonnet movies for every one laser movie

It sounds horrible, yes, but keep in mind you're still trying to convince her that you're a "sweet, sensitive guy." If you really want to go the extra mile, watch your one laser movie allotment in private (a bathroom, at work, etc.)—that way, she'll think you're *only* interested in the bonnets.

ENGAGED: Three bonnet movies for every one laser movie

Still not great, but we're making progress. Remember, you're trying to get her to actually go through with the wedding at this point. Of course, if you don't want to go through with the wedding, then a "guys' weekend" featuring the first 48 episodes of *24* would do the trick.

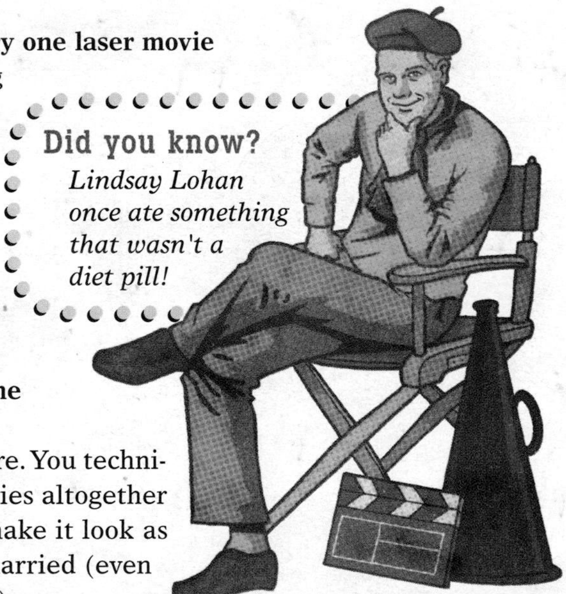

Did you know?

Lindsay Lohan once ate something that wasn't a diet pill!

MARRIED LESS THAN FIVE YEARS: One bonnet movie for every one laser movie

All right, now we're getting somewhere. You technically could eliminate the bonnet movies altogether at this stage, but you don't want to make it look as if you changed the second you got married (even though that's exactly what happened).

MARRIED MORE THAN FIVE YEARS:
No more bonnet movies

Congratulations, you've finally reached the promised land. Most likely, you're not getting lucky much anymore, so why bother risking the hell of a bonnet movie just for the off chance that hell will freeze over? The odds are about the same as for a big Powerball win, but instead of just risking a dollar, you're risking an entire night.

Did you know?
Sean Penn isn't joking when he comments on politics.

MARRIED WITH CHILDREN: No more movies, period

Once you have children, both the bonnet movie *and* the laser movie give way to something far more insidious and creepy: the talking animal movie. I'll have to cover how to get out of those in the next book.

HAVING YOUR CAKE AND EATING IT, TOO

After years of experience, I can unequivocally tell you that the only way to stomach a bonnet movie is to rent it. Sure, the theater offers all of those delicious treats, but it also offers public displays of crying women (lots and lots of them) and comatose husbands all pathetically trying to look interested while thinking, "Yes, yes, Lady Butterchurn loves Mister Winterbottom who loves Countess Thornwhistle . . . big manor house . . . horses . . . *when does this thing end?*"

Persuading her to *rent* the movie instead is a big advantage for a couple of reasons. First, since your home is likely the place where the coveted sex would happen, just being *in* your home already is a great first step. Second, if you play your cards just right, you may actually get lucky without even having to watch the stupid movie! Here's how it works:

1. Make sure the room where you'll be watching the movie is dark. Very, very dark. And quiet too.
2. If you followed number 1 closely, then it's almost a guarantee that she'll be asleep within ten minutes, or by Emma Thompson's first appearance—

whichever comes first. Once that happens, a small window of hope opens up, but you've got to act fast.

3. Extract yourself from whatever crazy, tangled position she's put herself in (usually one that's most comfortable for her but allows you no use of your arms or hands), and get up from the couch. For inspiration, think back to when you were 14 and you'd *slowly* try to get your arm around the girl next to you at the movies. Well, just do the same thing, but in reverse. (That's really the only difference between being an awkward teen and an awkward husband—everything is backward now.) But be careful. Like a game of "Operation," if you wake her up, you lose—and this game doesn't feature buzzers, it features bonnets . . . three hours' worth.
4. Eject the bonnet movie, and put in the laser movie. Lower the volume, or splurge and use headphones.
5. When the movie's over, gently wake your wife up and say, "I can't believe you slept through (insert name of bonnet movie here) . . . it was really beautiful." For added points, pretend to wipe away a tear from your eye. If you're successful, you'll get the *credit* for the bonnet movie but the *awesomeness* of the laser movie!
6. Cash in your points! If your wife is too tired after the movie (a common occurrence), then make sure you remind her of your sacrifice the next night as you make a pitch for some action. If she's still too tired (or is feeling bloated, or has to get up early, or hurt her big toe, or—sorry), then save your points. They don't expire! At a minimum, you can cash them in for a laser movie some other night or to escape a mundane chore.

Lifetime Achievement Award: JACKIE CHAN—*The Sir Laurence Olivier of "Laser Movies"*

Best Picture Ever: Tie between *TANGO & CASH* and *PLANET OF THE APES* (non–Marky Mark version)

Most Overrated Actor: SEAN PENN

Actor I Most Want to Throw Garbage At: Also SEAN PENN

Actress Most Likely to Serve Me with a Restraining Order: JESSICA ALBA

Sweatiest Actor: MICHAEL MOORE

SCAM + TECHNOLOGY = MUCH BETTER SCAM

I have an idea that's so simple, yet so revolutionary, that it could literally change the way men and women rent movies together. If I wasn't already a little busy at work, I'd honestly start a company around this idea, but since I can't, I'm offering it to you. For free. You're welcome.

Video stores should start creating special "couple's cut" sections. I'm not talking about a black curtain hanging in the back corner of the store (you know, the ones that are just thick enough to block the view inside unless you walk by really fast so that the breeze pushes it to one side slightly, thereby offering you a brief but tantalizing look at both the goods and, paradoxically, the bearded men in trench coats renting them). No, I'm talking about an entirely new concept.

All of the DVDs in this new "couple's cut" section would feature bonnet movies. Bonnets, bonnets, everywhere. But here's the trick. Fifteen minutes in (which is about five minutes after she's fallen asleep), the movie quietly goes to black. After a minute of darkness (which is your safety net in case she awakens—"Damn this broken DVD!"), a new movie starts. And there's not a bonnet to be found.

No, this new movie has fast cars, spaceships, or ninjas (preferably all three)—yep, a good old-fashioned laser movie. Think about it—you could finally rent *A Room with a View . . . To a Kill!* You win, she wins, but most of all, *you* win!

The whole key to this plan working is that women must never know about the existence of this section of the video store. Therefore, we need a universal indicator for men to tell quickly if it's a "couple's cut" movie, something that seems innocuous to the uninformed (her) while standing out to the enlightened (us). And I have just the idea. The "man sign" should be a made-up actress's name (I vote for "Emma Winslet") listed on the DVD. If you see the name "Emma Winslet" printed on the back, you can forget about what's on the front, because you'll only be enduring 15 minutes of it.

Genius? Yes, I know. Together we can save mankind. Now, go treat your wife to a movie.

Did you know?
Joan Rivers has had "a little" work done.

Chapter 11

Media Bias: An All-New Fairness Doctrine

THIRTY-NINE YEARS. THREE WORDS. EIGHT DAYS. DONE.

Don Imus had insulted every group of people in every context imaginable for four straight decades. He'd been paid millions of dollars to do it. But when he called the Rutgers women's basketball team "nappy-headed ho's" he broke the unwritten rule: Don't be controversial during a slow news cycle (even if your contract mandates you to).

Am I the only one who noticed that the term "nappy-headed" was followed by the word "ho's"? The news media's focus was always on the racial part of the statement (because it made for the best tabloid headlines), but you'd think that basically calling college students "disease-riddled streetwalkers who sell their bodies for money" would be a little more of an insult than crudely describing their hairstyle.

It was a bizarre eight days. Person after person went on television to say how "strong" the Rutgers women were yet how "devastated" they must be by three words uttered by an 825-year-old talk-show host almost no one listened to live.

In reality, Imus kicked the proverbial cute little puppy. The Rutgers women's basketball story was a heartwarming one. They weren't anyone's enemy, and people were upset that some rich white guy would tear down their moment of second-place glory. But the legitimate annoyance at his comments turned into a road map of how to gain power and control. In the end, Imus learned that no matter how many Democrats he endorsed, no matter how many sick African-American kids he helped, the second that calling him a racist would help people obtain power, he was a racist.

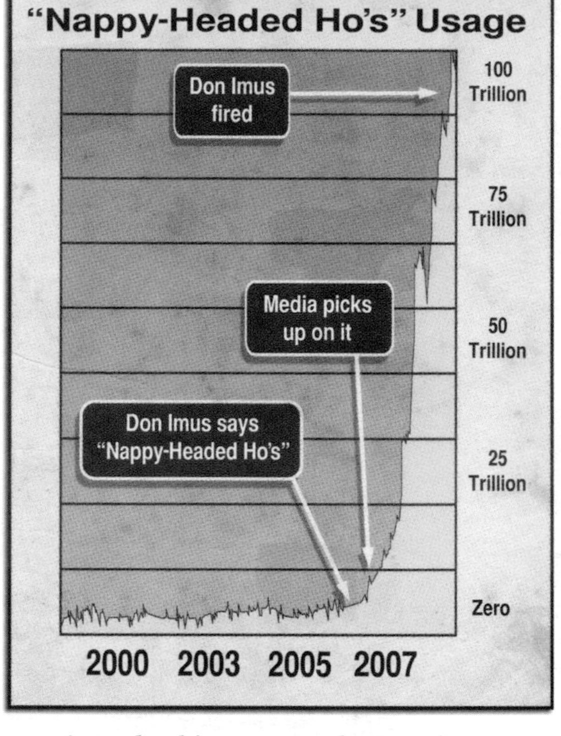

THE TELL-TALE HEART

During Imus's interview on Al Sharpton's radio show five days after the comment, Sharpton said, "The question is not whether you're a rabid racist with intent. If you commit a crime, intent may be an element, but the crime is still there."

First of all, let's remember that no criminal event occurred here, and even if there was, intent still plays a major role in determining punishment. That's why you can be charged with first-, second-, and third-degree murder, along with manslaughter.

But when it comes to racist words, it's *all* about the intent. After all, if it was *just* about the actual words, then wasn't Sharpton *also* a racist for repeating the phrase "nappy-headed ho's?" No, because we assume Sharpton's *intent* wasn't to slur his own people. Isn't it frightening that a man can be fired based solely on pressure groups and their best guess at his intent? Especially when the evidence is approximately five seconds of a 39-year career?

Lost in the debate and the shock over how quickly it all happened was how ridiculous our priorities have become. Both MSNBC and CBS Radio decided to fire Imus before or during his annual telethon, which routinely raises millions of dollars for children's charities. Why couldn't they have waited two more days? Do they really believe that off-color language by a radio host demands priority over curing childhood cancer and sudden infant death syndrome?

Did anyone notice that the Tennessee women's basketball team got the shaft in this story? I mean, they *won* the game. They were the world champions, and absolutely no one paid any attention to their achievement. (Coincidentally, that is the same reaction the winner of the women's basketball championship gets every year.)

A.D.D. MOMENT

As the circus escalated, those who were thrilled to appear on Imus's show to sell their book or promote their candidacy just days before took turns retroactively elevating themselves to the high road. But that was basically just the human survival instinct kicking in; the bigger problem was the media themselves.

REPORTEDLY REPORTING

The Imus story revealed massive holes in our media landscape that show no sign of closing anytime soon. Here are just a few of the incredible errors and unbelievably misleading reports that surrounded the demise of Don Imus's career.

- *Time*'s cover story on the controversy theorized that one of Imus's problems was that while "Howard Stern may be offensive . . . he's also self-deprecating, making fun of his own satyrism, looks and even manly endowment. Imus doesn't take it nearly as well as he dishes it out. His shtick is all cowboy-hatted swagger."

Had anyone at *Time* ever even listened to Imus? His show was almost entirely based on how ugly, old, crotchety, and miserable he was.

The *Time* story about Imus included a series of racially charged quotes from different public figures that were assigned an "outrage factor" on a scale of 1 to 10. The higher the number, the more trouble it brought to the person who said it. The point was seemingly to highlight the fact that the line of "who can say what" is hard to understand. While that's true, the pattern they missed is that you can apparently say a lot more if you're politically associated with the left than if you are with the right.

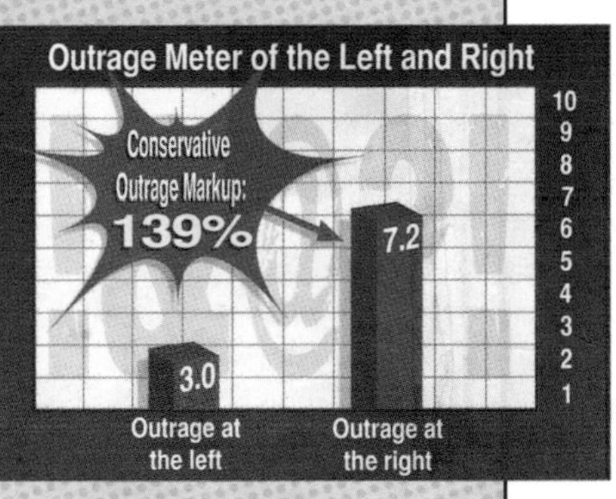

- Over and over again, Imus's commentary on Gwen Ifill (he supposedly called the black journalist a "cleaning lady") was repeated as case-closing evidence that he had a long history of hate-filled comments. Did anyone even bother to look at the context of the Ifill remark?

Imus explained it like this: "We had a bit on the radio called 'Imus in Washington,' which is like fake news. And I had a fake . . . David Duke character . . . and this David Duke-like character, reflecting the philosophy and the attitude of the Reagan administration, said, isn't it great that Gwen Ifill's been invited back to the White House as a cleaning lady. And for years people have said I said that. I didn't say that . . . that was satire . . . a reflection of the racism we perceived of that administration."

So, not only was Imus not being racist, he was using a character to make the point that the *Reagan administration* was racist, an opinion that almost everyone who criticized Imus's Rutgers comments would have stood up and applauded. I would vehemently disagree, but the point is that if you criticize Imus for comments made in character, then you might as well call everyone who's ever played Hitler in a movie a genocidal anti-Semite.

Right or wrong, shouldn't Imus's explanation have found its way into every story that used the Ifill comments against him? It's not as if his defense was hard to find; he gave it in the middle of the now infamous Al Sharpton interview—it was even fully transcribed for easy access by the *New York Times*.

☢ The *Los Angeles Times* reported that Imus called the Conway and Whitman show on Los Angeles radio station KLSX and vowed: "I plan to be on the radio. I plan to work again. I'm not going to sit around like an old woman."

Brian Whitman, one of the show's cohosts, is not only a close friend of mine, but he's also done a dead-on voice impersonation of Imus for years. Could Brian have actually fooled the *Los Angeles Times?*

Yep.

A few days later, they apologized (in that *Los Angeles Times*, nonapology sort of way): "For the Record: . . . The comments were not made by Imus but by the program's cohost, Brian Whitman, who was doing an impression of Imus. Imus was not a guest on the program."

I'll give the *Los Angeles Times* a little credit—at least they made the effort to correct it. How many others make similarly enormous mistakes and just ignore them? Remember, these aren't small local papers or high school newsletters; these are major media organizations seemingly not even bothering to understand what they're reporting.

ACID INGESTION

Who cares if a couple of newspapers get their facts wrong—everyone makes mistakes! True, but when it comes to the media, these mistakes become amplified over and over again by the process of "ingestion."

When you put a piece of news video or a report into the main computer system, they say it has been ingested. That's a microcosm of the process that occurs with today's media and our wired world. Once something has been ingested as fact, it's infinitely repeated across the internet and throughout the media until, right or wrong, it simply becomes the truth.

When Sheryl Crow wrote a blog about how we can all do our part to stop global warming by using only one square of toilet paper, dozens of credible newspapers reported on it. When I saw those reports, I assumed that they'd done their homework, and I repeated the story on my radio and television shows. Later that evening, I read the full blog entry myself and realized that, taken in context, her toilet paper comment was obviously a joke.

I take full responsibility for my part in repeating the story. Quite honestly, when I first read the story, I just assumed she was really that ignorant about global warming. I didn't question the media or do my own homework, and I allowed myself to be influenced by the cartoon version of liberal entertainers that I have in my mind. While that vision is built on a long line of their incontrovertible stupidity, it's not fair to apply it to *every* instance of *every* entertainer promoting a liberal cause.

The next day, I corrected the story on both TV and radio, but most of the other sources that reported it didn't bother. Later, Crow thanked me for correcting the story, even though she still surely thinks I'm completely insane about global warming (a feeling that is obviously reciprocated).

I understand that this is just a small, inconsequential example. Obviously, it's not exactly vital to national security if we think Sheryl Crow is slightly crazier now than we did before, but regardless of what side of the argument you're on, the truth *does* matter.

The number of people who now want to shake Sheryl Crow's hand has dropped by about 80 percent, because much of the world still believes that she seriously proposed "one person, one square."

A.D.D. MOMENT

CONTEXT MATTERS

Admittedly, I'm probably a little more sensitive than the average person when it comes to words being misused to fit an agenda. There is literally an entire industry now set up through big-named Democratic financiers to force me and others with a conservative point of view off the air.

I believe this is a sign of liberal talk-radio surrender. Since those shows and networks couldn't win in the marketplace, they've resorted to slanderous calls of racism and bigotry by taking words out of context. Here are a few of my favorite examples.

It's hard to get the real meaning of the Gettysburg Address when you report on it in chunks and sound bites.

But when it comes to my remarks about Katrina survivors, they went even further—shortening what I said to just one word in some cases.

A few blogs have even gone so far as to break down my statements into syllables by quoting me as simply calling Katrina victims "scum."

Glenn Beck Says "Katrina Victims Are Scumbags"

I say a lot of stupid things, but this was not one of them. Unfortunately, that hasn't stopped it from being used by those who either want to intentionally lie to the public to further their own agendas or those who haven't spent more than 30 seconds researching it.

While the insinuation that I hated people suffering from the worst natural disaster in our country's history makes for a nice little headline, the facts are just laughable.

First, what most people quote, including "journalist" Keith Olbermann, is a grand total of one word out of a 20-minute monologue.

Second, the topic of the monologue that morning was the fact that many people had started to get "Katrina fatigue." The news was littered with reports of people shooting at rescue helicopters and children's hospitals and video of looters stealing flat-screen televisions (I specifically pardoned anyone looting essential supplies throughout the week). I used the monologue as a plea for Americans to ignore those people, to look past the looters and murderers (or, more accurately, "the scumbags") to the real victims and dig deep.

Why did I say dig deep? Because that morning, we were broadcasting from the parking lot of a restaurant as part of our fundraiser for Katrina survivors. People could pull up and make their donations right through their car windows on their way to work. All told, we raised more than $160,000 for Katrina survivors. If I really thought these people were scumbags, I doubt we would've bothered.

Third, remember the whole "context mat-

Analysis of the diligent research of one of the main organizations that attempt to highlight offensive content on my show (by hiring liberal activists to listen to every minute) has turned up two interesting statistics.

First, I began being monitored by this organization (why give it any publicity by actually naming it?) in May 2004, but—judging by the number of alerts they've sent out—I apparently became much more offensive after being hired by CNN. I'm *sure* it's not simply because they decided I was a bigger target.

Second, since this organization's sole purpose is to point out offensive things they hear from conservatives in broadcast media, one can reasonably assume that when they hear something offensive, they report it. So we decided to calculate exactly how much of my program is offensive to hard-core liberal activists.

ters" discussion? If these people had bothered to listen to the rest of the monologue, they would've heard me say that I was only referring to—and I quote myself—a "small percentage" of "0.2 percent" of the survivors. That means I had expressed somewhere in the area of a 99.8 percent approval rating of Katrina survivors.

Fourth, I was also ripped for saying, in the same monologue, that I was annoyed at "around 10" of the families of the more than 3,000 9/11 victims because I felt that Americans had given until it hurt, and a few families seemed to be using their tragic position and America's sorrow for political and/or financial gain. Essentially, I was criticized for having a 99.7 percent approval rating of 9/11 families. If you can name *any* group of people, including your own family, and honestly tell me that you approve of at least 99.7 percent of their actions, then I'll be happy to call you a liar.

There was at least one positive that came out of this whole mess. The few people who did bother to actually look into the details realized two important things: (1) I'm not the personification of evil on earth; and (2) those who reported these quotes outside their original context have absolutely zero credibility.

Glenn Beck Wants to Nuke the World!

This one has to be my personal favorite, because it's a great example of how those who don't like your politics will sell their soul to the fourteenth level of Hell just to try to destroy your career.

For some reason, we were talking about *American Idol* that day, and one of my producers (Stu) began playing a horrible Clay Aiken song. Reacting to the overwhelming femininity of the moment, I told him to give me something "butch" to talk about. He said, how about "blowing up Iran?" So, in my gruff, stereotypically alpha-male character voice, I said, "I say we nuke the bastards!"

Reasonably intelligent people without an agenda might say that I wasn't making a serious policy statement, considering it was done in a character voice over a crappy Clay Aiken song, but that didn't stop blog after blog from reporting it as if it were serious.

In fact, the very *next* thing I said was, "In fact, it doesn't have to be Iran, it can be everywhere! Any place that disagrees with me!" Did anyone *really* think that I was advocating the nuclear annihilation of every country on the planet that doesn't agree with everything I say? Of course not; they just knew that the people who read their blogs wouldn't bother looking into it any further. They have *that low* an opinion of their readership—and sadly enough, it's pretty accurate.

Glenn Beck Insults Muslim Congressman!

Here it is, the most poorly worded question of all time: *"You are saying, 'Let's cut and run.' And I have to tell you, I have been nervous about this interview with you, because what I feel like saying is, 'Sir, prove to me that you are not working with our enemies.' "*

That's what I asked Keith Ellison, the first Muslim ever elected to Congress in America. To his credit, Ellison has never attempted to exploit my flub—but others have happily stepped in for him.

Before I get too much farther into this, let's first back up and start with the basics. To believe that I'm some evil hatemonger who thinks that Ellison is a terrorist and that all Islam is evil, you have to ignore a lot of contradictory evidence. For example, you first have to believe that I was *only* telling the truth when I butchered that one question and I was *lying* when I made each of these other statements in the same interview:

- **Beck:** "What I feel like saying is, 'Sir, prove to me that you are not working with our enemies.' *And I know you're not.*"
- **Beck:** "I'm not accusing you of being an enemy."
- **Ellison:** "I don't need to—need to prove my patriotic stripes."
  Beck: "And I'm not asking you to."
- **Beck:** "I really don't believe that Islam is a religion of evil. I—you know, I think it's being hijacked, quite frankly."

- **Beck:** "You come from a district that is heavily immigrant with Somalians, and I think it's wonderful, honestly."
- **Beck:** "You could be an icon to show Europe, this is the way you integrate into a country."
- **Beck:** "I think the Somalians coming out and voting is a very good thing."
- **Ellison:** "If you were to gather Muslims up and ask them how they feel about this country, they'll talk about it being the land of opportunity, the place where they can worship their faith as they choose, a place where they can earn a decent living."
  Beck: "Yes. I agree with you. We don't have any argument there."

If you can jump through the hoops of believing that the enemy question was the only honest thing I said in the whole interview (and of course, you ignore the hundreds of other times I've talked about Islam as a religion of peace), then you probably already have your mind made up, so feel free to skip ahead and further dodge the truth.

Many Americans, including me, have asked the question "Where are the voices of Muslims standing up against terrorism and the people who have perverted their religion?" On my radio and television shows, we've now gone farther than just asking the questions; we give the answers. We've gone out and found dedicated, practicing American Muslims who *are* standing up, and we've given their voices the amplification they need to be heard. That's also why we spent almost half of our special on Islamic extremism highlighting the voices of reason in both the United States and the Middle East. But until those voices are heard with regularity, it's natural for people to have questions, and who better to answer them than the first Muslim congressman?

A.D.D. MOMENT **The Ellison** question seemed to have angered only bloggers. Maybe Mr. Ellison was offended, too. I don't know. He didn't appear to be. I think one reason for that is that good Muslims *want* the opportunity to look Americans in the eye and say, "No matter what you might think you know about my faith, and despite the grainy home videos recorded in caves you've seen of people who claim to be Muslim, *I am an American*. I love this country just as much as you, and one of the reasons I love it so much is that different people from different religions can work together to make it better. Islamic extremism angers me as much as or more than it does you, because it not only threatens my life, it makes a mockery of my religion. Politicians in the Middle East are trying to hijack the Islam that I know just as the Catholic church was hijacked in the Dark Ages, and I am on the front lines doing everything I can to stop them."

A.D.D. MOMENT On the bright side, this controversy finally put to rest one long-standing argument: Who is funnier, Jon Stewart or Stephen Colbert? Both shows did bits wrecking me for my awfully worded question. Jon Stewart's take was brutal but brilliantly funny. Stephen Colbert's bit? Ehh . . . not so much. Glad I could help give America an answer on this one.

Glenn Beck Says Something Else about Muslims!

Let's start with the quote: "Muslims need to start saying, 'Hey, you know what? There are good Muslims and bad Muslims. We need to be the first ones in the recruitment office lining up to shoot the bad Muslims in the head.' "

I guess I can clarify one thing in case you're confused. In this context, "bad Muslims" doesn't refer to Muslims caught stealing Baby Ruth bars at a 7-Eleven; it refers to Islamic extremists who are plotting to blow up really tall buildings and kill lots of innocent people. With that said, let me be clear: Like Japanese-Americans who fought harder than anyone in World War II, "good Muslims" should be first in line to shoot "bad Muslims" in the head. Period.

Glenn Beck Calls Jimmy Carter a "Waste of Skin"!

This one is just plain accurate.

THE MORAL OF THE STORY

So what does all of this tell us? I mean, who cares if some overweight (but still oddly sexy) radio and TV host is unfairly treated, right? You should, and here's why.

While there have always been completely partisan organizations funded by political opponents to spread disinformation, the access and credibility these organizations now have with the mainstream media are unprecedented thanks in part to McCain-Feingold and their fancy campaign-finance reform. The media also have fewer and fewer resources to do their own homework these days, and the result is that many "journalists" turn to these hackish blogs and political action groups as real sources (or in Keith Olbermann's case, his *only* source—allegedly . . . I read that on a blog).

When those with obvious agendas and horrible track records for honesty and accuracy are treated as if they are seasoned, nonpartisan reporters, you wind up not being able to trust the news at all. Unfortunately, I fear that's exactly where we are headed.

MY SOLUTION

Attention, John McCain and Russ Feingold: There's no way to stop people from exaggerating, twisting facts, and making stuff up when political gain is on the line. George Soros and people of his awful ilk have enough money to promote lies about their political enemies and turn them into racist, bigoted hatemongers. There's just no way to stop the spread of information, even if it's completely false, outside of totalitarianism (which still isn't working in China, even when assisted by Google. Thanks, guys!).

The only way to solve the snowballing falsehoods of today's media landscape is to do some reporting of your own. You have to keep a little mental record of who's telling you the stories that check out and who's spinning them for their own purposes. Then, when you catch someone stretching the truth beyond recognition, you need to hold them responsible by calling them out and going somewhere else.

We already do this to some degree. For example, conservatives have always been skeptical of what they hear from the mainstream media, so when Dan Rather started reporting memos about George W. Bush's military record that were basically sketched with crayon on a napkin by the credibility equivalent of the head of the DNC, no conservative was surprised that it didn't check out. But as the Internet continues to foster the spread of lies and misleading commentaries faster than a computer virus promising nude pictures of Jessica Alba, we all have to be more vigilant.

Aside from outright lies and distortion, the media are also developing a problem with being completely honest about the prism they're presenting the news through. That's what I don't understand about people like Keith Olbermann. It's not as if people *don't know* he's a liberal. It's as obvious as the fact that I love pastries. So why not just admit it? It's not a dirty word, and you shouldn't be ashamed to say, "I see most things from a liberal point of view, so when I tell you this next story about Karl Rove and Dick Cheney murdering puppies, keep that in mind." After all, Olbermann provides a cute little service every night with his one-hour review of the day's liberal blog entries. Why even bother acting like a real journalist?

I'm not a journalist, but you don't have to be Bob Woodward to figure that out. Just because I'm on a news network doesn't mean that I'm a news person. My goal is to digest what *actual* journalists report and give you my opinion on it, an opinion that is proudly and openly from a conservative point of view. You know that right up front, and you can do with it what you want.

I think America appreciates that level of honesty. Unfortunately, people like Keith Olbermann apparently do not, and that's why he's today's Worst Person in this Book.

Chapter 12

You Can't Say That!

The Politics of Correctness

"Although (political correctness) arises from the laudable desire to sweep away the debris of racism and sexism and hatred, it replaces old prejudice with new ones. It declares certain topics off-limits, certain expressions off-limits, even certain gestures off-limits.

"What began as a crusade for civility has soured into a cause of conflict and even censorship. Disputants treat sheer force—getting their foes punished or expelled, for instance—as a substitute for the power of ideas.

"Throughout history, attempts to micromanage casual conversation have only incited distrust. They have invited people to look for an insult in every word, gesture, action. And, in their own Orwellian way, crusades that demand correct behavior crush diversity in the name of diversity."

WHEN PRESIDENT GEORGE H. W. BUSH included those words in a 1991 commencement speech, he knew how serious the consequences of political correctness were, but he couldn't have possibly predicted how quickly and how intensely we'd feel them. Less than two decades later, people seem to have absolutely no idea what they can say and when or where they can say it.

Here's how bad it's become:

- After suicidal, nut-job Islamic terrorists Mohammed Sidique Khan, Shehzad Tanweer, Germaine Lindsay, and Hasib Hussain blew themselves up on London's crowded buses and tubes (killing 52 and injuring 700) in July 2005, the BBC called them "misguided criminals."
- In an article about people starving in Zimbabwe, the hungry were referred to as the "food insecure."
- Washington's governor, Chris Gregoire, turned down a request to include a nativity scene at the state capitol building because attorneys advised that, with only a week until Christmas, they didn't have time to "research the matter." Governor Gregoire and her attorneys apparently didn't have the same concerns earlier in the week when she lit a menorah with a group of rabbis, saying it celebrated the cultural diversity of the state.
- The *London Daily Telegraph* reported on a classified European Union handbook that advises government spokesmen not to link Islam and terrorism in their statements, banning words such as *jihad, Islamic,* or *fundamentalist.*

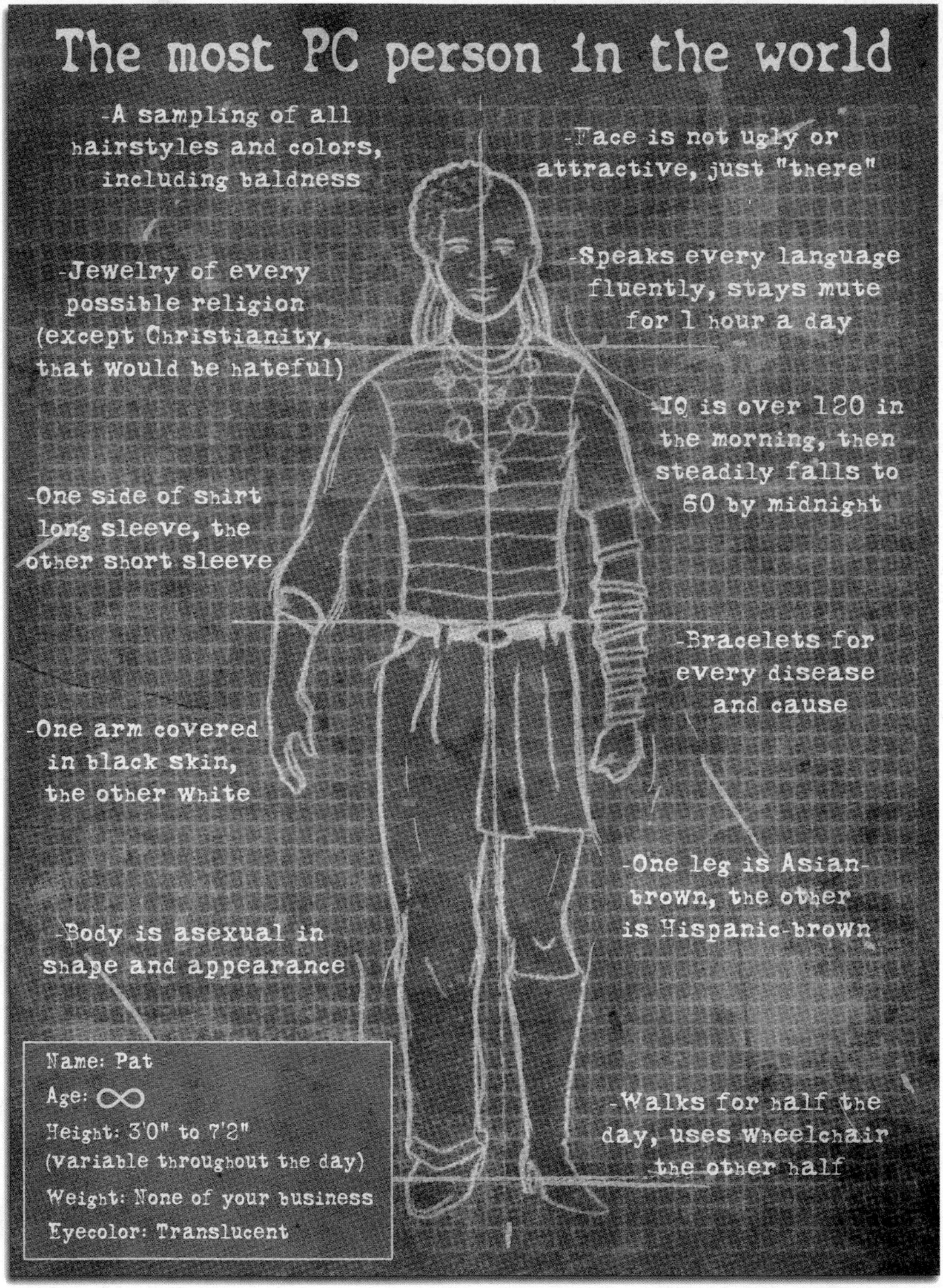

The most PC person in the world

-A sampling of all hairstyles and colors, including baldness

-Face is not ugly or attractive, just "there"

-Jewelry of every possible religion (except Christianity, that would be hateful)

-Speaks every language fluently, stays mute for 1 hour a day

-IQ is over 120 in the morning, then steadily falls to 60 by midnight

-One side of shirt long sleeve, the other short sleeve

-Bracelets for every disease and cause

-One arm covered in black skin, the other white

-One leg is Asian-brown, the other is Hispanic-brown

-Body is asexual in shape and appearance

-Walks for half the day, uses wheelchair the other half

Name: Pat
Age: ∞
Height: 3'0" to 7'2" (variable throughout the day)
Weight: None of your business
Eyecolor: Translucent

As much as I hate to admit it, my name is Glenn Beck, and I was part of the problem. I actually bought into this PC nonsense when it first hit the scene, partially because I have a daughter with "special abilities." The logic made sense to me. Why say something that may be demeaning to a handicapped child when there's an easy alternative?

The problem was that I never actually stopped to ask my daughter if *she was* offended by being called handicapped. I should have. I would have learned much earlier that she was far stronger than I had ever imagined.

Unfortunately, by not taking the time to figure out if the people we're trying so hard to protect are actually offended, we usually hurt their cause. For example, I opened *USA Today* not long ago and saw the unbelievable headline "After years as 'dirty word,' 'poverty' a campaign issue again."

Politicians are starting to use the word *poverty* again because the replacement words they'd chosen were basically sanitized jibberish. That made them powerless. The problem was never "those suffering from bank-account malnutrition," the problem was, and remains, poverty. Ironically, the people who have suffered the most from American politicians spending decades sugarcoating the issue are the same ones they're trying to help: *those who actually live in poverty.*

I think the key question to ask here is: Huh? When did the word *poverty* become offensive or a "dirty word"? Isn't it just a category used when measuring income? I must have missed the whole era where we had to call people "currency deficient."

A.D.D. MOMENT

Isn't it insulting to those who truly live in poverty that we're talking about what word should be used to describe their lives instead of working to improve them? The important thing isn't the word used to describe the situation—it's the *situation itself.*

SCHOOL IS IN!

The actions of people who often have the best intentions at heart (such as the former PC me) have resulted in the admirable goal of sensitivity morphing into mindless worldwide management of feelings. That's not being sensitive; that's being stupid and shortsighted.

A few years ago, the media began noticing that teachers had started using purple ink to correct papers instead of the classic red ink. Why? Sharon Carlson, a middle-school teacher, explained to the *Boston Globe:* "If you see a whole paper of red, it looks pretty frightening." Leatrice Eiseman, author of five books on color (and I was proud of *my* book deal), added, "Red is a bit over-the-top in its aggression."

Noooo, the Taliban is over the top in its aggression—red is just a motionless, inanimate, nondangerous, unthreatening color.

Just because your new purple ink may not have the same "Wrong, dummy!" connotation of red ink now doesn't mean that it won't in the future. If today's kids are corrected in purple, they'll think purple is frightening, and we'll have to keep switching colors every other week. Our kids don't benefit from that, because it teaches them that people will change or remove whatever makes them feel bad. In fact, the only one who does benefit is Crayola.

Words and phrases (and even evil aggressive colors) have power to offend because *we give them that power.*

Unfortunately, ink color isn't the only example of PC idiocy when it comes to schools:

- A teacher in a U.K. grade school split her large class into two groups and labeled them 1a and 1b. Parents of the kids in group 1b complained because they feared their children would be perceived as academically inferior to the 1a kids, even though the split was done alphabetically.

  A.D.D. MOMENT There *is* someone who is academically inferior in this story, and it isn't the kids.

- A government-backed survey in England revealed that more and more teachers were not teaching the Holocaust for fear of "offending Muslims." Some teachers have even stopped teaching the Crusades, because the lessons often contradict what is taught in mosques.

☢ Not to be outdone, universities are giving it "the old college try" to compete with public schools for who can be the most politically correct. In 2005, the NCAA set out on a mission to ban any team with a nickname it deemed "hostile or abusive" to Indians or other minority groups. The University of Illinois became one of the latest victims when their mascot, Illiniwek, was forced into retirement. The NCAA had deemed Illiniwek an "offensive use of American Indian imagery" for the way students would dress in classic Indian garb and dance a ritual at halftime of home games. (Incidentally, he'd been portrayed that way since 1926.)

Let me take a minute to announce that no one would catch me complaining if the Fighting Caucasians had a white boy dancing horribly at halftime. **A.D.D. MOMENT**

These universities are attempting to *compliment* you by paying tribute to your heritage. That's something the Seminole tribe understood when it fought the NCAA side by side with Florida State to make sure the name of the tribe would *remain* that university's nickname. The NCAA eventually reversed its earlier ban, and sanity scored a rare victory.

The end result of this sanitization of life that our kids now receive from kindergarten through college is nothing less then the creation of an entire generation of future sissies.

A.D.D. MOMENT Am I still allowed to use the word *sissies?* Well, don't check the dictionary for an answer, because the actual definition doesn't matter anymore. (Just for the fun of it: "a timid man or boy considered childish or unassertive.")

YOU'RE THE BEST!

Politically correct behavior such as changing ink colors in schools, not keeping score, and trying hard never to tell students they're wrong has resulted in another phenomenon: Our kids are addicted to praise. Parents, teachers, and families spend all day telling each child how great an athlete, architect, speaker, and painter he or she is (even though they never got a hit in Little League, couldn't get a Lincoln Log structure to stand, are mute, and paint worse than I do). It's created a generation of ego-inflated praise-oholics—and now we're paying the price. Just watch the auditions for *American Idol* if you need evidence of that.

The *Wall Street Journal* ran an article recently titled "The Most Praised Generation Goes to Work." It started, *"You, you, you—you really are special, you are! You've got everything going for you. You're attractive, witty, brilliant. 'Gifted' is the word that comes to mind."*

Does that not sum up perfectly the way our kids are treated? But now, as these kids start to trickle into the "real world," they're finding it difficult to adapt. Surprised? Me neither.

To cope, companies are using "praise consultants" who talk about using compliments instead of discipline. Don't reprimand that employee for showing up late! Just wait for him to show up on time, and then commend him for it.

> **I would** like to formally suggest "praise consultant" as the new PC name for pastor, priest, or bishop.
>
> A.D.D. MOMENT

Praise addiction works just like gambling, alcoholism, or any other addiction. The praise is empty and always needs to grow, so when the high is gone, you're left even emptier inside. Since we haven't taught our kids how to recognize their own strengths and weaknesses and adapt to them, they lose their way, and eventually, they lose hope. In essence, they've become *reality-challenged.*

PC PREDICTIONS

I said it earlier: Political correctness is a vicious circle. Changing words because someone thinks they're offensive is a pattern that will never stop. Here's how some of the more popular PC terms of today will probably evolve as special interest groups take turns being insulted.

- ~~Crippled~~ → ~~Handicapped~~ → ~~Handi-Capable~~ → Handy-People → (*People without hands complain*) Hearty-people → (*People without hearts complain*) → People.

☢ ~~Retarded~~ → ~~Mentally Retarded~~ → ~~Mentally Challenged~~ → ~~Learning Disabled~~ → Patient Learner → (*Sounds like someone admitted to the hospital*) → Selective Learner → (*What about those not "selected"?*) → Picky Learner → Learner.

☢ ~~Terrorists~~ → ~~Insurgents~~ → ~~Freedom Fighters~~ → ~~Misguided Criminals~~ → High-Risk Offspring of Mediocre Parents → Infrequent Law Practitioners → Malcontents.

☢ ~~Our Lord and Savior Jesus Christ~~ → ~~Jesus Christ~~ → ~~Jesus~~ → That Guy on the Cross → That Person on the Cross → That Person → Who?

☢ ~~Illegal Aliens~~ → ~~Illegal Immigrants~~ → ~~Undocumented Workers~~ → ~~Migrant Workers~~ → ~~Guest Workers~~ → ~~Imported Low Wage Workers~~ → Temporary U.S. Citizens → MexAmeriCanadians → Bob.

MARXIST MADNESS

Unless you're a fan of concentration camps, gulags, long lines, and shared wealth, communism hasn't exactly been the source of many enduring ideas. But there is one notable exception: political correctness. Yes, it was those zany Marxist Communists like Georg Lukacs (no, not the *Star Wars* guy), Theodor Adorno, Max Horkheimer, and Felix Weil who helped lay the foundation that would later become political correctness.

Lukacs believed that the biggest obstacle to achieving a Marxist "Happy Fun Land" was Western culture, so he started a war on it. He called it "cultural terrorism."

First up on the docket: a Madonna-like sex education program. The program encouraged "sexual promiscuity" (that's PC for acting like Lindsay Lohan) and "free love" (that's PC for acting like Paris Hilton). The idea was to create a new "all inclusive" society that would promote all sexual lifestyles as equal—a very PC concept, indeed.

I bet Deb Lafave wishes she were teaching during the old Georg Lukacs days, huh?

A.D.D. MOMENT

Later, his line of thinking caught on with fellow Marxist thinkers at Germany's Institute for Social Research (ISR). When the ISR fled from Hitler and moved to New York City with the help of Columbia University in 1933, the culture war continued here in

FUN LAND PARK MAP

WORK HARD, PLAY HARD AT MARX PARX!

America. ISR members such as Adorno and Herbert Marcuse focused on promoting ideas such as "inclusion" and "multiculturalism" in an effort to water down American culture.

Since then, other organizations with similar socialist/communist ideals have taken note of the philosophy and are (successfully) employing the same tactics.

Take the ACLU. They attack Christianity every chance they get by suing to have displays of everything from the Ten Commandments to Christmas nativity scenes removed. They claim their goal is to be inclusive, to treat everyone equally, but we know their real agenda: to water down American culture.

MY SOLUTION

I believe that political correctness is the biggest threat this nation faces today. Sure, you won't see newspaper articles about the nuclear program it's working on, but it's an enemy nonetheless.

Think of it as a poison that was dumped into our water supply years ago by our enemies. They knew that it would take time for the entire country to be affected, but they were patient, and now the entire country has been poisoned, and most don't even know it.

The only antidote for this toxin is for everyone to stop sitting down and taking it like French soldiers at war. We all have to start being open about the fact that political correctness not only exists but is killing us. The first small step in doing that is becoming aware and suspicious of the people and groups who are always trying to ban certain words or otherwise restrict your freedom of speech. Let's call them the *linguistically intolerant* or the *opposing-viewpoint-averse.*

When you see them, stop and ask yourself a simple question: Why?

Why does the ACLU want that Ten Commandments display gone? Why does CAIR lash out at someone (okay, me) for suggesting that good Muslims must stand up and speak out against those who've perverted their religion? Why do the NAACP and their subset groups sue to mandate that diverse candidates be afforded an equal number of job interviews, regardless of whether those candidates are the least bit qualified for the job?

It's time to take back the First Amendment. Everyone from Imus to Rosie should have taught us that freedom of speech—no matter how ignorant or distasteful that speech may be—is the most important right we have. Sure, you might be offended

You've been mugged by someone you identify only as a "400-pound Eskimo." Which of the following police lineups would be the most appropriate?

Common Sense Version

Politically Correct Version

from time to time, but wouldn't you rather know that the guy who lives next door is a racist so that you can avoid him instead of inviting him over to poker night every week? When everyone plays his cards face-up on the table, it's a lot easier to figure out whom you'd rather not brunch with.

People go justifiably crazy protecting the Second Amendment. Anytime someone so much as infers that you shouldn't be allowed to keep a street sweeper in your closet, Ted Nugent (okay, and me too) waves his guns around on television and chants, "From my cold, dead hands!" How about we start having that same kind of passion for the First Amendment?

Maybe we've all become a little spoiled on the free-speech front over the years. If Americans were forced to live like North Koreans, maybe we'd come to see the next time a comedian says something horrendously offensive in a comedy club as a tribute to the fact that we even *have* comedy clubs. Or, for that matter, comedy.

A.D.D. MOMMENT I sincerely doubt that North Koreans or Cubans get the pleasure of enjoying two-for-one drinks at amateur night every Wednesday.

But aside from standing up for free speech every chance we get, we also have to look at how we're training our own children, and we have to lead them by example. If your kid is called a "nappy-headed ho" or a "Macaca," don't go crying to the school. Sure, you might have to turn down the litigation lottery as a result, but guess what, that's okay. In fact, it's more than okay—it's great, especially if your child learns a lifelong lesson from it.

Being politically correct is not just a cutesy attempt to make people feel better; it's a larger, coordinated effort to change Western culture as we know it. Early Marxists designed their game plan long ago and continue to execute it today: Control the argument by controlling the language. Those with radical agendas understand that plan well and are taking advantage of an oversensitive public.

How can we expect to win the war against radical Islam when we can't even use the word *terrorist* when talking about mass murderers who kill to honor some perverted version of their religion?

Unfortunately, proponents of political correctness defend it under the guise of diversity. It's an effective argument, because no wants to be called a racist or per-

While this is one of the hardest problems in this book to solve, it's also one of the most important. Look at almost every other problem we address, and you'll be able to find political correctness as the culprit. It's weird how a communist idea can do that to a capitalist society. **A.D.D. MOMENT**

ceived as intolerant; we all want to be "inclusive." But in my experience, "diversity" does more to exclude diverse opinions than anything else.

In order to promote real diversity *and* diversity of opinion, we have to allow *every* opinion to be spoken, no matter how ugly or unpopular it may be. That's the very essence of free speech. No one ever said it would be easy, but if we don't keep pushing the envelope, if we don't accept that some people's views or ideas of a joke may be different from ours—*and that's a good thing!*—then we might as well just turn the country over right now to the special-interest groups that want to control the message and set this country's agenda.

I started this chapter with the prescient words of George H. W. Bush from a speech he gave in 1991, and I'm going to end it the same way:

> *"Men and women must feel free to speak their hearts and minds. We must build a society in which people can join in common cause without having to surrender their identities.*
>
> *"You can lead the way. Share your thoughts and your experiences and your hopes and your frustrations. Defend others' rights to speak. And if harmony be our goal, let's pursue harmony, not inquisition."*

Chapter 13

Gratuities: I've Reached My Tipping Point

"TO INSURE PROMPT" SERVICE. That's what old Merriam-Webster says is the definition of *tip.* But if you ask me, the definition of tipping is more like a heady cocktail of guilt management and a guarantee that some occupations will never be paid the minimum wage. Plus, I end up feeling pressured to pay more than my fair share—whether or not the service I received was prompt (or even satisfactory).

Now, let's get something straight right from the beginning: I'm a *great* tipper. I say that now because everything you're about to read will suggest that I'm not. But the truth is that I don't always understand *why* I tip. Like democracy, tipping seems an imperfect system, and just because I'm willing to play along with both doesn't mean I can't occasionally complain about it. In fact, if I didn't complain, then I'd be out of a perfectly good career.

> **A.D.D. MOMENT**
>
> **Tipping a waiter** is considered *insulting* in Japan. That's the kind of wisdom I'd like to import to the United States. That and all the bowing. The bowing seems really nice. And the national obsession with the Catholic schoolgirl outfits.

According to my exhaustive research (thank you, Wikipedia!) the custom of tipping dates back to either sixteenth-century English coffeehouses or seventeenth-century European feudal lords. The only real consensus is that there's no consensus. No one has any idea why some people tipped other people and when they started doing it. Actually, there might be a consensus, but my research window was closing when the commercial break was over, so I didn't have time to explore too much further. But whatever the origin, the practice of tipping has become so completely out of whack that it's hard to imagine it was ever rooted in anything logical. In fact, what we now call "tipping" was probably once called "bribing."

THINK BEFORE YOU TIP

As I said, I'm no cheapskate—I understand the importance of compassion and generosity, even when it's not Christmas—sorry, "holiday"—time. But the problem is that we've all become like a bunch of robots, mindlessly doling out an extra 15 percent on top of what we're already paying, without giving any thought to whether the *quality* of our experience was worth the extra cash. I actually can't believe we still do it; I can't believe there hasn't been some sort of grassroots revolution by now. Well, I'm mad as hell, and I'm not going to take it anymore—or shall I say I'm not going to *give* it anymore? The revolution starts now.

A.D.D. MOMENT

The next time you're having dinner in a big group and the check comes, fork over exactly what you owe, and explain to everyone that you don't believe in tipping. Then email me and let me know how that worked out for you.

In New York City, where I work, there are all kinds of situations that result in people sticking out their hands, looking for a little "extra." Fortunately for you, most of these don't apply in the "real America" (remember, Manhattan is a strange island just off the coast of America), so I'll give you an example.

Taxis. Here's the scenario: I hail a taxi and get inside. The backseat may or may not be covered in powder from the CSI squad that last dusted for fingerprints. Let's say it's a good day, and I snag a "clean" one that has only used hypodermic needles and a small pool of blood in it. Then let's also stay optimistic and assume that the driver speaks something resembling English and isn't playing a Haitian radio station, some Bangladeshi disco eight-track, or an Islamic chant where I'm pretty sure I can make out the words "Death to Beck the infidel." So far, so good.

I tell the driver where I want to go, and he takes me there (with blatant disregard for both the speed limit and the laws of physics that say you cannot pass through another solid object even if it is making a right turn from the left lane), and I arrive at my destination.

For this service, there is a fee. I'm comfortable with that. After all, I knew the cost before I even got into the cab, since it's plastered right on the door. There's also a convenient meter in case I ever forget. Why should I be expected to give a tip on top of that fee? I was driven somewhere for a prearranged amount. What's the extra payment

THE FIVE STAGES OF ~~DYING~~

TIPPING!

Denial

"I'm not here, this isn't happening!"

I had no idea she'd order the lobster and a shrimp cocktail. Who did I take to dinner—Orca? The tip is more than my rent.

Anger

"Why Me?"

How dare you do this to me! I never should've taken you to such a nice place. I bet she didn't even bring her wallet!

Bargaining

"If I do this, you'll do that."

If I leave a big tip then maybe she'll be "generous" after dinner?

Depression

"I can't put my family through this."

We'll be back to this place some-day; I don't want "the Chef's special" marinade.

Acceptance

"This is going to happen."

I'm ready; I just don't want to struggle anymore. This tipping thing is bigger than I am...one man can't make a difference. I'd leave 18%, but I'm so bad at math, so I'll just leave 20%.

for? Why have we decided that cab drivers are one group of people who should receive a tip automatically, regardless of the quality of the ride? That sort of thing has got to stop; it's institutionalized tipping, and it's actually *bad* for service. Here's why.

LOOK HOW SMART I AM

When tipping becomes an expected part of the payment, service suffers. After all, why try harder when society has decided that you're getting a tip anyway, with the default setting at 15 percent? When you start *expecting* a tip, you stop *earning* a tip.

A.D.D. MOMENT My favorite line is "For your convenience, an 18 percent gratuity has been added to your check." My convenience? Is that really convenient for me? That's about as insincere as "Your call is very important to us."

The system is broken, and in my opinion, it's waiters and waitresses who broke it. Being served at a bar or restaurant is where most of us get held up for a tip. I hate tipping waiters and waitresses. I'm using the word *hate* here. I know, I know, "they're not paid the minimum wage, so they depend on their tips to get by." Boo-frickin'-hoo—you're breaking my heart. Guess what, genius—it's not as if the "no minimum wage" part was a surprise before you applied for and subsequently accepted the job waiting tables, now, was it? No one is *required* to work at Applebee's. You willingly trade less pay for *the hope* of getting tips and making more. Your eyes were wide open.

Don't like what being a waitress pays? Well, "Susie" who works at the diner near my office and writes "Thanx!" on the check and signs her name by dotting the "i" with

Glenn Beck's "Tips" for getting a Bigger Tip from Glenn Beck:

1. Refill my glass of Coke Zero. Then refill it again . . . and again . . . and again.
2. When refilling my glass of Coke Zero, say, "Aren't you TV's Glenn Beck?" I'll pretend to be irritated, but my ego is way out of control, and I'll eat this up.
3. Say something folksy that's not funny at all, such as: "Be sure to save room for dessert—the chef's Death by Chocolate is to die for!" I love fatally delicious desserts almost as much as I love thinking about dessert while I'm still eating my appetizer.
4. You guessed it—more Coke Zero.

a little smiley face (hypothetically speaking, of course), I guess you should have been an investment banker or a brain surgeon instead of a waitress. Those jobs pay considerably better than waiting tables, and you don't have to keep an eye out for who needs their waterglass refilled (as mine did for 26 minutes yesterday).

Am I just angry and bitter? Of course I'm angry and bitter! Not so much about tipping but because more of my life is behind than in front of me. But tipping is part of it too. Do you have any idea how profitable owning a successful restaurant is? Can you imagine the wealth of Mr. Bennigan, Denny, or the genius behind the shrimp lover's feast at Red Lobster? Being a restaurateur not only sounds awesome when being introduced at a party, but it's a goldmine as well (jalapeño poppers are delicious, and they sure ain't free). So why are we, the dining public, subsidizing the payroll of every restaurant in America by allowing their owners to pay their servers less than minimum wage just so we can make up the difference? It's like a pyramid scheme that we're all playing along with when it should be exposed as a scam on *60 Minutes!* I'd like to see Mike Wallace tackle that.

CAPITALISTS . . . AM I RIGHT?

It's no secret that we don't have the work ethic of our grandparents—they had the Great Depression to scare them straight, and we had . . . well, *M*A*S*H* got canceled. But I pray we still have some of their good old-fashioned common sense. It seems to me that workers in this country have lost sight of the greatest tip of all: not getting fired.

I know the Democrats are solving all of America's problems now that they're in control of Congress, but there's still such a thing as unemployment, right? I mean, a tip is supposed to make sure that people do the best job possible, but if they're not doing their best, why not just fire them and hire someone who will? That's a more effective lesson than giving 10 percent instead of 15 percent, don't you think? It should be, because that's the marketplace working, survival of the fittest. Capitalism rewards good workers and punishes the bad. It's a good system. Why muck it up with this tipping lunacy?

According to the website stainedapron.com, which is definitely *not* run by agonizingly bitter servers, here are some good tippers: Tom Brokaw, Bill Murray, Mark Chesnutt, Willie Nelson, Morgan Freeman. And here are some not so good tippers: Mark McGwire, Usher, Al Gore, Sharon Stone, O. J. Simpson, Jimmy Buffett. I guess Gore is paying too much in carbon offsets to give his breakfast waitress a little extra. Can't argue with him on that one.

A.D.D. MOMENT

It's also a reality that some people earn more money than others. Perhaps tipping helps massage some of our guilt over this simple truth. But just because I can afford to have someone serve me a meal doesn't mean that I need to feel guilty about it. The service industry is there to serve—there's no value judgment involved, it's merely part of the economic cycle. Don't feel guilty for not tipping the delivery guy; if he doesn't like his wage, he can quit his job and find one that pays better. Eventually, if enough delivery people quit, the company will have to pay its employees better in order to stay in business. If they do, great. If they don't, they go out of business. That's the way capitalism works, and from the pushcarts of the first street merchants to the multinational corporations of today, it's been effective.

The Glenn Beck Tip Calculator

CHECK	TIP
$0.00 -- $4.99	$0.00
$5.00 -- $9.99	$0.00
$10.00 -- $14.99	$0.00
$15.00 -- $19.99	$0.00
$20.00 and up	18% x $0.00

MY SOLUTION

Business owners, let's make a deal: You pay your staff, and I'll pay for the food. Cab companies pay the drivers; I'll pay the fare. Pizza places pay the delivery guy; I'll pay for the Meat Lover's Deluxe with Crazy Bread and CinnaSticks. If we all just started demanding that employers paid their own employees, then we'd be allowed simply to pay for the goods and services we want without any "good service" surcharge (that should be part of the purchase price anyway).

The next time you find yourself in a situation where some worker either literally or figuratively has a hand out looking for "More, please" like some Dickensian waif (look it up—it's an eloquent reference), stop and think: Did you even get what you paid for, let alone anything above and beyond that's worthy of a tip?

If the answer is yes and you feel like taking a big sip of the guilt-flavored Kool-Aid, then fine—tip. But don't be afraid to stray from the accepted 15 percent. Until the day business owners finally liberate us from the needless burden of tipping, take matters into your own hands and give what—if anything—feels right. That's what I'm doing!

> **A.D.D. MOMENT**
>
> **Have you** noticed how the "tip jar" has weaseled its way into *every* kind of profession imaginable? Just because there's a transaction happening in the vicinity does not mean a tip jar is required. Hear me, Dr. Ross? Your physicals are good, but they're not *that* good.

Okay, the tough love part of this chapter is over. Remember, outside of brash talk in books, ol' Glenn is a pretty good tipper, so to all you single moms raising your three kids on tips from IHOP, I support you (a lot more than that deadbeat husband of yours does). The reality is that I usually overtip, especially if I'm with my wife. She apparently waited tables in college and is kinda sensitive about the whole issue. So, if you don't mind, let's keep this little chapter just between us, okay?

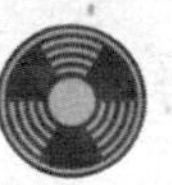

Chapter 14

Child Molesters: A Fiery Solution

IT WAS A MOMENT WITHOUT POLITICS. Despite the fact that Barack Obama was running for president and threatening to implement the exact opposite of every policy that conservatives believe would help the country, no one cared. Those who'd heard what happened were immediately transformed from Democrats and Republicans into mothers and fathers.

A website run by an admitted pedophile had posted pictures of Obama's children. Next to each child was a rating of their "cuteness."

A.D.D. MOMENT The site goes on to compare the struggle of the "girl lover" to the "emancipation of slaves" and the fight for "civil rights for minorities." I'm sure the most credible black presidential candidate in American history really appreciated that comparison.

Perhaps even more horrifying, though, was the section of the site called "Sugar and Spice." Designed in pink and blue pastels, it looked as if it could easily be the "My Little Pony" website. There was no doubt about the target audience: little girls.

"Sugar and Spice" featured an area called "Touching," which included this message to young girls, written in purple text:

> "You have to start being careful when you start kissing your special friend. While a quick kiss is almost always OK, if you start French kissing your special friend, some people might try to punish your friend. This is because they interpret the law in a way that suits only them."

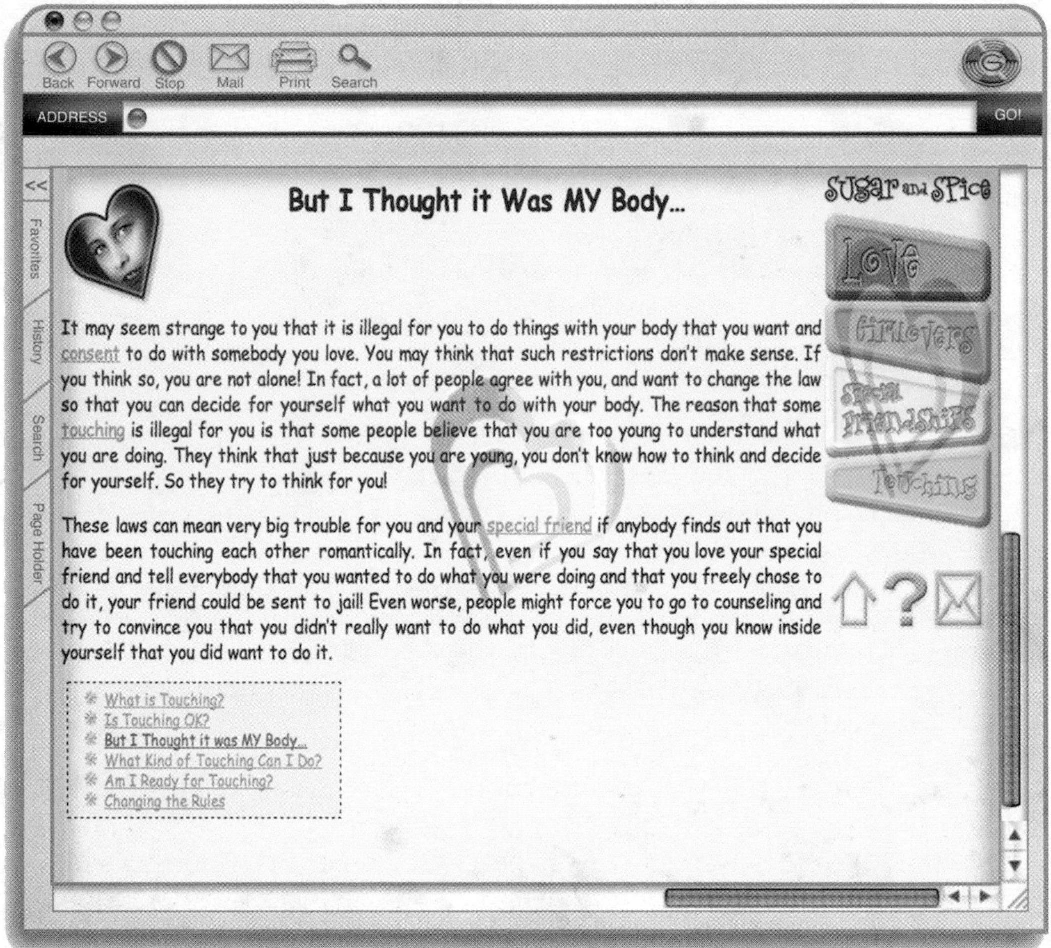

But I Thought it Was MY Body...

It may seem strange to you that it is illegal for you to do things with your body that you want and consent to do with somebody you love. You may think that such restrictions don't make sense. If you think so, you are not alone! In fact, a lot of people agree with you, and want to change the law so that you can decide for yourself what you want to do with your body. The reason that some touching is illegal for you is that some people believe that you are too young to understand what you are doing. They think that just because you are young, you don't know how to think and decide for yourself. So they try to think for you!

These laws can mean very big trouble for you and your special friend if anybody finds out that you have been touching each other romantically. In fact, even if you say that you love your special friend and tell everybody that you wanted to do what you were doing and that you freely chose to do it, your friend could be sent to jail! Even worse, people might force you to go to counseling and try to convince you that you didn't really want to do what you did, even though you know inside yourself that you did want to do it.

- What is Touching?
- Is Touching OK?
- But I Thought it was MY Body...
- What Kind of Touching Can I Do?
- Am I Ready for Touching?
- Changing the Rules

It went on to tell the girls not to worry because “there are no laws against hugging . . . snuggling with each other on the couch is also OK.”

Snuggling on the couch? Am I the only father who would have a very tough time not taking advantage of the Second Amendment if someone told my daughter that?

It gets worse. This predator realized that the final step of breaking down an innocent child's last line of defense is discrediting us, the parents. He wrote: “You may have learned about good touching and bad touching. Probably you have been told that touching in the private parts of your body is ‘bad touching.’ This is not always the case.”

That really puts partisan political differences into perspective, doesn't it?

When Obama's lawyers got wind of the sickening website, they sent the monster a letter. He mercifully removed the photos but remained indignant on several other requests. The "Sugar and Spice" and "Touching" sections of the website remain online.

It's natural for all of us to hope that this sort of thing is an isolated incident; the work of one deranged man who acts out his repulsive fantasies online. After all, the website was hosted in Panama, and the target was a very visible national figure. Something like that could never happen to *my kids* . . . right?

HITTING CLOSE TO HOME

Puyallup. Bellingham. Bellevue. Skagit County. Even my Mount Vernon. Those names might not mean anything to you, but they mean a lot to me. They are all areas I remember from my childhood, places my parents brought me to celebrate holidays, go to the fair, and go shopping.

They also were among the areas that popped up on the website of 45-year-old, unemployed, living with his parents, admitted pedophile Jack McClellan. What he did with his spare time (which he apparently had a lot of) was to visit different area events such as school plays, skating rinks, carnivals, and even Easter egg hunts, and write reviews about which ones provided the best access to "LGs." If you weren't in the middle of a chapter about child molesters, you'd probably never believe it, but "LGs" means "little girls" in the pedophile dictionary.

McClellan's website, the self-anointed "premier site of the girl-love revolution," states that its primary purpose is to "promote association, friendship; and legal, non-sexual, consensual touch (hugging, cuddling, etc) between men and prepubescent girls."

Sure it is. I wonder, given how "legal" the whole thing is, why McClellan posted the jail time and fines for each offense that one might run into as a (perfectly legal) girl lover. For example, there's "communication with minor for immoral purposes" (0–1 year in prison, $0–$5,000 fine); "luring" (0–5 years, $0–$10,000); "child molestation in the first degree" (0–life, $0–$50,000); and, of course, everyone's favorite, "rape of a child in the first degree" (0–life, $0–$50,000).

McClellan's website reads like a pedophilia nightlife guide, highlighting the best places and times to stalk young girls.

Public libraries: "You can get quite close to LGs there (they've sat next to me at Internet terminals)."

Elementary schools: "I've been surprised at how close you can get to some and how long you can loiter there without being noticed. . . . If the kids aren't out on the playground, the next recess will probably be in less than 2 hours!"

Nude beaches: "An email correspondent said that there are sometimes nude children here."

Halloween: "This is the one day of the year when the LGs might come to your place."

Tutoring programs: "I've thought about trying to get into a program like this (including volunteering for Girl Scouts), but I believe they are on high alert for pedophiles. . . . I'd probably be out of there the first time I tried to hug a LG."

Big Brothers/Big Sisters: "An email correspondent recommended 'mentoring' programs (I think Big Brothers/Sisters have them) where you get to pick up the child and take them on outings on a one-on-one basis, but he also said that they usually pair the adult with a child of the same sex."

The site even featured a section titled "International cities where unsupervised girls can be found on the streets." Included

This book was designed to inject comedy into serious topics, but I'm having a little bit of trouble with that on this particular subject. I guess the best thing we can do for now is laugh at the pedophiles themselves.

A.D.D. MOMENT

Therefore, I present to you a word-for-word review of the television series *Full House* that was posted on the website of Seattle pedophile Jack McClellan. May God have mercy on our collective souls.

Full House: This is arguably one the most subversive series produced by broadcast television because there were originally only 3 men and 3 prepubescent girls in the house. That situation began to deteriorate when Rebecca (Lori Loughlin) was introduced as Jesse's (John Stamos) love interest (Tanner vs. Gibbler, Oct '88), and completely ended when she moved in as his wife (Fuller House, Feb '91). The trend toward conformist nuclear-family normalcy continued when she gave birth to twin boys (Happy Birthday, Babies, Nov '91)—at which time the p****-whipping of Stamos' character was complete, and he had become almost unwatchable. I don't watch the episodes later than May '93 because Jodie is beyond my age of attraction, and I never thought the Olsen twins were that hot. Airs most days on ABC Family and Nick.

was this profile of Buenos Aires: "I saw a number of panhandling LGs. . . . I talked with and cuddled several without any problems from the cops."

Like a stereotypically bad movie, the entry closed with a picture of one of the young girls, holding the pudding and coins that the pedophile had given her.

Have we talked about the Second Amendment yet?

Whether it's the location of area Build-A-Bear Workshops or reacting to a missing 10-year-old girl by writing "she's cuter than she appears in the FBI poster," there's an incredible amount of shocking material on McClellan's site. But what may be almost as disturbing is what the police said when the story of this website came out: They knew all about it but couldn't do anything.

As illogical as that may sound, the reason was that there was no real proof of any illegal activity. Despite everyone's deep suspicion that McClellan would commit a crime and that the site he ran almost definitely inspired others to commit crimes, they

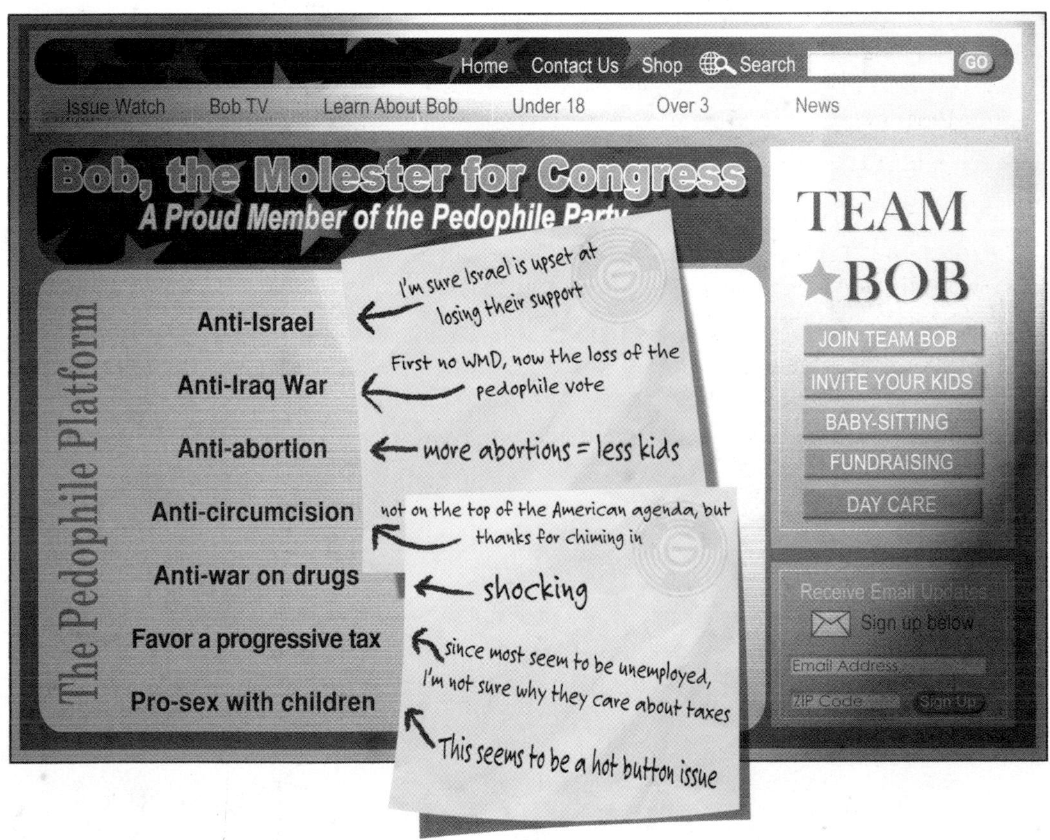

> **Many of** these pedophiles act like attorneys and try to exploit every legal loophole they can find. For example, did you know that it's perfectly legal to look at nude pictures of children online? In order for something to be officially classified as child porn it must specifically feature the child "lasciviously exhibiting their genitals or pubic area" as conveniently pointed out on Jack McClellan's website. As long as the dirtbag doesn't cross that line, everything is just fine.
>
> A.D.D. MOMENT

couldn't prove it. This isn't, after all, a *Minority Report* type of world where you can arrest people based on future acts.

Therefore, Jack McClellan, an admitted pedophile, was able to talk publicly about his "erotic arousal" by girls ages 4 to 11 without fear of reprisal, while the parents who lived in my hometown felt as if their families were literally being held hostage. After a media firestorm, the website's hosting company finally shut it down. Yet less than three months later, McClellan was back online with a similar site, this time based in Los Angeles.

Some of you may be wondering why we can't just arrest him if he's admitted on camera that he's a pedophile. That's because *pedophile* in his mind just means that he *wants* to touch little girls sexually, not that he actually *has*. Riiiiight. I guess he's claiming to be what I would call a letter-of-law pedophile. (Some might say that he just doesn't want to admit on a website to anything patently illegal.)

We all respect and honor our First Amendment, but handcuffing law enforcement to the point that it is forced to ignore an obvious danger to our kids doesn't make sense at all. There has to be a better way, a middle ground where the Jack McClellans of the world can be stopped without free speech coming under attack.

But how can we even talk about dealing with dirtbags like Jack McClellan, who at least claim to be tightroping on the right side of the law, when we don't even know how to deal with the pedophiles who *aren't* operating in the gray area?

THE MOST PREVENTABLE DEATH IN U.S. HISTORY

Let's play a little game called "Name That Child Molester." I'll give you the facts, you guess his name:

- In 1978, during one of his many burglaries, he was accused of putting his hand over a girl's mouth and then kissing her. He received 10 years in prison but was out by 1980.

- In 1991, he approached a five-year-old girl, who invited him to jump on her trampoline in her backyard. He then asked her to play hide and seek, exposed himself to her, and sat the girl on his lap (according to his own confession). When her mom came out and yelled for her, he ran away. After his confession, he received the maximum sentence for attempted molestation: five whole years. He was out on parole after just two.
- He had been arrested more than 20 other times on charges such as larceny, burglary, drug possession, and DUI—and had violated his parole frequently.

Did you guess who it is?

John Evander Couey—and unbelievably, everything listed above happened *before* you met him as the killer of Jessica Lunsford.

> **A.D.D. MOMENT**
>
> **John Couey** wrote in court documents surrounding his 1991 conviction for attempted molestation, "I know what I done was wrong and I know I will have to pay for it but I will be doing it with Jesus in my life and I will let the light shine in me." I'm not a biblical scholar, but I am a thinker—so here's my religious lesson of the day: Contrary to some people's misconception, nowhere in the Bible does Jesus advocate child molestation. I don't care what that little voice in your head tells you. I promise—it's not in there.

In Couey's most famous act, he took Jessica out of her bedroom and brought her to his trailer in the middle of the night. Then he raped her multiple times, made her stay in the closet so that no one in the trailer would know she was there, and went to work at Billy's Truck Lot. She stayed silently in the closet for the better part of three days.

When police and media attention about Jessica's disappearance began to pick up, Couey forced her into plastic bags and buried her alive in a shallow grave about 150 yards from her home.

After Couey led investigators to her burial site, they found that her body was well preserved, except for the two fingers she had managed to poke through the plastic bags as she struggled for a breath of air. She died holding her favorite stuffed animal, a purple dolphin.

John Couey wasn't alone. The nearest big city to him was Tampa, Florida (the area I used to live in), and we've put together a map (see page 180) showing all the sex offenders in just this one city, which always seemed to me to be relatively safe.

Infuriated yet? Just wait. It gets worse.

In his previous molestation arrest, Couey told police that "this was not the first child he had ever touched, however, this is the first time he was caught." He also admitted to previously molesting his ex-wife's daughter. The ex had said she wouldn't report the crime as long as they divorced and he left the house.

Sex Offenders Living in the Tampa Area

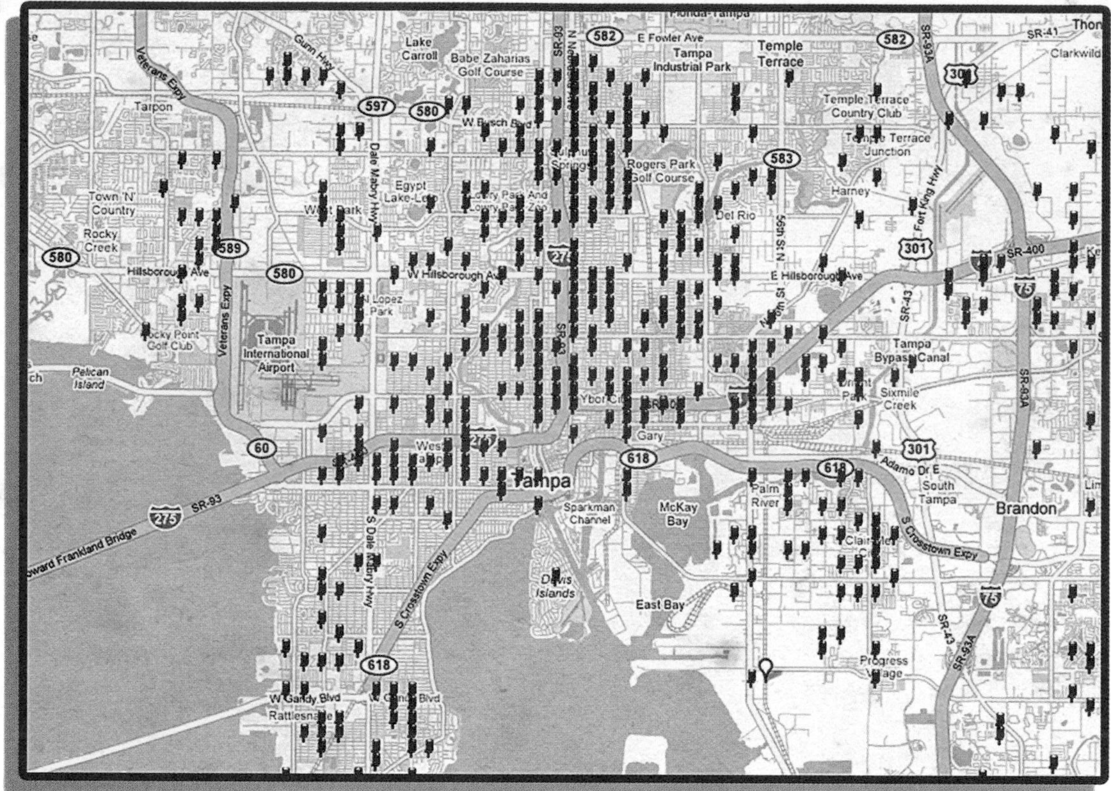

Source: mapsexoffenders.com

Couey's half-sister, in whose trailer the Lunsford attack occurred, told authorities that he'd exposed himself and inappropriately touched two of her daughters. Yet, inexplicably, she not only still allowed Couey to move in, she actually helped him escape. When she heard he was wanted by police, she gave him $200 and had one of her daughters buy him a bus ticket out of town.

But even after all of those missed opportunities to put Couey away for good, authorities still had one last chance to save Jessica. Just four months earlier, state law enforcement had sent a letter to the Citrus County sheriff's department saying that Couey had not responded to a letter to verify his address as he was required to do as a sex offender.

Had that letter been followed up on, Couey could have been charged with a felony and put away long enough to have prevented the Lunsford murder—at least that night. Unfortunately, no one in the sheriff's office could remember ever seeing the letter, which stated that Couey was just one of 58 sex offenders in Citrus County alone who hadn't reported their addresses as required. It also said: "Address verifications on these subjects may be more than 1 year overdue." That is how poorly we are keeping track of many convicted sex offenders.

Finally, in the ultimate failure of the system, a failure that would be ironic if it weren't so tragic, the letter requesting John Couey's address verification . . . was sent to the wrong address.

It's not as if the system didn't do anything to punish Couey for his various extracurricular activities. His driver's license had been suspended for 99 years. Sure, he was out of prison . . . but at least he couldn't drive! I mean, we all know that *driving* is the key to child molestation.

A.D.D. MOMENT

"DON'T OVERREACT"

I'm not trying to say that law enforcement in general doesn't do its job when it comes to stopping pedophiles—after all, they can only work with the laws and resources we give them. The real problem is that this country simply doesn't take child molestation seriously. Sure, we *say* that we do, but our actions tell a vastly different story.

There is actually a contingent of people who simply believe that we're *too tough* on child molesters. The *Christian Science Monitor* wrote that while "so many state and local governments have been tightening laws relating to child molestation," they "need to watch that they don't overreact." As evidence, it pointed to a policy in Miami Beach that "banned convicted child molesters from moving to within 2,500 ft. of schools, school bus stops, day-care centers, parks, and playgrounds. It effectively bans sexual molesters from moving to the city." Oh, the humanity! What would a city do without sexual molesters!

I never thought I would have yet *another* reason to move to Miami Beach, but there it is. If you think these laws are unfair, there's at least one sure way to avoid them: Don't molest children.

THREE

Three years. That's how long the average convicted child molester spends in prison. They receive an average of a seven-year sentence, but only three of those years are actually spent in jail. Does that sound like a society that's serious about protecting its children?

If that doesn't convince you that we're soft on pedophiles, consider this:

- About one in five child molesters in prison has previously been arrested for a sex crime against a child.
- Child molesters and statutory rapists had between a 23 and 81 percent chance of being rearrested for any crime within the next three years, depending on how many times they had previously been arrested.
- About half of child molesters who are released have more than three years left on their sentences.
- About 1 in 20 child molesters released from prison was rearrested for another sex crime within just *three years.*

Some see that last statistic as a positive because the rate of recidivism for child molesters is lower than that of perpetrators of many other crimes over the short term. But there are two factors that those people ignore.

First, you have to remember that pedophiles generally believe there is nothing wrong with having sex with children. That makes them pretty open about their opinions (at least, until jail is on the line). Remember those websites I quoted from earlier? They're shocking, but part of the reason they're shocking is because of how honest they are. Pedophiles don't see child molestation as a disease or a criminal act; they see it as a sexual preference.

Many of these people are able to spend a few years avoiding trouble, but their urges continue to push and push them until, one day, weakness and opportunity collide. Remember, it took John Couey 14 years after his 1991 molestation arrest before he killed Jessica Lunsford. The study that champions of molester reform like to cite is irrelevant, because it only looks at the first three years after release from prison. That might be fine for crimes such as burglary or drug dealing, but it's not a fair measurement of pedophilia recidivism.

The second unique factor is that, unlike a crime such as breaking and entering, you can't always tell when a child has been molested. In reality, everything has to go just right for one of these freaks to get caught. It's a crime that happens behind closed doors, and the victims are generally encouraged not to disobey adults; depending on the level and timing of the offense, there may be very little or no physical evidence; and the people like John Couey who do it pull out all the stops to make sure they aren't reported by demeaning, intimidating, and threatening their victims. The truth is that many child molestations don't even show up on the stat sheet. How many thousands of victims have we missed?

The BBC illustrated how difficult it is to catch rapists by reporting these dismal estimates for sections of the U.K.:

- About 80 percent of rapes are never reported.
- One-third of those reported are not recorded by police.
- Only one-fifth of those recorded ever reach trial.
- Only half of those tried result in conviction.

If you do the math, the result is that only 1.3 out of every 100 rapes result in a conviction. What kind of message does that send to the victims? The truth is that sex crimes are very hard to detect and even harder to prove, and it only gets worse in the many instances where children are attacked by trusted family members or friends.

This chapter is really depressing me.

MEGAN'S LAW

Our current solutions to these problems are quite simply a joke. We know that three years in prison is woefully inadequate, but defenders of the way we do business today will point to such things as Megan's Law (named after child rape and murder victim Megan Kanka) to show that we've made progress.

Unfortunately, despite the best of intentions, Megan's Law makes a mockery of Megan's memory.

Is it better than nothing? I guess, but the main function of Megan's Law is to require sexual offenders to register where they are living so that people in those neighborhoods are aware that there's a sexual predator in their midst. Unfortunately, that means we're ignoring the most basic of facts: If these people are so dangerous that we agree everyone should know where they live, then why did we let them out of prison in the first place? We wouldn't need a national registry if they all lived at the same address.

Even if you like Megan's Law, you certainly can't be happy with the gigantic holes in it. Sometimes offenses such as possession of child pornography, using the Internet to lure kids, and conviction in another country of a sex crime won't even land you on the list. Plus, the process of how offenders register varies from state to state, with

It's Megan's Law
"Who's On First!"
This person is a dangerous child molester.
So he's in prison?
No he's on this website.
What does the website tell us?
That he's a dangerous child molester.
So why is he not in prison?
Because he's not that dangerous.
But I thought he was a child molester.
He is.
So how is he not that dangerous?
Because he served about a third of his prison sentence.
Oh, so he's cured?
Nope.
Is he a third cured?
We can't say that. That's why he's on this website.
So he's "website" dangerous, just not "prison" dangerous?
Exactly.
This is a government plan, isn't it?
Exactly.

many locations actually depending on the child predators to register themselves. We already depended on them not to molest children, and we saw how well that worked out.

A.D.D. MOMENT We should give Chris Hansen an entire channel to do non-stop live versions of *Dateline: To Catch a Predator.* If you figure 12 pedophiles busted per hour, that's more than 101,000 child molesters a year (figuring two weeks' vacation, which seems fair given the importance of the job). Plus, we all get some high-quality television. Everyone wins!

MY SOLUTION

Child molestation is a difficult crime to detect, and it lingers inside the demented mind of the attacker for decades. That's why we must show absolutely no tolerance for the ones we do catch. If we are ever going to take this crime seriously, there must be a one-strike-and-you're-out policy. If you molest a child, you go to prison until you die, period. There's no excuse, and, more important, there's no cure.

That doesn't mean that we put an 18-year-old high school student in jail for life after a prom-night escapade with his 17-year-old girlfriend. There is a line somewhere between the prom king and John Couey that we need to find, but once we do, the price of crossing it is a lifetime supply of freedom.

Aside from the legal punishments, we also have to make sure that everyone really understands what we're facing. The Internet doesn't just provide a resource for perverts to contact our children; it also provides a haven for them to convince themselves that they're not freaks. When they read the sites I quoted from earlier (along with the hundreds of others that haven't been publicized), they begin to believe that they're not alone, that their thoughts are somehow normal. When there is less shame, there is more action.

HOW TO DEAL WITH A
CHILD MOLESTER
ACCORDING TO STU...

Find guilty child molester.

Place inside incinerator.

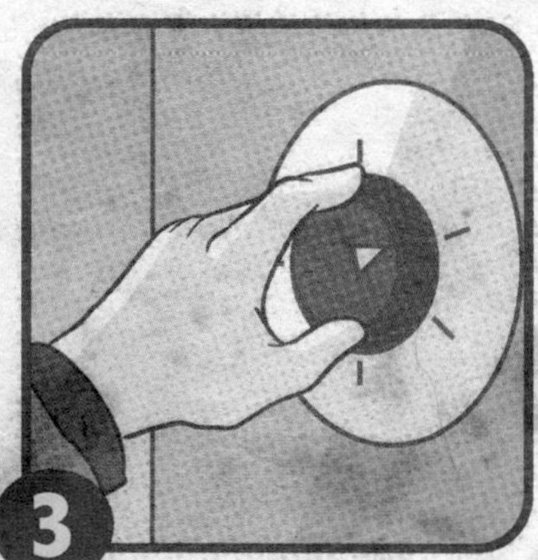

Reduce possibility of their future molestation to zero.

Throw a pizza party!

There is one way we can definitely lower the number of children who have been molested. Just change the definition of what is underage! Perhaps we should adopt the plan of the Philippines and lower our age of consent to 12! Sounds ridiculous, but that is the direction groups like the North American Man/Boy Love Association (NAMBLA) want to go in, and you shouldn't doubt that they'll slowly but surely achieve it. Look back to the 1950s, and you'll see that everything that was thought of as wrong or immoral back then—from divorce to premarital sex, cohabitation, and pornography—is now accepted and even embraced today. I'm so glad we have progressives to give us such progress.

A.D.D. MOMENT

The good news is that America is generally on the right road, and we (as usual) are leading the world in solving the problem. While we're complaining that Megan's Law doesn't do enough, Great Britain decided that its equivalent version of the law was just too mean to child sex offenders because it could lead to vigilantism. In case you're keeping score, that's not alerting parents of the location of a sex offender on the off chance that doing so might inspire an otherwise law-abiding citizen to attack *the sex offender*. Sounds reasonable.

Even something seemingly as unifying as the fight against child pornography is sorely lacking backbone around the world. In 2006, the Commission on Security and Cooperation in Europe passed a resolution called Combating Trafficking and the Exploitation of Children in Pornography. Sponsored by the United States, it virtually begged nations around the world to pass comprehensive laws fighting child porn.

As of summer 2007, only five countries out of the 186 the commission measured had acceptable laws in place dealing with child porn, and 95 countries unbelievably lacked *any* child porn laws at all. Of the countries that addressed it, 43 did not criminalize possession of child porn, and 55 countries lacked any legal definition whatsoever. It's hard to get convictions without legally defining what the crime is.

The United States is different. After John Couey brutally murdered Jessica Lunsford, varying versions of Jessica's Law were passed around the country requiring punishments as high as a 25-year prison sentence and a lifetime in a monitoring bracelet. Going even further, Louisiana, Oklahoma, South Carolina, Georgia, Montana, and Texas have allowed for the use of the death penalty in child-rape cases even if there is no charge of murder.

It's unclear what the courts will do with these death-penalty laws for child rape. The Louisiana Supreme Court recently upheld the execution of a 42-year-old man for the rape of his companion's eight-year-old daughter. However, in 1977, the U.S. Supreme Court struck down the death penalty for a rapist claiming the punishment didn't fit the crime. Experts say the Supreme Court may rule on the Louisiana case in 2008.

A.D.D. MOMENT

Ankle bracelets, employment checks, national online databases (and maybe having the words "I molest children" painted in red paint on molesters' foreheads) are all moves in the right direction. But none of these things can ever fully protect your child. There are still thousands of convicted molesters out there who will be legally grandfathered out of many of these punishments and thousands more who either haven't yet begun terrorizing children or haven't yet been caught.

That's why we must be vigilant with our children. Here's something that today's supersensitive parent isn't supposed to tell you: Feel free to read your kids' email. Know every single website they go to. Keep track of every letter they type on that keyboard you bought in that home that you own. Don't worry about your child's privacy—they'll have about six decades to have a private life, but only if you keep them safe now.

Let your kids know they can tell you about incidents that make them feel uncomfortable, no matter how uncomfortable it is for you. As parents, we're the last line of defense. It's our responsibility not only to guard the castle walls but also to make sure we build those walls as high and thick as possible for those times we can't be there.

After all, Chris Hansen can do only so much.

Chapter 15

The UN: Truth, Justice, and the Anti-American Way

I HAVE A POSTER HANGING in my office that has an iconic image of the UN building along with the slogan "The United Nations: A Rampart of Peace." Although I certainly admire the sense of humor, the only thing the UN is a rampart of these days is incompetence, bureaucracy, and corruption.

Like Rosie O'Donnell stepping on a scale, the UN's problems are too large even to register with most people anymore. We've come to almost *expect* the scams and the scandals, the backroom deals, and the unabashedly anti-American agenda.

But it doesn't have to be that way. The UN problem *can* be fixed, and I'll show you how.

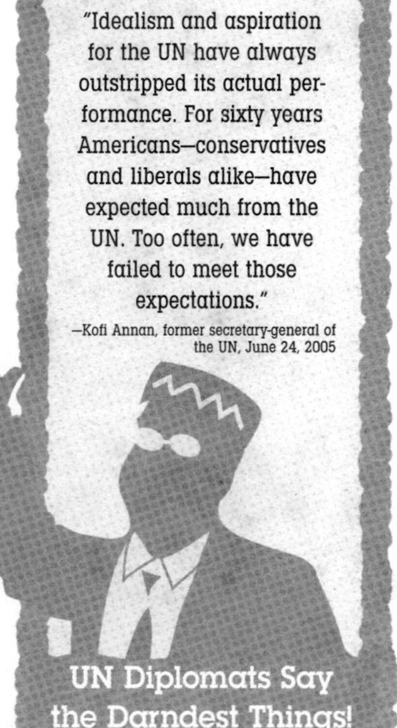

"Idealism and aspiration for the UN have always outstripped its actual performance. For sixty years Americans—conservatives and liberals alike—have expected much from the UN. Too often, we have failed to meet those expectations."
—Kofi Annan, former secretary-general of the UN, June 24, 2005
UN Diplomats Say the Darndest Things!

THE MOST UNPRODUCTIVE HOUR OF MY LIFE

My UN corruption journey started with a task that no real American should ever have to endure: paying $13 directly into the pockets of the malignant beast and taking a tour of their massively ugly Manhattan headquarters.

Charging people money to tour this hell hole should be an international war crime itself. When it came time to pay, my arms and hands were literally fighting with my mind. How could I possibly fork over cash to those morons? Would I actually be contributing to their agenda? Would my $13 somehow get funneled through the system and end up supporting some terror attack?

Probably—but I had a book to write, so on with the tour (which, in typical UN fashion, started 15 minutes late).

ONE SWEET GIG

After touring the UN, you can't help but feel a sense of loftiness in the air. UN employees have an arrogance about them, almost as if they think everything they touch turns to gold. (Which is really kind of ironic, since everything they touch actually turns to more of a bright orange color. And it flickers. Sometimes it even glows.)

Have some time to kill? Just punch "UN fails to" into Google, and you'll have hours of material to choose from.

A.D.D. MOMENT

Part of that lofty, I'm-better-than-you attitude comes from the fact that many people at the UN are diplomats who go around being called "Excellency" and "Ambassador" all day. After "work"—and I use that term loosely—these diplomats are whisked away by their drivers and brought to their posh Manhattan townhomes, which are often provided by their (in many cases impoverished) home countries.

"There are times when other diplomats get up and read their anti-American statements and then they come rushing up to the United States delegation and say, 'You know, I just had to read that,' and they slap you on the back, give you a handshake, and say, 'When are we going to lunch?'"

—Anonymous member of U.S. delegation, from *The U.N. Exposed*

UN Diplomats Say the Darndest Things!

Being a UN delegate has another great perk: diplomatic immunity. Since the UN is not technically in the United States, diplomats can't be taxed or charged under normal U.S. laws for, well, just about anything. In fact, despite their obvious love of big government, many UN employees are living the tax-free (including property tax) dream. It's no wonder these fat cats aren't exactly leading the charge for reform.

But it's not *all* champagne and caviar. These people are here to do important things. Like racking up parking tickets, for example. Diplomats from UN member nations owe about $18 million in unpaid parking tickets to New York City.

Leading the way are those crazy pranksters from Egypt ($1.9 million in fines) and Kuwait ($1.3 million). I almost expect that kind of behavior from Egypt—Cairo is so overcrowded that it makes Manhattan look like Wyoming—so it makes sense if they don't pay attention to where they park. But I expect more out of the Kuwaitis. We spent hundreds of millions of dollars and sacrificed the blood of our own soldiers to stop a madman from taking over your country; the least you could do is feed our meters.

When New York mayor Michael Bloomberg announced a plan to recoup the parking fines, Ban Ki-moon said he

Glenn's UN Tour Highlights
UN Security Council
Shockingly, they weren't working on anything when I stopped by.
This painting, a gift from France, symbolizes that no one country should feel dominated by any other. That made me throw up, which is exactly what this painting looks like.
This ivory sculpture, a gift from China, was carved from the tusks of eight elephants. I know what you're thinking, but don't worry: the elephants were hurt (quite a bit) in the process.
The ceiling was left open as a symbol of "the world's work never being completely done." I think the unfinished ceiling is a better symbol of a typical UN project.
EVERYONE HAS THE RIGHT TO REST AND LEISURE, INCLUDING REASONABLE LIMITATION OF WORKING HOURS AND PERIODIC HOLIDAYS WITH PAY.
This was our guide's favorite "human right" (#24). I think it's likely the UN's favorite as well.
"His Excellency."
I guess it's appropriate to have Mr. "Oil for Food" immortalized. In oil.
VANUATU

supported it. But what's lost in the discussion about a few million dollars in parking tickets is the fact that the United States contributed $423 million to the UN's general budget last year alone. That's 22 percent of its entire budget—the most of any country, and that's not even counting U.S. contributions to UN peacekeeping missions, which amounted to more than $440 million dollars in 2005.

IT'S THE THOUGHT THAT COUNTS

After World War II, in which more than 62 million people died, the winning countries got together and said, "Yeah, so I was thinking that after about five more world wars, there won't be any humans left on the planet. Whaddya say we go ahead and address that little issue now?"

With the League of Nations already dismantled, the Allied forces decided that the best thing to do was, in essence, form another League of Nations. So, in 1945, the United Nations—with 51 founding member countries—was born.

Although we could never have known back then just how bad things would turn out, the UN's list of goals probably should have sounded some alarm bells. I'm all for having lofty goals, but this list sounds as if it was put together by a bunch of delusional socialists. Wait a second—

In a nutshell, the UN's world-tastic agenda is to end all wars, safeguard human rights, balance global interdependence, blah blah blah. It's really the perfect scam. You beg for money to fight problems that are impossible to solve, and if anyone speaks up and tries to stop the funding, they look like blackhearted, evil monsters. "See? You hate poor people. I bet you *want* poverty!"

No, I'm not pro-poverty, I just happen to be a realist. Most of these problems aren't going to be "solved" under

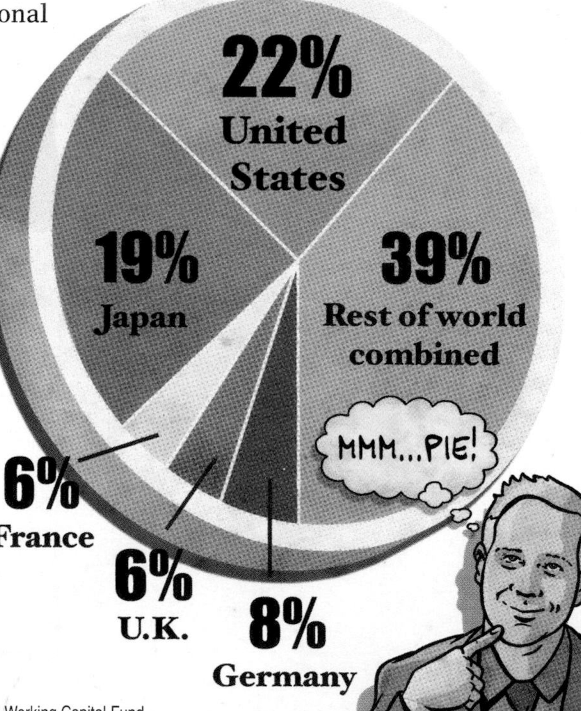

*Advance Contributions to 2006-2007 UN Working Capital Fund

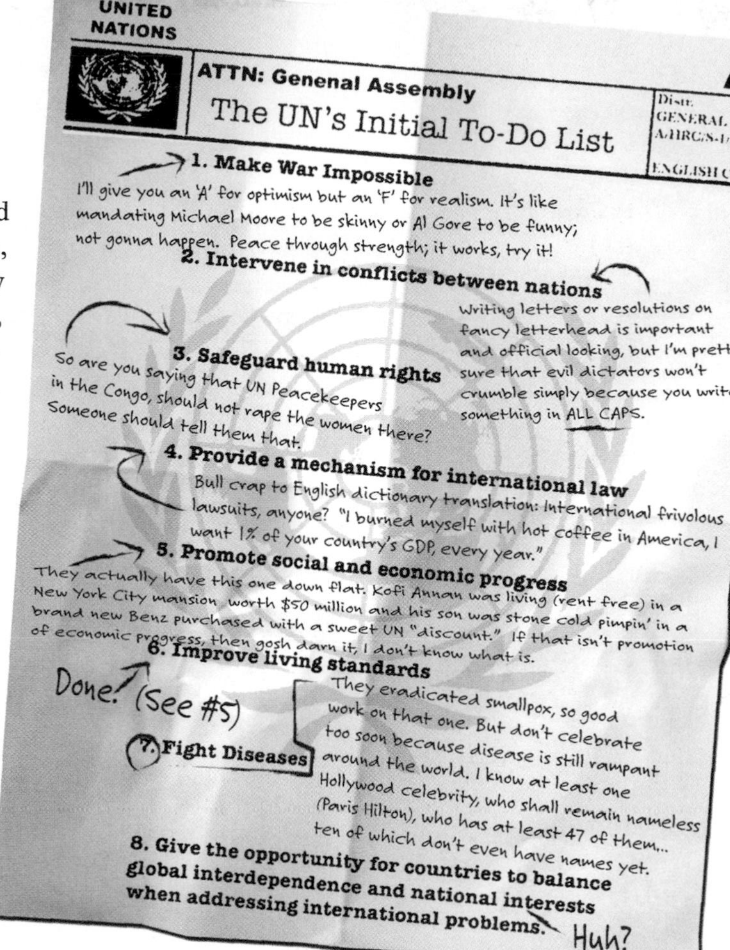

UNITED NATIONS

ATTN: Genenal Assembly

A

The UN's Initial To-Do List

Distr.: GENERAL A/HRC/S-1/NGO

ENGLISH ONLY

1. Make War Impossible

I'll give you an 'A' for optimism but an 'F' for realism. It's like mandating Michael Moore to be skinny or Al Gore to be funny; not gonna happen. Peace through strength; it works, try it!

2. Intervene in conflicts between nations

Writing letters or resolutions on fancy letterhead is important and official looking, but I'm pretty sure that evil dictators won't crumble simply because you write something in ALL CAPS.

3. Safeguard human rights

So are you saying that UN Peacekeepers in the Congo, should not rape the women there? Someone should tell them that.

4. Provide a mechanism for international law

Bull crap to English dictionary translation: International frivolous lawsuits, anyone? "I burned myself with hot coffee in America, I want 1% of your country's GDP, every year."

5. Promote social and economic progress

They actually have this one down flat. Kofi Annan was living (rent free) in a New York City mansion worth $50 million and his son was stone cold pimpin' in a brand new Benz purchased with a sweet UN "discount." If that isn't promotion of economic progress, then gosh darn it, I don't know what is.

6. Improve living standards

Done! (See #5)

7. Fight Diseases

They eradicated smallpox, so good work on that one. But don't celebrate too soon because disease is still rampant around the world. I know at least one Hollywood celebrity, who shall remain nameless (Paris Hilton), who has at least 47 of them... ten of which don't even have names yet.

8. Give the opportunity for countries to balance global interdependence and national interests when addressing international problems.

Huh?

the best of circumstances, and with the UN leading the charge, we should just be happy if they don't get much worse. After all, we're talking about an organization that's made up of 6 main bodies, 13 subsidiary bodies, 14 programs and funds, 5 research and training institutes, 8 functional commissions, 15 specialized agencies, 17 departments and agencies (under the secretariat), 5 regional commissions, 4 "related organizations," and 9 "other" entities and bodies.

Confused yet? Well, don't worry, because the UN has made things easy for you with acronyms! For example, if the United Nations Office of the High Representative for the Least Developed Countries, Landlocked Developing Countries and Small Island Developing States is too hard for you to remember, try UN-OHRLLS! There's also UNICEF, UNCTAD, WHO, UNESCO, DPI, DM, ECA ECE, UNITAR, UNOPS, INSTRAW, DSS, UNOG. Got it? You should be ROTFLOL at this point. Or maybe just crying.

YOU'RE (NOT) FIRED!

Under Jack Welch, General Electric was famous for firing the bottom-performing 10 percent of its employees each year. That policy helped ensure that GE retained only "the best of the best," and seeing that GE's market value increased by $400 billion during his tenure, it seemed to work out pretty well. So when an institution with as many problems as the UN fires only 40 employees (out of 23,000) during the first eight years of Kofi Annan's tenure, you know something is wrong.

MAKING THE UN WORK FOR YOU.

The Situation: You're a humanitarian worker for Latvia's government.

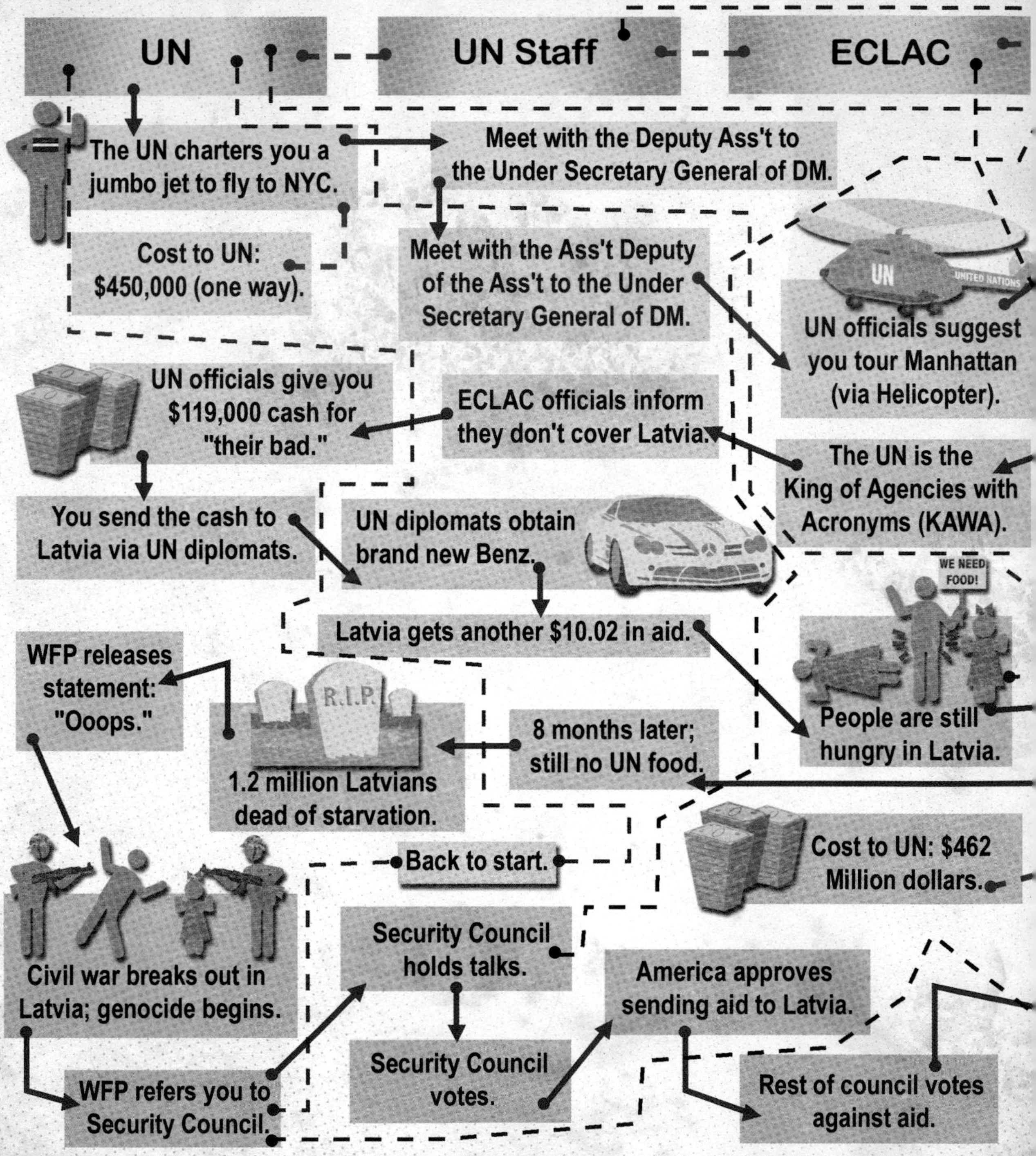

UN

UN Staff

ECLAC

The UN charters you a jumbo jet to fly to NYC.

Meet with the Deputy Ass't to the Under Secretary General of DM.

Cost to UN: $450,000 (one way).

Meet with the Ass't Deputy of the Ass't to the Under Secretary General of DM.

UN officials suggest you tour Manhattan (via Helicopter).

UN officials give you $119,000 cash for "their bad."

ECLAC officials inform they don't cover Latvia.

The UN is the King of Agencies with Acronyms (KAWA).

You send the cash to Latvia via UN diplomats.

UN diplomats obtain brand new Benz.

Latvia gets another $10.02 in aid.

People are still hungry in Latvia.

WFP releases statement: "Ooops."

1.2 million Latvians dead of starvation.

8 months later; still no UN food.

Cost to UN: $462 Million dollars.

Back to start.

Civil war breaks out in Latvia; genocide begins.

Security Council holds talks.

America approves sending aid to Latvia.

Security Council votes.

WFP refers you to Security Council.

Rest of council votes against aid.

People are starving in your country and you appeal to the UN for help.

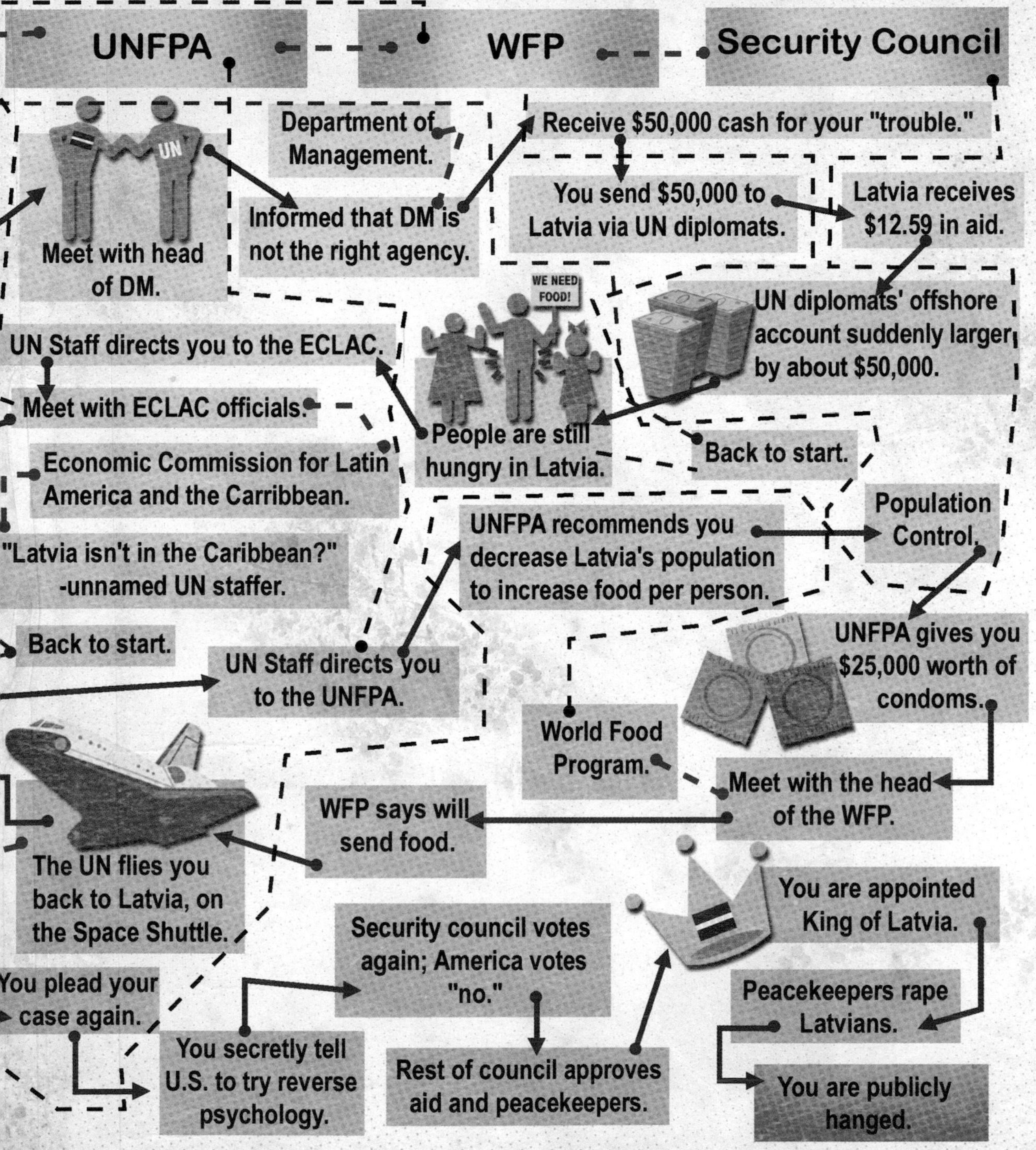

If we applied the same standards to staffers at the UN that were used to chase Paul Wolfowitz out of the World Bank, then the UN headquarters would be the emptiest office building in all of Manhattan.

A.D.D. MOMENT

The UN makes firing a tenured schoolteacher look like Brad Pitt trying to pick up drunk women. A job at the UN is a job for life!

Normal human beings would probably be punished, perhaps even fired (gasp!), if they bought a personal Mercedes in the name of the secretary-general just to get a big discount and free shipping. But if you're Kojo Annan (Kofi's son), the sentence for doing just that is your dad telling the press, "Kojo disappointed me."

Well, that'll teach him a lesson.

KOJO'S CONNECTIONS

A Swiss-based company named Cotecna Inspection Services SA held a $10 million contract with the UN from 1998 to 2003 to monitor goods arriving in Iraq under the infamous (more on that later) Oil for Food program. In a *completely unrelated* event, Cotecna also hired Kojo Annan at the oh-so-experienced age of 22.

Kojo stopped working for Cotecna in 1998 (the same year it landed the Oil for Food contract), but he continued receiving payments (upward of $400,000) from Cotecna until 2004. Now, I'm certainly not saying that Kojo Annan used his influence to land his company a huge UN contract, then took hundreds of thousands in kickbacks, but I'm not *not* saying it either.

Cotecna's website says it's a "family-run business"—they obviously mean that in more ways than one.

A.D.D. MOMENT

THE $100 BILLION SCANDAL

Under the Oil for Food program, Iraq sold $64.2 billion of oil to 248 companies, and in turn, 3,614 companies sold $34.5 billion of humanitarian goods back to Iraq. Sounds fair, right? Iraq had lots of oil but was pretty hungry, and the rest of the world was fat and lazy but a little short on black gold.

Unfortunately, the UN can screw up even the most straightforward programs. Under its "leadership," the Iraqis pocketed an extra $228 million in illegal income between 2000 and 2002 alone by adding 10- to 30-cent surcharges to each barrel of oil they were selling. That was enough to buy Saddam a few more statues of himself or some really nice drapes for their torture rooms.

Billbored FOR WEEK ENDING JUNE 29, 2007

The UN's Greatest Hits

Compiled by world dictators.

THIS WEEK	WKS. ON CHART	Hit	Category
1	2	Kim Jong Il ***No.1***	Stealing UN Cash
2	*	Genocide	Mega-death
3	*	Child Soldiers	Child Abuse
4	**	Peacekeeper Rape	Rape
5	250	Oil for Food	Stealing UN Cash
6	250	Kojo Annan	Abuse of power

*Since UN inception.
**Since invention of rape.

The surcharges happened because the UN allowed Iraq to actually choose which countries to sell its oil to. Saddam Hussein may have been a monstrous dictator, but he wasn't stupid. Iraq sold oil to the countries it felt were most sympathetic to its cause. I'm sure it's just a coincidence, but many of those countries also happened to be permanent members of the UN Security Council. Saddam's idea, of course, was to curry favor and support from UN members with the hope of getting the economic sanctions that had been imposed on him overturned.

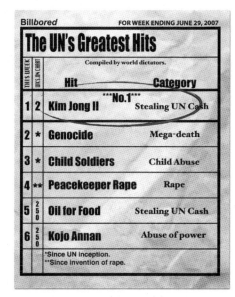

Surprise, surprise! Russian companies were the biggest beneficiaries. They got nearly 33 percent of the action. French companies were second. If those two names ring a bell, it's because they're also the same ones that later tried to stonewall our military action in Iraq. Hmmm.

Saddam's crazy scheme actually worked. He was able to trade oil for UN votes against the United States—and he would have gotten away with it too, if it weren't for those pesky kids (and the fact that he was later hanged and is currently no longer alive). But, aside from that small technicality, things couldn't have worked out better for Iraq at the time. The UN's negligent oversight helped strengthen a dictator and laid the foundation for what later turned out to be a group of corrupt allies who rallied against the United States and helped fuel anti-Americanism throughout the world. Thanks, guys!

"GETTING SOME" PEACE IN THE CONGO

The UN has been in and out of the Congo since 1960. Unfortunately, I mean that in more ways than one.

UN peacekeepers have committed horrible sex crimes in the Congo since at least 1999, when they were deployed to help monitor a ceasefire agreement. Of course, in typical UN fashion, the "peacekeepers" weren't able to keep the peace, and nearly 3.8 million people were killed during a three-year civil war. Incidentally, the Congo's president was also murdered in 2001.

Perhaps the *reason* the UN couldn't keep the peace was that its people couldn't keep their "guns" in their pants. Most notable was Frenchy-Frenchman senior UN logistics officer Didier Bourguet. This guy actually took pictures and video of himself having sex with scores of adolescent girls (some as young as 12) that he later put on the Web or sold. One photo reportedly shows Didier molesting a preteen girl who can clearly be seen crying. I don't know what fancy acronym the UN has for that, but where I come from, it's simply called rape.

But if this were just about Bourguet, then we could chalk it up to one disgusting pedophile. Unfortunately, this was more like an epidemic. Hundreds of women and girls, some as young as 11, came forward to allege they were sexually assaulted by the "peacekeepers." One woman, Aimee Tsesi, of Bunia, reportedly claimed that her 15-year-old deaf and mute daughter was raped and impregnated by a UN soldier from Uruguay. The UN turned her away when she originally tried to report the incident.

But, to their credit, peacekeepers didn't always resort to rape; sometimes they actually paid for the sex. Despite a strongly worded sign reminding troops that it was against the UN code of conduct to visit prostitutes or have sex with girls younger than 18 (what other organization would need a *sign* for that?), peacekeepers were visiting prostitutes at a rate that would embarrass Charlie Sheen.

Money wasn't much of an issue either. If troops didn't have any cash handy, they would just offer food. In one case, two Russian pilots traded jars of mayonnaise and jam for sex with two young girls.

Faced with these unbelievably disgusting acts, the UN showed the world its outrage by imposing a "tough" dusk-to-dawn curfew. Oh, and it also handed out condoms (and not condiments) to troops so they wouldn't get HIV/AIDS.

A total of 50 UN peacekeepers were eventually charged with 150 separate sex crimes in the Congo, including rape at gunpoint, pedophilia, and prostitution. And let's not forget about the hundreds of impregnated prostitutes (and rape victims) who now have children fathered by deadbeat UN soldier dads. I doubt any of those women will be seeing child-support payments anytime soon. And no, Russia, jars of mayonnaise don't count this time.

A.D.D. MOMENT

In early 2007, the executive director of UN Watch delivered some "tough love" in a speech to the UN Human Rights Council: "Faced with compelling reports from around the world of torture, persecution, and violence against women, what has the Council pronounced, and what has it decided? Nothing. Its response has been silence. Its response has been indifference. Its response has been criminal."

Ouch. But it was the response from the UN Human Rights Council president that proves how far gone they really are: "I am sorry that I'm not in a position to thank you for your statement. I should mention that I will not tolerate any similar statements in the Council."

Silencing dissent. Stifling free speech. Threatening critics. Not exactly what you'd expect from the "Rampart of Peace."

LEFT SIDE, RIGHT SIDE, WE ALL DANCE FOR GENOCIDE!

In 1993, the UN decided it had a lot of nice short acronyms but still lacked a really, really long one. With that in mind, it established UNAMIR, the United Nations Assistance Mission for Rwanda. It was supposed to help ensure that something called the Arusha Peace Agreement would be adhered to, but when reports of militias stockpiling weapons came to light, the UN refused to endorse a preemptive strike. (Sound familiar?)

By April 1994, the extermination, which ended up killing upward of a million people, had begun. Although the UN already had forces on the ground in Rwanda and even though UN Canadian Lieutenant General Romeo Dallaire made repeated requests to engage the enemy, the UN wouldn't allow it.

A.D.D. MOMENT They say Nero fiddled while Rome burned, but he had probably just called in the UN to oversee things.

The genocide finally ended when a rebel group called the Rwandan Patriotic Front was able to take control of the government from the Hutus, who fled to eastern Zaire, now the Congo, which eventually plunged into its own civil war after hatred between the Hutus and the millions of people whose loved ones were killed by them predictably boiled over into violence.

A case can therefore be made that the UN's inaction in Rwanda cost not only the lives of nearly a million people in Rwanda but also those of millions people in the Congo. But I suppose UN members can still hold their heads high because they later designated April 7 as Rwandan Genocide Reflection Day. Forget about bullets and bombs; the best way to stop future genocides is to reflect on the past ones. If nothing else, the UN gets that.

CURRENT UN FLAG

PROPOSED UN FLAG

Kofi Annan said that inaction in Rwanda was one of his biggest regrets as secretary-general. I sure hope another one is Darfur.

The UN won't even define what's happening in Darfur as genocide, even though as many as 500,000 people have already been slaughtered there. Honestly, if they learned anything from Rwanda, it should have been that classifying mass murder isn't quite as important as *stopping it.*

Although the Darfur conflict started in July 2003, it wasn't until late 2006 that the UN finally created Resolution 1706 calling for 22,500 peacekeeping troops to be dispatched there. To facilitate the deployment, the UN took the heavy-handed approach of sending a letter. Sudan's president, Omar Hassan al-Bashir, didn't reply, and the UN said it was really "frustrated" by that—but you know how slow that darn Sudanese mail service can be.

THE SOLUTION

Entire books have been written about the UN's ineptitude, so this chapter is just scratching the surface, but the question remains: How do we fix it?

Well, as a tribute to the UN, I think we should take a multilateral approach: First, I will go to Home Depot and buy as many shovels as I can afford. I will then make an on-air plea that everyone who despises the UN should meet me in New York City for a "project" that could rid us of UN corruption forever.

Many schools around the world use a Model United Nations to teach kids about diplomacy and international conflict resolution. Perhaps the real United Nations should study their methods. I'm just sayin'.

A.D.D. MOMENT

When the millions of people inevitably arrive, we'll dig along the property line until the UN building is no longer connected to Manhattan. Then we'll collectively shove it out into the East River.

If the whole thing sinks, that would be a bonus of sorts. If it floats, we'll use a barge to push it to the polar ice shelf so that the penguins and polar bears have somewhere to go once this damn global warming melts all of the glaciers.

I know, dare to dream. But if we aren't successful in physically severing the UN from the U.S. mainland, maybe we should just sever our ties. You know, cancel our UN membership, stop writing checks. I know that might sound a little dramatic, and I'm sure I'll be called all sorts of bad names for even mentioning it, but many experts believe it would spell certain doom for the UN if we left (remember, we do pay 22 percent of its budget).

The UN may have good intentions, but its socialistic means of achieving them are just flat-out wrong. The main, intractable sticking point between the United States and the UN is this: The UN simply does not believe that a global superpower like the United States should exist. Period. That puts us in a pretty difficult spot.

The UN believes power should be spread around the world as evenly as possible.

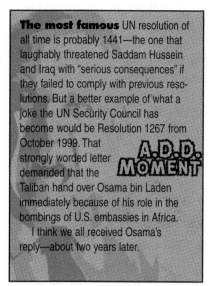

The most famous UN resolution of all time is probably 1441—the one that laughably threatened Saddam Hussein and Iraq with "serious consequences" if they failed to comply with previous resolutions. But a better example of what a joke the UN Security Council has become would be Resolution 1267 from October 1999. That strongly worded letter demanded that the Taliban hand over Osama bin Laden immediately because of his role in the bombings of U.S. embassies in Africa.

I think we all received Osama's reply—about two years later.

A.D.D. MOMENT

That's why the Iraq War met such strong opposition. It wasn't the nature of the mission or the weapons inspectors needing more time; it was a power play by UN member nations to minimize the United States' status in the world.

Why should we be a part of an organization that, because of its core beliefs, will naturally be at odds with us nine times out of ten? Why should we support an organization that is more interested in empowering capricious nations like France then working toward a true world consensus? Why not put that $423 million annual fee toward something we actually believe in?

The *American* system is the one that's worked time and time again, and we need to trust in it. In 200 years, it's taken us from 13 colonies and a ragtag army to 50 states and the most prosperous and peace-loving country (except for those damn Swiss) on earth. I think the Founding Fathers were on to something, don't you?

The UN is on to something too, but it's more like a twisted version of Robin Hood, where they take money and goods from the rich and powerful and give them to the poor and powerless. But somewhere along the way, they forgot about the middlemen, the unscrupulous dictators and politicians who grab what they can before it ever gets to the people.

Since they aren't willing to use the necessary force to prevent these evil leaders from ruining their countries, they continue to throw money (most of it ours) at problems. That generally results in some sort of scandal, which, in turn, requires more money to fix. Well, I don't know about you, but I'm tired of throwing money down the socialist drain.

UN, it's been fun (no, I *mean* that) but alas, it's time to go. Good luck without us! You're going to need it.

"It's payback time for the U.S. At the UN you can say anything, vote any way you want, and, at the end of the day, it doesn't really matter that much. It's easy to grind your ax, it's words and resolutions. Countries that either do not have the guts or ability to stand up to the U.S. at other international forums . . . find the UN a convenient place."

—Anonymous UN ambassador, from *The U.N. Exposed*

UN Diplomats Say the Darndest Things!

Chapter 16

How to Remember Names, by Glenn-something or other

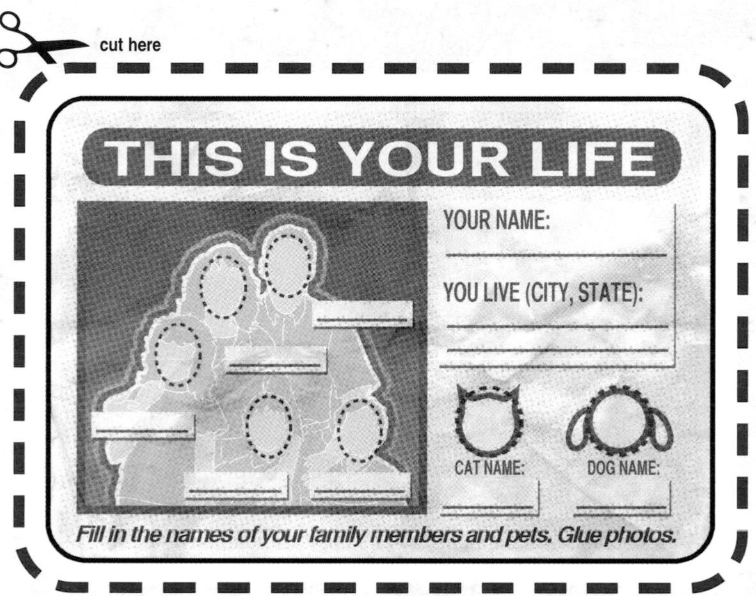

cut here
THIS IS YOUR LIFE
YOUR NAME:
YOU LIVE (CITY, STATE):
CAT NAME:
DOG NAME:
Fill in the names of your family members and pets. Glue photos.

A FEW DAYS AFTER my youngest daughter was born, a couple of friends dropped by the house to pay us a visit. Proud new dad that I was, I answered the front door holding my bundle of joy, swaddled snuggly in her pink blanket.

"Oh, she's simply adorable." The guests oohed and aahed. "What's her name?"

My mind instantly froze. At that moment, I was unable to recall the name of my very own child. In a state of panic, I did what any self-respecting man would do: I fabricated a kitchen emergency and fled, leaving them alone on the porch.

If I were to tell you that I'm terrible with names, I'd be lying. *Terrible* would be way too generous. I'm spectaculawful, tremendorrible, horrendastic.

> **Attention Big Pharma**
>
> New product: Remembra. For people suffering from NRD (name remembrance disorder). I don't care what the side effects are, just get it on the market and give me 6 percent for coming up with the name.

THE WRONG LINE OF WORK

My radio staff witnesses my trouble with names on a daily basis. On the air, I'm constantly treading water, filling valuable airtime with "umms" and "aaaaahs" as I probe my mind in vain, desperately trying to recall the names of powerful, important people. It usually fails, which is why I end up referring to them as "Senator What's-his-name" and "that guy, the one from that state. You know, the one with all the cheese." I leave it to the listeners to fill in the blanks, and I think they appreciate it. It's kind of like an involuntary game of MadLibs: "You know, What's-his-face from over in the place with the stuff going on. The one who signed the bill about the thing."

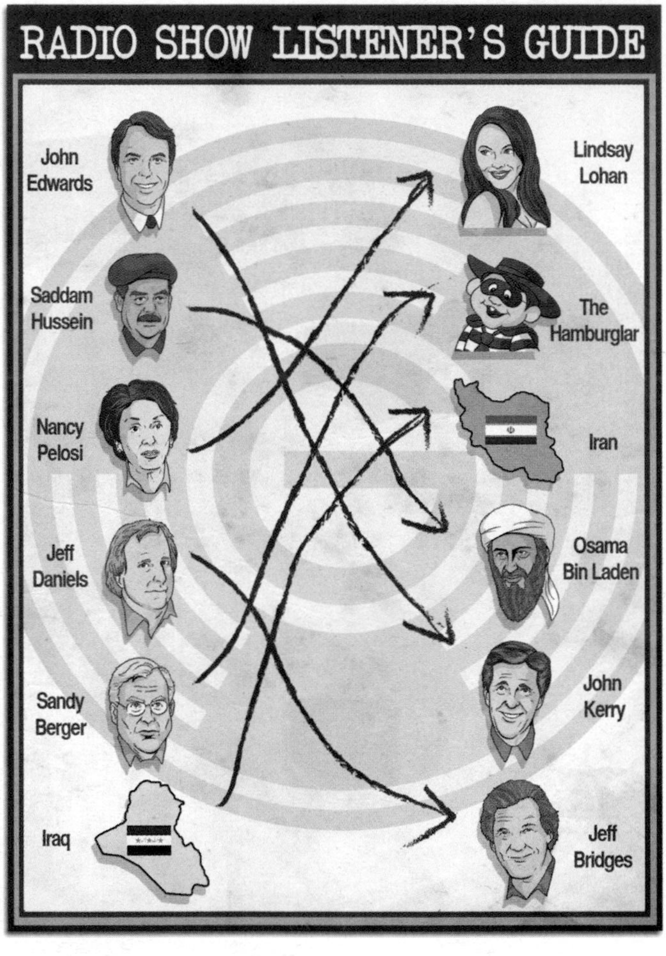

RADIO SHOW LISTENER'S GUIDE

John Edwards
Saddam Hussein
Nancy Pelosi
Jeff Daniels
Sandy Berger
Iraq
Lindsay Lohan
The Hamburglar
Iran
Osama Bin Laden
John Kerry
Jeff Bridges

I'm even worse with celebrities. All of a sudden, these people I've never seen before are on the front pages of the tabloids, and I have to hear about what they're wearing, what nightclub they were thrown out of, and which rehab clinic they're signing themselves into. It's impossible to keep track of these people.

A.D.D. MOMENT Maybe it's presumptuous of me, but I believe we should change Andy Warhol's renowned prediction to: Everyone will be famous *in* 15 minutes

The point is that I *should* remember their names, and I don't. Maybe it's the A.D.D. Maybe I just don't listen. Unfortunately, I'm not exactly in a line of work that makes it easy to cover up that shortcoming.

AN EASIER WAY

I know I'm not the only person with this problem, and I think it's because we all have way too many people in our lives these days. They had it easy back in the horse-and-buggy days; there was no MySpace, no reality TV to turn drunk kids into celebrities, and, most important, there were about 10 first names. Odds were, even if you didn't remember someone's name, you could still guess and probably get it right. "Nice to see you again, Ebenezer." "How are your crops this season, Jebediah?" "Lovely beans, Noah." Nowadays it's all different—we're exposed to more people than ever before, and lots of them have strange foreign names like Kenyatta, Jerzy, or Laxmi. It seems as if there's some secret contest to give your kid the funkiest, hardest-to-remember name you possibly can. But what these contestants don't realize is that the prize for first place for best name is a lifetime of therapy for your kid.

Stu's real name is actually Steve. (I think.) I kind of remember telling the story of why I call him Stu in my first book, which was called *The* —hold on, it's on the tip of my tongue. This is bad. I wonder if someday I'll be writing a third book and I won't be able to remember that the title of this one is —oh, no, this can't really be happening. I've got to call my editor.

A.D.D. MOMENT

Glenn's first book was called The Real America, and it's sad that Glenn forgot the title. "Ernest Glenningway" left all the verbs out of his first draft, so the publisher "outsourced" the revisions to a ghost writer who'd never even heard of him. It's a great book, but it was a nightmare.

—Stu, Editor

Of course, when names started becoming more varied, strategies for remembering them naturally evolved. One trick that really took off in the Roaring Twenties was calling everyone by the same nickname. "Governor" and "Chief" are my personal favorites, but there were also "Doctor," "Boss," "Captain," and many more. The beauty was that everyone used those names without any regard to a person's real name, so no one could possibly be offended. In fact, most times, I don't think people ever bothered to learn real names; they just didn't matter. You'd say, "I saw Babycakes the other day," and your friend would assume he knew whom you were talking about.

Jebediah is one of those names that only old people have. Same thing with Mildred and Edna. Come to think of it, I've never met a Mildred who wasn't at least 90 years old. I wonder if they house them all in some "elderly name" farm until they're old enough to be let loose. Then again, if Capri pants can come back into style, I have no doubt that Mildred and Bertha will have their day as well.

A.D.D. MOMENT

But soon the handful of nicknames gave way to the even better strategy of using one name for everybody. Frank Sinatra was really the pioneer; he just called everyone Toots. Of course, he was Frank Sinatra, so you were happy to be called Toots—but nowadays, a moniker like that would probably get you clocked in the mouth.

GUILTY BY ASSOCIATION

A few years ago, I was flipping through the channels when I came across a show where they were interviewing a guy who called himself "one of the world's most renowned memory experts." I can't recall his name . . . but I do remember him saying that "the key to remembering someone's name is to associate a word with their face." He suggested that you look the person in the eye, concentrate really hard, say their name over and over, and then come up with a word or object that reminds you of them. Simple enough, right?

The next day, I was going to a small cookout. I told myself that, no matter what, I was going to apply that trick and learn every single person's name at that party. People would be amazed, and for once I'd be referred to as "that guy who remembered my name!" as opposed to "that pale, bloviating jerk!"

The first person I met that afternoon was a guy named John. We struck up a conversation, and as he talked, I concentrated really hard, repeating "John" over and over again in my head. I looked him right in the eye, thought of an object, and took a little memory snapshot of it, just as What's-his-name on TV had suggested.

Of course, I was so busy associating his name with an object that I didn't hear a single word he said. I couldn't tell you what he did for a living, what he thought about any issue, how many kids he had—nothing. Even worse, I had forgotten his actual name and only remembered the object I'd associated his name with: a toilet. So much for word association. Later, when Toilet approached me to introduce his wife, I panicked and said I had to go to the bathroom.

An Inconvenient Name

Sure, Al Gore says the science is settled and that man-made CO_2 levels are driving our recent warming, but has he investigated the possibility that parents who give their sons names that start with CA may be the real cause of the warming? Our research shows that the names Caleb, Caden, Carter, Cameron, Carlos, and Calvin, among others, seem to be the main cause of this planet's bleak future.

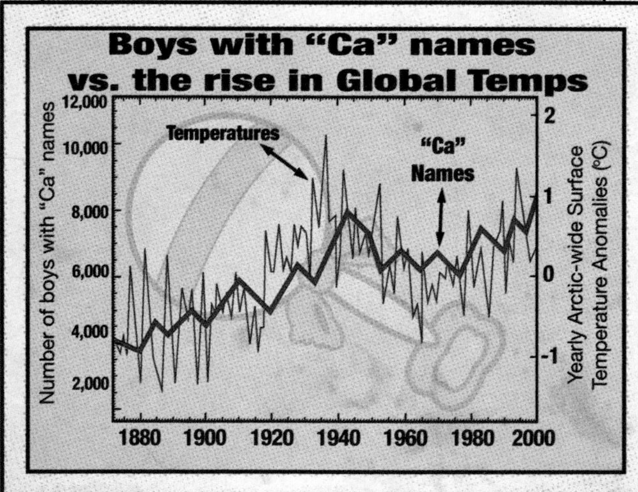

Attention, parents: Save the earth. Name your child Bob.

It wasn't until hours later that I found out he's my father-in-law. Can you say embarrassing?

LEARN FROM MY MISTAKES

Perhaps I'm going about this memory problem all wrong. Maybe the answer is for all of us to stop the charade and admit once and for all that we just don't know each other's names. Imagine how liberating that would be! Finally, you'd have the freedom to say, "Hi, I know I've met you about a hundred times, and our two families even vacationed together for a week on the Cape, and I think you might actually be the godmother to my third child, but I can't for the life of me remember your name," without any embarrassment. Think of all the aggravation that would save.

Trick 17 for Remembering Names

Repeat it often.

GLENN: Hi, I'm Glenn.

AMANDA: Hi, my name's Amanda.

GLENN: Amanda, Amanda, Amanda, Amanda, Amanda, Amanda, Amanda, Ama—

AMANDA: Please stop doing that. *(Calls 9-1-1).*

When my wife and I go to a party, she always has to stay within arm's reach so that I can quickly call her over to find out the name of the person I've been talking to for the last 20 minutes. It usually goes something like this:

1. I am in the middle of a great conversation with Some Person. Sensing that the end is coming, I give my wife . . . um, don't tell me, don't tell me . . . Tania! Yeah, that's it. So then I give Tania (who's engaged in a separate conversation nearby) the secret signal.
2. Tania excuses herself from her conversation and barges into the middle of mine.
3. Tania: "Hi, I'm Glenn's wife, Tania. What's your name?"
4. Some Person then says, "Hi, Tania, I'm Fred Tanner. Pleasure to meet you."
5. Me: "I'm sorry, Fred, I'm so rude—I should've introduced you."

It works almost every time. The only exception is when the mark uses the same trick. If you're reading this and we've had a conversation that Tania suddenly interrupted, I apologize.

Unfortunately, this scheme does have one big weakness: Tania isn't always with me. That leaves me to fend for myself more often that not, including at the dreaded "work party." That's always a particularly dangerous occasion, because you must have conversations with people you barely know but are forced by cruel fate to spend lots of time around, people who are often extra chatty thanks to all the booze.

Fortunately, there is one surefire method I've developed to get through the evening relatively unscathed; it's called the "plaster cast" strategy. The day before the party, wrap one of your arms in plaster. As you meet new people, simply ask them to sign your cast. Voilà, a running logbook of everyone you've met is literally being kept right on your body. Yes, it really is that easy—you're welcome.

A.D.D. MOMENT Sometimes people will approach me and say, "Hi, Glenn, it's ———. I met you back in 1998. I had the green jacket on—don't you remember me?" The answer is: "Yes! Absolutely. But I need to run."

MY SOLUTION

I hope you agree with my premise that there's nothing wrong with simply admitting we don't know each other's names. So why don't we just celebrate it? If we all acknowledge we have a problem, then we can all come together in supporting my solution: a modern-day version of the trustworthy name tag.

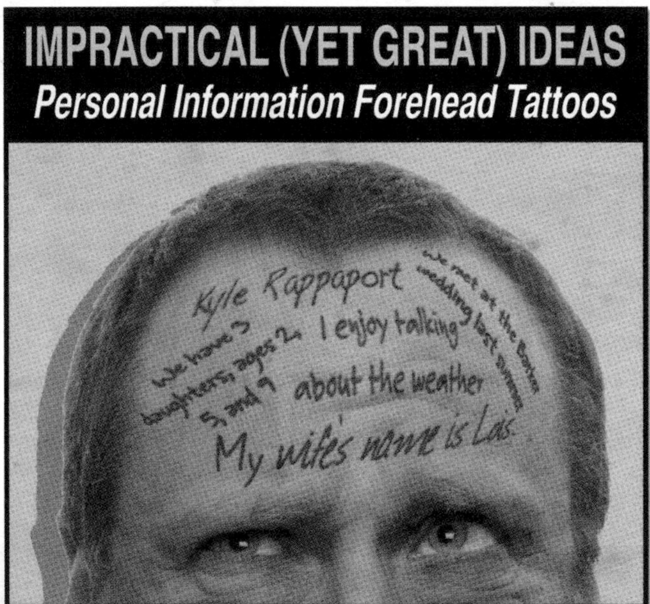

IMPRACTICAL (YET GREAT) IDEAS
Personal Information Forehead Tattoos

Now, I know what you're thinking: Who wants to wear some dorky piece of paper on their chest every day for their entire life? I agree—I sure don't, and that's why I've come up with a sane alternative to the name tag, and it's guaranteed not to peel off. I call it the forehead tattoo.

At birth, we all would have our full names permanently tattooed just above our eyebrows. There would be no exceptions allowed. Umbilical cord cut, name tattooed on. Yes, the actual procedure would be incredibly painful, and yes, if you ever decided to change your name, it would create immeasurable complications, but I think the convenience outweighs the problems.

Now, I'm not a complete idiot. This plan will probably never work—at least, not right away. It could take years to implement, and we'd need to rally support from congressmen who probably not only hate needles but also would claim that this plan sounds "a lot like the Antichrist." Of course, we could always bribe them through some pro-Antichrist lobbying firm, but that would cost a lot of money, and honestly, I don't care about this plan enough to spend my own cash on it.

If the front of your head is the "forehead," why isn't there a name for the back of your head? Rearhead? Backhead? Let's get this going.

A.D.D. MOMENT

Maybe the solution isn't as complicated as I'm making it; maybe we should all just use basic telephone etiquette in everyday life. When I call someone, I don't expect them to remember my voice. They answer the phone and say "Hello?" I respond with, "Hi, it's Glenn." It works every time. Even my father—who's known me for 43 years—says, "Hi, it's Dad," when he calls me.

If you're not expected to remember the voice of someone you've known for their entire life, should you really be expected to remember their face? Of course not! Unless, of course, that face is connected to the body of, oh, let's just say Jessica Alba.

Yes, there's an exception to every rule.

Remembering Names: An Alternative Solution

Step 1. Meet someone.

Step 2. As they leave, pat them hard on the back, simultaneously implanting a microchip.

Step 3. Next time they're within 20 feet of you, a radio signal will broadcast their name every 15 seconds through another implanted chip in your ear.

Step 4. Develop ear cancer because of the constant radio waves.

Step 5. Realize that ear cancer is better than forgetting names at a party.

Step 6. Realize that this is another tactic that the Antichrist might use.

Step 7. Weigh the options: living the Book of Revelation vs. remembering all names.

Step 8. Realize that untold famine, plague, war, and death are still better than forgetting names at a party.

Chapter 17

Minimum Wage, Maximum Politics

THE FEDERAL MINIMUM WAGE SHOULD BE $0.00.

I know what you're thinking; that's exactly the opening line you expect from a conservative, low-skill-worker-hating, free-markets-at-all-cost, right-wing blowhard, right?

Yes, but in this case, it also has the benefit of being true.

The minimum wage is the Holy Grail if you're looking for an issue to illustrate just how differently liberals and conservatives see the world. Liberals say a rising minimum wage helps low-skilled workers; conservatives say it hurts them. Conservatives say it hurts economic growth; liberals say it helps. But the real beauty of this issue is that *both* sides get to use plenty of stats, studies, and personal anecdotes to prove their cases.

For every study "proving" that an increase in the minimum wage has no impact on unemployment, two other studies say it does. For every statistic "concluding" that a rising minimum wage doesn't affect poverty levels, there's a senator with his arm around a young minority worker who says that it most certainly does.

It all adds up to the minimum-wage issue being a classic example of the saying "Statistics don't lie, but liars use statistics." So, instead of contributing to that, I want to expose this issue for what it's really all about: politicians pandering to voters while trying to win elections.

POLITICAL WAGERING

After taking control of Congress for the first time in 12 years, the Democrats made the minimum wage a centerpiece issue of their first 100 hours in session. Why? Was it more important than debating the Iraq War, fixing the illegal immigrant invasion from Mexico, saving Social Security, or reforming health care? No. But it was a heck of a lot *easier* than any of those things and it met the three main criteria that none of those other issues did:

1. *Broad support.* Polls showed that 80 percent of Americans favored an increase in the minimum wage—which just shows what a great job Democrats have done marketing it.
2. *Guaranteed quick approval.* With Democrats controlling both houses, that was a no-brainer. President Bush also publicly announced he would sign it before the debate even started.
3. *Grandstandable.* OK, I made that word up, but it means an issue that allows one party to hammer the other for ignoring it because that party supposedly hates the people it would help.

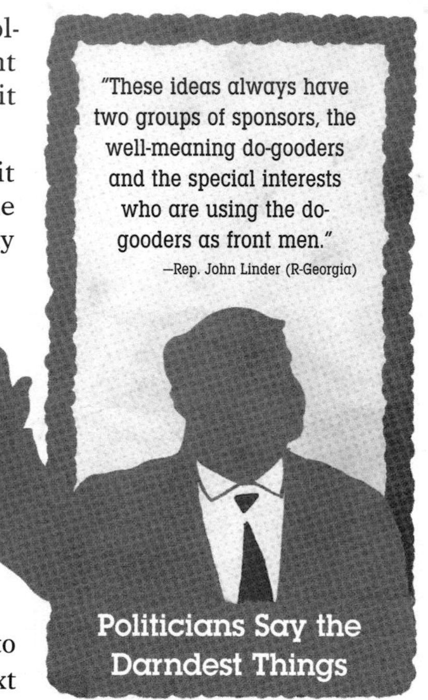

"These ideas always have two groups of sponsors, the well-meaning do-gooders and the special interests who are using the do-gooders as front men."
—Rep. John Linder (R-Georgia)
Politicians Say the Darndest Things

Check, check, and check. The minimum wage is the ultimate "common compassion" issue, something that seems to be common sense while also tugging at our heartstrings, begging us to be compassionate. I mean, who *doesn't* want to help that struggling, hardworking family get ahead? Who *doesn't* think that almost 10 years is too long to wait between raises? No one—and that's exactly why, on January 10, 2007, the House voted 315 to 116 to raise the federal minimum wage from $5.15 to $7.25 an hour over the next two years. (After the Senate made some changes, House Democrats attached the minimum-wage hike to the Iraq emergency war-spending bill to force Republicans' hands. It worked—the bill passed.)

The number you can't stop hearing about: $5.15 an hour (the old minimum wage).

The number you've probably never heard before: $17.00 an hour (the *average* wage of an hourly worker in the United States).

Although the House vote wasn't very dramatic, the speeches afterward were. New Majority Leader Steny Hoyer promptly took to the cameras to milk the victory for every ounce of political gain: "On Monday, we commemorate the life of a great American, Dr. Martin Luther King Jr., and Dr. King once said: 'Equality means dignity. And dignity demands a job and a paycheck that lasts through the week.' Today, we heed those words."

News flash to the geniuses in Washington: Great television sound bites don't equal great public policy. If they did, Jesse Jackson would've been president by now. And by the way, dignity does *not* demand a job. It's the other way around: A job helps build dignity.

"We think (raising the minimum wage is) both the right thing and good politics."
—Rep. Steny Hoyer (D-Maryland)
Politicians Say the Darndest Things

STENY HOYER IS REALLY OLD

It may have taken only seven days to pass the minimum-wage bill, but politicians packed an unimaginable amount of manufactured passion, meaningless statistics, partisan politics, and outright lies into one week. And it was all led by Mr. MLK Jr. himself, Steny Hoyer.

When Steny was first elected to Congress, I was 17 years old, the space shuttle *Challenger* wouldn't explode for five more years, and President Reagan had just taken office. Suffice it to say, the man's been in Washington a long time. And somewhere in those 26 years, he apparently picked up a thing or two about how to give a good speech. Here's what he had to say from the House floor during the minimum-wage debate: "In the United States of America, the richest nation on earth, workers should not be relegated to poverty if they work hard and play by the rules."

A.D.D. MOMENT Ohhh, so all people have to do is "play by the rules" to get ahead, according to Steny Hoyer. That's funny, because he got an F– grade for his policies on border control and interior enforcement from the Americans for Better Immigration group. Steny wants you to believe that he's standing up for hardworking Americans, but at the same time, he's apparently okay with illegal aliens who break the law to get here and then take jobs away from those hardworking Americans. That makes sense.

That's a taste of the "manufactured passion" I was talking about. Who exactly is relegating these workers to poverty? Me? You? The government?

It sounds as if he's claiming that a bump in the minimum wage will get these hardworking people out of poverty. That, of course, is a lie. Government handouts don't get you out of poverty—hard work, education, and determination do.

Congratulations! Your exciting platform of higher taxes and finger pointing has won over the hearts and minds of the American people.

But now things get tough. You can't just ridicule the Republican Party's ideas anymore; you actually have to come up with your own. I know, I know—that's just not what we do, but I'll show you how to fake it.

OK, first things first—we need to find you an issue. Go buy today's newspaper (preferably the LA or NY Times since we own them).

Alright, now skip past the first few pages—that's where all the controversial stuff is—and look for an issue that seems like common sense. If nothing stands out, raise the federal minimum wage and then accuse Republicans of hating the poor—that always works.

After that passes, raise everyone's taxes just for fun.

Pg.183

The Official Democratic Handbook

Rep. John Dingell (D-Michigan) left the passion aside and moved right on to the partisan politics: "It is our job to represent the American people, and I am proud that the new Democratic majority is getting the job done. We will succeed in raising the minimum wage during the first hundred hours of the 110th Congress—an accomplishment that the Republican majority could not—or shall I say cared not to—achieve in 10 years."

Actually, John, the only "job" you're getting done is putting more people out of them. Sorry, sorry—I swore this chapter would stick to the politics, and now I've broken my own rule. Dingell (I just like saying his name) says that it took the Democrats less than 100 hours to do what the Republicans couldn't do in 10 years. That's quite the television sound bite—Dingell's speechwriter deserves a raise—but it's only partially true.

The "Republican majority" Dingell refers to was actually in place when the wage was last increased in 1997, so that kind of blows his (sorry, Dingell's) cute little argument that it's always the big, bad GOP that's keeping the low-wage workers lowly waged. In addition, in 2006, Republicans actually allowed a vote to come up, but Democrats (yes, you read that right, Democrats) blocked it in the Senate because it was tied to a repeal of the estate tax.

I'd also like to take this opportunity to remind Mr. Dingell that Republicans presided over one of the greatest economic runs this country has ever seen. I don't want to speak for politicians, but maybe the old rule "If it ain't broke, don't fix it" somehow made its way to the hallowed halls of Washington. Nah, that would require too much common sense.

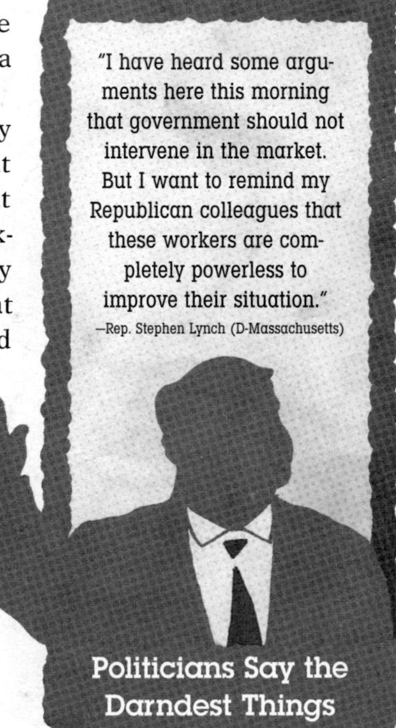

"I have heard some arguments here this morning that government should not intervene in the market. But I want to remind my Republican colleagues that these workers are completely powerless to improve their situation."
—Rep. Stephen Lynch (D-Massachusetts)
Politicians Say the Darndest Things

LAYING THE BLAME

Many of the politicians who spoke in favor of this bill ended up citing the exact same studies and stats. But the one that stuck out the most was the constant mention of America's CEOs; I counted at least 18 instances in just one debate. I won't bore you with them all, but here's a sampling so you get the idea:

The Democrats adopted a rule called "pay-go" in the House when they took over in 2007. It means that every time they cut taxes or increase spending, they have to raise taxes or cut spending somewhere else so that no extra money is spent. Makes sense, right? So why would they be so opposed to the Republicans' proposal to raise the minimum wage while cutting the estate tax? Don't worry, it's a rhetorical question. A.D.D. MOMENT

- REP. JOHN CONYERS (D-Michigan): "During this period in which Congress has failed to act to raise the wage of America's poorest workers, CEO and top-executive pay has soared: the average annual compensation for a CEO at a Standard & Poor's 500 company rose from $3.7 to $9.1 million."
- REP. JANICE SCHAKOWSKY (D-Illinois): "The CEOs of the nation's top companies made on average $10,712 in the first two hours of the first workday of the New Year . . . those CEOs make $5,279 an hour, $10,982,000 a year, or 1,025 times more than their minimum-wage employees. Those CEOs must really be special compared to the woman who changes their mother's diapers or cleans their toilets."
- REP. BETTY MCCOLLUM (D-Minnesota): "CEOs of top companies make in two hours what a minimum-wage worker makes in a year."
- REP. CORRINE BROWN (D-Florida): "You know, the sad thing is that a CEO before 12:00 earns more money than a person on minimum wage will earn all year long."
- REP. JAMES MCGOVERN (D-Massachusetts): "Right now the average CEO of a Fortune 500 company earns $10,712 in 1 hour and 16 minutes. It takes the average minimum-wage worker 52 40-hour weeks—an entire year—to earn the same $10,712."

A.D.D. MOMENT Let's step aside from talking about the minimum wage for just a second to appreciate $10,712 an hour. God bless America.

I think I speak for all Americans when I say: *We get it!* CEOs make a lot! Minimum-wage workers make . . . well, they make the minimum.

If this chapter were about debating the merits of the federal minimum wage (it's

> **None of this** is to say that CEOs shouldn't be responsible with their wealth. They absolutely should be—and many of them are extraordinarily generous (which, of course, doesn't make any headlines). But that's a *completely* separate argument from the minimum wage.
>
> A.D.D. MOMENT

not), I might take this opportunity to mention that most "CEOs of the nation's top companies" are highly trained, highly educated, highly skilled executives who have devoted their lives to a job. I might also mention that these same CEOs have (generally speaking) worked hard to increase shareholder value, thereby increasing the household wealth of millions of Americans. I might even mention that if it weren't for these CEOs running their companies effectively, there wouldn't *be* any jobs for the rest of us, including many minimum-wage workers.

But the key point is that these politicians all took the same stat (a top CEO makes an average of $10,982,000 a year) and regurgitated it in as many ways as possible: What do they make per hour? Per minute? Per second? Per millisecond? How many new Porsche SUVs could a CEO buy in one month of work?

> A.D.D. MOMENT A CEO could buy 21.1 Porsche Cayennes (at MSRP) after one month of work.

Who cares? It's like making the argument that your local soccer goalie should get a bump in pay because David Beckham just signed a huge contract. How are those two things possibly related? If your local goalie wants a raise, he should go train hard and try to be *as good* as David Beckham is.

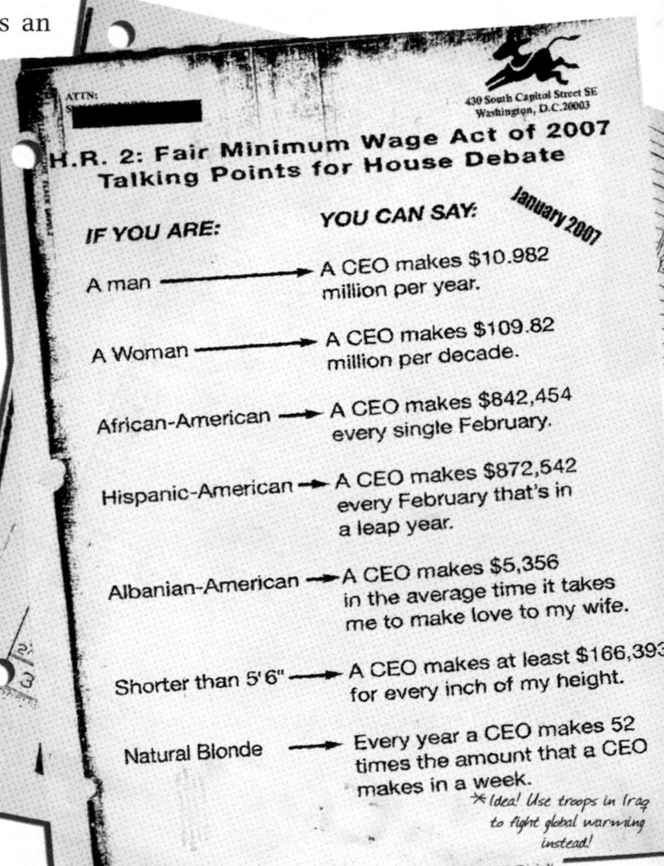

ATTN:

430 South Capitol Street SE
Washington, D.C. 20003

H.R. 2: Fair Minimum Wage Act of 2007
Talking Points for House Debate

January 2007

IF YOU ARE:	YOU CAN SAY:
A man →	A CEO makes $10.982 million per year.
A Woman →	A CEO makes $109.82 million per decade.
African-American →	A CEO makes $842,454 every single February.
Hispanic-American →	A CEO makes $872,542 every February that's in a leap year.
Albanian-American →	A CEO makes $5,356 in the average time it takes me to make love to my wife.
Shorter than 5'6" →	A CEO makes at least $166,393 for every inch of my height.
Natural Blonde →	Every year a CEO makes 52 times the amount that a CEO makes in a week.

*Idea! Use troops in Iraq to fight global warming instead!

A.D.D. MOMENT

The average top-company CEO makes $1.46 a second. That means they just made about $44.60 in the time it took you to read that last paragraph and another $17.52 in the time it's taken you to get this far into *this* paragraph. That's $62.12, which they could easily cash in for 151 U.S. postage stamps. Put another way, a CEO earned enough to mail 151 letters while you read this stupid joke. Now 211 letters. All while the average minimum-wage worker has to read two more lines just to afford to mail one. It's an outrage.

STATISTICS DON'T LIE—OR DO THEY?

While we're on the subject of stupid stats, politicians love quoting and misquoting all sorts of stats and studies about who really makes the minimum wage.

Rep. Jack Kingston (R-Georgia): "In 1980, 15 percent of the workers in America were on minimum wage. Today, it is 2.5 percent. Who are they? Fifty-two percent are teenagers. 30 percent are part-timers. And 40 percent have never held a job before."

He's basically saying two things: (1) Not very many people make minimum wage anymore, and (2) of those who do, a large portion are teenagers, part-time workers, or first-time employees. Got that? Okay, let's go to the blue corner.

Rep. Lucille Roybal-Allard (D-California): "Who are the workers in our country earning the federal minimum wage? Most are full-time hardworking American adults. Most have not had the educational and career opportunities of higher-wage earners."

Hmm, now, that's interesting. She says that "most" are full-time workers, which gels with what Mr. Kingston said—she just used the other side of the same statistic. However, the statistics she left out were more important than the ones she mentioned. Notice she never talked about teenagers and first-time employees. Why? Because that would have ruined her argument. Back to the red corner.

Rep. David Weldon (R-Florida): "The average minimum-wage earner lives in a household with income above $50,000 a year. Less than 1 in 25 minimum-wage earners are single parents who work full-time. Very few families rely on a minimum-wage job to support a family. Only one in five minimum-wage earners live

"As I left the Memphis airport, a hardworking man for Northwest Airlines said to me, 'Congressman, will you pass the minimum wage?' To him and many others, the thousands in District Nine, I say, yes, we will do that."
—Rep. Steve Cohen (D-Tennessee)

Politicians Say the Darndest Things

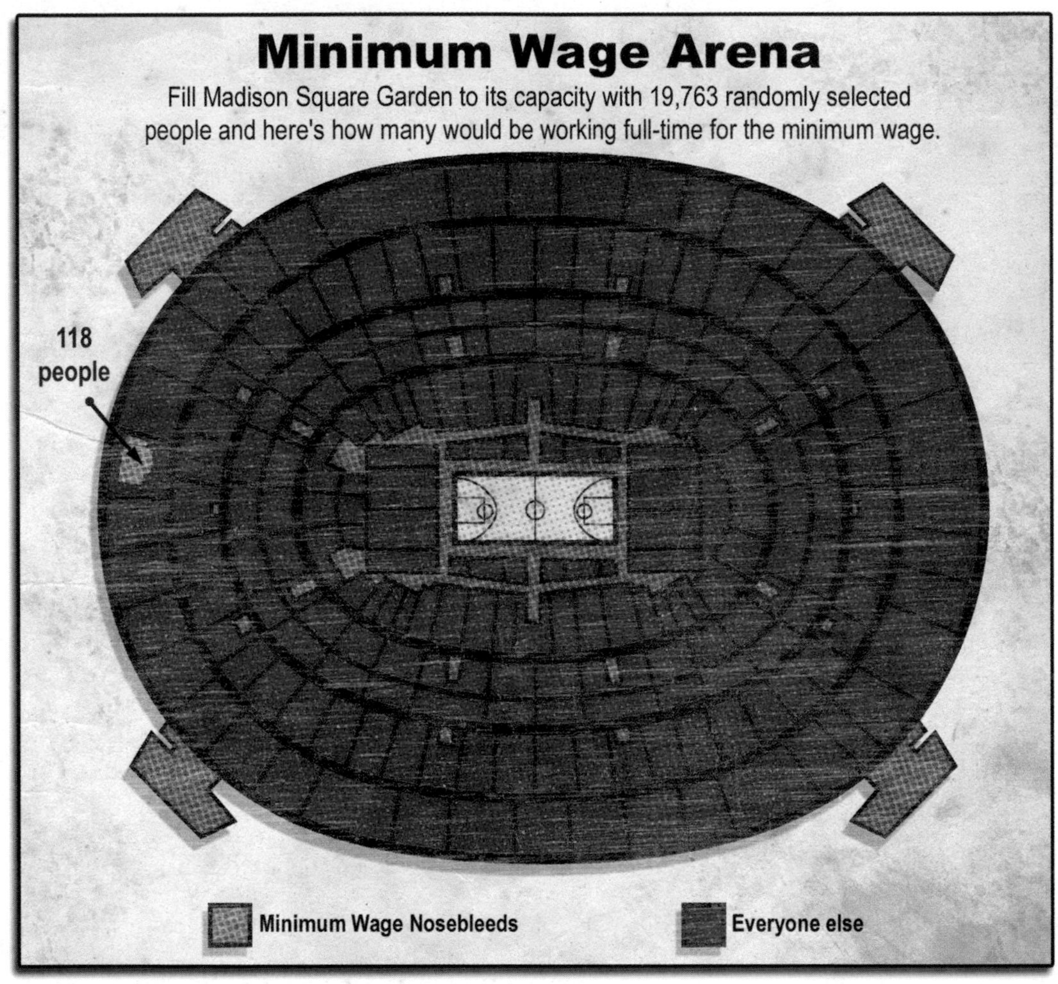

Minimum Wage Arena
Fill Madison Square Garden to its capacity with 19,763 randomly selected people and here's how many would be working full-time for the minimum wage.
118 people
Minimum Wage Nosebleeds
Everyone else

below the poverty level . . . 68 percent of Americans live in states that have a higher minimum wage. Sixty-seven percent of minimum-wage earners get a raise within the first year of employment."

Mr. Weldon introduces us to some new stats. Now we find out that household income of minimum-wage workers averages more than $50,000, and he further refines the full-time stat down to the level of single parents. In addition, he tells us that more than two-thirds of workers get a raise in their first year, which makes the minimum wage effective for one thing: getting people off it. Back to the blue corner for the final round.

> **I sometimes** wish that really controversial political issues could be decided once and for all with a Saturday-night pay-per-view steel-cage fight. We give Washington three months to solve an issue, and if they can't, each side picks one politician for the fight, winner takes all. Imagine: Charles Rangel versus John Boehner with an Iraq War timetable on the line. Tell me you're not paying $34.95 to watch that.
>
> **A.D.D. MOMENT**

Rep. Stephanie Jones (D-Ohio): "While opponents of increasing the minimum-wage often claim that minimum wage workers are largely middle-class teenagers, recent reports from the U.S. Census demonstrate that among those workers who would benefit from this legislation, nearly half (48 percent) are the household's chief breadwinner."

As any good magician knows, the most important part of any illusion is the setup. Politics isn't much different. The "breadwinner" claim sounds impressive, until you realize that she qualified it by saying "among those workers *who would benefit* from this legislation."

That's a completely different group of people from the minimum-wage workers this debate is about. The workers who "benefit" from this bill include everyone making less than $7.25 an hour (since they would all eventually get a raise), not just those who are making the minimum. That adds 7.4 million more people to the mix, and it drastically distorts reality. Think about it this way: If I proposed that we raise the minimum wage to, say, $20 an hour, I could then legitimately claim that something like 80 percent of the people affected by my new bill are their families' "chief breadwinner." It's great marketing, but it has nothing to do with the real issue.

After a close fight, the judges have decided that the loser is . . . the American people.

THE IRRELEVANT PERSONAL ANECDOTE

Rep. George Miller (D-California), from the House floor: "I cleaned out oil tanks; I cleaned out ships; I drove trucks in the pear orchards; I picked fruit; I worked in the canneries; and sometimes I did two of those at the same time. I worked at night in the cannery and in the daytime in the oil refinery. I worked at the minimum wage."

Somehow the fact that Congressman Miller once drove a truck in a pear orchard is supposed to give him personal insight into the plight of today's minimum-wage workers. But beyond the obvious irrelevance that his previous jobs have to a congressional debate, Miller's statements do actually prove a point: The minimum wage worked for him—he got off it!

At the danger of breaking my own rule on keeping this about politics (again), let me just say that people tend to forget that the minimum wage is the *minimum* wage. In other words, it's the floor, the bottom, the absolute least you can ever legally pay someone. But what seems to get lost in translation is the fact that *you're not supposed to make that salary forever.* You're supposed to move up, get a raise, and do better for yourself—and most people do. As Rep. Weldon said in the House debate, two-thirds of minimum-wage workers get a raise within the first year, and that raise *averages* 10 percent. For those who work full-time minimum-wage jobs, their average first year raise is even higher: 14 percent.

Rank-and-file members of Congress currently earn about $165,000 a year. That's $79.32 an hour. In just more than three weeks, they earn $10,712. It takes the average minimum-wage worker 52 forty-hour weeks—an entire year—to earn the same $10,712. Sound familiar?

A.D.D. MOMENT

"Why are you stopping at $7 an hour? If it is good for the economy and good for the workers, as we keep hearing over and over again, why do we stop at $7 an hour, this arbitrary number? Nobody can make a living at $14,000 a year. Why not go to $8 an hour, $9 an hour, $10, $20 an hour? Heck, if it is good for the economy, let us go to $50 an hour. And if we had a committee hearing, maybe we could have some answers on that."
—Rep. Jack Kingston (R-Georgia)
Politicians Say the Darndest Things

Despite the stereotype, minimum-wage jobs are not life sentences. By helping low-skill or young workers develop a track record, they provide a foundation for future success. But when you raise the floor, you not only decrease the number of jobs available, but you also take away the incentive that people have to help themselves.

Okay, back to the politics.

Democrats are always clamoring about helping the lowest-wage workers, yet—at the same time—they refuse to get serious about addressing the one issue that would help those people the most: illegal immigration. That just doesn't add up.

Rep. David Weldon (R-Florida), probably summed up this contradiction better than I ever could: "What has been absent from today's debate is a discussion about what the real downward pressure is on U.S. workers' wages—illegal workers. After the federal government cracked down on illegal immigrants working at meat-processing plants across the U.S., the company was forced to pay American workers a higher wage. Cracking down on illegal immigration, rather than granting amnesty to over 11 million illegal immigrants, will do more to improve the wages of the working poor than a law increasing the minimum wage."

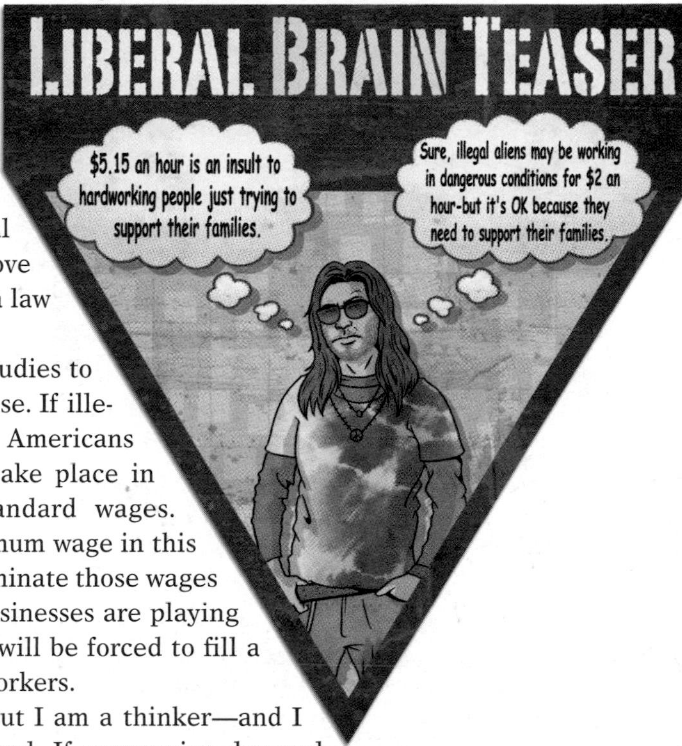

He's right, and you don't need studies to prove it—you just need common sense. If illegal aliens are "doing the jobs that Americans won't do," it's because those jobs take place in substandard conditions for substandard wages. *Those* wages represent the real minimum wage in this country, not $5.15 or $7.25. If you eliminate those wages from the marketplace (so that all businesses are playing by the same rules), then companies will be forced to fill a lot more jobs with minimum-wage workers.

I may not be Alan Greenspan, but I am a thinker—and I know the laws of supply and demand. If companies demand more workers, the price of those workers goes up. It's a simple way to use capitalism to give workers a raise, but Democrats either don't see that, or they're really socialists who only understand the Frenchy-French school of economics.

MY SOLUTION

Right off the top, I said that the federal minimum wage should be $0.00. But the key word was *federal;* it's the states that should be in charge.

Think about it: We set a national minimum wage as if life in New York City were the same as life in Topeka. Well, guess what, it's not. Consulting firm Runzheimer International looked at what it costs to live in 300 different U.S. cities by comparing what a typical middle-class family of four would have to spend to maintain the same lifestyle in each location.

The average U.S. city came in at $61,430. Manhattan, on the other hand, was—ready for this?—$146,060. That's 138 percent over the average. The rest of the top five (San Francisco, $122,007; Los Angeles, $117,776; San Jose, $108,506; and Washington, D.C., $102,589) were all at least 50 percent over the national average.

So let's go back to my question: Why set a uniform national wage when the cost of living is anything but uniform? If Steny Hoyer thinks $5.15 an hour doesn't go far in Annapolis, he should spend a week in New York City—he'd be shocked.

The people who know the economic and living conditions in each state the best are the leaders *of each state*. Let them look at indicators such as their states' unemployment rate, job growth, inflation rate, and cost of living and set their minimum wage accordingly. If people don't like their state's wage, then do the same thing people do when they don't like their state's income tax, or gun laws, or highway congestion: Move.

The good news is that many states already do set their own minimum wage. At the time of the House vote, 29 states, plus Washington, D.C., had a higher minimum wage than the federal one. I guess they were doing the job the federal government just wouldn't do.

By making the states solely responsible, you'd finally make each state's wage *relevant* while doing something even more worthwhile: making Washington politicians *irrelevant*. I'm not sure which accomplishment would be more gratifying.

Unfortunately, it will never happen. Why? Because it wouldn't allow politicians to drag out this issue every time they need to win an election. It's really that simple.

"I have asked my staff to draft a measure I call the Obesity Reduction and Health Promotion Act. Since Congress will apparently not be restrained by the laws and principles that naturally exist, I propose that the force of gravity, by the force of Congress, be reduced by 10 percent. Mr. Speaker, that will result in immediate weight loss for every American. It will immediately help reduce obesity problems in America."

—Rep. Bill Sali (R-Idaho)

Politicians Say the Darndest Things

Plan B

Here's the problem: I believe this is nothing but a political issue. So how can politicians prove me wrong? Well, it's two-for-one solution day, because I have an idea: Index it.

If you *really* care about doing what's best for workers and the economy (and not just your own campaign), then tie wage increases to some standard measure of inflation, such as the Consumer Price Index.

Never again would politicians have to plead that wages hadn't kept up with inflation. Never again would they have to call press conferences and invoke the words of great leaders to champion their "cause." Never again would this country have to waste valuable time and money on legislators taking to the floor of Congress to recite the same irrelevant statistic that 14 other people already have.

And never again would this be an issue that would have any influence on an election.

And that's *exactly* why it will never happen.

Chapter 18

Aging: God's System of Depreciation

YOU KNOW HOW SOME old people say they're not getting older, they're getting better? Well, those people are liars. That tired, old (pun intended) saying may look good on mugs and T-shirts in the AARP Christmas catalog, but the grim truth is that we are all getting older, and most of us *are not* getting better. We're dying in slow motion. We can't change that by trying to "catchphrase" our way out of it.

Perhaps I'm getting cranky as I crest into my late 30s. Okay, fine, early 40s. All right, all right, mid-40s. Actually, I completely forget how old I am, which is ironically one of the few perks of old age.

I'll bet the people who say 50 is the new 30 were pretty lame when they were 30.

A.D.D. MOMENT

You don't have to be in Florida (God's waiting room) to realize that America is full of old people. As a whole, our country's population is older than it's ever been. That's because technology has made life easier on us, and medical advancements are allowing us to live and complain about the country's youth longer.

Historical Fact
. . . or Something I Made Up?

In 1887, the life expectancy was so low that you qualified for a senior citizen's discount when you were 11.

The average life expectancy in the United States is now 80 years. Compare that with just 100 years ago, when it was just, well . . . a lot less than 80. And 200 years ago? People died so young they were never even born.

Okay, that may be an exaggeration, but the point is that aging itself isn't the problem—science is solving that for us. The real problem is what aging does to us. Dealing with the ravages of time is the rent we have to pay for our extended stay on the planet. Although that rent may seem overwhelming at first, it's not insurmountable if you just take each of the side effects one by one.

Guys, we've *got* to start taking better care of ourselves. Our life expectancy is only 75 years—that's five years shorter than for women. Too often, we're taught to "man-up" and ignore pain when we might be disregarding real symptoms of actual health issues. The *Journal of the American Medical Association* (a big-deal thingy written by guys *even smarter than me*) says that women are twice as likely to schedule regular exams than men.

A.D.D. MOMENT

Since I'd rather amputate my own arm with a plastic fork than have a routine physical, I'm not about to lecture you, but you do have to find something that will motivate you to take control of your health. Some people think about their wife and kids, but that didn't work for me (sorry, honey). No, the only thing that got me to the doctor was realizing that just 10 years ago, there was no TiVo, and you couldn't get anything close to a 50-inch flat screen! We are living in a miraculous age, and I want to be around when 3-D holographic TV allows Jessica Alba, Charlize Theron, or Wilford Brimley to strut around my living room. Did I say that out loud?

HAIR

As we get older, time gets a kick out of making hair stop growing where we *want* it to and start growing *where we don't*. In my 20s and 30s, I used to have a long, thick, flowing mane—like a roadie for Lynyrd Skynyrd. Nowadays, I have irregular groupings of white and gray "hair" strands—like a roadie for Abe Vigoda or something.

A.D.D. MOMENT I know Abe Vigoda probably doesn't travel with an entourage of roadies. In fact, he probably doesn't travel, period. I realize this is not the best analogy in the book.

Thinning hair and baldness are conditions that deal a tremendous blow to the male ego (while also helping to sell more sports cars than any commercial could ever dream of). Much like Samson, we men attach a sense of strength and virility to the presence of our hair. Imagine Fabio bald. Exactly. He'd be just another lonely Italian guy living on his mom's sofa.

As our hair abandons us, we feel the need to compensate with leather seats and horsepower and SUVs that can drive up mountains at 90-degree angles—if only we'd ever let them leave the road, which you don't when you spend 80 grand on a car. Yes, it's pathetic, and yes, we know it. (Personally, I'm packing about 550 horsepower—although I have approximately 21 kids now, so that's spread out over four minivans.)

I guess toupees are kind of a solution, but honestly, they just make things worse. Going the toupee route is like deciding to hide a pimple by painting your whole face red. Sure, no one will notice the pimple anymore, but that's because you've diverted their attention to something far worse.

At the height of the 1970s, when open shirts were all the rage, you could actually buy a "toupee" of chest hair, commonly referred to as a "Travolta."

I hate to ruin the ending of this chapter for you, but the truth is that in all of life money is the great equalizer. Donald Trump is not only getting older and fatter, but his hair gets more and more ridiculous with each passing second. Yet, inexplicably, his wives keep getting younger and hotter. Does he score because he's a good person, a charming conversationalist, a warm and loving soul? Nope. I can think of—oh, I don't know—a *billion* other reasons he always gets the girl. The moral of the story is that if you're not a handsome man, invest.

A.D.D. MOMENT

Toupees are the one self-improvement accessory that a man *doesn't* want you to notice. The new BMW convertible in the driveway? Absolutely. The speedboat that can part the ocean? Sure. The new full head of "hair" that he came back from "vacation" with? Not so much.

It's a cruel fact of life that men go bald, but there is a bright side. Studies show that a surprisingly high percentage of women say they find bald men attractive. Unfortu-

nately, the studies never tell you what those women look like. Regardless, if you're bald, it doesn't hurt to also be rich—since those studies never track how many women are attracted to *poor* bald men.

When it comes to hair sprouting up from—or shall I say out of—places we'd rather it didn't—such as our nose and ears—there's only one solution: the love of a good woman. See, as guys, we're not a whole lot different from our caveman ancestors. We're ruled largely by our primal desires (sex, food, more sex), and personal appearance ranks very low with men, unless they're stars of a reality show on Bravo.

We need guidance, and you'll find no one more eager to help you remake yourself than your wife or girlfriend. Women love to look good, and part of that is not looking bad by association when being seen with a schlub. That'd be you. It's in their best interest for you to not embarrass them in public. In fact, any married or soon-to-be-married man has a section in his closet devoted to clothes he's now forbidden to wear—all the apparel acquired in those glorious years when he was young, on the prowl, and incapable of dressing himself.

Reason #236 That Women Are More Evolved Than Men

Men fall in love with women they're attracted to, while women become attracted to the men they fall in love with.

It may sound contradictory, but it's the women who love us the most who keep us from morphing into a less talented version of Jerry Garcia. True love means many things, but one of the most important is alerting us when a forest has begun growing out of our ears and nose. If you really want to know whether your marriage will survive, then skip the counselors and go—right now—to the bathroom. Look in the mirror. If you have a "mustache" that could be taken care of with a good nose-hair trimmer, then you're doomed, because she's stopped caring.

WEIGHT

Even though you haven't started eating like Mindy Cohn (that fat girl from *The Facts of Life*—go ahead, Google her, hate me briefly for making fun of a husky teen star from the '80s, then laugh—I'll wait), your body's metabolism slows as you age, making it a lot easier to pack on a few (dozen) pounds.

As we get older, our lives become busier and more complicated. It's hard to make time for playing football in the park, running, or taking the stairs instead of the elevator. Not that I actually did any of those things when I was younger, but I'm just sayin'—I can imagine how tough they'd be to do now. Especially now that everything hurts. If it's not throbbing, it's prickly or numb.

A.D.D. MOMENT I was actually more of the "sit in the house by myself and become a social misfit" type of kid than the "go out and play with lots of friends" type. I know, you're shocked.

Historical Fact

. . . or Something I Made Up?

In the 1930s, Dr. William Tecte discovered that the hotter the food you eat, the faster your metabolism runs. The dessert industry, which was primarily serving ice cream and popsicles at the time, suffered an immediate and catastrophic crisis as a result. Fortunately, some quick thinking averted disaster as fried ice cream, baked apple cobbler, and the short-lived Habañero-'n'-Tabasco Blueberry Cheesecake were invented and rushed into the marketplace.

If you really want to lose weight, forget about all the diet pills, shakes, herbs, and other voodoo remedies (like exercise) out there, because there's really only one thing that works: Get yourself a TV show!

When I was just doing radio, I was a pale misfit—like the Pillsbury Doughboy but more doughy and less attractive. But within minutes of signing the contract for the TV show, my enormous ego kicked in. It wouldn't dare let me get in front of the camera without shedding the extra 5, 10 . . . or 65 pounds that I'd put on over the years.

A.D.D. MOMENT

Remember that fancy *Journal of Medical Blah, Blah* I told you about before? Well, they also say that preventing weight gain and alcohol abuse during midlife are the two major factors in determining whether we stay healthy as we ripen into old age. In my 30s, I was an overweight alcoholic (not exactly the combo they recommend), but fortunately, midlife to them doesn't start until 40, so I think I'm off the hook.

I jumped on the Atkins train, and now I look slightly less grotesque than I used to. As when on any diet, I still have moments (or hours) of weakness, but now I'm able to run over to the TiVo, watch my double chins from the night before in slow motion, and step away from Tania's lasagna with only minimal harm done.

Please note: This "get your own TV show" plan for staying thin has not worked for Oprah. If you are Oprah and you're reading this book, please disregard and move on to the next section. But consider adding this book to your book club. And send me some money.

PLASTIC SURGERY

This is always a bad idea. Need proof? Just check out Joan Rivers. Once you've stopped vomiting, check out Melanie Griffith, then Meg Ryan, then Michael Douglas, then Susan Lucci, then John Travolta, then most of the *Desperate Housewives,* then the poster child for plastic surgery, Jocelyn Wildenstein. (Yes, it's worth another Google; I'll wait again.)

Tragically, too many women, and an increasing number of men, seem to think that having the small things made bigger and the big things made smaller is the key to looking and feeling young. Invariably, these people want us to pretend that they look mysteriously younger and more fabulous, when in actuality they look like spooky freaks who got tired of only feeling insecure on the inside and decided to show some of it on the outside as well. I make fun of these people, and I encourage you to do the same.

A.D.D. MOMENT

If I were a psychologist, I would tell someone who desperately wanted plastic surgery that they were "externalizing deep-seated feelings of insecurity" or something smart-sounding like that. Then I'd charge them $300 and tell them to come back in two days.

HEALTH

Back in the day, my generation's drugs of choice were cocaine, whiskey, Quaaludes, and hashish. And there was no Big Pharma, just Big Lou, and you didn't need a prescription, just cash. Nowadays, my generation is grooving on Lipitor, Ambien, Propecia, and Viagra. And while medicine has done a lot to help slow the body's inevitable decay, it has failed us in one crucial way: nighttime peeing.

What does it say about the pharmaceutical industry that we've made greater strides in curing erectile dysfunction than prostate or testicular cancers—big-time killers of the over-50 set? If profit is their motivation, then maybe someone should inform those learned men of science that nobody has less sex than dead guys. (Except for maybe Al Franken.)

A.D.D. MOMENT

I'm literally turning into my grandparents—I must get up five times a night to go to the bathroom. I don't know what it is; no matter how much or how little I drink during the day or evening, I spend more time in the bathroom at night than I do in bed. I'm actually thinking of bringing a pillow in there to save myself some time. Wait a minute—I'm having another one of my incredible ideas: a pillow for nighttime potty breaks, the "Pee-low"! This is going to be huge—I've got a nose for these sorts of things.

But that can wait. Now, where was I? Oh, right . . . my body's slow but unyielding decline.

Besides my incredibly shrinking bladder, I've had chest pains and lower-back aches, migraines and shortness of breath, the sweats, the chills, and all the major and minor health concerns of a guy who's fort—let's just say no longer in his 20s. The only solution is to do our best to stay in good health and wait for some dorky super-genius to figure out how we can all live forever.

Alzheimer's Fact/A.D.D. Moment

A good indication that you're getting older is the inability to focus. Of course, I already have A.D.D., so it's a lethal combination. I don't think homeless guys in New York should smoke when cigarettes cost $8 a pack. I'd like to meet Neil Armstrong. Mint chocolate chip is probably the best ice cream flavor going. I hate elevator conversations.

But hey, while I said at the beginning of this chapter that catchphrases weren't going to help us with this aging thing, I do believe this: If getting older depresses you, "Just think of the alternative." (*Cha-ching!* I smell a T-shirt gold mine!)

They also say that youth is wasted on the young, but the other side of that coin is that wisdom is wasted on the old. We usually tend to get smarter, more confident, and more

Makes a great gift!

the Pee-Low!

You can sleep in the bathroom, but you can't pee in the bedroom!

Show your bladder who's boss!

Z Z Z

In Stock Now!

MADE FROM SPACE-AGE TECHNOLOGY!

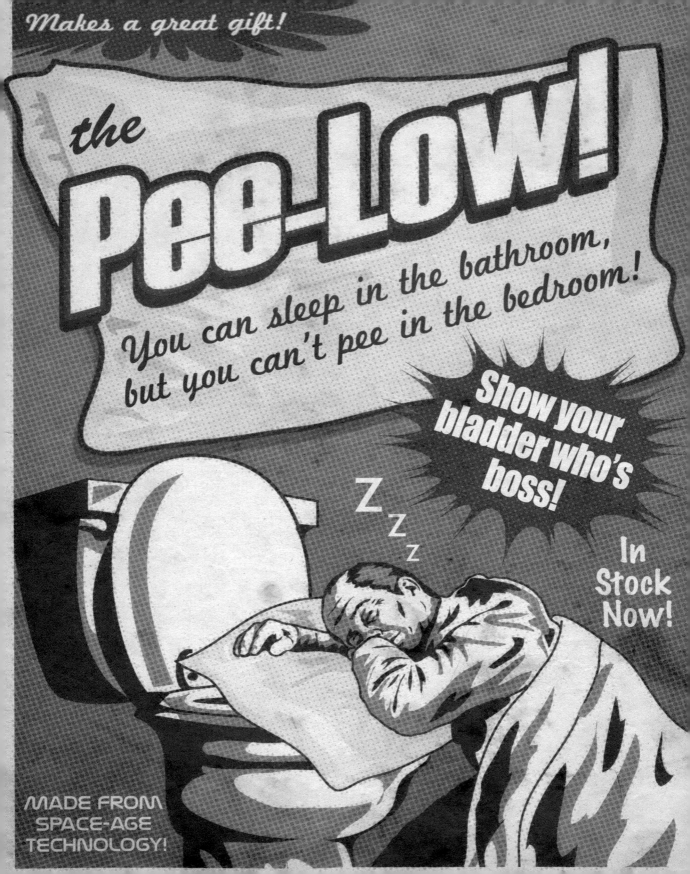

emotionally secure as we get older, and I think that's a pretty fair trade for smooth skin and a flat stomach. I mean, would you *really* go back to being 18 if you could?

Of course, getting older won't be a total picnic if illegal immigration continues to drain this country's vital resources and I'm left without Social Security. Or . . . maybe I'll slip and break my hip while reaching for the Ho-Hos, and I won't be able to get help because the emergency room near me has been closed because of public funds having been reallocated because of failed border security. I know, I know, this doesn't have anything to do with what I'm talking about. But getting to complain about stuff is a perk of old age. That and getting to take a nap whenever you want. Plus, movie admission is cheaper. And I can save 15 percent at Wal-Mart on Wednesday mornings. Actually, aging has some pretty good upsides.

Now, if you'll excuse me, I have to use the bathroom again.

Chapter 19

Opinion Polls: Our Country's Real Leader

THE POLITICAL BATTLE LINES WERE DRAWN. While each side scavenged tirelessly to line up allies, the rest of the nation turned its attention to inside the Beltway, where a vicious partisan battle to repeal the Public Affairs Act of 1975 was taking center stage.

Like almost every high-profile issue that passes through Washington, opinion polling was vitally important. The *Washington Post* commissioned a national survey, and both sides waited with bated breath, knowing that the results would undoubtedly shape the future of their parties.

After a seemingly interminable wait, the results were finally announced: By a slim 5 percent margin, Americans favored repealing the Public Affairs Act of 1975.

There was just one small problem: There was no such thing as the Public Affairs Act of 1975.

Almost half of those polled by the *Post* (43 percent) had no problem offering up an opinion on something they had never even heard of.

But wait, it gets worse.

The original wording of the poll question was "Some people say the 1975 Public Affairs Act should be repealed. Do you agree or disagree with this idea?"

Twenty-four percent of respondents agreed, 19 percent disagreed, and 57 percent were actually honest enough to admit they had no frickin' idea what it was.

But just for fun, the *Post* asked the question two other ways to see how much personal political ideologies influence opinion. First they asked: "Republicans in Congress believe the 1975 Public Affairs Act should be repealed. Do you agree or disagree with this idea?"

Suddenly, the mythical Public Affairs Act of 1975 became a deep-seated partisan issue. Republicans overwhelmingly embraced the repeal by a margin of 35 percent to 14 percent, while Democrats demanded the Public Affairs Act continue to stand, 45 percent to 13 percent.

When the question was posed as President Clinton's idea, Republicans completely reversed themselves and fell in love with the idea of repealing the act by a 40- to 17-percent margin. Clinton, who had yet to unleash Operation Human Humidor and fully endear himself to his party, managed only a split from Democrats, but the experiment's results were clear: Many people mirror the partisan hacks they hold in such disdain. Even without any information, they'll gladly give opinions that toe the party line the very first chance they get.

DUMB, DUMBER, DUMBERER, AND PEOPLE TAKING POLLS

Allow me to shake your faith in humanity even further for just a second. A few decades ago, a man named Philip Converse began studying opinion polls and found that 88 percent of people had no semblance of a coherent opinion on supposedly important public issues and no idea where political parties stood on those issues.

A.D.D. MOMENT No, that wasn't a misprint; it really was 88 percent. Well, I assume it wasn't a misprint. If there was an error in printing this book and it says something other than 88 percent, then it *was* a misprint. Although if they misprinted it the second time I wrote "88 percent" and it was replaced with the same number as the first misprint, then you'd never know the original was a misprint. I'm 88 percent sure that didn't happen, though.

When interviewed, Converse found that most people had no rational system of beliefs, and many presented an entirely different set of opinions the next time they were asked. Over and over again, the analysis pointed to two unquestionable conclusions:

1. Most people are simply making up their opinions on the spot, mainly to prove they aren't stupid for not having them.
2. After inventing new opinions, people act overly passionate about them in order to hide their ignorance.

As unsettling as those conclusions are, at least they help explain every infuriating conversation about politics you've ever had at work.

EXIT POLLS EXIT THE REALM OF CREDIBILITY

It was a glorious several hours. Democratic operatives, the media, and bloggers, the media's new unquestioned source, celebrated with all-knowing smirks on their faces, comfortable in the knowledge that George W. Bush would not serve a second term as president of the United States.

Oops.

Why were they so wrong? Well, wrong is what they do best—but the real problem was that they'd all based their premature glee on exit-polling data.

After Voter News Service failed so miserably in 2000 and 2002, the National Election Pool took over in 2004. Even though they specifically asked the media not to leak the initial results and held a conference call during the day to say that the data looked sketchy, the leaking and the smirking didn't stop.

"The sum total of what we got today is enough to suggest that there should never be exit polls again."

—John Zogby, Zogby International

Polling Experts Say the Darndest Things

In reality, as many as 59 percent of those sampled in the exit polls were women, which skewed all of the data toward John Kerry. Once the final numbers came in, all of the smirks were wiped away and moved over to the other side of the aisle—at least until 2006, when they all combined to live as one gigantic grin on Nancy Pelosi's face.

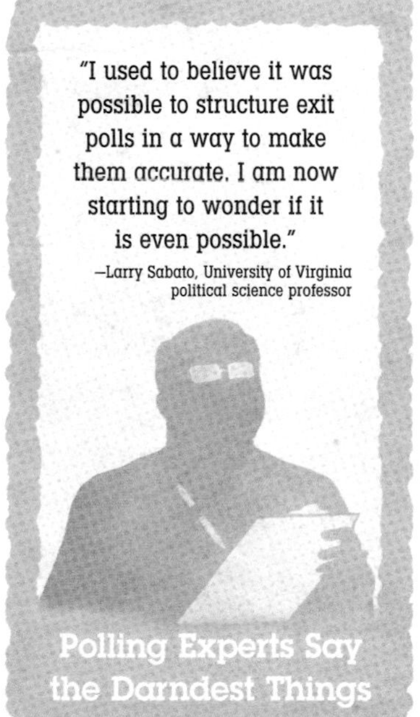
"I used to believe it was possible to structure exit polls in a way to make them accurate. I am now starting to wonder if it is even possible."
—Larry Sabato, University of Virginia political science professor
Polling Experts Say the Darndest Things

	Exit poll result	Actual result
Iowa	Kerry by 1.0%	Bush by 0.1%
Nevada	Kerry by 1.4%	Bush by 2.6%
New Mexico	Kerry by 4.2%	Bush by 0.8%
Ohio	Kerry by 6.5%	Bush by 2.1%
Minnesota	Kerry by 14.3%	Kerry by 3.5%
New Hampshire	Kerry by 15.0%	Kerry by 1.4%
North Carolina	Bush by 3.6%	Bush by 12.4%
Pennsylvania	Kerry by 13.8%	Kerry by 2.3%
Wisconsin	Kerry by 5.7%	Kerry by 0.4%

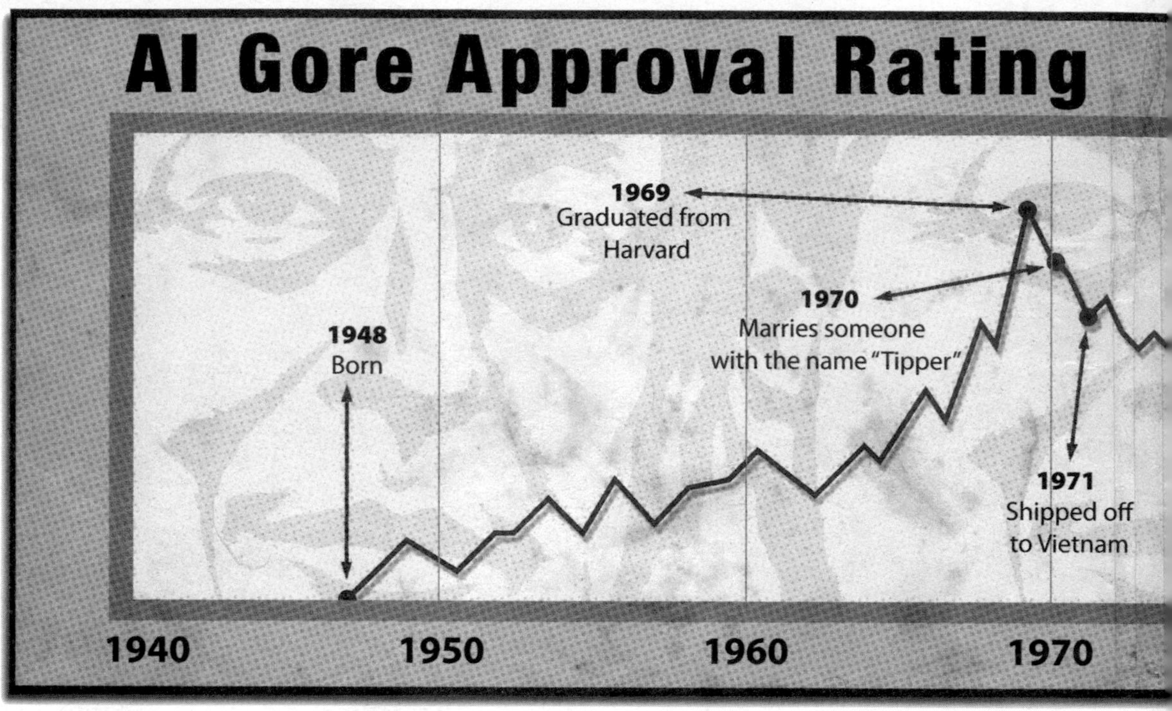

Our experience with exit polls should teach us all a larger lesson: Polls of all types, while valuable in certain circumstances, have an incredible amount of inherent problems. Once you start looking into them, you'll realize that polls should be taken not just with a grain of salt but with an entire Pacific Ocean's worth.

LARGER MARGIN THAN YOU'D THINK

How do pollsters predict the opinion of the entire country's population of more than 300 million people by talking to 1,000? They can't. But in theory, they should at least be able to get pretty close. That's where the margin of error comes into play.

People seem generally to understand the concept of "margin of error" (unless, of course, they're making it up to seem smart), but frequently they don't get an accurate picture from the media of what it actually means. For example, how many times have you heard something like "In our latest poll, the McGriddle holds a lead of 51 to 46 percent over the Crossanwich. That falls outside the survey's four-point margin of error."

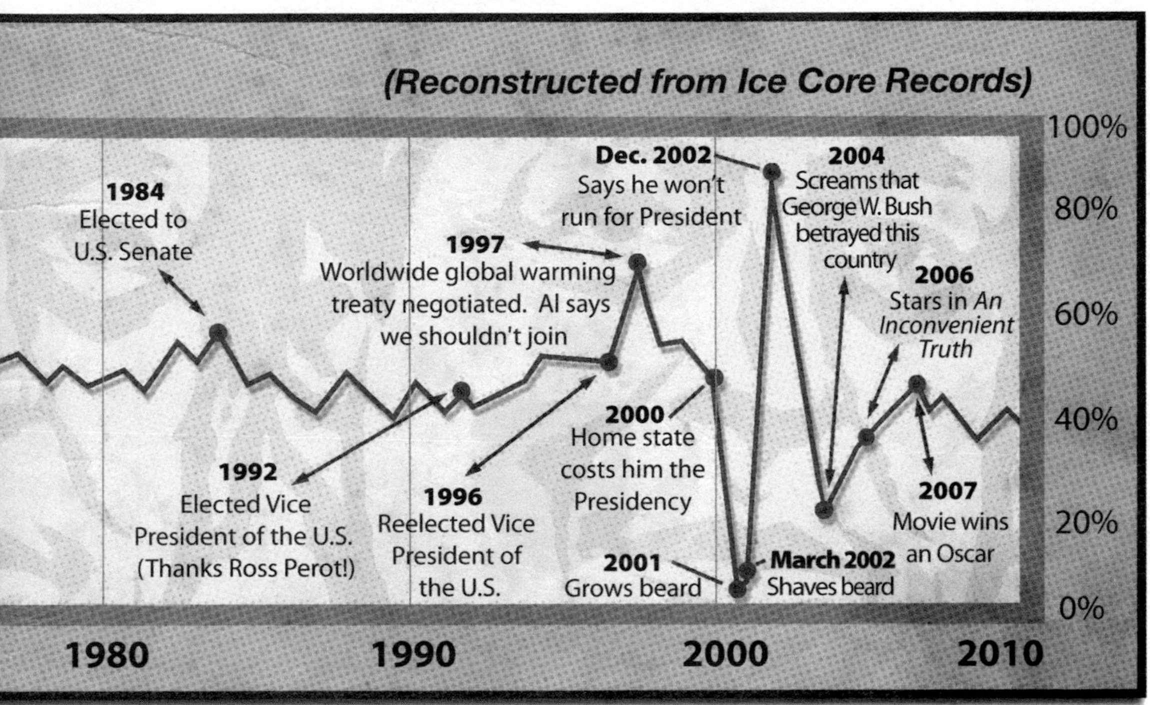

Actually, no, Mr. Fast Food News Anchor, it doesn't. You have to apply the margin of error to *both* sides. The McGriddle's support may actually be anywhere between 47 and 55 percent, while the Crossanwich's favorability could fall anywhere between 42 and 50 percent. That means the McGriddle could be the favorite breakfast treat by a convincing 55 to 42 percent margin, or there's an equal chance that the Crossanwich could actually be winning the hearts, minds, and arteries of America by a 50 to 47 percent margin.

Yes, those are the statistical extremes, but those extremes can and do happen. That makes me wonder why we listen to any opinion poll that's even remotely close.

> **A.D.D. MOMENT**
>
> **This is,** of course, a completely fictional example of America's opinion of breakfast sandwiches. I believe the sweet and salty goodness of the McGriddle would handily triumph over the buttery cheesiness of the Crossanwich. However, if the poll also asked about the availability of "cheesy tots," then the King would rapidly close the gap.

I HAVE NO CONFIDENCE IN YOUR INTERVAL

While most media sources will at least acknowledge the margin of error, there is another measure of a poll's accuracy that is just as important yet completely invisible to everyone who spent their college years at keg parties instead of statistics class: the 95 percent confidence interval.

The *Los Angeles Times* says that the confidence interval is "such a standard measure that we usually don't even mention it." And while it's true that 95 percent is a standard number, it's far from standard knowledge that it even exists.

It basically means that one out of every 20 polls don't even fall within the margin of error. Or, to translate even further, one out of every 20 polls is complete bullcrap.

Now, I don't have any fancy polls of my own to prove this, but I would venture to guess that the polls the media hype the most—which are usually the ones that show drastic changes or unexpected results—are more likely to be part of that 5 percent group that's fatally flawed. (To be fair, the margin of error on that guess is 3 percent, but my confidence level is 100 percent.)

Not Representative of the Population

All the rules that bring the fabulous accuracy we've grown to know and love from opinion polls go completely out the window when the sample is either not truly random or not representative of the population. Sometimes this sort of thing is just an innocent limitation of the system. For example, about 1.5 percent of the population older than 18 isn't generally surveyed because they can't speak English.

Judging by the way people answer polls, I sometimes wonder if that number isn't actually a lot higher.
A.D.D. MOMENT

Another 5 percent of the population never gets surveyed because they don't have a phone. No phone at all. And *you're* embarrassed that you can't attach a file to an email.

Even though innocuous oversight can be blamed for a lot of polling irregularities, sometimes you have to wonder if certain polls are tainted for other reasons. For one example (among billions), look at the October 2005 CBS News poll that (poorly) attempted to measure the approval rating of George W. Bush.

The media rejoiced in reporting on a poll that showed Bush's approval rating drop to all-time low levels, while ignoring the fact that the polling sample was nothing short of ridiculous. Out of the 1,018 people CBS polled, only 25 percent were Republicans, 40 percent were Democrats, and 33 percent were Independents (use your imagination about what the other 2 percent were). Does that sound like a fair sample that's representative of the U.S. population?

Afterward, they did weight the totals, showing 28 percent Republicans, 37 percent Democrats, and 34 percent Independents.

October 2005 CBS News Poll

	Unweighted	Weighted	2004 voters
Total Republicans polled	25%	28%	37%
Total Democrats polled	40%	37%	37%
Total Independents polled	33%	34%	26%

If you extrapolate the CBS poll to reflect the 2004 exit-poll party weightings, Bush's approval rating jumps from 34 percent to 38 percent. While that's not exactly George Washington territory, it takes away the "worst since" angle of the story and makes it just one more boring poll. A boring poll that does very little to help the media organization that commissioned it.

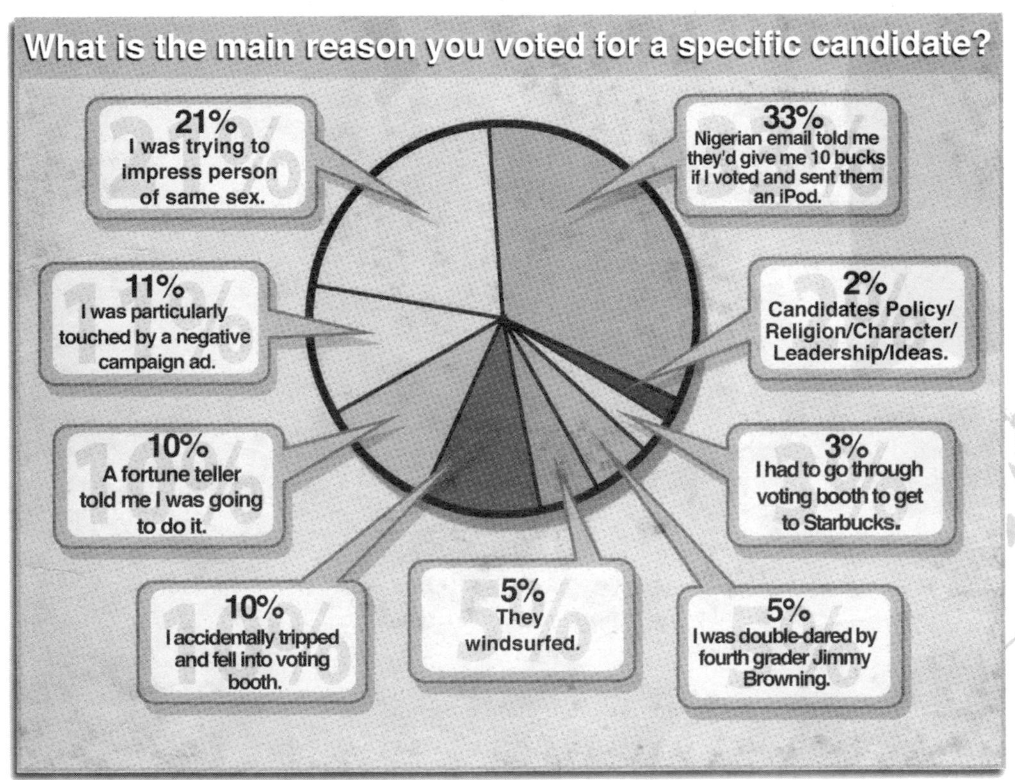

CBS News' excuse is that they don't weight poll samples by political party, just demographics such as race and age. But isn't there (or, at least, shouldn't there be) a moment before you release the results when you realize that your sample is so bad that you should just trash the whole thing and start over?

THE NEW GUY IN THE OFFICE

One of the odd simplifications the media like to present is that opinion is "changing" when a poll shows a higher or lower amount of support for an issue or politician. For example, if support for future President Lindsay Lohan is 53 percent one week and 48 percent the next, newscasters will undoubtedly state that support for the Lohan administration (of the Party Party) fell by 5 percent after her "no undies" exit from *Marine One.*

Put aside for a second all of the other problems I've already pointed out that make the poll itself dubious at best because the media's characterization of the results isn't even accurate.

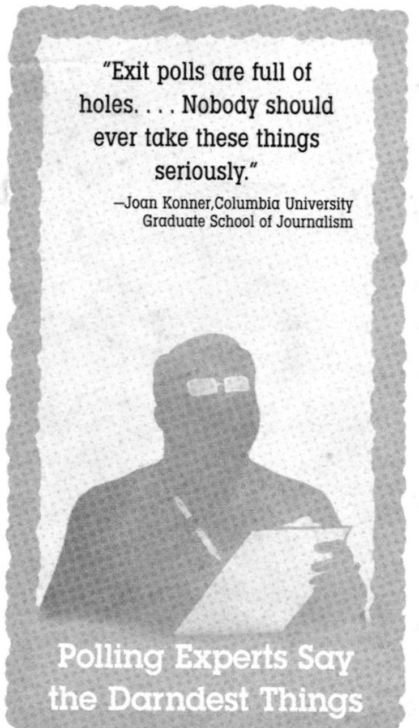

"Exit polls are full of holes. . . . Nobody should ever take these things seriously."
—Joan Konner, Columbia University Graduate School of Journalism
Polling Experts Say the Darndest Things

To show you what I mean, I'll counter the Lohan simplification with an even greater one: Let's say there's a new guy who starts working at your office. You want to find out how popular he is, so you go around and ask 10 of your coworkers if they like him or not. Seven out of 10 say yes, giving him an approval rating of 70 percent.

A month later, after the new guy was caught urinating in the coffee room and copying his extremities on the digital document center, you decide to take a new poll to see how much his approval rating has changed. How would you do it? Would you go ask an entirely new group of 10 people, or would you go back to the same 10 people from the first poll to see if their opinion had "changed?"

Professional pollsters would go to an entirely new group of people, even though they have no idea if those people liked him in the first place. Seemingly, you'd get a much better feel for actual "change" if you picked a representative sample group and then just kept asking them every week. Unfortunately, that would probably create a new industry of special-interest groups that would find out who is in the samples and start lobbying them for votes.

RESPONSE RATES

One of the main questions I have when I see a poll is this: What kind of person has a life that is so boring that spending 25 minutes on the phone answering questions from a complete stranger seems like a good idea? Aren't they likely the same people who are currently paying a few thousand dollars to the son of a former Nigerian king who promises to give them half of his family's fortune?

The percentage of people who actually participate in polls is pretty well known to be only about 30 percent. That's a significant problem.

Studies have shown that when the response rate is increased to just 60 percent, the average difference in answers provided is about 2 percent. It might not sound like much, but remember that Bush defeated Kerry in 2004 by just 3 percent nationwide.

CAN YOU HEAR ME NOW? GOOD

The same general concept that stops businesses like Bills Stucco Siding and Toilet Repair from calling you on your cell phone also stops pollsters from getting your opinion for their worthless surveys. And because many people (as much as 10 percent of the U.S. population and growing) have already converted to a cell-phone-only lifestyle, millions and millions of people are left unmeasured by polling groups.

Initial surveys from Pew show that those polled on cell phones are younger, more liberal, less affluent, less likely to be married, and more likely to be a member of a minority group than those surveyed on land lines. (You have to love the irony of doing a survey to assess the inaccuracies of your surveys.) However, one of the unexpected results was that young cell-phone users were also more likely to support President Bush than young land-line users.

> A.D.D. MOMENT
>
> **Cell phone users** were about half as likely to participate in the poll, although those who did were twice as likely to be using those stupid Bluetooth ear pieces and annoying the people they were sitting next to.

That's yet another small example of how something that's seemingly unrelated can chip away at a poll's credibility. Of course, "small" in this context refers to the complete elimination of the opinion of tens of millions of people.

LOOK ME UP NEXT TIME YOU'RE IN TOWN

Many of the polls you hear about in the media were done using listed phone numbers instead of the polling-geek-approved system of random-digit dialing. It doesn't sound like a significant difference, but using the phone book eliminates those with unlisted phone numbers. That excludes approximately 30 percent of the entire population, including 100 percent of those who've faked their own deaths to avoid uncomfortable calls resulting from drunken one-night stands.

I'M OUT OF ORDER? THIS WHOLE POLL IS OUT OF ORDER!

Could the American public hold opinions so pathetically shallow that they can be affected dramatically by simply changing the order of the possible options for their answers? (Sigh.) Yeah.

To test this phenomenon (and I don't mean that in the good sense), a poll was done in which respondents were asked what issue mattered the most in deciding which politician to vote for.

When "health care" was the first option listed, it was chosen as the most important voting issue by 24 percent of respondents. When it was listed last, it dropped to just 15 percent. When "family values" was moved to the top of the list, it increased from 10 percent to 20 percent. Only the issues listed in the middle stayed around the same. (For example, "the environment" was last both times. Sorry, Al Gore.)

Issue That Mattered Most in Deciding Vote

Issue	Choosing as Most Important When Listed in This Order	Choosing as Most Important When Listed in Reverse Order
Health Care	24%	15%
Federal Budget Deficit	25%	17%
Abortion	13%	11%
Education	12%	13%
Economy/jobs	41%	44%
Environment	4%	7%
Taxes	12%	17%
Foreign Policy	7%	9%
Family Values	10%	20%

Note: Percentages total more than 100 because of multiple responses. Adapted from Mitofsky and Edelman, 1993.

STICKS AND STONES MAY BREAK MY BONES, BUT WORDS WILL NEVER HURT ME

Whoever came up with that saying obviously wasn't a pollster, because the wording of a question might be the single largest factor in skewing a poll from mildly accurate to as irrelevant as the presidential aspirations of Joseph Biden.

For example, when people were asked about our missile-defense system, it was supported by a wide 61 to 29 percent margin. But when the same question was asked with the caveat that "some scientists believe it's unlikely the system can ever work," people *opposed* it 56 to 25 percent. When instead told that the system might have "a good chance of working," support became almost universal (71 to 12 percent).

But it's not just complicated issues such as missile defense that cause confusion. A 1993 poll showed that 34 percent of Americans either questioned whether the Holocaust ever happened or straight-out denied its existence. That's a shockingly high response, right? Yes, but it was the confusing way the question was asked that led to the ridiculous results. The question was phrased "Does it seem possible or does it seem impossible to you that the Nazi extermination of the Jews never happened?" Huh? That question is filled with more double negatives than the coming life of Anna Nicole Smith's baby.

A.D.D. MOMENT **The nonson** of Anna Nicole Smith, Dannielynn, may never get a chance to undo the negative consequences of her nonfather not living until she doesn't become a senior citizen. Dannielynn will never not forget the issues and non-issues surrounding the downfall of her mother and the undoing of a positively negative upbringing. The only nonlying parental nominee, Larry Birkhead, will never not be unhappy with Howard K. Stern for not denying he wasn't the father of the baby, unless lawsuits help him disallow himself from being unrich.

Once the wording was cleaned up (i.e., once the idiot who wrote it was fired), more than 95 percent of people said the Holocaust either "definitely" or "probably" did happen. The other 5 percent were either brain-dead, a former Nazi prison guard in hiding, or named President Ahmadinejad.

Because so many people are making up their opinions on the spot, the wording of poll questions is vitally important yet so subjective that it renders an incredibly high number of polls completely worthless.

PEOPLE ARE CALCULATING BASTARDS

People are calculating bastards, and while a lot of them are not informed on the topics they're being questioned about, that doesn't mean they're stupid. They know how polls get used, and they think about that when they answer.

For example, let's say you had a one-night stand with one of the Proclaimers, and a pollster asks you if you think the greatest band of all time is the Rolling Stones, U2, the Beatles, the Proclaimers, or Chumbawumba.

A.D.D MOMENT You know, the Proclaimers! The band that sang that "I Would Walk 500 Miles" song? Nothing? Remember, they had nerdy twins who looked like the result of a botched stem-cell research project as their lead singers? Still nothing? You'll have to take my word for it.

A.D.D. MOMENT You know, Chumbawumba! You don't remember them either? "I get knocked down, but I get up again, you're never gonna keep me down!" Still nothing? Remember, it felt like something you'd hear from the bottom of a drunken soccer stadium stampede? Am I the only one?

Now, obviously, you don't think the Proclaimers are better than the Beatles, but since you now have a 14-year-old son with geeky glasses and a ridiculously exaggerated Scottish accent, you vote for them anyway. Now, thanks to you and your horrible judgment on whom to be a groupie with, the poll has incorrect results, and your kid is incredibly odd-looking.

A.D.D. MOMENT

If you want a more scientific example than a hypothetical story about bad one-hit wonders, then go back and reread the Republican and Democrat responses to the repeal of the Public Affairs Act of 1975 at the beginning of this chapter. If you want a real challenge, try to read it while listening to the Proclaimers.

SPIRAL OF SILENCE

What a nice little circle the media have put together. They report only the bad news from the war, portray the religious as a bunch of snake-charming nut-jobs, and present every conservative policy, from Social Security reform to tax cuts, as hateful, racist, and uncompassionate. Then the same (supposedly neutral) organizations call people and ask if they support the policies they've been describing as evil.

Shockingly, many average people feel some social pressure to give the "correct" answer and avoid appearing like hatemongers. That skews the polls against many issues supported by conservatives.

But the best part is still to come. The media, the same group that influenced the opinion and then measured it, will now go and report on their own poll results as fact, thereby creating yet another story that will help persuade the next round of poll responders to hide their real opinions.

Polling geeks call this type of reaction the "spiral of silence." I call it "how America works."

MEDIA COVERAGE OF POLLS

Ever wonder why you start suddenly hearing a random song from someone like Randy Vanwarmer on the radio again, seemingly out of nowhere?

Most likely, it's because his song "tested" well in the surveys that radio stations do with their listeners to find out what they want to hear. Occasionally, an older song tests really well, and you'll start to hear it every 20 minutes for a month. Then, invariably, new research will come out revealing that the old research was a fluke, and the station goes back to playing the same crap it was playing before.

Research can be valuable, but only when good, experienced radio people interpret it. Making a station "Your Randy Vanwarmer Source" for three weeks is not a good idea, no matter what the data say. The same thing is true of public opinion polls.

A.D.D MOMENT You know, Randy Vanwarmer! Oh, come on, you've got to be kidding me! "Just When I Needed You Most"! No, not the one by Dolly Parton, that was a cover version. Still nothing? I give up.

For example, the ubiquitous "direction of the country" poll is universally looked at as yet another measure of the president's performance. But think of a conservative who's more than happy with the president but might be concerned about the direction of the country because of how it's turning away from religion.

In fact, Republicans are routinely about 30 percentage points less positive on the future of the country than they are on the performance of George W. Bush. But it's all about how you translate the poll to the public. A less experienced person might look at the data and conclude that Republicans have turned on their leader, while a more seasoned person might realize that other things are in play besides a simple referendum on the president.

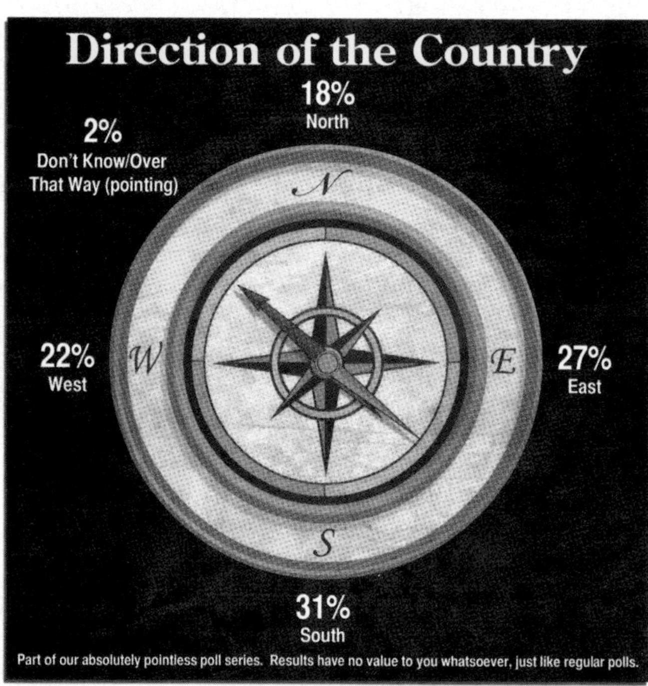

Another way the media control the message is by hand-selecting which polls get reported. For example, on March 18, 2007, two different polls of Iraqi citizens were released. The first, from *USA Today*, reflected typical media optimism about Iraq, including such positive stats as nine out of 10 Iraqis saying they lived in fear, along with uplifting antecdotal evidence such as a 38-year-old Iraqi woman saying, "There is no life at all."

On the same day, the Sunday *Times* reported on a poll with a sample size more than twice as large as the *USA Today* poll that painted quite a different story. It showed that "by a majority of two to one, Iraqis prefer the current leadership to Saddam Hussein's regime, regardless of the security crisis and a lack of public services." The poll also revealed that "contrary to the views of many western analysts, most Iraqis do not believe they are embroiled in a civil war." In fact, only 27 percent of Iraqis reported feeling that way.

Guess which poll was widely reported by the U.S. media?

SO . . . WHO CARES?

Who cares if polls are unreliable? Aren't they basically just a little blurb in the bottom corner of the newspaper?

No—polls aren't just *measures* of opinion, they *move* opinion.

Because most people base their views on so little information, polls wind up moving polls. When the only real piece of knowledge people have is a poll that shows overwhelming approval of an issue, they tend to approve of it too. Like the two-thirds of all Yankee fans who live outside New York, these people have fallen victim to what pollsters call "the bandwagon effect."

What's funny is that most Americans who look at polling results joke about those who answer "I don't know" or "No opinion." But, unlike the majority of respondents in most surveys, at least those people are being honest about their ignorance. The rest of us try to bluff our way through it.

A.D.D. MOMENT

If we could use the peer-reviewed science of *American Idol* results as an example—remember Sanjaya? No? Seriously? I need to stop making pop-culture references. He was the weird-looking Indian kid who couldn't sing but became a minor sensation for a couple of months as he kept surviving the nationwide vote every week. Why? The bandwagon effect. He was surviving because he received all the press attention, and people started to believe he wasn't just that season's sideshow. If *American Idol* was political, there surely would have been a media circus proclaiming that America was yearning for terribly voiced, androgynous, half-Indian leaders with crazy hair. (Which, in comparison with many of our current leaders, doesn't sound too bad.)

MY SOLUTION

Unlike many of the problems in this book, this one is incredibly easy to solve. It doesn't involve any technical fixes for polls themselves—it just requires that the people who use them (mainly our leaders) get back to that outdated concept of common sense that many have somehow forgotten.

HOW LEADERS SHOULD HANDLE POLLS

1 Take the poll before reading it and fold it lengthwise.

2 Fold it widthwise.

3 Take the folded poll and insert it into the cylindrical can where you previously threw your ketchup stained Arby's wrappers.

4 Lead your state, country, or branch of the PTA based on your knowledge, research, and gut. That's why people elected you.

If you're a leader, here's what you do when a poll arrives on your desk.

Real leaders don't need to read polls. They don't need to hire a polling consultant to interpret them or change their whole personality and agenda based on their results. And they especially don't need to follow polls to keep their paychecks coming in for another two, four, or six years.

No, *real* leaders live and die by what they think is right, and eventually the polls follow *them.*

Chapter 20

Poverty Prozac

PICTURE A POOR person in your mind right now. What does he or she look like?

I see a Tiny Tim clone, complete with soot on his face and a barely understandable English accent. "Allo, I'd like some more chocolate, please. And please stop dressing me like Mark Twain circa 1918. Is it me, or are these knickers made of burlap?"

Maybe you pictured a frail child batting away flies in some horrifying landscape of a Third World country. Maybe you even saw Sally Struthers standing next to him, chomping on a Double Bacon Western Barbecue Burger while begging you to send your daily coffee money to a country that will use it to fund the nineteenth palace of a corrupt dictator.

Regardless of the details, the poor person you pictured was probably:

- hungry
- unable to pay the bills
- lacking a satisfactory entertainment system
- without shelter
- smelly

A.D.D. MOMENT

The only stereotype that applies in America is the stench. Being a man who has stood in his fair share of elevators, I know that odor is an American epidemic that penetrates both our culture and my nose—and it's rampant no matter the income level.

In many places on earth, those stereotypes may be true—but not in America.

That's not to say that real hunger and poverty don't exist in America—they clearly do, and each case is as significant as it is devastating. But once you hear the facts, you'll realize that the crisis is infinitesimally small compared with what you've been led to believe. I hope that will serve as a giant dose of antidepressant Poverty Prozac.

Bill Gates
Net Worth
56 Billion

$43,000
Average
American

$30,100
Average Frenchy
French Man

$10,600
Average
Mexican

$9,979
American
at Poverty Line

$8,900
Average
Iranian

$8,800
Average
Turkmenistan-ian

$8,600
Average
Brazilian

$8,200
Average
Macedonian

$7,800
Average
Belarusian

$7,300
Average
Azerbaijanian

$6,900
Average
Venezuelan

$6,400
Average
Peruvian

$5,500
Average
Swaziland-ian

$4,600
Average
Jamaican

$4,000
Average
Syrian

$3,000
Average
Bolivian

$1,300
Average
Burkina
Faso-ian

$900
Average
Yemen

$600
Average
Malawian

$600
Average
Somalian

Glenn Beck
1st Year of
Employment
$27.31
Paid in Pastry

Sam
The Poorest
Person in
the World

someone at the U.S. poverty line is better off than 85% of the rest of the world

WHAT'S FOR DINNER, I'M STARVING!

Hunger is not truly an American problem.* In fact, it's almost insulting to the rest of the world to allege that, as even a cursory glimpse at their reality makes our worst problems seem like incredible blessings.

Of those Americans defined as poor by the U.S. Census, an astounding 89 percent had enough food to eat throughout the year, and only 2 percent had bouts with hunger on a regular basis. Overall, just 1 out of every 400 children skips one or more meals per month because of lack of cash. In fact, the biggest food-related crisis for America's poor *is eating too much of it.*

This country's porker problem doesn't discriminate between rich and poor, and studies have shown that people's intake of fat, vitamins, minerals, and protein is almost identical across class lines. America truly is the melting pot of pot bellies.

THE CHECK ACTUALLY IS IN THE MAIL

Sure, maybe the poor are figuring out a way to eat, but they can't possibly be paying their bills every month, can they? After all, I've never thought of myself as poor, but there have been months where I've missed payments, shifted debt, and stolen from my pimp to make ends meet.

While those things certainly happen to the poor more than the general population, seven out of 10 poor households were able to meet all of their essential expenses (mortgage or rent, utility bills, and important medical care) for the entire year. About 96 percent of poor households avoided having their utilities shut off because of lack of payment, and 99 percent avoided eviction because they couldn't come up with mortgage or rent money.

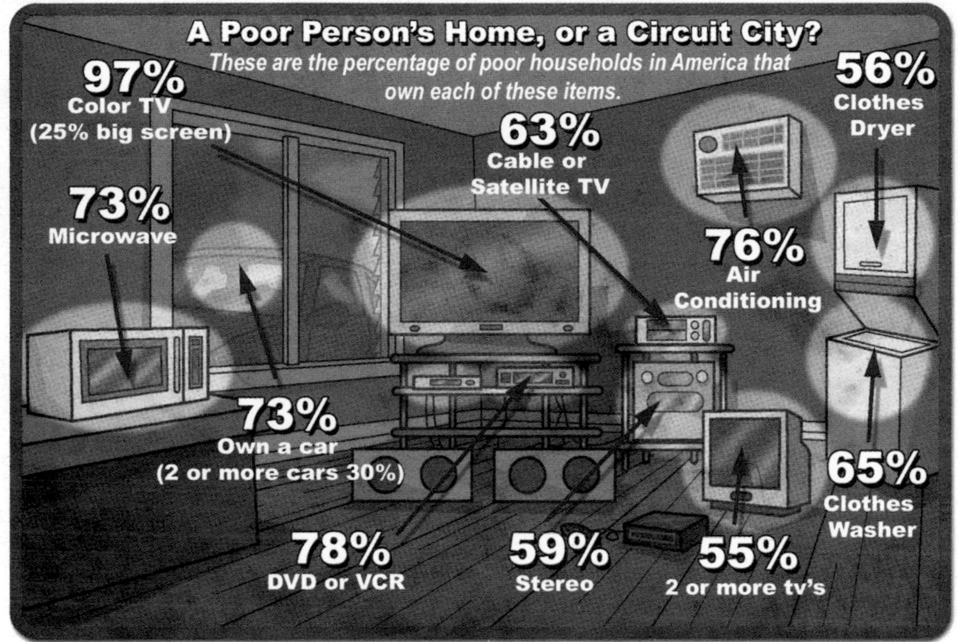

Not only do almost all poor people have shelter, paid bills, and a decent living room full of electronics, but almost half of them actually own their own homes. In fact, the average dwelling of the American poor person has more square footage than the average overall residence in every European nation except Luxembourg.

Remember, that's not the average *poor* person in Europe, that's the *average person*. And it's not as if the homes our poor live in are rat-infested hell holes; only 2 percent of them have "severe physical problems," and just 9 percent have "moderate physical problems."

America's poor live in homes 30 percent larger than that of the *average* Frenchy-French person. I just had to throw that in.

A.D.D. MOMENT

A.D.D. MOMENT While a "moderate physical problem" might sound bad, it actually includes such devastating conditions as not having a full kitchen. And the most common "severe physical problem" was having to share a bathroom with another unit. Obviously, that isn't exactly ideal, but it's far from life-threatening. By that definition, doesn't almost every college dorm in America have "severe physical problems"?

America is incredible for its short attention span. Many of the problems that we think are overwhelming today were facts of everyday life just a few decades ago. But instead of acknowledging that we've gone a long way toward solving them, our government scares us, our media depress us, and there's absolutely no one with the motivation to recognize how far we've really come.

I'm not trying to give you a rose-colored-glasses view of the world. Just because a problem is small doesn't mean that it's not still a problem. Fortunately, this one is actually solvable, and the solution is simple, but I'm going to have to whisper it because it's way too politically incorrect.

Shhhhh . . . the solution is . . . "work."

The average poor household in America runs on only about 16 hours of work per week. But it's not because there aren't any jobs; the 16 hours figure actually remains about the same regardless of how good or bad the economy is.

If we could somehow get that number to 40, which is generally considered to be full-time (either through one household member working 40 hours a week or two members working 20 hours each), number crunchers say that almost three-quarters of children in poverty would be immediately lifted out. It's at this point my mind starts to wander to the phrase that's constantly thrown around during the illegal-immigration debate: "jobs Americans just won't do."

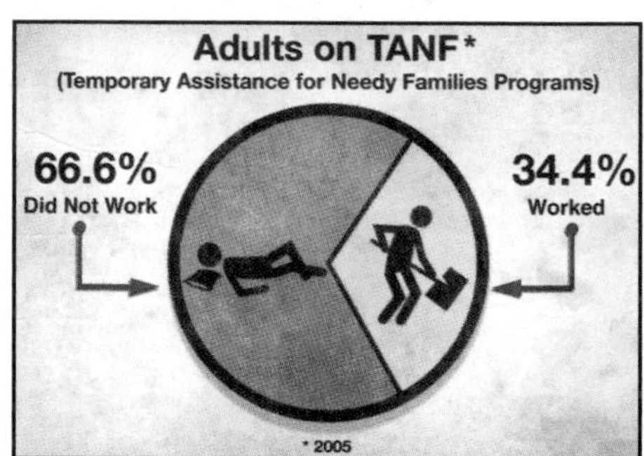

EXTREME MAKEOVER: CARDBOARD-BOX EDITION

Did you know you're almost homeless? According to Melissa Zowaski, a struggling mother, you are. She told *CBS News,* "Most Americans are just a paycheck away from being on the streets or being in a shelter."

Sorry, Melissa, that's just not true. Most Americans are definitely *not* a paycheck away from being on the streets. But if you think CBS would bother to point out that Melissa is unquestionably wrong, you don't know the media very well. They ran her quote unchallenged, exploiting a struggling mom who was emotionally projecting her unfortunate situation onto the rest of America.

Having even one person homeless is dramatic enough; why perpetuate a false impression of nationwide doom? Maybe it's because most of the media believe it's their job to make you feel guilty for shoveling Hot Pockets into your mouth while watching that new plasma TV in your nicely heated home while someone somewhere is struggling.

POVERTY WINS ELECTIONS

Most major problems in America eventually wind up on the desk of the head honcho. If the public perceives that the president or Congress won't solve them, then they eventually make a change to the other party to give them a shot. But for whatever reason, poverty just doesn't work that way.

When cities suffer through decades and decades of the worst poverty America has to offer, they tend just to keep electing the same people with the same ideas over and over and over again. Sounds like a *poor* idea to me.

Here are the American cities with the highest poverty rates along with the percentage of time since 1965 that a Republican mayor was running them.

		Poverty rate	Time a Republican was mayor since 1965
1	Cleveland, OH	32.4%	38.1%
2	Detroit, MI	31.4%	0.0%
3	Miami, FL	28.3%	31.0%
4	Atlanta, GA	26.9%	0.0%
5	Buffalo, NY	26.9%	0.0%
6	St. Louis, MO	25.4%	0.0%
7	Cincinnati, OH	25.0%	19.0%
8	Milwaukee, WI	24.9%	0.0%
9	Newark, NJ	24.8%	0.0%
(tie) 10	Philadelphia, PA	24.5%	0.0%
(tie) 10	New Orleans, LA	24.5%	0.0%

The grand total? Republicans have run the cities with the worst poverty problems in America only eight percent of the time since 1965.

For cities with nonpartisan mayoral races, the party the mayor was most closely associated with before, during, and/or after his or her term was used. In the case where partisan information was lacking (El Paso), the city was excluded. This exclusion is unlikely to have any significant effect on the results, as El Paso County is generally a Democratic-leaning county, being one of the few counties in Texas to support John Kerry for president in 2004 over George W. Bush. Kerry received 56 percent of the El Paso County vote while managing only 38 percent of the overall Texas vote.

DON'T SAY "HOMELESS," PLEASE USE "RESIDENCE ASPIRANT"

The government has estimated that there are about 754,000 homeless people in America. That's less than 0.3 percent of our population. While that means that more than 99.7 percent of Americans are *not* homeless (something that is never pointed out, of course), it doesn't mean we shouldn't take it seriously. But taking it seriously includes putting the problem into perspective, ideally in a sober, nonhysterical fashion. That doesn't generate ratings or sell books, but hey—you already bought this one, so what do I care if you think it's interesting? So, without the pressure of ratings or sales, here's the unadulterated truth.

Counting homeless people isn't exactly the easiest thing to do. While some homeless advocacy groups believe the government's estimate of 754,000 is too low, there is real reason to believe that it's actually much too high.

Consider these qualifications buried in the report's footnotes:

- Some communities are "making upward adjustments to the numbers" and/or "counting people who are not literally homeless."
- More than "one-fifth of the total number of unsheltered persons in families in the nation were reported by just two (communities)."
- One community reported "14,000 unsheltered persons in families based on a survey finding that **two out of 1,001** households had homeless families living on their properties. The sample size used to produce the estimate is extremely small."
- The second community "appears to have included doubled-up families in its estimate."
- Some communities reported that their estimate included people considered to be "at risk of homelessness (e.g., doubled up) but not currently homeless."

Even with these and other limitations included on both sides of the equation, the most comparable number of homeless in America is this: In 1996, there were 842,000 homeless people in America; in 2005, there were 754,157.

That reduction of about 10 percent can't be relied upon enough to say confidently that we've decreased homelessness by that exact number, but it's at least safe to say there was no *increase* in homelessness during that time. To look at it another way,

You know those little annoying yappy dogs that irritating celebrities always own? Intense research has uncovered an incredible trend. Ninety-five percent of their owners are either rich heiresses, celebrities who are inexplicably famous, or white trash (which is, of course, exactly what the rich heiress celebrities would be without the money). Look at this incontrovertible evidence.

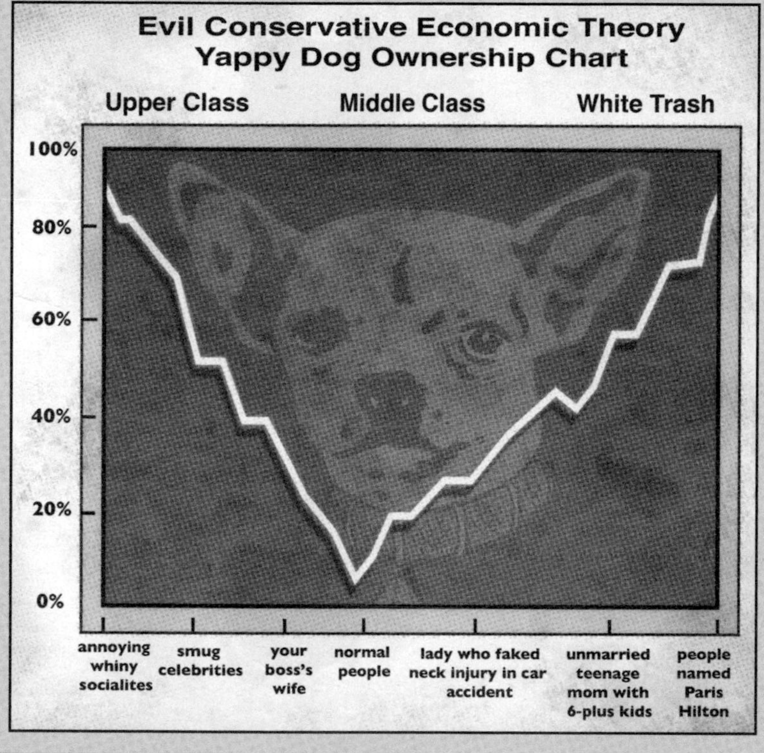

between 1996 and 2005, we added 31 million people to this country. It's almost as if none of them became homeless.

But that's not the end of the story. The vast majority of the 754,000 homeless are *not persistently homeless*. In fact, only about 170,000 are chronically in that state.

Horrible circumstances can happen to everyone at some point in their lives. When wealthy persons have enormous financial difficulty, such as uncovered medical bills or losing a job, they dip into their savings. Those in the middle class might run up their credit cards. It's those who are already extremely poor who risk homelessness. While most are *still* able to avoid that outcome, about 77 percent of those who do wind up homeless don't stay that way.

Take a moment to admire yourself, America. The country that you've worked so hard to build, the country that you're constantly told has so many problems, can proudly say that just 0.07 percent of its entire population is chronically homeless.

BEDTIME STORIES

The pessimism patrol isn't going to be derailed by some evil conservative analysis saying that the problem of homelessness in America is comparatively microscopic. To counter, they quickly jumped on a claim that there are 300,000 more homeless people than there are available beds in shelters.

There's only one problem with that assessment: *The beds we have aren't full.*

Honestly, they're not even really that close to full. On any given night in America, tens of thousands of beds that exist specifically for use by the homeless go empty.

But wait a second! CBS said there are "three-quarters of a million homeless people, filling emergency shelters through the year and spilling into special seasonal shelters in the coldest months." Right—well, the "seasonal shelters" they mention as if they're a bad thing are actually a simple result of supply and demand. During colder months, when more people want to get out of the weather, more shelters are added. In other words, the seasonal beds aren't needed the rest of the year.

If someone would have gone through all the trouble of actually reading a couple of more paragraphs of the same report, they might have learned that emergency shelters were about 91 percent full for individuals and 87 percent full for families. Transitional housing for individuals was just 85 percent full and 72 percent full for families. Overall, *about 16 percent of the beds we have for the homeless go empty every night.* That amounts to about 90,000 beds, not including the 30,000 more that the same government report said were in development as of early 2005.

Are certain areas not properly equipped? Absolutely. Can resources be moved around and applied more efficiently to meet specific demand? Of course. But, as you can see, the impression of a crisis caused by lack of space for the homeless is a media mirage—much like the career of Ashton Kutcher. (Yes, I realize he still has a better career than I do.)

HEADLINE NEWS CRIBS

It was like a really crappy version of *Headline News Cribs* when we took our television cameras out to cover the story of a homeless man who had staked out a grate in front of a posh Manhattan antiques store as his new home. The owner of the store had filed a $1 million lawsuit against four homeless people, claiming they were blocking his window and verbally harassing prospective customers (not to mention using the storefront as their own personal urinals).

My first reaction was to feel horrible for the homeless men, despite the fact that the sidewalk grate actually offered more square footage than most New York apartments. They must have no place to go . . . right?

Actually, New York City has a "right to shelter" law, meaning that the government essentially is *required* to provide shelter for the city's homeless . . . if they want it. But that's the key, because after looking at the stats, reading the laws, and talking to those who deal with the problem every day, there's only one sad conclusion you can draw: The people who sleep on the streets of New York City are choosing to do so.

There are varying reasons someone may choose to sleep on the street, but a key explanation is that many shelters have this crazy requirement that you have to be sober when you enter them. While I know it's shocking to hear someone say it, I promised you the truth, so here it is: Some homeless people would rather be drunk than in a bed. As a guy who pounded a gallon of Jack Daniel's a week for years, that "logic" isn't completely lost on me. You'd be surprised at what seems like a rational decision when you're in that state.

Homelessness in America is a quintessential example of the type of problem that humanity hasn't figured out how to deal with. It's a problem that is extremely small in scope but incredibly brutal to those it affects, and it causes an understandably emotional reaction that usually guilts us into throwing more money at the problem. When that solves absolutely nothing, the cycle starts all over again.

A.D.D. MOMENT

One way New York City is trying to persuade the homeless to use their services is through the creation of shelters where they *will* let you in even if you're drunk. While that idea has plenty of heart, it seems a little like running a lung cancer clinic where it's okay to smoke. Homelessness isn't a disease; it's a straight-line consequence of other problems, which oftentimes include alcoholism and/or drug abuse and should be treated as such.

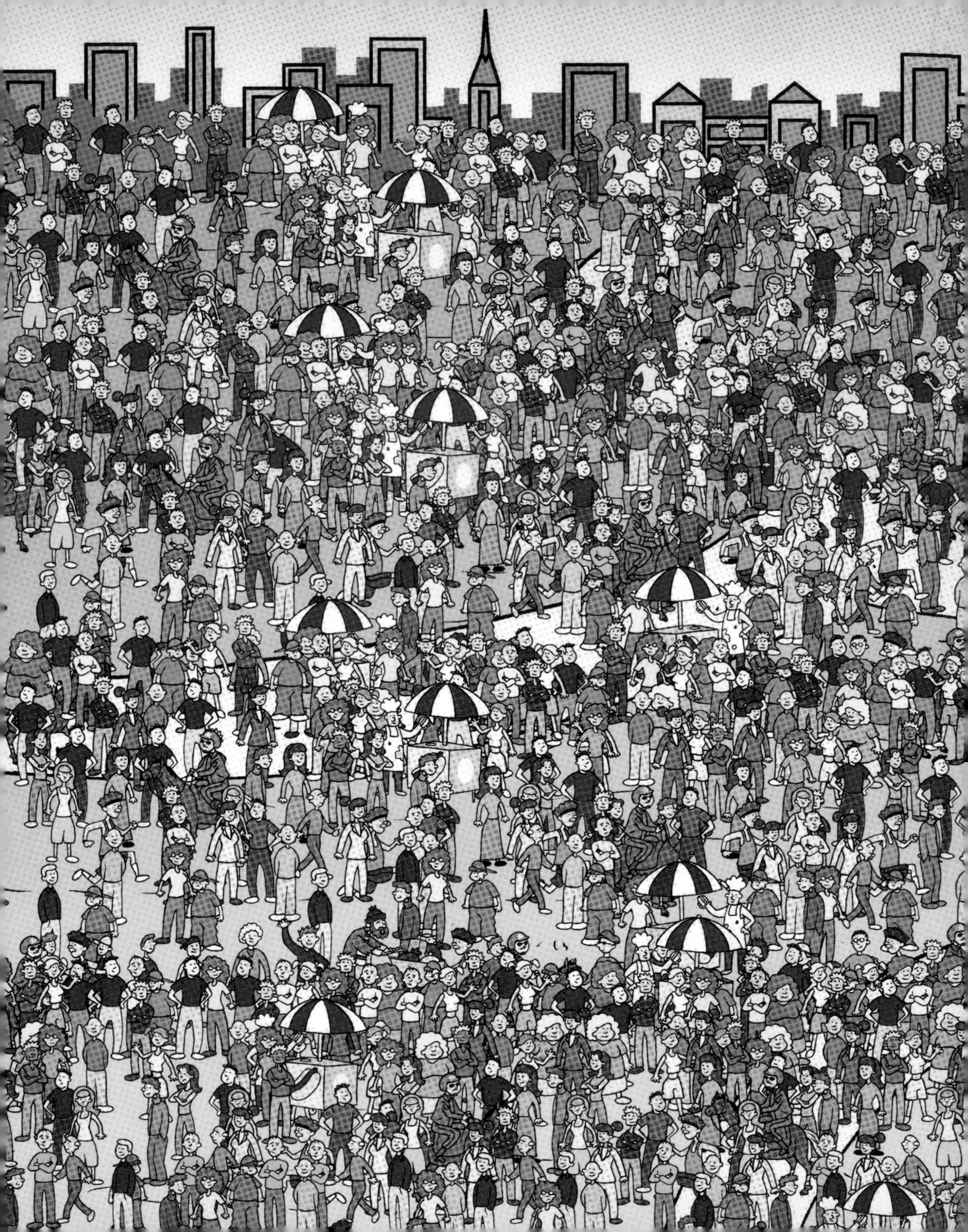

WHERE'S HOBO?
There are 2123 residents of New York
for every one that lives in the streets.
Can you find the hobo?

MY SOLUTION

Examples of how to solve this problem are everywhere. One Friday in October 2006, we were sitting in our daily meeting to prepare our radio show, and we saw an obvious target for ridicule: the Nobel Peace Prize. We were sure that the winner would be some human shield from the Kashmir region who took a bullet in the abdomen to prevent it from striking a tulip. After all, how could the award celebrate anything *but* some worthless gesture in a miserable region of the world that did absolutely nothing to bring peace to anyone?

A.D.D. MOMENT For example, I'd like to introduce you to the 2004 Nobel Peace Prize recipient: Wangari Maathai, a Kenyan environmentalist who won the award for her campaign to plant trees in Africa. Maybe I'm just an evil warmonger who doesn't understand the path to peace, but trees don't exactly make me want to kill people any less. In fact, it's just the opposite—trees give me a resource to create baseball bats to kill people more efficiently. Maybe that's why we went into Afghanistan and Iraq; there weren't enough trees to make us feel peaceful. If Saddam would have just lined the border with a few weeping willows, he might still be in power.

In 2002, the Nobel Peace Prize went to Jimmy Carter. That's how ridiculous this award usually is. A.D.D. MOMENT

But our Nobel-bashing plans were derailed by the 2006 award winner, a guy named Muhammad Yunus. The interesting thing to me wasn't that I didn't know how to pronounce, or spell, his name—that's nothing new—no, the amazing thing was that he was a businessman.

Yunus had built a huge company that pioneered a form of lending called micro-credit. He makes thousands and thousands of very small loans in extremely poor areas of the world. Loans as small as $9 and averaging only about $100. Believe it or not, that's enough money for a struggling family in these areas to start their own businesses.

One hundred dollars is also enough to park your car at the Time Warner Center in Manhattan for two days and nine minutes. (Really.) A.D.D. MOMENT

Banks can't usually be bothered with loans so small, especially when the money is going to people who are thought of as too risky to ever make the payments. But that hasn't turned out to be the case. Payback rates on Yunus's micro-loans have been as high as 98 percent, even with no collateral required, because the credit is given to large groups of families, and the entire group loses its chance at future credit if one family defaults. It's like peer-pressure lending.

But the best part of the story is that Yunus is making a difference within the bounds of capitalism. He's figured out an innovative solution that's not another pathetic attempt by a government to give money to a Thirteenth World country whose evil dictator will use it to buy fancy military uniforms to slaughter his people in style.

It's the *Dateline: To Catch a Predator* philosophy: It does a good thing, *and* it provides fabulous pedophile-bashing entertainment. It's the ultimate use of capitalism: *doing good while doing good business.* That's our responsibility, not as legally required taxpayers but as individuals. Enlightened capitalism gives as many people as possible the *opportunity* for success, which—despite campaign promises—is all this country owes you.

Over and over again, the private sector proves it is superior to the government. When Hurricane Katrina struck, it wiped out two bridges in the same general area. The bridge owned by a private railroad, CSX, was completely rebuilt and back in use within six months. The other bridge, owned by the government, was still about half a year away from a *partial* opening after 16 months. While all levels of government lumbered to assist the Gulf Coast, about 100 different companies donated at least $1 million. Wal-Mart, the pinnacle of evil to people who complain about poverty, donated $20 million, 1,500 trucks of free stuff, and 100,000 meals.

Those figures don't even include the hundreds of millions of dollars generously donated by individuals. Conservatives (you know, the people who are constantly preaching about personal responsibility) give about 30 percent more to charity than liberals. Of the 25 states that donate more money than the national average, 24 of them donated their electoral votes to George W. Bush instead of John Kerry. It's the people who truly believe in the power of personal giving who do it the most.

But more than just a political issue, charity is more accurately an American concern. A recent analysis of charitable giving by the Charities Aid Foundation showed that America gives more than double the amount to charity than its closest competitor studied, the United Kingdom.

A.D.D. MOMENT Americans give about 12 times more than the Frenchy-French, who, by the way, finished dead last. Again, I just had to throw that in.

But in some ways, I think our generosity has blurred our focus about what really works. We donate so much money that we wind up creating giant charitable bureaucracies that rival the government in red tape and ineptitude.

We need to get back to the philosophy of our grandparents. Back then, the neighborhood was king. People took care of each other because they *cared* about each other. Hunger, poverty, and homelessness aren't global problems, they're individual ones. The worst thing we can do is try to have some global entity solve them.

As for the relatively few who fall through the cracks in this ridiculously successful experiment that we call America, the answer is simple: Get smaller. Help your family and friends, and know your neighbors.

The answer isn't in Washington, it's in the local church, the community outreach, and, most important, the neighborhood.

Chapter 21

Parenting: The Case for Abstinence

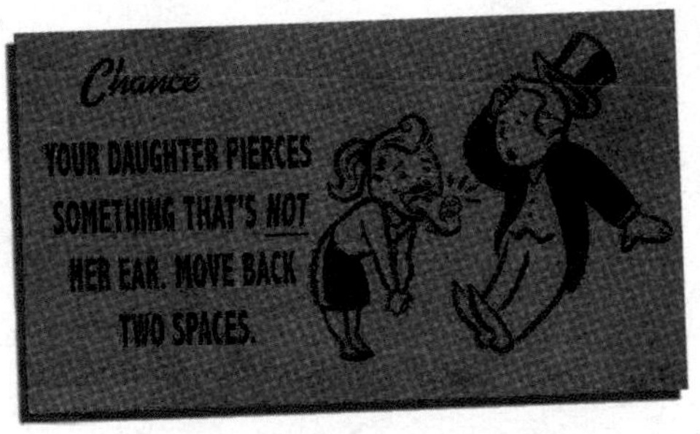

Chance
YOUR DAUGHTER PIERCES SOMETHING THAT'S NOT HER EAR. MOVE BACK TWO SPACES.

AS A PROUD PARENT of four healthy, beautiful kids from ages one to 18, I've learned a few things. The most important is that I have absolutely no clue what I'm doing. Never did. My whole experience with being a father is kind of like a script for a Sandra Bullock movie—I'm just making it up as I go along and hoping we can fix all major errors later. I love my kids more than anything, but even the most casual observer might say that I've screwed them up in every possible way.

I do *try* to be a good parent. If they had "good effort" medals for parenting, I think I'd at least get a bronze. But even though I'm not a perfect parent by any stretch of the imagination, there are millions and millions of Americans who know even less than I do (I'm talking to you, Ms. Spears) and sadly, they're the ones having all the kids.

> **A.D.D. MOMENT**
>
> **Actually,** I've found that it's harder *not* to screw kids up. One wrong word and twenty years later, they'll be on a couch telling Dr. Makesalot how one moment you don't even remember somehow destroyed their self-esteem and ruined them for life. Naturally, the doctor will back them up on that, because at $120 an hour, you simply nod your head and agree with the person paying you.

Apparently, the lower your IQ, the more fertile your loins. Even though you might want to write that off as their problem, it's really *not* their problem—it's our problem. Bad parents and the dysfunctional kids they raise are everyone's problem, especially when they become serial killers, nitwit socialites, or the waiter who never brings lemon for my Coke Zero even though I've asked 12 times.

We're up to our necks in unfit parents, and the problem seems to be getting much, much worse. You can see examples of it at schools, on television, and in the gossip pages. We're being assaulted on a regular basis by classless, impolite, ill-behaved, undisciplined little monsters. What's worse, someday their hormones are going to get the best of them, and they'll produce classless, impolite, ill-behaved, undisciplined little monsters of their very own.

It's a vicious cycle. Sometimes I wish I could be made sheriff of the Department of Children and Family Services for a day, because then I could be the lead actor in my own fantasy-land screenplay.

I know I'm not the only one who feels that something drastic needs to be done. And I, being the type of person who likes to take action—or at least likes to think about how I would take action if I got around to it—have a plan.

"Deputy Beck"
FINAL SCRIPT-DO NOT PHOTOCOPY

INT - FOOD COURT - DAY

INNOCENT BUT POORLY RAISED BOY
I want some Panda Express!!!

UNFIT MOTHER
You're not getting Panda Express—we're eating Sbarro's. (THWACK)

UNFIT MOTHER SMACKS INNOCENT BUT POORLY RAISED BOY. SUDDENLY, DEPUTY BECK ENTERS.

DEPUTY BECK
Ma'am...I'm going to have to ask you to unhand the boy...

UNFIT MOTHER
Who the heck are you?!?

DEPUTY BECK
Just a concerned American, Ma'am...I'm going to need you to hand over that calzone as well.

BOY STOPS CRYING. BYSTANDERS APPLAUD, GLENN STUFFS CALZONE IN HIS MOUTH. "UP WHERE WE BELONG" BEGINS TO PLAY.

DEPUTY BECK ORDERS ANOTHER CALZONE.

p.9

STEP OUT OF THE BED AND PUT YOUR HANDS ON THE NIGHT TABLE

I believe that prospective parents should have to apply for a baby license—a license to procreate, if you will—before any child-rearing is allowed. Sure, it sounds like the crazy plot of a really bad Charlton Heston flick or China's current family policy, but just think about it for a second: You need to fill out an application to rent *Gigli* at Blockbuster, you can't buy certain nasal decongestants without showing your ID to the pharmacist, and you have to prove you can park a car before they let you drive one, yet any drunken yahoo with an urge to merge can bring another person into this world without any sort of up-front screening process.

Most major transactions in life involve some kind of cursory inquiry into your worthiness, but the life-changing act of baby making? *Nada*.

I'd put an end to that immediately. With me in charge, the procreation license would become mandatory. And as much as I hate government bureaucracy, this is so important to me that I believe it warrants a new behemoth federal agency to oversee it all, the U.S. Department of Parenting. They can even create it overnight, without any planning or foresight, just as they did with the Department of Homeland Security. After all, this is an emergency.

A.D.D. MOMENT

Actually, there is one evaluation that takes place, but it's really more of an instruction, and it's useless because it happens after the baby is already born. The nurse comes in and tells you to watch a video on *not shaking your baby.* Really? That's a bad idea? So, should I just use a pillow over its head to quiet it down next time?

And before the Left Coasters start whining, I'm not talking about regulating just the lower end of the socioeconomic strata. Sure, Debra DeProne and her six kids by six different daddies make me physically ill, but so does Tiffany McSpoiled and the children she "raised" with the help of her 12 nannies. With my grand plan, everyone is equal under the law, and all prospective parents will be subject to the same scrutiny prior to mating.

In fact, the Department of Parenting would actually give you a taste of parenting *before* you even conceive the baby. Here's how it works: A DOP agent would come by, wake you up at two in the morning, and keep you awake until four. Then he'd let you sleep for an hour before waking you again and keeping you up until it's too late to go back to sleep. Then he'd yell all morning, take a nap, and—just as you were starting to doze off—he'd wake you up, start shrieking again, and not tell you why.

This would go on for, oh, say, about three months. If you're still interested in parenting after that, you move on to another agent who will ask some simple questions to determine how fit you are to be a parent.

Assuming the interview goes well, you're free to book a room at the Ramada for you and your significant other. Then, nine months later, your dream of not getting a good night's sleep for the next 18 years will finally come true.

Sample DOP Interview Questions

Do you have a job?

Will you attempt to dry your child in the microwave?

What do you think about leaving the child in the car while you go to work?

How many children do you already have?

How much time can you devote to raising your child?

Do you chew with your mouth open?

Do you plan on giving your child a stupid name?

Will you let your child roam the restaurant or insist he or she stay seated?

Children, bathtubs, and hair dryers—a good combination?

Why is the sky blue? Why, why, why?

Unfortunately, unless I'm elected president or I seize power in a bloody coup, my licensing proposal won't be debated in Congress anytime soon. So, in the meantime, if you're one of the millions of people determined to have kids and you won't just take a cold shower or imagine your significant other as Joy Behar or Carrot Top instead, I've got some parenting advice for you. Of course, I'm fully aware that my wife is the brains of the parenting operation, and I'm little more than a flesh-and-bone jungle gym and entertainment system, but here's what I've gleaned so far from my job as father of four.

THE GOO-GOO YEARS (DOODY DUTY)

I know there are two Spocks. One was a babyologist and the other a Vulcan. I only know the Vulcan. Most of my "formal" education on parenthood came from best-selling books by comedians (*Parenthood* by Paul Reiser and *Fatherhood* by Bill Cosby). The nice part about books like those is that they don't dwell on the small stuff, such as whether the baby should sleep on its back or stomach, or how often to feed it. No, they get right to the point: Infants mean poop, tears, and poop. Constantly. Poop, tears, and poop. When the baby stops crying, it's only because it's getting ready to poop. Then it starts crying again. About the poop.

No one is really ever prepared for this.

Nor is anyone prepared for how much control an infant has over your life. Considering how small and utterly helpless it is, an infant is totally dependent on you, yet it's also the boss of you. It's really not fair.

I suppose in that respect, they're a lot like cats.

A.D.D. MOMENT I really hate cats. I mean, I *really* hate them.

THE TODDLER YEARS (DANGER, DANGER EVERYWHERE!)

Assuming the DOP did its job and you were a competent parent who actually fed your child properly, didn't leave it in the sun, and didn't sell it to gypsies, you'll wind up with a toddler. The good thing about raising toddlers is this: You haven't completely wrecked them yet. Your little progeny is like an uncarved stone—an uncarved stone that poops itself and smells accordingly—but an uncarved stone nonetheless, just waiting for you to sculpt it, with your parenting savvy as the chisel. Don't use a real chisel, of course. (I hope they showed you that video after the "don't shake the baby" one.)

The best piece of advice I can give you about raising a toddler is to think of it like

License to Procreate Application

U.S. Department of Parenting

S E A1-6

UNITED STATES DEPARTMENT OF PARENTING

Please provide the following personal information: PLEASE RETURN TOP COPY

NAME: Ruthie Bicher

SOCIAL SECURITY NUMBER: 4-Got

ADDRESS: 3 bloks away

DAYTIME PHONE NUMBER: 555-02 sumthing

AGE: aboot 20??? **SEX:** Call ME!

DENIED

Answer the following questions to the best of your ability:

YOUR CURRENT OCCUPATION: ~~Docter~~ Barfly

OTHER PARENT'S NAME: Hmm -- could be this dude Roy or Flava Flav

OTHER PARENT'S OCCUPATION: X-Box playa

ARE YOU MARRIED OR DO YOU INTEND TO MARRY? Helllllllz no

REASON YOU WANT TO HAVE A CHILD: Their sooooooooooooo cute!!!!

THE MOST IMPORTANT SKILL A PARENT NEEDS TO HAVE IS: Upper body strengf

BABIES LIKE TO EAT: Fruity Pebbles and soder

IF A BABY IS CRYING, YOU SHOULD: Shut the dor or turn up the musik louder

AS A PARENT, I WOULD TEACH MY CHILD THAT ~~Yes~~ **:** hottnesss and sexiness is the most improtant thing in the world!

OFFICIAL USE ONLY!

REVIEWED BY:

1 2 3 4 5

A162-11544.556464-300.000-17

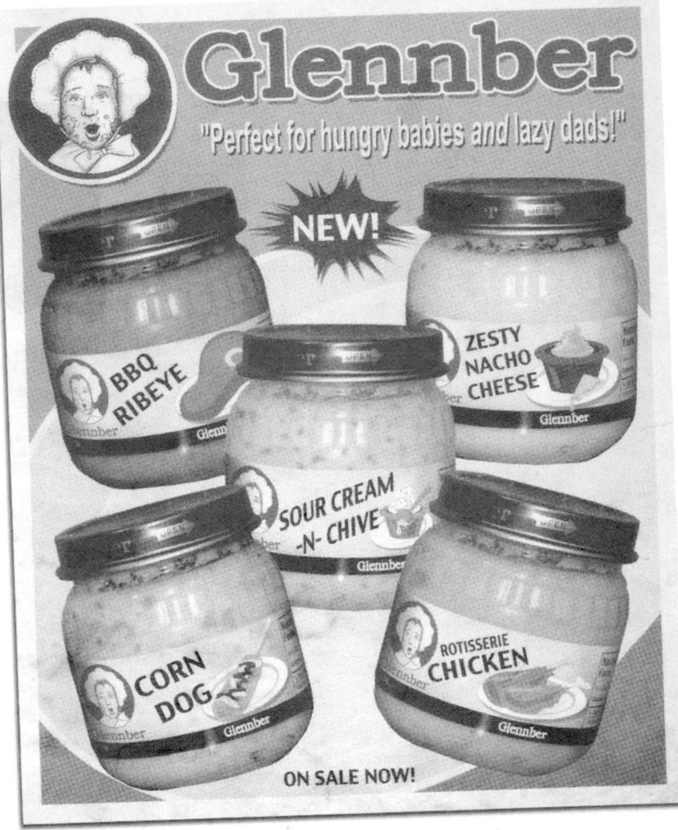

a tiny little danger magnet. A lot of people say that children are actually a lot more harmless than you think, that they're almost indestructible, but I'd like to tell you right now that those people are dead wrong. Once toddlers start walking, they will gravitate toward anything that is remotely dangerous. Items that most people would never think of as hazardous suddenly take on new meaning. *Get that Chiclet out of here!* From the moment these children wake up in the morning until the moment they fall asleep, they're only thinking one thing: "What's the best way to hurt myself?"

Glennber
"Perfect for hungry babies and lazy dads!"
NEW!
BBQ RIBEYE
ZESTY NACHO CHEESE
SOUR CREAM -N- CHIVE
CORN DOG
ROTISSERIE CHICKEN
ON SALE NOW!

Michael J. Fox once said that as soon as a child starts walking, the parents are on suicide watch for the next couple of years. He's right. As the parent of a toddler, your mission is very simple: *Keep them alive!* Sure, it's also nice to clean up their poop, read them bedtime stories (like they'll ever remember), and feed them on occasion—but all of that is secondary to keeping them poison-free and unelectrocuted.

There may be something in between toddlers and teens. I'm hoping to find a book by Ray Romano that covers it.
A.D.D. MOMENT

The real fun begins in a few years when those uncarved stones turn into teenagers. That's when you finally begin to see the fruits of your incompetence. What was once a little bundle of joy is now a pimpled, sarcastic drama-bot who wants you to know how unimportant you are in his or her life. A toddler calling you names is funny, but a 13-year-old? Not so much.

Chance
TAMPAX
YOUR DAUGHTER ASKS
YOU TO BUY HER TAMPAX.
LOSE A TURN...AND
YOUR DIGNITY.

TEENS: THEY'RE NOT HUMAN

"Anything you say can and will be used against you." It's what all suspects hear when they're arrested. It's also a fact about parenting teens.

I know that I'm going to pay for everything I say to my kids. It could be three years later; it could be 20. But even as the words are coming out of my mouth, I can hear Dr. Makesalot's cash register ringing 20 years in the future after my kid just spent 45 minutes on his couch.

"Then Daddy said this." *Cha-ching.*

"Then Daddy said that." *Cha-ching.*

That *cha-chinging* gets especially loud and frequent when you're the father of a teenage girl (or, in my case, two of them, with another one just about a dozen years away). It's as if I'm being Punk'd . . . for three straight decades, only there's no hope of a B-list actor jumping out at the end to tell me it was all a big joke. Just the Reaper.

For me, the fun of raising my daughters began during the era that I like to call the Trifecta of Awkwardness. That's bras, tampons, and boyfriends.

The first two issues I can easily pass off to their mother—after all, I don't know how to put bras *on,* and frankly, tampons frighten me. No man needs to contend with those things. But the boyfriend thing? That was all on me.

Unfortunately, having been one, I know boys. I know how they think; I know what they think about; I know how they operate; I know how they lie. And, at the risk of being labeled a reverse sexist, I know that *all boys are bad.*

I tried to relay that information to my girls during the infamous "preemptive talk," but it was painful . . . for them. It was the "birds and bees" thing, sure, but I went off on tangents and involved too many bad analogies. There were birds and bees and wolves and snakes and Zeus watching their every move with a lightning bolt at the ready. There were clowns, Big Brother, witches, and something about a shamed koala named Dooley.

YOUR SON COMES HOME FROM
COLLEGE WITH HIS "FRIEND"
STEVE AND SAYS HE HAS

AT DINNER. LOSE A TURN.

It didn't go well.

For a while afterward I thought my speech had been so awkward and convoluted that it

MOVE INTO A NUNNERY.
MOVE AHEAD 3 SPACES.

might actually have worked. Maybe my daughters would just forget the whole dating idea and become nuns or volunteer for a women-only mission to Mars. Or perhaps they'd enter into a loveless, sexless marriage for the sake of their political careers—that would have been fine with me.

Then it happened: "Dad . . . I'm going out tonight," my oldest daughter said. "With 'Stanley.' " (Names have been changed to protect the innocent.)

Breathe, Glenn, breathe. Deep breaths, that's right; nice and slow. Find a happy place. Pretty birds, pretty birds—look at all the pretty birds.

Sorry—flashback.

After the smelling salts were administered by my wife and I woke up from my "unplanned nap" caused by hearing that sentence, I started planning. Fortunately, my line of work has allowed me to get to know certain people. People who can "take care of things"—if you know what I mean.

I know, you're probably thinking Kim Caldwell or Danny Bonaduce, but I'm actually talking about John Walsh from *America's Most Wanted*. John and I don't know each other that well, but he's been on my television show, and I figured that was more than enough of a friendship to ask for his help on something this important. So I pitched him my plan, and he agreed.

When my daughter's "date" came to pick her up, I answered the door and with my best tough-parent act said, "Hello, Stanley, could I have a word with you alone?" It was a rhetorical question.

He sat down on the couch, and I did an old lawyer trick, which is to sit in silence and stare, the idea being to unnerve the other person into saying something. I didn't want poor Stanley to say anything, though; I just wanted him to be unnerved.

Once the atmosphere was sufficiently uncomfortable, I leaned forward and, in the friendly but scary tone of a Mafia warning, I smiled and said the following: "You know John Walsh from the show *America's Most Wanted,* right, Stanley?" He nodded. "Well, he just wanted me to tell you that I have a

Community Chest
YOUR SPOILED-ROTTEN
KID LEAVES EVERY LIGHT
IN THE HOUSE ON.
WHAT AM I, MADE OF MONEY? I MEAN, WHEN
I WAS YOUR AGE, MY DAD WOULD HAVE GOTTEN HI

gun, a shovel, lots of property, you'll never be missed, and he promises to never put my face on television. Have her back by eight."

Needless to say, a romance between my daughter and Stanley never blossomed. Perhaps they lacked a spark, or perhaps it was because I threatened to set him on fire; I guess we'll never really know.

Now maybe you're starting to understand why I think I'm screwing up my kids so bad.

MY SOLUTION

If you're seriously looking to me for a solution on parenting, we're in bigger trouble than I thought. I came up with the licensing thing—that's really all I've got.

What I've learned, though, is that there is no manual for bringing up children the right way. Every day is a new adventure, every night a torturous battle between you and your wife to determine who gets up next. In the meantime, all you can really do is love your kids, listen to them, and pray that insurance will cover the Prozac.

Chapter 22

Illegal Immigration: Behind the Lies

"Give me your tired, your poor, your huddled masses yearning to breathe free. The wretched refuse of your teeming shore. Send these, the homeless, tempest-tost to me, I lift my lamp beside the golden door!"

THOSE SPINE-CHILLING WORDS by Emma Lazarus, engraved into a plaque on the Statue of Liberty's pedestal, have greeted immigrants to America for generations. Boat after boat, decade after decade, from country after country, they've come here to make a better life for themselves and their families.

They are our great-grandfathers, our grandmothers, our uncles, and our parents. They are our teachers, our doctors, our scientists, and our leaders. They brought with them new ideas, old traditions, and fresh perspective. America is not just *better* because of them; America is *America* because of them.

This chapter is not about those people.

RACIST!

Let's make something else clear right off the top: People who want this country to secure its borders are not racist. Nor are they bigots, hatemongers, xenophobes, or un-American. (Yes, I've been called every one of those things.) There is a difference between the law-abiding Ellis Island immigrants and those who come here in the dark of night and slip into the shadows; but it's not the color of their skin.

I wish this whole illegal-immigration debate *was* as simple as racism and the big bad conservatives hating minorities (please finish reading this sentence before the blog alerts go out), because then this issue would have been solved a long time ago.

Unfortunately, the reality is that it's much more complicated than that, and many of the people who want to make this about racism actually have far different intentions from what you might imagine.

THE FIVE W'S

"Thousands of Mexicans Illegally Cross U.S. Border Each Month."

It's probably not surprising *where* that headline was published (the *Los Angeles Times*), but what may be surprising is *when* it was published: 1950.

President after president—Democrat and Republican alike—have, with varying degrees of public embarrassment, failed to stop the flow and fix the problem. Jimmy Carter wanted to give illegals amnesty but didn't have the votes. Ronald Reagan had the votes and required employers to pay large fines for hiring illegals, but he also gave amnesty to millions, and that did nothing to stem the flow. George H. W. Bush opened the front door wider by increasing the level of legal immigration by 35 percent but did nothing about the illegal side. Bill Clinton tried to focus on border security and started building a fence, and George W. Bush made the fence a little longer—but neither was ever really serious about doing it right.

But none of them—including three two-term presidents with nothing left to lose—was able to use his power to solve this once and for all. None of them—despite leading a Congress where they held the majority of both houses, along with the will of the people—sealed the border or addressed the fate of the millions of illegals already in the country.

Why?

While countless pages have been written about the who, what, where, and when of illegal immigration, from the massive security concerns to the impact on our economy to the loss of our nation's identity, the question of why has gone largely unanswered.

After countless hours of research, numerous interviews with experts, and a little bit of logical thinking thrown in for good measure, I believe I have the answer—and by the end of this chapter, so will you.

A.D.D. MOMENT

As far as I'm concerned, the only acceptable term is *illegal alien*. Every year, the advocacy groups give us some new politically correct term such as *undocumented worker, citizenship-less citizen*, or *unauthorized migrant*, but please, the more we sugarcoat the issue by wordsmithing it, the more trouble we're in. A malignant tumor doesn't sound so bad if you call it a cellulosed grouping, but you're a lot less likely to take it seriously that way.

MEET YOUR NEW GOVERNMENT

Let's start with a few of the excuses that you *have* heard a thousand times.

> "It is easier to believe a lie that one has heard a thousand times than to believe a fact that one has never heard before."
>
> —Robert S. Lynd

- Our borders aren't sealed because the Republicans cater to the big businesses that fund their campaigns and demand access to cheap labor.
- Our borders aren't sealed because the Democrats cater to Hispanic-American voters, a group with significant influence on elections.
- Our borders aren't sealed because some of the terrain makes it simply impossible—or too costly—to build a fence there.
- Our borders aren't sealed because of the special-interest groups that frighten politicians and the public alike with calls of racism.

Every one of those explanations contains a kernel of truth, which is why they are so convincing, but think about it. Are any of those reasons really enough to prevent generation after generation of our leaders from getting together and doing something that vast majorities of the American public support? Politicians literally live and die by poll numbers. Why would they choose to ignore their guidance on only this one issue?

They wouldn't—unless the politicians themselves aren't really the ones in control.

Let me introduce you to some other facts, ones that you probably *haven't* heard a thousand times before.

The Security and Prosperity Partnership of North America (SPP)

On March 13, 2005, U.S. Commerce Secretary Carlos M. Gutierrez met with Mexican Secretary of Economy Fernando Canales and Canadian Privy Council Assistant Secretary Phil Ventura. Ten days later, at a trilateral summit in Waco, Texas, the leaders of Mexico, the United States, and Canada announced the formation of the Security and Prosperity Partnership of North America.

> "A conspiracy is nothing but a secret agreement of a number of men for the pursuance of policies which they dare not admit in public."
>
> —Mark Twain

Here's how it was described that day by Canadian

Prime Minister Paul Martin: "The world is not standing still; new economic powerhouses, such as China and India, are rising and we face new opportunities—but we also face new challenges. And this requires a new partnership, stronger, more dynamic, one that is focused on the future. We are determined to forge the next generation of our continent's success. That's our destination. The security and prosperity partnership that we are launching today is the road map to getting there."

The destination is the next generation of North America's success, and the SPP is the road map. That certainly makes it sound like a pretty important initiative. But if it's so important, why is it so secret?

There doesn't appear to be any law authorizing the creation or funding of the SPP, and no congressional committee has any oversight of its activities. Many congressmen don't even know that the SPP exists, let alone the fact that it's formed numerous working groups that are reporting serious recommendations to cabinet-level executives in all three countries.

MexAmeriCanada:
It's Not All Bad!
Dept. of NAU Propaganda
1024 Lincoln Ave.
Washington, D.C.
20003
- QuebecTexMex cuisine yields burger topped with American cheese and Canadian bacon, using quesadillas for buns!
- Border Patrol can focus on the coasts, where illegals are easier to spot because they're swimming with suitcases.
- Free migration of Shakira.
- Potential NFL franchise in Cabo.
- New City Names!
Maricopa + Tijuana = Marijuana
- Much easier to traffic drugs
This message furnished by the Dept. of NAU Propaganda.
"Live Three or Die."
Congressional Authorization # TBD

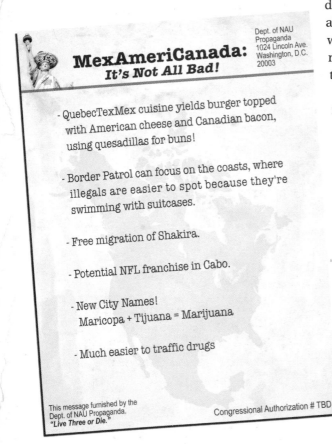

Before the Paranoia Express gets too far from the station, let me disappoint the staged-moon-landing crowd and make it clear that I do not believe the SPP is masquerading as some sort of unified North American government. Yet. But I certainly do believe that MexAmeriCanada could easily evolve over time. Think of the SPP as a trial balloon—if all the readings come back positive, then the real work gets under way.

Howard Phillips, chairman of the Conservative Caucus and a major SPP critic, seems to share my concerns. He likens the SPP to the initial stages taken by the supporters of the European Union, saying that the "economic route being pursued behind closed doors by SPP working groups is a replay of the exact stealth route taken in Europe. . . . By leading with economics, SPP is crafting a North American regulatory structure that transforms U.S. regulations by 'harmonizing' them with Mexican and Canadian regulations, all without specific congressional approval."

If he's right, if leaders in each of the three countries are hoping that SPP-initiated economic reforms will whet each country's appetite for integration in other areas, then everything the SPP is doing has to be examined under that light. And it all starts with those SPP "working groups" that Phillips mentioned.

SPP Working Groups

Just 90 days after it was formed, the SPP released its first "Report to Leaders." (If only "official" government agencies could work that fast.) It announced the creation of 10 "working groups" that would identify "concrete, forward-looking strategies and initiatives." Ironically, one of those working group's first recommendations was to create a *new* working group, called the North American Competitiveness Council. Here's how they describe it:

"You asked us to examine ways to strengthen the SPP to ensure its continuity and success. To that end . . . Ministers officially launched the North American Competitiveness Council (NACC). Our three governments recognize that private sector involvement is key to enhancing North America's competitive position in global markets and is the driving force behind innovation and growth. As such, the creation of the NACC provides a voice and a formal role for the private sector."

"Facts which at first seem improbable will, even on scant explanation, drop the cloak which has hidden them and stand forth in naked and simple beauty."

—Galileo Galilei

Ah, yes, the private sector. Remember earlier when I suggested that it may not be the politicians who are fully in control? Well, I'm not saying that elite corporate leaders are; but I'm not *not* saying it either.

The NACC membership list reads like the guest list of a Fifth Avenue Christmas party that I'll never be invited to: Joseph Gilmour, New York Life; William Clay Ford, Ford; Rick Wagoner, General Motors; Raymond Gilmartin, Merck; David O'Reilly, Chevron; Jeffrey Immelt, General Electric; H. Lee Scott, Wal-Mart; Robert Stevens, Lockheed Martin; Douglas R. Conant, Campbell's Soup; James M. Kilts, Gillette; Herman Cain, Whirlpool.

That's just a sample of U.S. participants; the participants from the Canadian and

Mexican business communities are equally impressive. Again, I hate to spoil the party, but is anyone bothering to ask why? What's the point of bringing so many wealthy, influential, and powerful people together under the guise of some working group?

The classic American cocktail party ice breaker is "So . . . what do you do for a living, Bob?" But NACC parties must be different, since everyone there already knows what everyone else does. I imagine they break the ice with lines like "Love your soup, Doug" and "Big fan of your Propecia, Ray."

A.D.D. MOMENT

I believe there are two answers, and they were both provided to us right in that first Report to Leaders: *continuity and success.*

Speaking at the official launch of the NACC, Commerce Secretary Gutierrez pretty much confirmed the continuity aspect: "The purpose of this meeting was to institutionalize the North American Security and Prosperity Partnership (SPP) and the NACC, so that the work will continue through changes in administrations."

It makes sense. If you're planning to be the founding father of a brand-new continental government, you've got to make sure it has time to evolve. You can't let those pesky popular elections get in the way of progress.

The success element of the NACC's involvement is harder to gauge because of the secretiveness surrounding it all. The mainstream media have largely been kept in the dark about it all, and the only real account of the NACC's work can be found in an exposé done by a reporter for *Maclean's* who spoke with some of the participants of the NACC's first meeting.

The Naked Capitalist by W. Cleon Skousen is a must-read if you're interested in learning more about the organizations behind this.

A.D.D. MOMENT

She wrote that the government leaders in attendance asked participants for help in overcoming the "bottlenecks" created by all (those annoying) laws and regulations that *our elected representatives* passed on our behalf. In her article, she described the group as a "cherry picked group of executives who were whisked to Cancun in March by the leaders of Canada, the U.S. and Mexico, and asked to come up with a plan for taking North American integration beyond NAFTA."

According to Ron Covais, president of the Americas for Lockheed Martin (which happens to be the largest weapons manufacturer in the world): "The guidance from the ministers was, 'tell us what we need to do and we'll make it happen. . . . We've decided not to recommend any things that would require legislative changes because we won't get anywhere.' "

Good thinking, Ron. We certainly wouldn't want any of those checks and balances mandated in our Constitution to slow you down. Annette Verschuren, president of Home Depot Canada, also seemed to have a good time in the sun and sand of Cancun. She said the meeting was "an intimate discussion" and "a lot of fun [because] there were no reporters, just a freewheeling discussion on the things that drive you crazy."

No one really knows exactly what the group is up to (which is exactly the problem), but the chair of the Canadian contingent, Linda Hasenfratz (CEO of auto parts maker Linamar), summed up the plan pretty plainly: "Let's get some low-hanging fruit to give the thing some momentum, but let's not lose sight of bigger-ticket items."

"Secrecy is the beginning of tyranny."
—Robert A. Heinlein, American writer

I guess the people who believe the things you hear a thousand times would probably think she's referring to "bigger-ticket items" such as new trade agreements or reduced tariffs. But if you'd hop aboard the Paranoia Express with me for a second, I'd remind you that the whole reason this group exists is to advise our leaders on how to take North American integration "beyond NAFTA." Call me crazy, but I don't think she's talking about better shipping rates for vegetable trucks.

"The sovereignty fetish is still so strong in the public mind, that there would appear to be little chance of winning popular assent to American membership in anything approaching a super-state organization. Much will depend on the kind of approach which is used in further popular education."

—Council on Foreign Relations, 1944

Council on Foreign Relations

If you don't have your tin hat on yet, please get it ready, because we're about to take another step down the rabbit hole.

> **A tin-foil hat** is actually a crude approximation of a Faraday cage. If you tell folks you're wearing a makeshift Faraday cage, as opposed to a tin-foil hat, they'll know you're smarter than the average tin-foil-hat-wearing nut-job, and they won't run away (as abruptly).
>
> A.D.D. MOMENT

As I said earlier, I don't believe that the SPP itself is meant to be a new North American government. As secretive as it is, it's still a government program, which means that things such as "Freedom of Information" requests can cramp their style. The NACC, as a "round-table" working group, solves some of those problems, but to make real progress you need to have private organizations on board. They can create blueprints and road maps with almost no public scrutiny, thereby providing an invisible barrier to accountability for any controversial recommendations—barriers that elite government officials are quite fond of.

Enter the Council on Foreign Relations (CFR). (Yes, I know, there's a lot of acronyms to remember—that's why I made the "Guide to Your New Continental Government" chart . . . you're welcome.) Founded in 1921, the CFR is "a nonpartisan and independent membership organization" that has counted some of the nation's most powerful and influential people as members. (The current membership is said to include Dick Cheney, Fred Thompson, Condoleezza Rice, Colin Powell, George Soros, Jimmy Carter, and others.) The group claims to be "dedicated to the belief that the nation's peace and prosperity is firmly linked to that of the rest of the world," but many believe the true agenda is quite a bit more far-reaching.

The late Georgetown history professor Carroll Quigley, who Bill Clinton has said was his mentor and a major influence on his life, wrote the following in his book *Tragedy and Hope:* "The Council on Foreign Relations is the American branch of a soci-

The Amero
Your exciting new currency!

CFR: Council on Foreign Relations
Complicated times demand a covert Congress.

Council of the Americas
"...a continuous conversation about the issues that define and challenge the societies of the Western Hemisphere."

NAF: The North American Forum
Business leaders creating a new Continental Congress over Continental breakfast.

NACC: The North American Competitiveness Council
Official trinational working group of the SPP, organized to "drive the integration process through changes in government in all three countries."

NADB: North American Development Bank
Created under NAFTA, this bank's catchy slogan is: "Transboundary problems, bilateral solutions."

NASCO: North American SuperCorridor Coalition, Inc.
"Dedicated to developing the world's first international, integrated and secure, multi-modal transportation system..."

Pastor, Robert
MexAmeriCanada's unassuming founding father. Sure, he denies it, but that's just because he's humble.

PTP: Ports-to-Plains Corridor Coalition
"...a multi-lane divided highway that will facilitate the efficient transportation of goods and services from Mexico, through West Texas, New Mexico, Colorado, and Oklahoma, and ultimately on into Canada..."

A Reference Guide for All MexAmeriCanadians!

ety which originated in England [and] believes national boundaries should be obliterated and one-world rule established."

The CFR has been the target of suspicions from the New World Order crowd for decades, but instead of reciting all of the suspicions, I want to focus on something more recent and relevant to the idea of a North American Union.

In 2005, the CFR released a report titled "Building a North American Community." Written by a CFR-sponsored independent task force, the report was vice-chaired by Professor Robert Pastor (remember that name; there will be a test later), and its findings were presented to Congress.

"We're grateful to The *Washington Post,* The *New York Times, Time* magazine and other great publications whose directors have attended our meetings and respected their promises of discretion for almost forty years. It would have been impossible for us to develop our plan for the world if we had been subject to the bright lights of publicity during those years. But the world is now more sophisticated and prepared to march towards a world government."

—David Rockefeller, chairman of the CFR (1970–1985)

Why is this report important? Because the report's introduction confirms, "The Task Force is pleased to provide specific advice on how the [SPP] can be pursued and realized." Translated, it means this "independent report" is directly connected to the SPP and that the people behind the SPP will ostensibly be looking at the report's findings as a road map for the future.

Look Who Agrees

Enrique Berruga came pretty close to pinpointing the same MexAmeri-Canada time frame as the CFR report. In a panel discussion on U.S.-Mexico relations in November 2006, Berruga flatly said a North American Union was not only needed but must be finished before the U.S. baby-boomer retirement wave hits in eight years. So, is Enrique Berruga just another conspiracy nut? Nope, he's Mexico's ambassador to the United Nations.

The report is 70 pages long, but it all basically comes down to one major recommendation: "The Task Force proposes the creation by 2010 of a North American community to enhance security, prosperity, and opportunity. . . . Its boundaries will be defined by a common external tariff and an outer security perimeter within which the movement of people, products, and capital will be legal, orderly, and safe. Its goal will be to guarantee a free, secure, just and prosperous North America."

I don't know about you, but when something that unbelievably arrogant and threatening is supposed to be used as a blueprint by a government program, alarms bells start going off in my head. Of course, being paranoid isn't exactly a new phenomenon for me, so the real question is whether any of the report's recommendations will actually be taken seriously.

Unfortunately, yes. In fact, they already have.

The report recommended the creation of "A North American Advisory Council [that] should be composed of eminent persons from outside government . . . to provide a public voice for North America . . . along the lines of the Bilderberg conferences."

A.D.D. MOMENT Mentioning Bilderberg, one of the most secretive gatherings of elite power brokers in the world, didn't help their chances with the Black Helicopter crowd. Why not throw in a Bohemian Grove reference while you're at it?

OK, sure, the name is off by one word, but the North American Competitiveness Council was launched by the SPP less than one year after the report was released.

The report called for "the freer flow of people within North America." (You really don't have to worry about illegal immigration if no one is illegal—or an immigrant—anymore.)

Lots of great progress on this one. The government is working to start a pilot program that will allow Mexican trucks to travel freely in the United States for the first time in 25 years, and it is fostering private concerns that are looking to build a "NAFTA Superhighway" running from Mexico, through the United States, into Canada. Government officials, of course, say they have no plans for a superhighway, yet the North American SuperCorridor Coalition (NASCO) has received $2.5 million in earmarks from the U.S. Department of Transportation.

There are plenty of other examples of recommendations made in the CFR report that the government and SPP have subsequently acted on (air travel, energy, disease outbreaks), but the real question shouldn't be *if* they're following the CFR's road map but how far they'll go.

Follow the Leader

Pop quiz: Name the person I highlighted earlier as the vice chair of the task force that authored the CFR report. If you're part of what he calls "the xenophobic or frightened right wing of America that is afraid of immigration and globalization," then you probably remember his name well: Robert Pastor.

When he's not promoting a continental government or following the playbook by equating border-security conservatives with racists, Robert Pastor is professor of international relations at American University. (And yes, I do see the tremendous irony in that.)

As one of the country's foremost experts on "North American integration," Pastor was called on by both the Canadian Parliament and a Subcommittee of the U.S. Senate Foreign Relations Committee to talk about the CFR report. Although he consistently asserts that the conspiracy theorists are nut-jobs and that "nobody is proposing a North American Union," his comments in Canada certainly seem to indicate otherwise:

"The three governments remain zealous defenders of an aging conception of sovereignty whereas the people seem ready to entertain new approaches."

An "aging conception of sovereignty"—hmm, you mean like we have our own constitution, borders, and government? If so, then I guess I'm one of those zealous defenders. Oh, and by the way, you don't have to make any conspiratorial leaps of faith to figure out what he meant by "new approaches," since he covered a few of them right in his speech:

- GIVE THEM MONEY! "A North American Investment Fund to invest $20 billion a year for a decade in infrastructure—roads, ports, railroads, communication—to connect the southern part of Mexico with the lucrative North American market."
- PROTECT THEM! "The Department of Homeland Security should expand its mission to include continental security."
- NEW ROADS AND RAILS! "Develop an integrated continental plan for transportation and infrastructure that includes new North American highways and high-speed rail corridors."
- WE'RE ALL NORTH AMERICANS! "Instead of stopping North Americans on the borders, we ought to provide them with a secure, biometric Border Pass that would ease transit across the border like an E-ZPass permits our cars to speed through toll booths."
- CHANGE OUR LAWS! "The United States and Canada should begin to merge immigration and refugee policies."

All great ideas, Bob, really; and I can definitely see why you say that people are crazy for thinking that you're advocating any kind of North American Union.

Pastor ended his testimony in Canada with some brown-nosing and a plea: "Canada has played a key leadership role in so many issues. I sincerely hope your government will take the lead in defining the path toward a more collaborative relationship. I cannot say that the United States government will respond positively, but I think Mexico would consider such an approach positively, and if the two neighbors of the United States were to make a persuasive case, *influential sectors* in the United States would encourage the Administration to take them very seriously."

We've covered a couple of those "influential sectors" already, but there's one more group you need to be aware of—and Pastor is the key link between them.

"I am now convinced that the president's true objective is the absorption of the United States into some sort of borderless 'North American Union' with Canada and Mexico. That's why they have done nothing to secure our borders. That's why they seek to grant amnesty to millions of illegal aliens."

—Rep. Tom Tancredo (R-Colorado)

The North American Forum

Don't let the boring name fool you. The North American Forum (NAF) is an unbelievably secretive group of extremely high-level "elites." It's also, according to U.S. Consul General John Nay, a "sister organization" and "parallel structure" to the SPP. You probably wouldn't be surprised to hear that no public records are kept and no announcements have been made about the group's activities.

The NAF's 2006 meeting, at the Banff Springs Hotel in Alberta, Canada, was kept quiet, but at least one participant, who felt that the meeting was an affront to democracy, leaked the guest list and agenda. It turns out that about one-third of those on the task force that wrote the CFR report were invited, and two other names should also ring a bell: our friend Robert Pastor (who served on a panel titled "A Vision for North America: Issues and Options"), and Ron Covais, the Lockheed Martin Americas president who is also a member of the NACC. Of course, there were also numerous other high-level politicians, executives, and military personnel in attendance.

If nothing else, the NAF is smart about its secrecy. Members make donations to fund the meeting, and everyone pays for their own travel arrangements. That makes it a private event that no one, including politicians who attend, are mandated to announce publicly.

Confession

Many years ago, I too was involved in a highly secretive group that kept no public records and operated in secrecy. However, I promise you that the Glenn Beck and Friends Found a Musty Copy of *Playboy* organization was disbanded shortly after it was formed in the attic in 1976 and was never particularly influential.

Alternative Name Idea

Sure, "North American Forum" is catchy and all, but it's a little generic, don't you think? How about something that's a bit more clear? I suggest "The Really Rich People Who Design the World's Future in Secrecy While Eating Free Continental Breakfast Forum."

John Larsen, an NAF spokesman, tried to explain the private nature of the forum, but I think he just made things worse: "You can imagine that if this was all televised or open to public scrutiny, the nature of the conversations and ultimately what you would be able to do with those conversations and how far you might be able to advance the solutions around it would be different."

Right—and isn't that sort of the point?

Creative Insults

The people who believe that the North American Union is nothing but a drummed-up conspiracy theory don't hold back their vitriol for people like me. Michael Medved, a conservative talk-radio host (and someone I generally agree with), is one of those people. In a column blasting those who fear an EU-style union for North America, Medved was extraordinarily creative with his insults. I've put them into alphabetical order for your convenience (remember, he used all of these in *the same* article . . . that's impressive):

Bastards
Brain-dead fantasies
Charlatans
Childish
Cranks
Creeps
Crooks
Demagogues
Drunks
Exploiters
Fringies
Groundless frenzy
Hysterics
Ill-informed
Jerks
Jug-heads
Losers
Ludicrous
Lunatics
Manipulative
Miserable cretins
Opportunists
Paranoid
Psychotics
Reprobates

Follow the Money

Elitists are also capitalists, and none of this would be happening if money and profit weren't at stake. For Canada, it's having increased access to the huge American markets. For Mexico, it's increasing its standard of living through trade and more "flexible" immigration policies. And for the United States, it's mostly about energy.

Remember: *Canada and Mexico are this country's top two suppliers of oil.*

Then again, that shouldn't come as much of a surprise to anyone who's been paying attention. At the now infamous Waco summit where the SPP was set up, President Bush, standing next to President Fox and Prime Minister Martin, said, "Yes, we're using a lot of [energy] and we need to conserve better in the United States. . . . We appreciate the fact that Canada's tar sands are now becoming economical, and we're glad to be able to get the access toward a million barrels a day, headed toward two million barrels a day . . . that's, by the way, an advantage for open trade; the American people must understand that when there is open trade, it helps solve our energy deficiency."

"The real truth of the matter is, as you and I know, that a financial element in the large centers has owned the government of the U.S. since the days of Andrew Jackson."

—Franklin D. Roosevelt, 1933

Maybe everyone is so focused on a so-called war for oil happening overseas that we're all missing the "sovereignty for oil" trade happening right in front of our eyes.

But it goes even deeper than oil and profits. The people who support a North American Union also support a common currency. Our friend Robert Pastor is one of them, of course, but so is someone a little more influential: Bank of Canada Governor David Dodge. He said that it was "possible" that North America might one day welcome a single currency modeled after the euro.

Welcome to the amero.

A.D.D. MOMENT The euro was great for about 10 minutes when one dollar was equivalent to approximately one euro. It made calculating things easy. But now one dollar is something like 0.742 euro. That's the kind of math that keeps me from traveling to France—besides France itself, of course.

No, I'm not kidding. Originally proposed in a 1999 report by a Canadian think-tank to counterbalance the euro, the amero idea has picked up some steam over the years

(along with an endorsement from our good friend Robert Pastor). Last year on CNBC, an international currency trader broached the subject on national TV, resulting in the hosts coming back the next day and laughing at his expense.

Unfortunately, they probably should stop laughing and start researching. The amero might seem like some wild pie-in-the-sky scheme now, but you probably would have said the same thing if I told you 15 or 20 years ago that countries such as Germany, France, Ireland, Italy, and Spain would all be using the same currency. Laughing at the idea is exactly what they want—because "evolution by stealth" is exactly what they crave.

"Does it not seem strange to you that these men just happen to be CFR and just happen to be on the Board of Governors of the Federal Reserve, that absolutely controls the money and interest rates of this great country without benefit of Congress?"

—Former U.S. Sen. Barry Goldwater, from his book *With No Apologies*

MY SOLUTION

I started by asking a simple question about illegal immigration: Why? Why has no leader bothered to solve the problem once and for all? Why does a Republican president ignore his base and fight for amnesty for millions of illegal aliens?

Why?

The question is simple, but—as you've seen—the answer is anything but. Superelites in our government are conspiring to sell out our sovereignty by skirting around the series of checks and balances mandated by the Constitution—a series that our forefathers set up to prevent this exact scenario from happening.

I want to reiterate: I do not believe that the SPP is already masquerading as some North American Union government. In fact, I don't even believe that most of the people involved in the SPP or the NACC believe that.

But that's the whole problem—only the superelites are privy enough to see the whole picture, how all the puzzle pieces fit together. The Department of Transportation can flat-out deny that a NAFTA superhighway will ever be built, and the Department of Homeland Security can talk about border enforcement and fencing—and they can do it all with a straight face because, as far as they know, they're right. It's plausible deniability at its finest.

As with so many other problems we face, the solution can be found right in the Constitution—the very document the elites are trying to circumvent. And it's right in those first three magic words: "We the People."

"This is how the future of North America now promises to be written: not in a sweeping trade agreement on which elections will turn, but by the accretion of hundreds of incremental changes implemented by executive agencies, bureaucracies and regulators."
—Luiza Ch. Savage, *Maclean's*, reporting on the first NACC meeting

We have to *demand* accountability and transparency from our leaders. We can't sit idle as "private" working groups form recommendations during secret meetings, and we can't stay silent when those recommendations turn into actions.

A good example is the immigration bill proposed in the spring of 2007. The Secure Borders, Economic Opportunity and Immigration Reform Act of 2007 (love that name) contained references to both the SPP and to something called the Partnership for Prosperity, which was a precursor to the SPP from 2001.

The bill stated, "It is the sense of Congress that the United States and Mexico should accelerate the implementation of the Partnership for Prosperity."

Political Irony

The name of a bill in Congress is often in direct contrast to what the actual bill does. The Social *Security* Act now puts us at risk of identity theft, and the *Can Spam* Act actually increased junk email. Congress apparently loves irony almost as much as it loves issuing pay raises to itself.

A.D.D. MOMENT "Sense of Congress"? They like irony even more than I thought.

I'll bet most elected representatives don't even know what the SPP or Partnership for Prosperity is, let alone be willing to vote that it's their "sense" to accelerate it. If supporters are really not trying to be covert about these programs, then why bury those references on page 231 of a 347-page piece of legislation that they know virtually no one will read?

Fortunately, there is a surefire way to leverage our collective power and beat the elites at their own game.

1. *Build two fences.* One along the entire north border and another along the entire south border. They should have double layers of fencing with a road in between for patrols, concrete vehicle barriers, surveillance cameras, and tunneling sensors.

It would likely cost upward of $20 billion.

If that sounds expensive, consider that 9/11 cost the City of New York alone at least $90 billion. Believe me, the fences are a bargain.

Then again, the price tag—along with calls of racism and claims that it wouldn't help anyway—are just misleading tactics that the critics use. I'm not really interested in their propaganda anymore; if you haven't noticed, it's gotten us nowhere. Not to mention, the critics have forgotten one of the key rules of real estate: Fences make good neighbors.

When I asked Rudy Giuliani about illegal immigration, he basically said that the bottom line is that we've got to know the identity of each and every person in the country. Call me crazy, but that seems like common sense, and I bet that if you polled the country on just that question, 90 percent of people would agree.

A.D.D. MOMENT

2. *Hit the employers hard.* Hardworking Mexicans come here for jobs and money. Those jobs (which, by the way, often involve work in substandard conditions for illegal wages) are provided by American companies. That has to stop.

By mandating that employers who are caught knowingly hiring illegal workers be hit with crippling fines, we would send a message to every business owner that it will no longer be tolerated. Once the supply is cut off, the demand will dry up.

After those two things are done (and by "done" I mean that the fence is built, not just included in some bill), then, and only then, can we talk about things such as amnesty, guest-worker programs, or a path to citizenship. To commingle them is like picking out a new paint color for your kitchen while it's still flooding from a broken pipe. You've got to fix the leak first and stop the flooding—then you can worry about everything else.

The other benefit of building fences and fining employers is that those solutions are the kryptonite to the elite's power. The last things they want are fences or stricter immigration policies. In fact, those very things would ruin the goals they've been working toward for decades.

After all, it's tough to have a unified North American government with 7,000 miles of double-layered fencing in the way.

ACKNOWLEDGMENTS:

THE LISTENERS, VIEWERS AND READERS—you make everything we do possible. Insiders, you're the nicest group of people I've ever been lucky enough to call fans. ☢ **CHRIS BALFE**, my business manager, who will most likely be living in the Caymans while I, penniless, find a dry spot under a bridge somewhere. ☢ **KEVIN BALFE**, who is responsible for the quality of so much of our work at Mercury. Sorry, no refunds on this book, but at least you now have a name to attach to any class-action lawsuits. ☢ **STU BURGUIERE**, my vegetarian radio Executive Producer, who keeps me on track every day and who, I believe, is part of a liberal sleeper cell. (This was my only opportunity to get that message out since Stu won't read any book I recommend.) ☢ **ADAM CLARKE**, who works every hour I do and never gets recognized for it. Here's the recognition you deserve—don't expect anything financial. ☢ **MY TELEVISION AND RADIO CREWS**, along with everyone behind the scenes at **MERCURY RADIO ARTS**—thanks for all you do to make me look and sound good. I'd like to see each of you in my office this Friday afternoon. ☢ **MY FLOOR AND MAKEUP CREW**—you make wrecking television for millions every night fun. My publisher, **LOUISE BURKE**, for believing in me from the beginning and always standing behind my vision. ☢ **GEORGE HILTZIK**, my agent and my friend (in that order). ☢ My editor, **MITCHELL IVERS**, for putting up with me through two books' worth of changes, spelling errors, and last-minute revisions. Here's to many more to come. (I mean books, not revisions). ☢ My good friend **KRAIG KITCHIN**—living proof that good guys do finish first. ☢ **DAN METTER** and **JULIE TALBOTT**, why are you reading this? Shouldn't you both be selling? ☢ **MY CHILDREN**, who give me hope for a better tomorrow. ☢ All my **PARENTS**, who raised Tania and me. Thank you for making it through the struggles and teaching us what's really important: family. ☢ **CITY BAKERY** (1898–2006). Everything of value I learned in the back of our family's shop. ☢ The **FLY-OVER STATES** for not only getting it, but living it every day. Thanks for seeing that the answer always lies with "We the People." ☢ My **HOME WARD**, for being such a blessing. You're the most generous, well-grounded group of people I've known. ☢ **ROGER AILES, RUSSELL M. BALLARD, JOEL CHEATWOOD, PAT GRAY, MARK MAYS, SUZANNE SCOTT, BILL SHINE, GRESHAM STRIEGEL**, and along with **EVERYONE ELSE** I've undoubtedly forgotten—thank you for believing in me.